PERFORMANCE MANAGEMENT
Strategies • Interventions • Drivers

SRINIVAS R. KANDULA

Global Head (Human Resources)
iGATE, Bangalore

PHI Learning Private Limited

New Delhi-110001

2011

Rs. 275.00

PERFORMANCE MANAGEMENT: Strategies—Interventions—Drivers
Srinivas R. Kandula

ISBN-978-81-203-2988-1

The export rights of this book are vested solely with the publisher.

Fifth Printing   ...   ...   **January, 2011**

Published by Asoke K. Ghosh, PHI Learning Private Limited, M-97, Connaught Circus, New Delhi-110001 and Printed by Mudrak, 30-A, Patparganj, Delhi-110091.

CONTENTS

PREFACE

Of all the human resource management functions, performance management has a special place since it is a strong determinant of organizational excellence. Organizations of contemporary era have realized that human resource needs to be continuously excited and provided with opportunities for gratification of motivational needs in order to sustain business growth. Performance management as a concept and practice has substantive potential to fulfil business demands of an organization by integrating its growth with motivational needs of human resource.

Performance management as a distinct discipline is gaining ground slowly but firmly. However, most efforts are focused on exploring and explaining performance management in bits and pieces. As a departure, this book is an attempt to capture the comprehensive picture of performance management from a practitioner's perspective. It has been written keeping in view two important reasons. First, performance of human resource cannot be managed effectively by using piecemeal approaches such as goal setting, monitoring, appraising and rewarding achievements. Performance management is much more than these pieces as this book unfolds. Second, performance management is more a practice than theory and more a reality than rhetoric. Therefore, it can be discussed only in a practitioner's language, that too in an organizational context.

The book, which is patterned after motivational structure of human resource, comprises seven performance management strategies, 14 interventions and 140 drivers. An organization can be sure of achieving business excellence apart from attaining maturity and status of performance centric entity, once it is through with implementation of all the drivers in an evolutionary manner. The journey from first driver to the last driver at times can be painful, long drawn and involves persistent efforts. After all, breakthrough achievements can come only from years of untiring efforts.

This comprehensive book is the outcome of my years of study, observation and participation in design and execution of performance management strategies in business organizations over a decade with a mixed experience of success and failure. Throughout the book, I have made sincere efforts to present performance management in practical manner to managers intending to pursue it in a systematic fashion. Special features like theoretical foundations, case studies, best practices and discussion questions are also added to address the needs of university students.

Friends continued to be real support in my professional journey. I am indebted to Vinod Baxla who has supported and extended all help while writing this book. I am also thankful to K.V.V. Satyanarayana, Sandeep Chatterjee and Ritu Tather for their encouragement and suggestions in enriching the quality of the book.

Srinivas R. Kandula

Chapter One
INTRODUCTION

OVERVIEW

Performance management has assumed a pivotal role in the face of rapid changes such as globalization, liberalization, technological and market changes. It is the backbone of human resource management for any organization intending to produce a high performance and leverage its human capital. Human resource management during the last two decades has shifted its focus from maintenance and administrative kind of function to that of a value added role. In this process, performance management has occupied a centre stage. In other words, all people management efforts are directed towards enhancing performance of employees and thereby improving the bottom line of organizations. However, more often than not organizations are saddled with human resource strategies and interventions that are piecemeal and fragmented. These isolated and individualistic practices have not only failed to produce any positive results at the bottom line of organizations but also caused ineffectiveness and chaos in management of people. Therefore, performance management efforts in organisations should be distinctly integrated and every sphere of human resource management activity must be integrated vertically and horizontally to deliver significant positive business results. This book is an attempt in that direction. An integrated framework is presented in the following chapters by aligning seven core performance centric strategies such as reward, career, team, culture, measurement, competency and leadership.

OBJECTIVES OF THE BOOK

The objective of this book is threefold:

- To present the theory and practices of performance management in an integrated perspective.

- To present performance management strategies, interventions and drivers that help in nurturing and institutionalizing high performance work orientation in organizations.
- To equip readers to develop customized performance centric strategies, interventions and drivers suited to their organizations.

DESIGN OF THE BOOK

An attempt is made to present theory and practices of performance management in an integrated and pragmatic style. This book consists of 7 strategies, 14 interventions and 140 drivers: all these cumulatively are expected to make an organization not only performance centric, but also make performance management a fundamental system of organizational management. Each of these strategies is presented in chapters 2 to 8 in the following text. The definitions of strategy, intervention and driver as used in this book are described as follows.

STRATEGY

Strategy in the context of this book is defined as *an activity which is comprehensive in nature consisting of fundamental and advanced level interventions with an objective to nurture and institutionalize performance management as a natural way of organizational functioning.* The book is woven around seven principal strategies of performance management as shown in Figure 1.1. These are:

- Reward-based performance management
- Career-based performance management

FIGURE 1.1   Seven strategies of performance management.

- Team-based performance management
- Culture-based performance management
- Measurement-based performance management
- Competency-based performance management
- Leadership-based performance management

Intervention

Intervention is defined as *an initiative structured with fundamental, contemporary and advanced level drivers, implementation of which adds a substantive value to an organization's effort in embracing performance management*. A set of two interventions forms the body of a strategy as shown in Figure 1.2. In total sum, this book consists of 14 interventions.

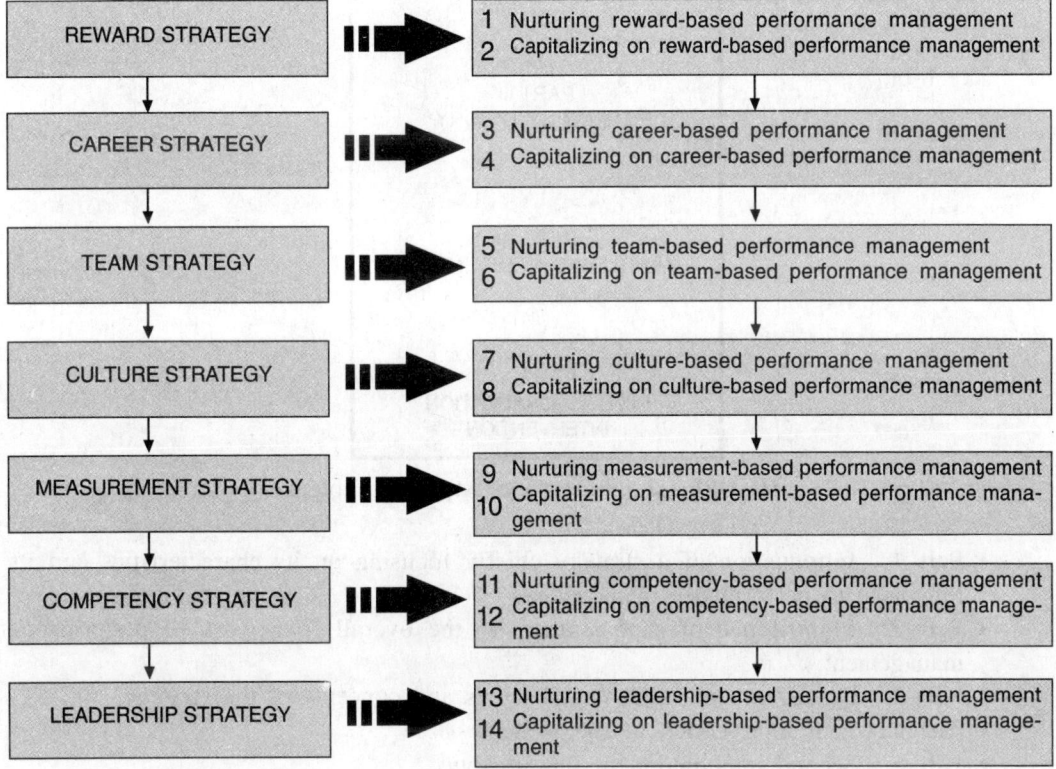

| REWARD STRATEGY | 1 Nurturing reward-based performance management |
| | 2 Capitalizing on reward-based performance management |

| CAREER STRATEGY | 3 Nurturing career-based performance management |
| | 4 Capitalizing on career-based performance management |

| TEAM STRATEGY | 5 Nurturing team-based performance management |
| | 6 Capitalizing on team-based performance management |

| CULTURE STRATEGY | 7 Nurturing culture-based performance management |
| | 8 Capitalizing on culture-based performance management |

| MEASUREMENT STRATEGY | 9 Nurturing measurement-based performance management |
| | 10 Capitalizing on measurement-based performance management |

| COMPETENCY STRATEGY | 11 Nurturing competency-based performance management |
| | 12 Capitalizing on competency-based performance management |

| LEADERSHIP STRATEGY | 13 Nurturing leadership-based performance management |
| | 14 Capitalizing on leadership-based performance management |

FIGURE 1.2 Strategies and interventions of performance management.

Driver

Driver is *a combination of actions initiated as a part of implementing a performance centric intervention*. A set of 10 drivers forms the structure and content of an intervention. There are 140 drivers in this book, each beginning and ending with a meaningful task.

STYLE OF PRESENTATION

Style of presentation followed while discussing the seven strategies chapterwise is identical. There are five parts in each of the strategies focusing on issues as indicated here and shown in Figure 1.3.

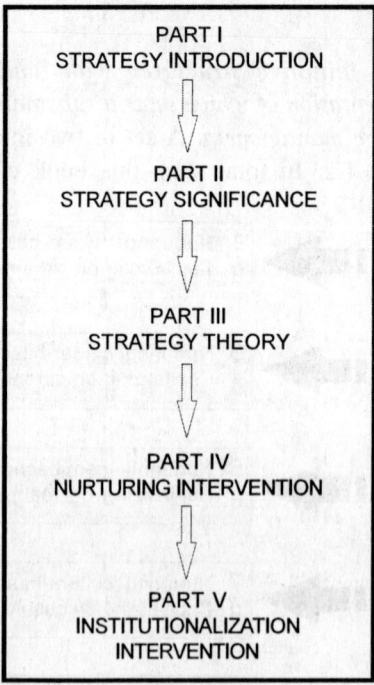

PART I
STRATEGY INTRODUCTION

PART II
STRATEGY SIGNIFICANCE

PART III
STRATEGY THEORY

PART IV
NURTURING INTERVENTION

PART V
INSTITUTIONALIZATION
INTERVENTION

FIGURE 1.3   Presentation style of chapters.

- Part 1: Introduction of a strategy chiefly focusing on its characteristics and its relevance to performance management.
- Part 2: Significance of such strategy to the overall framework of performance management.
- Part 3: Description of fundamental tenets and concepts of the strategy.
- Part 4: First intervention of the strategy.
- Part 5: Second intervention of the strategy.

Some of the best performance management practices, a few case studies and questions for discussion are added at the end of every chapter to enable users of this book to reflect on and relate to the issues covered in real-life work situations.

USERS OF THE BOOK

Teachers and Students: Teachers using this as a textbook, either for a main paper or optional in postgraduate course may need to allocate 45 hours (30 sessions) of coaching time to cover all the strategies, interventions and drivers of performance management. Each strategy requires about six hours of teaching (four sessions) that includes 45 minutes for wrap up and summing up the discussion, i.e. 42 hours for seven strategies and three hours (two sessions) for the introductory chapter. Teaching this subject as a main course helps management students a great deal as more and more organizations are looking for management professionals with knowledge of performance management issues. Currently, courses in the area of human resource management/development are focused on generic and traditional themes that are progressively losing their relevance to the industry. In this backdrop, this book aims at preparing management students as performance management specialists.

Professionals: Management professionals, particularly those in the area of human resource management can be immensely benefited using this book. Contents and structure of this book help them not only to gain a deep understanding of performance management theory and practices, but also enable them to draft organization specific performance enhancement interventions. In a nutshell, this book can be a one-stop shop for all performance management related issues, whether conceptual or practical.

PERFORMANCE MANAGEMENT

Performance management is a process of designing and executing motivational strategies, interventions and drivers with an objective to transform the raw potential of human resource into performance. All human beings possess potential within themselves in a few or more functional areas. However, utilization and conversion of this potential into deliverable performances is often suboptimal due to a variety of reasons. Performance management acts as an agent in converting the potential into performance by removing the intermediate barriers as well as motivating and rejuvenating the human resource.

WHAT IS NOT PERFORMANCE MANAGEMENT?

Performance appraisal system is often confused with performance management and mostly misunderstood as synonymous. *Performance appraisal is a singular activity that is employed to assess performance of employees for a predetermined duration on a set of parameters.* As opposed to this, performance management is an integrated activity that aims to nurture and institutionalize performance management as a fundamental system of an organization. In this parlance, performance appraisal is considered as one of the tools that is used in measuring actual performance of employees on an assigned task. Similarly, performance management is viewed as an activity of goal setting and monitoring achievement of goals. Performance management in this sense is viewed as another form of management by objectives (MBO). In fact, management by objectives is one of the important features of performance management. In contrast to the popular misbelief, performance management is a comprehensive discipline that consists of strategies to address the entire motivational need structure of human resource such as physiological, security, social, self-esteem and self-actualization through appropriate interventions and drivers.

SIGNIFICANCE OF PERFORMANCE MANAGEMENT

Performance management has the potential to fulfil strategic and operational requirements of an organization and personal as well as professional needs of employees in a number of ways. A few of them are presented pictorially in Figure 1.4.

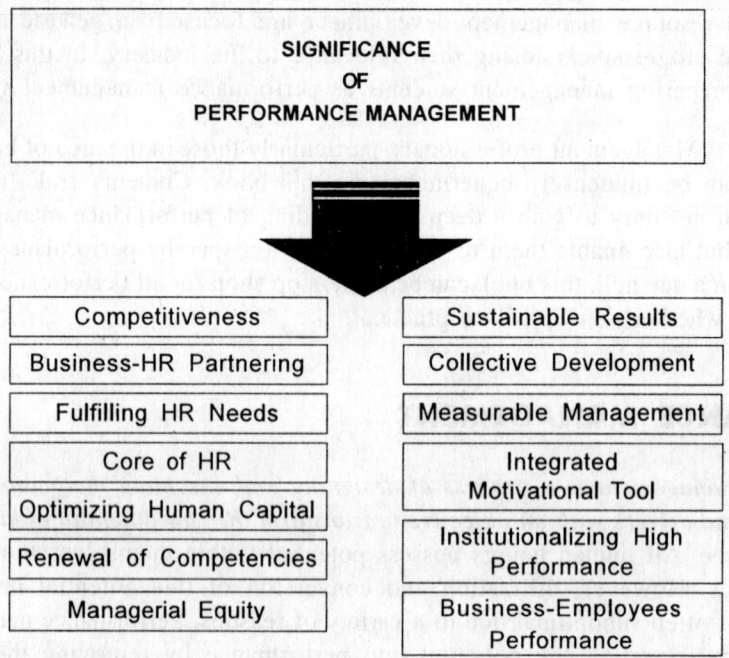

FIGURE 1.4 Significance of performance management.

Competitive Business Environment

Present day organizations are required to deal with performance-related issues more than in the past due to increasing competition and the need to do more with fewer resources. In an uncertain business environment, human resource is the only asset that can make organizations survive, exist and succeed. Hence, more performance-oriented human resource management practices are preferred than those of maintenance and collective bargaining.

Business-HR Partnership

There is a growing pressure on human resource professionals to establish the worth of human resource function mainly in two forms: firstly, its contribution to the bottom line of organizations in terms of profits, sales, turnover and earnings per share. Secondly, the utility of human resource function and its practices to the effective functioning of organizations in terms of work culture, employees' performance and availability of human resource competencies and skills. Value addition could be attained only when performance management practices are given a high priority.

Fulfilment of Human Resource Needs

In the motivational hierarchy, most employees in business organizations are placed at the level of self-esteem and self-actualization. They look forward to (i) perform higher-level tasks and handle professional challenges with freedom and flexibility, (ii) seek appropriate rewards for their efforts, more of non-monetary nature, (iii) consistent updation of competencies, (iv) a performance inducing work environment that includes teamwork and (v) seek open communication and transparency. These demands could be met only by applying performance-oriented human resource practices.

Performance Management as Core of HR

Performance driven practices such as reward, career, team building, culture, performance measurement, competency development and leadership, lie in the heart of human resource management. These practices are capable of leading human resource function into the strategic domain of organizations. Wherever and whenever human resource function has succeeded in meeting the employees and organizational demands, it is due to the priority accorded to higher-level human resource practices known as *performance driving activities*.

Integrated Motivational Tool

Performance management consists of a set of motivational tools that are capable of obtaining superior performance of employees. They also facilitate conversion of latent potential that exists inside human beings into tangible and contextual performances. These performance-oriented practices are largely built on the framework of well-established motivational theories such as Maslow's hierarchy of needs, Herzberg's hygienic-motivational factors and Vroom's valence-expectancy framework. Implementation of these performance-oriented practices also progresses in the same pattern as that of these motivational frameworks. Therefore, performance management is the key to motivating employees.

Capable of Institutionalizing High Performance Work Culture

Performance management practices are centred on creating a distinct and salutary work culture. It promotes openness, trust, collaboration, proactivism and empathy. All these are essential ingredients for leading people to maximize their performances. It means performance management is a combination of a set of practices and processes called in this book as strategies, interventions and drivers. Practices guide as to what is to be done, whereas processes show how it is to be done.

Long-Lasting Impact and Sustainable Results

Long-lasting positive results for both employees and the organization can be achieved only through implementation of performance management initiatives. This is because performance management balances both short-term and long-term requirements of the organization and its people. It is also possible to achieve a good fit between basic and higher-level interventions. For example, each performance driver and intervention will have a short-term goal like meeting current skill requirements and long-term objective of building substantive organization specific competencies to take care of future needs.

Individual and Collective Development

Performance management makes both individual and collective development possible in organizations. An employee as an individual and also as a team member will have accessibility to all performance driven interventions. It means an employee will have the opportunity to perform and grow with a distinct identity and also as a team player wherever task execution involves interdependence. Work in modern organizations requires both individual and collective form of performances and there must be harmony between them. Traditional human resource practices fall short in creating such a balance. Performance management with its integrated and comprehensive approach to people management successfully fills that gap.

Measurable Management

There is a widespread agreement that something which is not measurable, is not manageable. No benefit can be accrued from something that is not manageable. The biggest criticism conventional human resource management practices encounter is that they are non-measurable and therefore, their efficacy is doubtful. As opposed to this view, strategies, interventions and drivers of performance management are highly measurable, quantifiable and demonstrable in results.

Optimizing Human Capital

Organizations generally own reservoirs of human potential. However, optimizing these potentials, channelizing them towards a defined objective, translating them into meaningful skills and competencies and using them smartly for business gains are real challenges. These challenges form the centre of performance management activities. Various strategies, interventions and drivers employed within the gamut of performance management, systematically ensure optimization of human capital. Human resource is stimulated to discover their inner capabilities, and organizations are equipped with soft competencies to achieve the set objectives.

Consistent and Continuous Renewal of Skills and Competencies

The ever changing face of technology, fluctuating market demands and decreasing product life cycles presuppose renewal of human skills on a continuous basis. Functional and organizational-level competencies also need to be redefined in tandem with changing business realities. Such skill and competency renewals are possible only when an organization pays adequate attention to performance-oriented strategies, interventions and drivers. In other words, these performance-based practices can lead organizations to be contemporary and competitive even in the midst of rapid technological and market changes.

BUSINESS PERFORMANCE EQUALS EMPLOYEES' PERFORMANCE

It is well-established in practice as well as in theory that the level of business performance of an organization is just equivalent to cumulative performance level of its employees. This may not be true with other resources like capital, infrastructure and technology. Organizations with best of these can still lose to competitors. This is due to under utilization of these physical resources. It happens because human resource may be incapable of rightly exploiting them to the strategic advantage of the company. There is large-scale evidence in support of the view that competencies of employees come first in organizational effectiveness.

Equity in Management

Performance management has the potential to ensure equity in all spheres of organizational management. This equity concept may have a philosophical tone but it possesses enormous material benefit to people in particular and the organization in general. When people are assured of equality in terms of opportunities and growth, it infuses great organizational commitment and forms a fine social fabric.

CHALLENGES OF PERFORMANCE MANAGEMENT

Design and implementation of performance management strategies, interventions and drivers is easier said than done. This involves managing both macro and micro level challenges. These challenges are briefly discussed here and shown in Figure 1.5.

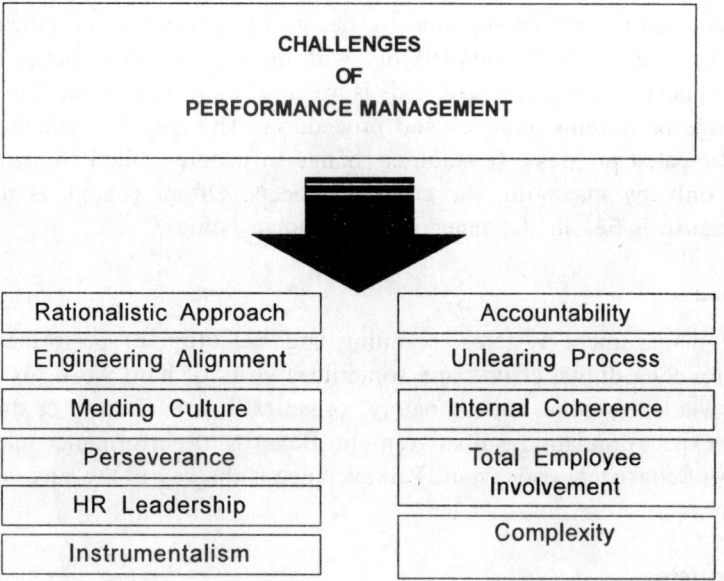

FIGURE 1.5   Challenges of performance management.

Rationalistic Approach

Performance management calls for a totally objective and rationalistic approach in adoption of various human resource practices and processes. There must be a superordinate purpose and theme running across all performance management efforts. Each and every human resource practice should carry a logical framework with well-defined deliverables at all stages. Often, such rationalistic management necessitates organization-wide revolution and process re-engineering. On the other hand, any substandard, subjective or piecemeal attempt to install performance management in an organization can cause counterproductive results.

Engineering Alignment

Performance management will gain purpose, direction and a firm platform only when its various strategies, interventions and drivers are sharply dovetailed with the business strategy of an organization. It means performance management must perform the role of catalyst in attaining short, medium and long-term objectives of an organization. This involves chiefly three aspects: firstly, making an elaborate study of business strategies and dynamics. Secondly, deciding methodology of alignment, implying how to achieve linkages between business and human processes and thirdly, developing appropriate content such as performance management strategies, interventions and drivers matching the pattern and structure of business strategies.

Melding Culture

Success of performance management largely depends upon its capability to blend various practices with culture. All organizations carry a kind of work culture that is identifiable, historical and nurtured for a long time by design or spontaneity. Challenge is, this work culture must have an absolute compatibility with the type of performance management that is either being planned or implemented. This is because application of performance management involves change in systems, policies and procedures. This physical change merely will not bring the anticipated progress. It requires change in people, called *transition*, which could be achieved only by managing the cultural aspects. Often, change is much easier than transition because it lies in the inner part of human beings.

Perseverance

Unlike other management systems, planning and execution of performance management system requires long drawn efforts and sometimes years of hard work. All employees must be involved wholeheartedly. Unfortunately, organizations backtrack or dilute their efforts because they expect dramatic results overnight. Benefits of performance management can be seen only out of consistent endeavour. Perseverance is the key to the success of performance management.

HR Competencies

Human resource leadership is highly critical to the effective practice of performance management. Human resource managers must hone their business skills as their soft human skills. They must be capable of using quantitative techniques as well as qualitative methods and should be information technology savvy. Human resource managers with either of these skills may not perfectly match the demands of this profession. The twin knowledge base of business and human resource science is a prerequisite. There is a dearth of such professionals who possess skills in both these areas.

Utilitarian Instrumentalism

Performance management is often seen as a product of utilitarian instrumentalism. It means performance management encourages (i) sourcing human resource as cheaply as possible, (ii) retaining them as long as useful and (iii) severance of the employment contract the moment utility is lost. Fact, however, is that art and science of performance management is built on the foundation of human resource as a natural resource with unlimited potential. Humanitarian perspective is the dominant propeller of various performance management practices. Therefore, the first effort of performance managers is to remove this misnomer and disseminate the philosophy of performance management abundantly and clearly.

Accountability

The basic purpose of performance management is to create relevant performance indicators, based on which people can monitor their own performance levels. This helps them to plan their activities, to initiate corrective measures and also pursue right methods to maximize their performances. In other words, it helps in defining the area of accountability in terms of value addition or business gains. Therefore, performance management should play itself as an ideal example by adopting a perfect system of accountability. This accountability must be in terms of deliverables to the development and well-being of people as well as to the organization. Creating such a framework of accountability is certainly a formidable challenge to performance managers.

Engineering Unlearning Process

Traditionally, many organizations follow maintenance-oriented, regulatory and administrative human resource management. This can become a stumbling block for introduction of performance management practices. Resistance in substantive measures can be expected. Such resistance may be potential enough to slow down the progress of performance management. Performance managers must begin their work by managing this resistance. Firstly, all human resource people must be motivated to unlearn the past practice and they must be imparted knowledge of strategies, interventions and drivers of performance management. Secondly, the policy of performance management should be developed with active participation of all employees. Thirdly, an evolutionary approach must be followed in execution of performance management. Fourthly, there must be regular reviews, appraisals and audit of performance management efforts in order to gain opportunities to renew them suitably.

Ensuring Internal Coherence

The biggest challenge of performance management is ensuring tighter integration among all strategies, interventions and drivers. There is empirical evidence that higher the internal coherence among various performance management strategies and interventions, larger the impact of these functions. Conventionally, most organizations pursued fragmented human resource practices on a stand-alone format. This is mainly due to the absence of overall focus and lack of a superordinate goal for the human resource function. Further, each of the functions is guided by their own pressures and mechanisms, sometimes conflicting within themselves and with other human resource functions. Therefore, to succeed in creating performance excellence performance management must bring strong integration among all its activities.

Encouraging Employees Participation

Effectiveness of performance management is contingent upon active involvement of all employees, particularly line managers. Unlike some human resource functions, in performance management employees are not only the target and beneficiaries, but also implementers and owners. The role of performance managers is that of facilitation, advisory and that of guiding through many phases of its journey apart from taking a leading act in periodical audit of the system. Therefore, the challenge of stimulating all employees to own the performance management system lies with performance managers.

Complexity

Both, development and execution of performance management strategies, interventions drivers are a complex exercise. This is because it involves soft and hard variants of human resource management, i.e. nurturing attitude and aptitude of human resource and translating them into tangible performances to achieve business excellence. It also requires application of specialized tools and techniques in diagnosis, application and evaluation of performance management. However, this complexity can be resolved with a clear plan and proactivism. In reality, when organizations try to be different, nothing can be free from complexity.

THEORETICAL FOUNDATIONS OF PERFORMANCE MANAGEMENT

Performance management as a concept and practice is not new to people and organizations. The only newness is that it has gained prominence as organizations struggled to find ways of improvement. As the subject is evolving, it has formed an integrated framework with the help of empirical evidences of efficacy. Customization and application thrust led to creation of new generation strategies, interventions and drivers. The fundamental structure of performance management is drawn from basic principles of well-established motivational and learning theories. Therefore, understanding these motivational and learning theories and their relevance is very important in order to grasp the underlying assumptions of performance management. In this part, important motivational and learning theories are discussed briefly.

MOTIVATIONAL THEORIES

HULL'S DRIVE REDUCTION THEORY

This model helps in the design and implementation of performance management strategies, interventions and drivers mainly in the areas of reward, measurement and competency management. Central learning of this model is that the goal of all motivated behaviour is to reduce the intensity of a drive/need. Unfulfilled drive creates loss of equilibrium in both internal and external terms to an individual. Therefore, people put in efforts to reduce the drive in order to stay in a state of equilibrium. For example, hunger disturbs the equilibrium, therefore, immediately we indulge in eating in order to reduce the drive of hunger. This process of reducing the drive is called *drive reduction*.

The implication is that habit tends to form when a relationship between a drive and the objective of reduction is established. It is like the relationship between hunger drive and eating. This relationship will be strengthened since eating fulfils the drive and brings back the balance. Over a period of time, this strengthened relationship contributes to the reduction method (eating) itself becoming a drive/motivating factor. In other words, eating itself becomes a drive. Chief contribution of this age old theory is that over a period of time work itself can be made the motivator in place of being the mere means of fulfilling biological and social needs. A high performance work culture can be built using this theory as a base. Clark Leonard Hull, Professor of Psychology at the University of Wales, proposed this model in his much acclaimed book *Principles of Behavior* published in 1943. This model is based on the principle that human body wants to stay in a homeostatic environment.

Murray's Manifest Theory

This is also an age old theory conceptualized and developed by Henry Murray in the 1940s, explaining motivational behaviour. This theory encompasses two broad motives consisting four needs, namely: (i) achievement, (ii) affiliation, (iii) autonomy and (iv) power. The first broad motive is called *directional motive* that guides people to behave in a particular manner and in a particular direction. The second motive is known as *intensity motive* that is represented by the intensity of need and energy level to fulfil that need. Murray also observes that needs are largely learned rather than inherited and activation of these needs is contingent upon the external environment. Hence, it is called *manifest needs theory*. For example, an individual might have learned a need to achieve high professional standards, but working oneself to achieve it will be dependent upon the environment that person lives in. It means environment plays a critical role in driving people to perform. This need-environment-performance linkages as brought out by manifest needs theory has great relevance to performance management, particularly in the development of culture and team-based performance management interventions and drivers.

Maslow's Hierarchy of Needs

Abraham Maslow is the architect of this theory. He proposed the need structure of human beings in a hierarchy in his paper titled "A Theory of Human Motivation" published in *Psychological Review* in 1943. The premise of this hierarchy is that once a need in hierarchy is fulfilled, human beings are driven to seek gratification of the next higher need. Therefore, this theory is called *hierarchy of needs*. This hierarchy consists of five major steps as follows:

Physiological Needs: It is the most basic level need in the hierarchy. Fulfilment of this level is sought to sustain human life itself. Needs here include food, water, clothing, sleep, sexual satisfaction and shelter.

Security Needs: This need is related to seeking certainty of future in terms of freeing oneself from the tension of being deprived of physiological needs. This means seeking permanence in possessing resources for fulfilment of physiological needs.

Social Needs: This is a need of belongingness. Human beings want acceptance, affection, love and recognition from other human beings in society/organizations. They will be driven by this need once their physiological and security needs are met.

Self-esteem Needs: This is an inner need. At this stage of need hierarchy, human beings are motivated on their own and strive to do things which make them feel proud of themselves. They are guided by their conscience.

Self-actualization Needs: This is on the peak of need structure. Human beings when they reach to this level of need structure, endeavour to realize their potential completely and seek outstanding accomplishments.

Basic assumption of this theory is that once a lower-level need on this hierarchy is fulfilled, the next level of need drives human beings. It means, the need that gets gratified loses its power of motivating people although that need continues to be in the background. Therefore, understanding this need hierarchy and also identifying and placing people where they stand on this hierarchy assumes critical importance in performance management. This is because motivating people is cardinal to the success of performance management. For this purpose, performance managers must clearly understand the motivational stance of people. As discussed earlier in this chapter, the structure of performance management is based on these motivational theories. Relevance of hierarchy of needs for performance management is illustrated in Figure 1.6 by juxtaposing both: hierarchy of needs vis-à-vis strategies of performance management. As shown in the figure, each of the strategies of performance management is patterned after hierarchy of needs.

HERZBERG'S HYGIENE-MOTIVATOR FACTORS

This is also called *two-factor theory* of motivation. Frederic Herzberg is the propounder of this theory and presented it in a detailed fashion in his book *The Motivation to Work* published in 1959. The model is well tested and explains the work behaviour of people in terms of job satisfaction and productivity. According to this theory, human motivational behaviour is governed by two types of factors:

Hygiene/Maintenance Factor: This is the primary level of motivation mainly consisting things of extrinsic value that include compensation (money), family, relationships, security

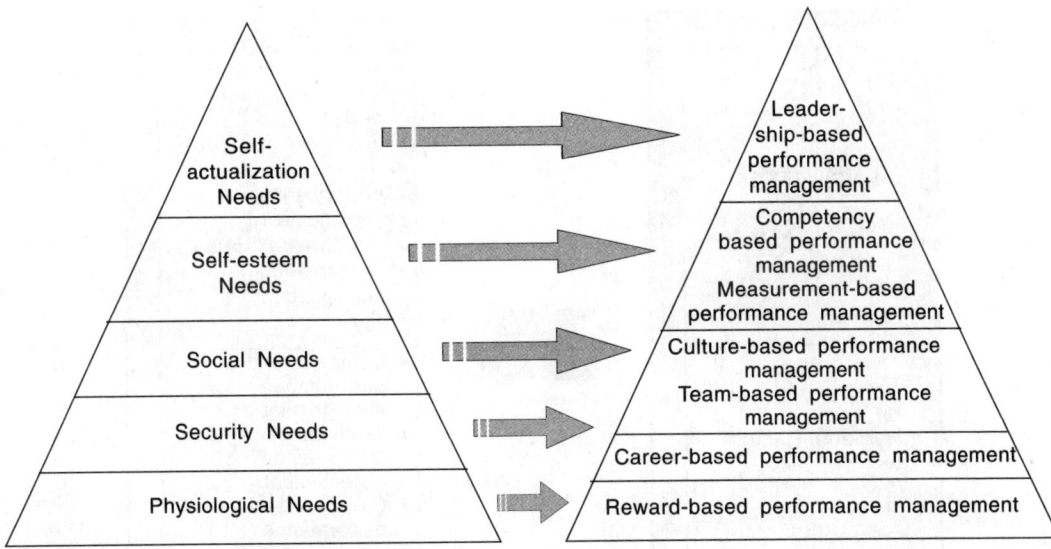

FIGURE 1.6 Maslow's hierarchy of needs vs. strategies of performance management.

of future/job/work, housing and owning other physical objects. This hygiene factor alone doesn't have the potential to motivate people to perform higher-level tasks, but possesses enough potential to demotivate in its absence. Therefore, it is like a foundation that is essential but cannot provide roof and room for living.

Motivators: This is at the higher level of motivational behaviour and has much to do with intrinsic side of people. It includes things such as inviting challenges, performing complex tasks, desire to achieve something that is uncommon, acquiring unique competencies and the drive to reach highest levels of one's profession/career. This factor works as a real motivator to produce performance excellence. Much of the demotivation and lack of job satisfaction among people is attributable to unfulfilment of this need. When organizations fail to provide opportunities to gratify this need, employees psychologically detach themselves from organization and look for its fulfilment outside.

The two-factor model has direct relevance to the theory and practice of performance management as shown in Figure 1.7. We need to ensure provision of hygiene factor and focus on motivators in order to maximize performance of people. Therefore, strategies, interventions and drivers of performance management are built around salient features of hygiene-motivator factors.

ALDERFER'S EXISTENCE-RELATEDNESS-GROWTH (ERG) THEORY

Clayton P. Alderfer is the father of this theory, who published the conceptual framework as well as empirical evidence of ERG model in his paper titled "An Empirical Test of a New Theory of Human Needs" published in the journal *Organizational Behavior and Human Performance* in 1969. Motivational behaviour of human beings has been explained using three core needs as a continuum.

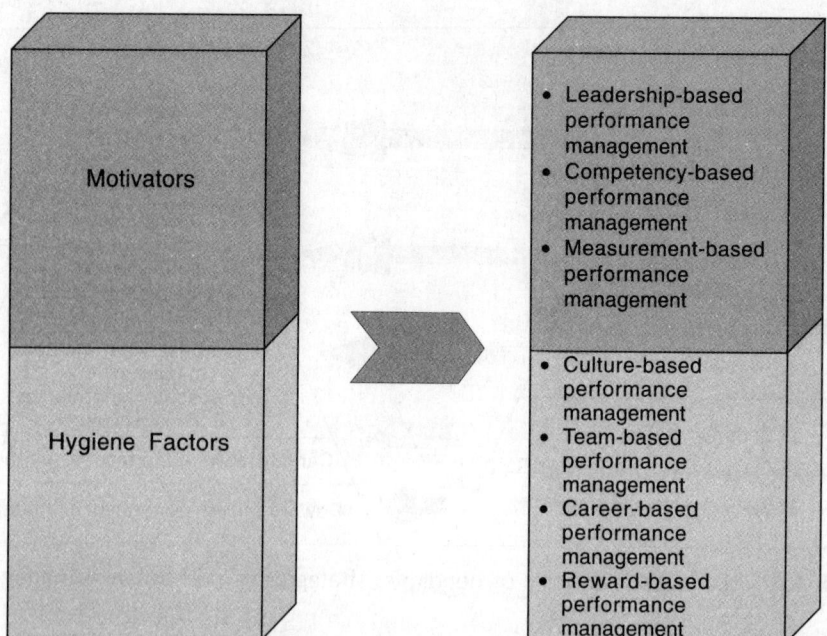

FIGURE 1.7 Two-factor motivational theory vs. strategies of performance management.

Existence: This is akin to physiological and security needs in Maslow's hierarchy of needs. It is concerned with fulfilment of basic requirements like food, shelter and clothing.

Relatedness: It is related to needs like interpersonal relationships, acceptance as a member in a group/society and family relationships. This is equivalent to social needs of Maslow's theory.

Growth: This need is pertinent to personal and professional growth of people and similar to self-esteem and self-actualization needs and motivators in Herzberg's two-factor theory.

Uniqueness of this theory in comparison to other motivational theories is fourfold. Firstly, it establishes that more than one need can be operative at the same time. It means all the three needs—existence, relatedness and growth—can be equally powerful and seek simultaneous gratification. Secondly, if the higher order level needs are blocked or opportunities are not provided for their fulfilment, the need to satisfy the lower-level need increases. Thirdly, it is not compulsory that a person seeks gratification of lower-level need before seeking the fulfilment of higher level need like relatedness. This is because cultural background of the person plays a role in it. Fourthly, this theory demonstrates that more the opportunities for satisfying the growth need, higher the frequency of seeking it. Relevance of ERG theory in design of performance management strategies is shown in Figure 1.8.

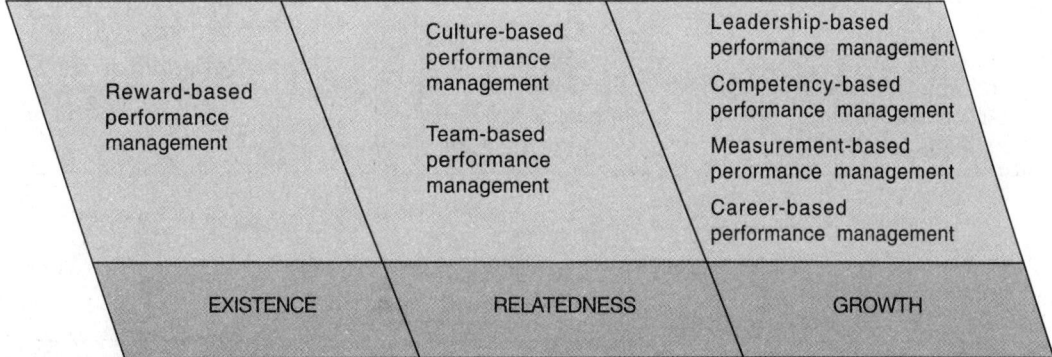

FIGURE 1.8 ERG theory of motivation vs. strategies of performance management.

VROOM'S VALENCE-EXPECTANCY-INSTRUMENTALITY THEORY

Vector Vroom's expectancy theory advocates that people will be driven to choose a particular task and carry it out in a particular mode because they expect such actions will lead them to attain something which they value. Therefore, the intensity of efforts people put in is generally equivalent to the sum of value they attach to the outcome of such efforts. This theory consists of three vital elements. These are:

Valence: It is the 'value of an outcome' of an effort. Degree of value to an outcome varies from person to person. For example, hike in annual compensation may not be valued equally by all people though the increase is same. Therefore, people who value hike in compensation are most likely to put in more efforts than those who value it less.

Expectancy: This is 'expectation' on the part of people that a particular action or a set of actions would lead to produce the outcome they desire to achieve, which in turn gets them what they value. For example, some employees may expect that performing beyond targets will help them climb the career ladder fast.

Instrumentality: It is concerned with 'mechanisms' people use to attain goals. For example, people who are interested to grow fast in their career may employ two mechanisms. Firstly, they choose to perform exceedingly well in their jobs with an expectation that this ensures them a quick promotion. Secondly, this promotion is perceived as a mechanism to reach higher level in the career. Here, performing exceedingly well is the first level outcome and promotion is the second level outcome.

All the three elements mentioned above are building blocks of performance management. This basic philosophy of expectancy is significantly used in two ways as shown in Figure 1.9. Firstly, it establishes the attractiveness of outcomes of goal/rewards for achieving the goals. Secondly, it manages expectations of people by ensuring logical association between degree of performance and type of reward that is appropriate to the need structure of people.

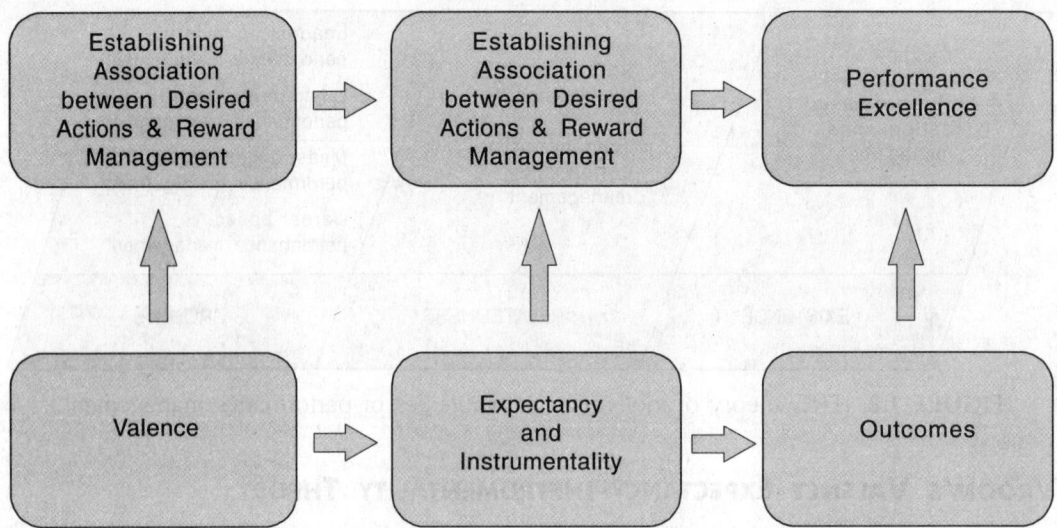

FIGURE 1.9 Vroom's motivation theory vs. strategies of performance management.

COGNITIVE EVALUATION THEORY

This theory proposed by R. Charms in 1968 has massive managerial implication for practice of performance management. It argues that excessive application of extrinsic rewards decreases the intrinsic motivation levels. For example, a higher compensation level drives people to perform activities which they may not like or are comfortable with or which their aptitude doesn't suit. Still they compromise their intrinsic value for the sake of extrinsic rewards. When people trade off their intrinsic motivation for external rewards, they will never be able to realize their potential implying low self-esteem and self-actualization levels.

The second important contribution of this theory is that extrinsic motivators and intrinsic motivators are not independent rather dependent on each other. As overemphasis on extrinsic rewards causes decline in the need for fulfilment of intrinsic motivations, the absence of extrinsic rewards such as a fair compensation, good working conditions can result in reduced desire for satisfaction of intrinsic needs like performing higher-level tasks/achievements and seeking broader responsibilities. Therefore, performance management should balance both extrinsic and intrinsic needs and their gratification as shown in Figure 1.10. Lack of semblance can contribute to under performance of organizations and their people.

PORTER-LAWLER MODEL

The first premise of this theory is that motivation automatically doesn't lead to performance. There will be many barriers between motivation and actual performance. These barriers may be in the form of individual's own abilities, traits and role perception. It means, an individual may not be successful in performing a task even if his/her drive to achieve is very high. The second premise that also has conclusive research support is that performance

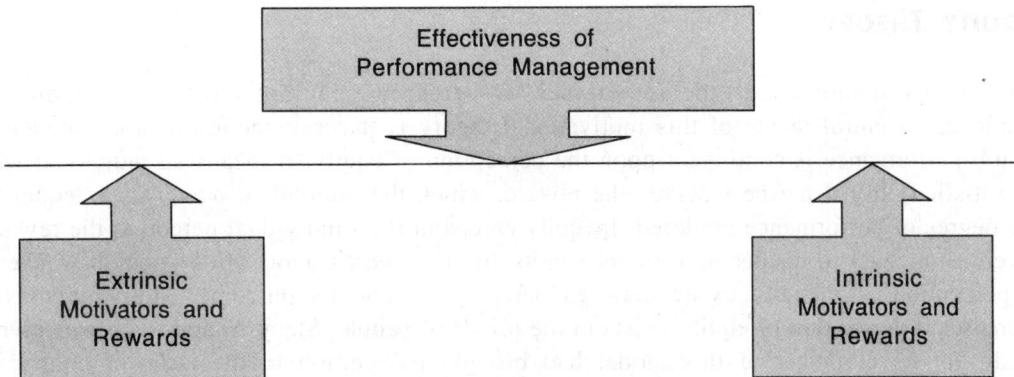

FIGURE 1.10 Cognitive theory of motivation vs. strategies of performance management.

doesn't automatically lead to satisfaction. This may be because of unattractive consequence of performance, i.e. rewards. This means reward management must be done in a way that ensures close linkage between performance and job satisfaction. The Porter-Lawler model has a significant relevance to the management of performance. The implication can be manifold but important among them is (i) removing intermediate constraints like incompetencies and facilitating correct job perceptions and (ii) ensuring sharp association between performance and satisfaction by aligning rewards.

PATTON'S MANAGERIAL MOTIVATORS

Arch Patton based on his extensive study on motivational behaviour of executives, identified six motivators that are commonly found among managerial staff. These are:

- *Challenging work:* Job responsibilities, autonomy and authority.
- *Status:* This includes titles, designations and symbols of prestige such as size of cabin, personal staff attachment, car and other material privileges.
- *Leadership:* The need to lead and occupy position of influence.
- *Competition:* This is characterized by the need to compete and secure a position. Lack of competition may dilute the drive to achieve higher-level goals and they may not provide real satisfaction even if such goals are achieved.
- *Fear:* Insecurity, fear of making errors, losing on assignments, probability of being fired and pay cuts represent this need.
- *Money:* Earning more money is real motivator of human behaviour in most of the contexts.

Patton presented this simple and practical model of managerial motivation in his book titled *Men, Money and Motivation* published in 1961. This model is relevant to various facets of performance management, especially while developing the strategies, interventions and drivers of performance management.

EQUITY THEORY

This theory demonstrates the importance of perception in motivational behaviour of employees. Central theme of this motivational theory is that satisfaction as a consequence of job performance is contingent upon the perception of equity. It means an individual will be satisfied only if he/she receives the reward, which that individual perceives as equal to the degree of performance rendered. Inequity creeps in if an individual perceives the reward given as unequal to his/her performance ratio. In other words, motivation strength weakens if perception of inequity exists between performance and its outcome. Motivation level increases if perception of equity exists in the minds of people. Stacy Adams, who was given credit for development of this model had brought recognition to the issue of equity in performance management. The equity principle has wide ramifications to the management of performance because it argues that equity should be ensured in design and implementation of various strategies, interventions and drivers of performance management.

McCLELLAND'S ACHIEVEMENT THEORY

David McClelland is the originator of this theory who presented it for the first time in his book *The Achieving Society* published in 1961. He found that some people are different from others. Their behavioural characteristics are represented by traits such as (ii) seeking complex tasks/assignments, (ii) taking calculated risks, (iii) determination to break standards and set new standards, always exert themselves on the tasks and (iv) do things better than what others do. They also seek immediate and frequent feedback about their performance and goal achievement. According to empirical findings of this theory, need for achievement can be cultivated among people. This theory, also called *theory of n Ach,* has made significant contribution to performance management, particularly in the management of star performers in organizations. Based on this theory, a few interventions and drivers of performance management are drawn in the areas of competencies, measurement, career and leadership-based performance management strategies.

ELTON MAYO'S INTERPERSONAL RELATIONSHIP-BASED MOTIVATION

Elton Mayo and his associates drawing insights from a series of experiments and studies on industrial human behaviour found that interpersonal relationships are far superior to any other variable in determining the motivation level of people. This theory argues that human beings should not be treated as mere collection of individuals but as members of an emotional group. Its implication is that managers who do not enjoy good interpersonal relationship with employees will not be in a position to motivate them. This theory is mainly originated from the experiments called *Hawthorne Studies,* conducted by Elton Mayo in the 1940s. This well-established theory points out the importance of culture, communication and teamwork in performance management.

LEWIN'S CLIMATE THEORY

Power of motivation depends upon organizational climate according to Kurt Lewin as brought out in his classic book *The Conceptual Representation and the Measure of Psychological Forces* published in 1938. Principle argument of this theory, also known as *field theory*, is that human behaviour is a function of a person and his/her environment. In order to understand and manage a person's motivation, we must understand that person's environment. This explains the differences between motivation levels of people. Therefore, organizational climate has enormous influence, to the extent that arousal and repression of motivation are subject to its cooperation.

LITWIN AND STINGER'S RESEARCH ON MOTIVATION-ORGANIZATIONAL CLIMATE RELATIONSHIP

Two researchers, namely Litwin and Stinger, based on their study of a number of managers in industrial organizations, found that motivational behaviour, particularly achievement motivation, is strongly correlated to a positive organizational climate. They found that strength of motivation is affected by organizational climate to a large extent.

McGREGOR'S XY THEORY

Douglas McGregor, based on his years of study of managers and human resource management practices, presented two distinct perspectives about people at work in the book *The Human Side of Enterprise* published in 1960. This theory known as *X* and *Y* assumptions of human behaviour has some significant cues for management of performance. Assumptions of *X* are centred on negative impression about people and *Y* is drawn from trust and positive orientation of human work behaviour. These assumptions are:

X Assumptions of Work Behaviour

- Average human beings have an inherent dislike of work and look to avoid work as much as they can.
- People need to be coerced, controlled, directed and threatened with punishment in order to be driven towards work, due to their dislike of work.
- Average human beings prefer to be directed, wish to avoid responsibility, possess relatively little ambition and seek security above all.

Y Assumptions of Work Behaviour

- Work in the form of both physical and mental efforts is natural to human beings. Work is considered as equivalent to play, recreation and rest.
- Average human beings continuously seek to learn, solicit broader responsibilities and enjoy challenges of work.
- Human beings are capable of exercising self-restraint and self-control in attainment of objectives to which they are committed.

- Control and punishment have limited influence in regulating human work behaviour.
- The degree of commitment of human beings to a task is proportionate to the rewards associated with achievement of such task.
- The capacity to exercise a relatively high degree of imagination, ingenuity and creativity in the resolution of organizational problems is widely spread in the population.
- The intellectual and creative potential of human beings is only partially used in organizations.

Both these perspectives present two worlds of human behaviour at work. No one assumption is complete without the other assumption in drafting strategies, interventions and drivers of performance management. Reality is that both the characteristics are evident in human behaviour. Hence, performance management also must comprise strategies matching the twin assumptions.

LESSONS OF MOTIVATIONAL THEORIES

Motivational theories underpin the structure and content base of performance management strategies, interventions and drivers. Unless motivational chemistry of human beings is rightly understood and managed effectively, no performance management could ever be successful. Performance excellence comes from people who are well motivated. The need structure of human beings as brought out by these theories can be classified into three types as follows:

- *Materialistic needs:* Represent physical, monetary and family needs.
- *Non-materialistic needs:* Represent achievement, competency, self-esteem and actualization needs.
- *Social needs:* Represent interpersonal relationships, communication and work environment and situations.

The foundation of performance management is built upon these three motivational spheres. A dual method is followed for this purpose. First method is, each performance strategy bears the imprint of all the three motivations in the form of interventions and drivers. For example, though the basis for reward-based performance management is inspired by materialistic motive, it still takes care of non-materialistic needs in the form of non-monetary recognition interventions and drivers and social need structure in the shape of team-based strategy. The second method adopted is that each motivational sphere drives a particular type of performance management strategy. For example:

- Materialistic motivation is the foundation for reward, measurement and career-based performance management strategies.
- Non-materialistic motivation is the propeller of competency and leadership-based performance management strategies.
- Culture- and team-based performance management strategies are drawn from the structure of social motivation.

LEARNING THEORIES

The second set of theories which wield considerable influence on the performance behaviour of employees and can help in development and execution of performance management strategies, interventions and drivers are learning theories. A performance management system which is built on the foundations of learning theories could be meaningful, matured and rational. Four most important and basic learning models are discussed below:

PAVLOV'S CLASSICAL CONDITIONING

Ivan Pavlov, a Russian psychologist, had propounded this theory in the 1920s. In the process of his experiments on the digestive system of animals he found that by associating two unconnected things/events (stimulus-response) a relationship could be established. It means, responses we give to various stimulations are learned rather than natural. For example, Pavlov observed that a dog salivating at the smell of food or at the sight of food is natural. Here the food is called as unconditional stimulus and saliva as unconditional response because association between them is natural and no learning is involved. But when he is repeatedly introduced to a bell ring before serving or showing the food, the dog started salivating at the sound of bell ring. This salivation at the sound of bell ring is learned and not natural because there is no natural connection between a bell sound and saliva. This means a conditioned/neutral stimulus (bell ring) can obtain an unconditioned response (saliva) when it is paired with an unconditioned stimulus (food). This became the basis for all human learning in organizational settings.

This seminal theory provides a great deal of understanding about human behaviour. Performance management strategies such as reward, measurement and competencies are developed in consonance with the principles of this theory.

SKINNER'S OPERANT CONDITIONING

This is also known as instrumental conditioning, operant conditioning consists of four elements. These are:

- *Positive reinforcement:* A process of encouraging desirable behaviour (performance) by way of paring it with a positive condition (reward) for the responder is called positive reinforcement. Behaviour that accrues rewards tends to be repeated and grows as habit. For example, when good performance (desired behaviour) is rewarded, performance behaviour gets repeated and the connection between performance-reward gets stronger over a period of time.
- *Negative reinforcement:* Process of encouraging a desired behaviour by stopping or avoiding a negative condition to the responder is called as negative reinforcement. For example, income tax payees who do not submit their tax returns by stipulated date are required to pay penalty. Therefore, they are encouraged to submit returns within the time schedule and whoever does so is not required to pay any penalty.

- *Punishment:* This is often confused with negative reinforcement. Punishment is a process in which a negative consequence to a responder will be used to weaken or discourage an undesirable behaviour. For example, all late submissions of tax returns entail penalty. The difference between negative reinforcement and punishment is that awarding penalty is used as a mechanism in punishment whereas avoiding penalty is used in negative reinforcement.
- *Extinction:* Process of discouraging a behaviour by not associating any positive condition (reward) to the responder is called extinction. For example, whoever submits tax returns after due date will not be entitled for special discount in tax payment.

B.F. Skinner, a Harvard professor who conducted numerous experiments, had popularized this theory. This theory has been widely used in behaviour modification and learning management. In performance management too, operant conditioning stands as a pillar in reward, competency and measurement-based strategies, interventions and drivers.

LAWS OF THORNDIKE

This is also known as *Thorndike effect,* named after its proposer Edward Lee Thorndike. This is one of the earliest and path-breaking theories that explain learning behaviour. There are three laws in this:

Law of Effect: First principle states that responses to a situation that are followed by a rewarding state of affairs, will be strengthened and become habitual responses to that situation. The second principle says that responses that are followed by discomfort are weakened.

Law of Readiness: A series of responses (stimulus-response) can be obtained together to satisfy a goal, which will result in annoyance if blocked. Linking incentives to productivity is based on this principle.

Law of Exercise: Association between two or more things gets strengthened with practice over a period of time and becomes weakened when practice of associating them discontinues. For example, repeat presentation of a stimulus (production rate) -response (incentive) combination would strengthen relationship between the two, and stimulus-response that is not presented together repeatedly will be weakened.

These three laws contributed towards the development of performance-based compensation and incentive system in organizations. This theory is drawn as a building block in proposing reward and measurement-based performance management strategies, interventions and drivers.

SOCIAL LEARNING THEORY

Julian Rotter, a clinical psychologist is the founder of this theory. Central focus of this theory is that personality is shaped by an individual's interaction with his/her environment.

Therefore, we need to understand the environment of a person in order to understand and manage that person effectively. This theory argues that change in a person can be brought about by changing the environment. The only difference is that larger the interaction of a person with environment (life experience), more will be the efforts required to make change happen within that person. There are four essential elements integral to this theory. These are:

- *Behaviour potential:* It is the likelihood of a person engaging in a particular behaviour in a particular situation/context.
- *Expectancy:* A subjective probability that a particular behaviour will produce a particular outcome. There can be high, moderate or low expectation on any outcome based on a person's confidence that a type of behaviour will or will not lead to the outcome.
- *Reinforcement value:* Reinforcement refers to the desirability of an outcome. Reinforcement tends to be high if a person is attracted to the outcome and it will be low if not attracted to the outcome.
- *Predictability:* Behaviour of a person towards a particular situation/context can be predicted with the help of above three elements.

LESSONS OF LEARNING THEORIES

Though learning theories help the development of performance management strategies, interventions and drivers in a number of ways, four critical contributions are discussed here:

- Learning theories establish that a large portion of human behaviour is learned. It means human beings can learn and acquire competencies, make modifications in their behaviour based on experiences and environment. Therefore, it is the responsibility of performance managers to provide the kind of environment, resources and systems that help people to produce performance excellence. Taking cue from this well-established fact, the strategies of performance management such as reward, measurement, competency, leadership, career and culture are proposed in the following chapters.
- Learning theories discovered that a neutral stimulus when positioned in the middle of an unconditional stimulus and an unconditional response could elicit a conditional response that is equivalent to unconditional response. Reward, career, measurement and competency-based performance management strategies are drawn using this fundamental principle.
- Power of positive reinforcement in (i) encouraging desirable behaviour, (ii) influencing negative reinforcement in choosing a path to avoid a negative condition and (iii) the role of punishment and extinction in pulling back from undesirable behaviour have offered great truth and laid the path for effective management of people. This reinforcement principle is adopted as a cardinal principle and backbone in performance management of people, particularly in reward and competency-based strategies.
- Social learning theory is drawn as the foundation for development of team and culture-based performance management strategies.

NURTURING ORGANIZATION SPECIFIC PERFORMANCE MANAGEMENT

Performance management is more an action-oriented and pragmatic tool than a conceptual framework, although its structure and content are drawn from the basic tenets of organizational behaviour and organization development theories. Therefore, a performance management system must be self-explanatory with regard to its course of action. A performance management plan should always be organization specific and must be tailor-made to fit to the requirements of each organization. Internal environment, business strategy, strengths, weaknesses, vision, mission, etc. of every organization are unique and exclusive to it. Therefore, an organization intending to pursue performance management for gaining competitive advantage, must develop its own performance management system based on the strategies, interventions and drivers presented in the following chapters. A three-dimensional framework is provided below using which an organization can decide its course of action for launching an organization specific performance management system.

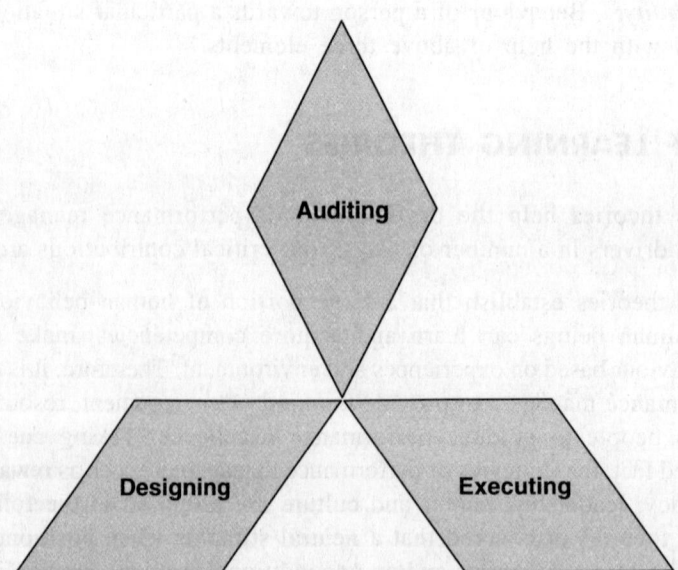

FIGURE 1.11 A three-dimensional approach to nurture organization specific performance management

DIMENSION I: AUDITING PREVAILING PERFORMANCE MANAGEMENT SYSTEM

Every organization manages employees' performance either through a formal or informal method. Some may not realize that what they are doing is indeed an act of performance management. Few organizations may be pursuing tools/techniques or functions of performance management in isolation like performance appraisal system, compensation revisions, setting up of key results areas, training, etc. The existing system, whether stand-alone or integrated, should be assessed in order to understand its current status. Primary techniques such as questionnaire survey, interview and critical incident techniques can be used to elicit views and perceptions of employees on existing performance-related management. Secondary tools like auditing policy papers, perusing pertinent records, analyzing decisions, studying financials of the company can be used to trace history and the system of performance management. This assessment should have clear objectives like:

- To what extent the existing performance management system is rational?
- Whether performance management initiatives have clear coherence among themselves?
- Whether performance management objectives have a clear linkage with business strategy?
- To what extent is performance management fulfilling needs of human resource?
- To what extent is performance management contributing towards achievement of organizational goals?
- To what extent are employees happy with existing practice of performance management?
- What is the overall focus of performance management initiative and is it in tune with organizational reality?
- How each of the performance management mechanisms, referred to in this book as performance management strategies (reward, career, team, culture, measurement, competency and leadership), are working? What is their level of contribution? Which are stronger and which are weak? How are these performance management strategies/mechanisms placed in comparison with other organizations in the same or related industries?

This dimension of performance management facilitates an organization to gain a feel of the present scenario of performance management.

DIMENSION II: DESIGNING ORGANIZATION SPECIFIC PERFORMANCE MANAGEMENT SYSTEM

Based on the results obtained at dimension I, efforts should be made to map an organization specific performance management system. Following seven chapters of the book can offer significant help in this regard. Organization specific performance management system must have the following properties:

- Sharp alignment between organizational strategy and performance management system.
- Performance centric practices capable of addressing and gratifying the entire range of human resource motivational needs.
- Internal coherence among all such performance management practices.
- Practices for institutionalizing performance management as a fundamental human resource management system.

Organizations may require a surgical approach and revolutionary change in the existing performance management system. It means the old system will be completely replaced with a new system. The second scenario can be incremental and involves strengthening the existing system in its content and direction. This may be more a renewal exercise as opposed to a surgical operation.

A performance management system so developed should be comprehensive and must comprise all related performance management strategies like reward, career, team, culture, measurement, competency and leadership development. Each of these strategies should also be very clear in their objectives, operational details, flow of activities, measurement indices, deliverables and accountability. These strategies must be positioned in such a way so as to contribute towards institutionalization of performance management individually and collectively. The following chapters focus on these issues in detail.

DIMENSION III: EXECUTING PERFORMANCE MANAGEMENT SYSTEM

Execution of performance management must proceed in a gradual, phased and evolutionary manner. Therefore, performance/human resource managers, subsequent to development of an organization specific performance management system, must decide on the plan for implementation. It is neither desirable nor feasible to install performance management system comprising all strategies/practices like reward, career, team, culture, measurement, competency and leadership at a time and as a single programme. It is ideal if the organization chooses a particular strategy like reward or team or leadership to begin with and gradually extends the implementation to all other strategies. An organization must opt for a particular performance management strategy as a main platform for launching performance management programme. This platform can be used as a launch pad for other performance management strategies in due course.

INSTITUTIONALIZING ORGANIZATION SPECIFIC PERFORMANCE MANAGEMENT SYSTEM

Mere execution of performance management strategies may not be sufficient to ensure its existence as fundamentally strong. The ultimate aim of a performance manager must be to make an organization performance centric with performance management as a fundamental management practice. Principles of performance management must be reflected in everyday working of an organization and at the same time be subsumed in the minds of people. In order to attain such a matured stage of performance management implementation, special efforts need to be made. This is called as the institutionalization effort. The institutionalization effort can be initiated in a number of ways. One definite method is integrating a particular performance management strategy with all other strategies as a part of the institutionalization process. The second method, more as a supplementary to the first one, is to make efforts to leverage on a particular performance management strategy to derive comprehensive benefits. For example, trying to achieve a salutary work culture using reward strategy. Similarly, initiating leadership-based performance strategy and leveraging it to achieve a performance centric reward system/ competency/career system likewise.

Therefore, in the following chapters, each performance management strategy is dealt with in two phases. The first phase is meant for nurturing that particular performance management strategy (for example, reward-based performance management) with the help of relevant drivers. The second phase is dedicated towards institutionalization of performance management as a fundamental system of an organization based on nurtured performance management strategy.

ROLE OF THIS BOOK

As discussed in the beginning of the chapter, this book contains seven strategies, fourteen interventions and one hundred and forty drivers of performance management. This encompasses the entire range of performance management practices. Specialty with content structure of this book is that each performance management strategy is developed as self-sufficient in itself. This means, an organization can pursue one performance management strategy out of seven and that will automatically lead to adoption of other six strategies in due course as a part of performance management institutionalization plan. Therefore, an organization in consonance with its comfort level can choose a particular performance management strategy presented in this book. Further, this book can be used by professionals in three different ways in tandem with growth stage of an organization as indicated here:

- *New organization*:   An organization which is in its infant stage can use this book for developing, executing and institutionalizing organization specific performance management system. Such organization must commence the performance management programme in the manner as presented and dealt with in this book. In other words, an organization can pursue the performance management programme with the launch of the first strategy, i.e., reward-based performance management and gradually extend it to the remaining six strategies. This gradual extension can be done as a part of the second intervention of the strategy, i.e. the institutionalization process. In comparison to an old organization, where some kind of performance system is likely to exist, institutionalizing performance management as a fundamental system of management is much easier in a new organization.
- *Established organization in which performance management is in nascent stage:* This type of organization is one which is established but performance management system is either absent or exists in an incomplete manner. This means, the organization may be having some kind of performance practices/tools which are incomplete and may not be related to each other. For example, having a performance appraisal system/training/compensation system without strong fundamentals and lacking holistic perspective. Such organizations need not follow the sequence followed in this book for initiating performance management programme. Instead, they can embrace a particular performance management strategy out of the seven strategies. However, an organization must embrace a particular strategy based on the strength of the existing performance practices/tools. For example, an organization can start performance management programme with team-based strategy if teams are strong in comparison

to other performance practices like reward, career, culture, measurement, competency and leadership.

- *Organization with strong performance management presence:* Third type of organizations are those where performance management system is strongly in place. Organization has the entire range of performance centric practices and they are reasonably related to each other. Such an organization can use this book for two purposes. Firstly, as check book referring to the existing performance management practices against seven performance management strategies dealt with in this book for possible improvement. Secondly, the book can be used for institutionalization of existing performance management system in order to transform the same to a fundamental system of organizational management. For this purpose, such organizations can use institutionalization interventions given in all the seven strategies independently.

SUMMARY

Performance management is an integrated and comprehensive framework that encompasses seven strategies such as:

(i) Reward-based performance management.
(ii) Career-based performance management.
(iii) Team-based performance management.
(iv) Culture-based performance management.
(v) Measurement-based performance management.
(iv) Competency-based performance management.
(v) Leadership-based performance management.

Each of these strategies comprises two interventions and twenty drivers. Put together, this book presents seven strategies, fourteen interventions and one hundred and forty drivers centred on nurturing and institutionalizing performance management as a fundamental system of organizational management. Principal objectives of performance management are threefold: firstly to convert human potential into performance through systematic planning and implementation of performance management strategies, interventions and drivers. Secondly to improve the bottom line of organizations and sharpen its competitive advantage in high velocity business environment and thirdly to meet the human resource needs in terms of personal and professional life.

Performance management offers multiple benefits to people and organizations. These include:

(a) Ensuring business-HR partnership.
(b) Fulfilling individual and collective needs of people.
(c) Institutionalizing high performance work culture.
(d) Facilitating long-lasting and sustainable results through measurable people management.

(e) Optimizing human capital through continuous renewal of human skills and competencies.

(f) Ensuring equity in people management issues.

(g) Helping organizations to exist, survive and succeed in a competitive, globalized and uncertain business environment.

However, conceptualizing and executing performance management in organizations encounters many challenges. Some of them are formidable and test perseverance of organizations in sustaining efforts. These are:

(a) Image of performance management as a science of utilitarian instrumentalism rather than a humanitarian model.

(b) Difficulties in alignment such as linking performance management strategies with business strategies and achieving coherence among strategies, interventions and drivers of performance management.

(c) Challenge of melding culture with performance management practice.

(d) Developing performance measurement indices.

(e) Wholeheartedly involving all classes of employees in performance management.

(f) Shortage of competent human resource professionals who can guide organizations through performance management.

(g) Complexity of performance management as an art and science.

Motivation and learning theories form the basic underlying theory and foundation for performance management. Understanding basic and advanced motivational theories, which include Hull's drive reduction model, Murray's manifest theory of motivation, Maslow's hierarchy of needs, Herzberg's two-factor theory, Alderfer's ERG theory, Vroom's valence-expectancy theory, Porter-Lawler model, Lewin's climate theory and equity theory of motivation is very important for performance managers, as they provide the fundamental structure to strategies, interventions and drivers of performance management. Likewise, grasp of implications and relevance of classical conditioning, operant conditioning, Thorndike's laws of effect and social learning theory helps in deploying customized yet scientific performance management solutions. These theories are time tested, well-established and have stood the scrutiny of critical evaluations worldwide. Most importantly, they provide the DNA of human behaviour that includes motivational and learning behaviour: two pillars of performance management. Ultimately, performance management is realized by nurturing and motivating people.

Development of a performance management system involves three dimensions:

(a) Assessing status of existing performance management system.

(b) Mapping desirable performance management system.

(c) Executing performance management system based on seven performance management strategies presented in this book.

KEY WORDS

Following are the key words discussed in this chapter:

- Performance management
- Intervention
- Integrated motivational tool
- Equity
- Alignment
- Melding culture
- Hierarchy of needs
- Drive reduction
- Valence-expectancy-instrumentality
- Achievement motivation
- Classical conditioning
- Laws of Thorndike
- Positive reinforcement

- Strategy
- Driver
- Utilitarian instrumentalism
- Rationalistic approach
- Internal coherence
- Unlearning process
- Hygiene-motivators factors
- Existence-relatedness-growth
- Manifest motivators
- Managerial motivators
- Operant conditioning
- Social learning
- Negative reinforcement

DISCUSSION QUESTIONS

1. Discuss the role of performance management in organizational excellence.
2. Managing performance of employees is easier said than done. Is it true? Discuss the challenges in realizing performance management in reality.
3. Compare and contrast performance appraisal with performance management.
4. Why is understanding motivational theories important for performance managers? Discuss the relevance of motivational theories to performance management.
5. How can learning theories/models contribute towards better understanding of performance management? Discuss four important learning theories that can have implications for design and implementation of performance management strategies, interventions and drivers?
6. What are the various strategies a rational performance management system must encompass? Why are these strategies required to maximize the performance of employees?
7. What is the equity principle and how less does it help in management of employees' performance?
8. Summarize all motivational theories using a three-tier classification.
9. Discuss the salient steps in development of performance management system.

CASE STUDIES

1. Babul works as an unskilled workman in an automobile workshop. His responsibilities include housekeeping, serving of refreshments, cleaning utensils and other errands. He belongs to low income group and has migrated from a rural area to urban centre for livelihood. He is a daily wager, whose employment is temporary in nature and is paid Rs. 30 per day. Now discuss:

   (i) Immediate motivational need of Babul based on Maslow's hierarchy of needs and Herzberg's two-factor theory.

   (ii) Draw a performance management strategy that would help in motivating Babul perform better than his present level of performance.

2. Sheetal is employed as a software programmer in a global blue chip computer firm. She serves high profile corporate clientele. Rupees two million per annum (on cost to the company basis) is her compensation package. She is also entitled for soft housing and conveyance loans. She is well received as a member of her team and recognized as a good performer in the company. Now discuss:

   (i) Where does she stand on the motivational structure of well-established motivational theories?

   (ii) What will be the appropriate performance management strategy/intervention/ driver that can maintain and enhance her performance levels?

   (iii) What kind of motivational unfulfilment can cause her performance to fall?

3. A new incentive scheme is launched in a financial services company. This scheme entails employees to draw ten per cent more pay per month if they meet the target of deposit collection to the tune of Rs 30 million in a quarter. Discuss whether it is positive reinforcement or negative reinforcement or punishment intervention.

4. Performance-based compensation structure is introduced in a fast moving consumer goods manufacturing company. According to this scheme, pay of any employee failing to achieve the agreed target will be deducted of proportionate pay. For example, fall in production target by 100 refrigerators a week causes employees to lose Rs. 100 a week. What type of reinforcement is this? Discuss with the support of related theory.

5. Whenever people sight a green flag and green light either on a railway track or at railway platform they expect a train to pass by within few minutes. How is the connection between green flag and arrival of a train established? What is this association called? Discuss the relation of this event with pertinent learning theory.

6. National Heavy Engineering Equipment Corporation is a state undertaking and functions under the control of the Government. The corporation employs 4000 engineers who were recruited through a national level competitive test. All engineers are bright professionals with outstanding academic record. They are paid handsome compensation, employment is permanent in nature and retirement life is also secured by way of pensions and medical insurance schemes. Further, their career progression

is also preplanned. According to the existing promotion policy, they are expected to be promoted to the next higher level on completion of four years of service in a particular grade. This is a hierarchical organization and flexibility on operations is limited. A survey conducted in the corporation recently reveals that morale of employees is low and so is their performance. Another survey conducted during the same period to establish the knowledge level of employees, found that the knowledge base is above average. It is ironical to this company that though the knowledge level of its engineers is above average, performance levels are poor. The issue has been discussed at a length in a high level management meeting with the help of a performance management specialist. Accordingly, they diagnosed that lack of proper performance management system is the reason for this poor performance.

Please analyze the situation based on the above details and discuss how performance management strategies could help to translate this knowledge base into performance.

7. Global Soft Solutions Ltd is a conglomerate of six business units. Top management of these units has taken a decision to merge all business units and give a new image and identity to the company. Accordingly, merger has taken place. The company is in the business of software development and has a global presence. It is profit-making and poised for phenomenal growth. Employees are white collared; highly qualified and average age is 30 years. The human resource department is given the responsibility to review and position a new performance management system across all the units, as there is a variation in the performance management practices among these units. A preliminary study revealed that performance management practices are fragmented and piecemeal in majority of the units. There are no linkages among various human resource practices like reward structure, career planning, teamwork, competence development initiatives, etc. First responsibility of human resource manager is to prepare and submit a plan for developing a tailor-made performance management system in-house for approval of board of directors.

Position yourself in the shoes of the human resource manager. Based on above details prepare a blueprint for developing a performance management system for approval of the board.

SUGGESTED READING

Adams, Stacy (1965). "Injustice in Social Exchange." In L. Berkowitz (Ed.), *Advances in Experimental social Psychology*. New York: Academic Press.

Alderfer, Clayton P. (1969). "An Empirical Test of a New Theory of Human Needs." *Organizational Behavior and Human Performance*, May, pp. 142–175.

Charms, R. (1968). *Personal Causation: The Internal Affective Determinants of Behavior*. New York: Academic Press.

Herzberg, Frederic, B. Mausner and B. Snyderman (1959). *The Motivation to Work*. New York: John Wiley.

Hull, Clark Leonard (1943). *Principles of Behavior.* Chicago: The University of Chicago Press.

Lewin, Kurt (1938). *The Conceptual Representation and the Measure of Psychological Forces.* The Duke University Press.

Litwin, G.H. and R.A. Stinger (1968). *Motivation and Organizational Climate.* Boston: Harvard Business School Press.

Maslow, Abraham H. (1943). "A Theory of Human Motivation." *Psychological Review,* July, pp. 370–396.

McClelland, David (1961). *The Achieving Society.* Princeton, NJ: Van Nostrand.

McGregor, Douglas (1960). *The Human Side of Enterprise.* New York: McGraw-Hill.

Murray, H.C. (1938). *Explorations in Personality.* New York: Oxford University Press.

Patton, Arch (1961). *Men, Money and Motivation:* New York: McGraw-Hill.

Porter, L.W. and E.E. Lawler (1968). *Managerial Attitudes and Performance.* Homewood: Irwin.

Roethlisberger, F and W.J. Dickson (1939). *Management and the Worker.* Cambridge: Harvard University Press.

Rotter, Julian B. (1954). *Social Learning and Clinical Psychology.* New York: Prentice Hall Inc.

Skinner, B.F. (1953). *Science and Human Behavior.* New York: Macmillan.

Thorndike, Edward Lee (1932). *The Fundamentals of Learning.* New York: Columbia University Press.

Vroom, V.H. (1964). *Work and Motivation.* New York: John Wiley.

Strategies
Interventions
Drivers

STRATEGY 1: REWARD-BASED PERFORMANCE MANAGEMENT

Monetary and non-monetary rewards are basic building blocks in the architecture of performance management. This is like foundation in the motivational behaviour structure of human beings. Reward is highly critical for effective performance of employees. Ineffective reward management or absence of adequate and equitable reward can cause other performance management strategies to collapse irrespective of how professionally these strategies are conceived and implemented. Reward whose basic function is to motivate and fulfil motivational needs of employees, can become a fertile source of demotivation if not properly addressed. An unprofessionally conceived and badly executed reward strategy often satisfies a section of employees at the cost of other sections of employees and sometimes at the cost of organizational health. A systematically evolved and applied reward strategy not only gratifies basic motivational needs of employees, but also enables employees to operate at higher motivational level.

In brief, reward management is cardinal for success of performance management and has unlimited potential in motivating employees to give their best performance. Managing reward and leveraging it as a performance management strategy requires a holistic approach and professional acumen. Reward is a double-edged sword. Reward must be made and extended keeping in mind individual and collective interests of employees, and at the same time it should have an intimate relationship and alignment with strategic objectives of an organization. Traditionally, interests of organization (management) and that of its employees as far as monetary rewards are concerned, are assumed to be conflictive. There is logic in such an assumption. However, modern economies, changing cultural ethos and ultra people management practices have altered this proposition to a great extent. As a result today there are practices like ESOPs, involvement, empowerment and partnerships offering to workforce. However, much remains to be done in this area. First priority for organizations is that they must reorient their compensation, incentive and recognition schemes to be performance focused. These individual and piecemeal practices should also be brought under the umbrella of reward management. In other words, reward must be used and deployed as a powerful corporate strategy to obtain superior employee and organizational performance. Keeping in view this first and important priority, this chapter presents reward-based performance management strategy as a precious instrument. This instrument is expected to enhance performance of employees and contribute towards creating performance excellence as a way of organizational life.

This chapter is presented in five parts. First part discusses what is reward management and what it is not in the context of performance management. Significance of reward-based performance management strategy in the overall framework of performance management is described in part two. Theoretical foundations of basic and essential reward management, both monetary and non-monetary, and insights into how these theories offer means for crafting an organizationally dovetailed performance centric reward management is illustrated in part three. The reward-based performance management strategy is developed encompassing twin interventions. The first intervention of nurturing reward-based performance management policy and practice is presented in part four. Part five captures the second intervention, i.e. capitalizing on reward-based management in institutionalization of performance management.

REWARD MANAGEMENT

Reward management in the context of performance management is defined as *an integrated reward system that ensures equitable avenues to employees for fulfilment of their financial and non-financial needs and recognition urge for their contribution to attainment of organizational goals*. Performance-stimulated reward system possesses the following characteristics:

1. Reward emphasizes not only financial compensation, but also non-financial rewards like enrichment of job, work autonomy/freedom, company sponsored family tours, best employee awards and popularization of employee achievements in house journals, etc.
2. Rewards must be offered in proportion to respective employee contribution/services in fulfilment of organizational responsibilities and achievement of organizational goals.
3. Reward must be equitable implying that there should be equilibrium in reward offered to an employee in comparison to others.
4. Reward must be integrated implying that there must be balance and comprehensiveness in design and application of the reward management strategy.
5. Reward should be capable of delivering dual results, i.e. fulfilment of motivational needs of employees and achievement of organizational objectives/goals.
6. Reward should be performance driven and create performance excellence through institutionalization of performance management systems.

WHAT IS NOT REWARD MANAGEMENT

It is equally important to clarify what is not reward in the context of performance management. Reward in the context of performance management is neither a simple monetary-based compensation management nor a socialistic patterned reward. Performance centric reward management, therefore, does not mean:

1. Mere monetary compensation for services rendered in organization that is devoid of non-monetary aspects.
2. Offering all employees same compensation regardless of their actual contribution.
3. Managing reward for the sake of reward implying reward as an independent system in the organization.
4. Reward management neither contributing towards employees satisfaction nor for organizational achievement.
5. Inequity in reward implying right pay/recognition for wrong person (position or wrong pay/recognition for the right person (position).
6. Absence of integration among various monetary and non-monetary reward practices vogue in organization.

SIGNIFICANCE OF REWARD IN PERFORMANCE MANAGEMENT

Reward as discussed in the beginning of this chapter is a key practice in the overall framework of performance management grand strategy. Reward strategy consists of two valuable properties in motivational behaviour of employees. First property is undoubtedly the monetary component of reward management which can fulfil employees' lower-level needs like hygiene factors or physiological and security needs. The second property is:

FIGURE 2.1   Significance of reward-based performance management.

non-monetary component of reward management consisting of recognition and job autonomy. This property has an enormous potential to fulfil higher motivational factors such as self-esteem and self-actualization factors. Employees can be motivated to offer peak performance on their jobs by tying their motivational need structure to the performance structure of an organization. Further, the significance of reward in creating performance excellence in employees and consequently in organizations can be traced in the following discussion.

Reward as Source of Organizational Effectiveness

Organizational effectiveness can be obtained only from high-performing employees. High-performing employees can make other resources perform highly. Reward is a proven and established means of stimulating employees to perform exceedingly well. Studies of all genres highlight that a poorly designed and implemented reward system can cause loss of morale among employees and this eventually can lead to organizational ineffectiveness. On the other hand, lessons of organizational excellence illustrate that reward is one of the basic strategies that ensures employee motivation hovers on the higher echelons on continuous basis. No organization can really aim to be effective unless its reward system is effective.

Reward as Medium between Organization and Employees

If there is any practice that brings organization and its employees together, it is reward. Therefore, successful management of reward is important to both organization and its employees. Reward has the capacity to perform the role of a medium. The top management of an organization can communicate importance of performance through reward and it can also lay the foundation for sound people management. Employees also tend to utilize reward as a channel to air their views and concerns on various performance-related issues. It has also been observed that employees tend to receive substantial rewards when organization's performance is great and get less when organization is slipping into the red. This illustrates how organizational health depends on the reward system.

Reward as Avenue of Multiple Motivations Fulfilment

An employee works in an organization mainly to (i) earn livelihood, (ii) acquire luxuries, (iii) secure future, (iv) secure a respectable place and (v) gain recognition in society and pride about self-performance and achievements. Reward strategy provides avenues and opportunities to all employees in an organization to fulfil these motivational needs to their satisfaction. An organization can transform employees potential into performance by systematically tying performance of employees to gratification of their motivational needs. Therefore, the reward strategy not only helps employees to earn their livelihood, but also enriches their work experience and provides them motivational satisfaction at all levels.

Reward as Factor of Motivation

Reward is a dynamic instrument. It not only creates opportunities for fulfilment of motivational needs as discussed above, but also enhances the intensity of motivation. This means, employee motivation doubles every time he/she is suitably rewarded. Enhanced motivation leads to higher performance, which in turn leads to higher rewards. This is a cycle of performance-reward-performance, which demonstrates the dynamic relationship between performance and reward. Therefore, organizations must effectively utilize this relationship for enhancing performance.

Reward as Performance Guide

Reward itself can guide the organization and its employees to perform at their best. Reward encourages healthy competition and collaboration among employees to perform well, which leads to innovation in the pursuit of reward achievement. This reward achievement is not the main motive for all hard work and great performance, as might appear on the surface. Rather somewhere during the journey, performance itself becomes the destination. In other words, as the reward needs of employees change from financial to a combination of financial-cum-non-financial to sheer non-financial, the performance contours also grow from simple skilled work to breakthrough innovations. This is like growing the needs of employees, thus driving them to grow in work performances. In this way, reward can guide performance excellence in organizations.

Reward as Source of Differentiation

General performance profile of a typical organization consists of a marginal percentage of high performers and low performers, and majority of average performers. Performance of average employees can be enhanced through suitably rewarding high performers and depriving reward from low-performing employees. This reward distinction not only helps to manage different performers differently, but also facilitates average performers who are generally fence sitters to jump into the bandwagon of high performers. The organization's inability to create this reward distinction can lead to poor performance since all employees tend to get rewarded whether there is performance or no performance.

Reward as Source of Employee Involvement

Employee involvement, participation and empowerment studies sufficiently establish that performance excellence can come from employees who are totally involved with organization. This involvement can be obtained only by creating opportunities for employees to involve themselves in organizational management. Reward is one potential source that can be effectively tapped for creating these avenues of involvement. There is agreement among academicians, consultants and practitioners of human resource management that an equitable and suitable reward system can encourage employees to get involved emotionally with an organization and shape their professional journey in tandem with the organizational plans. An unprofessionally conceived and applied reward system can cause great deal of frustration and consequential alienation of workforce from the core of organizational functioning. Further, a good reward system works as a strategy for retention of talented employees. No employee would ever attempt to sign off as long as the organization's reward system is equitable and up to the satisfaction of employees. In fact, the reward system when managed well creates a perception of security. This also creates an assurance in the minds of employees that here right and wrong are easily distinguished and recognized. Therefore, reward as a factor of employee involvement has a principal role in policy and practice of performance management.

Reward as Source of Innovation

Non-financial rewards generate a high degree of internal drive in employees to excel. Zeal to perform excellently paves way for innovation. Reward systems possess an inherent capacity to pump actualization drive in human beings. Therefore, well-designed and appropriately focused non-financial rewards provide right recognition to employees and mature as a source of innovation. Innovating capability is the indicator of the highest level of performance in any organization. Many employees possess aptitude that allows them to break the ceiling of norms and make breakthroughs, but due to lack of conducive environment in the form of adequate recognition system, employees unknowingly refrain from exploiting their own potential. A good reward system can bridge this gap effectively.

Reward as Source of Competitiveness

A common observation of human resource professional circuit is that (i) all high-performing organizations pay and recognize employee contributions well and (ii) low-performing organizations have a kind of unprofessional and blunt reward system that fails to recognize employee contributions. This observation has great truth in it. Organizations in order to attract formidable talent should have a robust reward system. In natural process, reward system itself contributes to organizational performance in a measure of proportion. Organizational competitiveness comes from sheer performance capacity of organizations. This capacity can be sharply evident when organizations encounter situations of crisis. Therefore, any organization that intends to strengthen its competitiveness must first focus on implementing a suitable reward system.

Reward as Source of Organizational Harmony

Traditionally, monetary rewards popularly referred to as compensation issues, are at the heart of human resource management and therefore at the centre of performance management. Lack of agreement/understanding between management and a section of employees on how compensation is to be administered is the most influential factor for a few organizations performing below normal. Every year, millions of man days are lost on account of compensation-related disputes and misunderstandings. This lack of understanding further breeds distrust among employees and stakeholders and has serious adverse implications for organizational performance. Even the best of technology can fail to deliver goods if industrial harmony is absent. Industrial unrest becomes a hurdle in implementing employee development interventions. In a situation where there is no trust, efforts to convert potential into performance fall flat. Reward that is managed well can be a great source of organizational harmony, which is a prerequisite for great employee and organizational performance.

THEORETICAL FOUNDATIONS OF REWARD-BASED PERFORMANCE MANAGEMENT

Theories pertaining to reward mainly revolve around basic motivational theories such as Maslow's hierarchy of motivation, Hergberg's two-factor theory, Alderfer's existence, relatedness growth theory and most importantly Vroom's valence-expectancy-instrumentality theory. These theories chiefly illustrate (i) the significance of equity in rewards, (ii) relationship between pay and job satisfaction, (iii) different types of rewards: financial, non-financial and indirect financial incentives, (iv) compensation strategies and (v) determinants/techniques such as job evaluation, gain sharing, variable pay that help in designing a scientific reward system. The second set of theories is behavioural, encompassing employment contract theory, job characteristics model, theory of equitable payment, and the goal setting theory.

LAWLER'S REWARD AND JOB SATISFACTION MODEL

Edward Lawler, based on his years of research on relationship between pay and job satisfaction, held that job satisfaction of an employee is contingent upon his/her perception of being paid proportionately to the service/effort rendered or work performed. Employees tend to be disappointed, culminating in job dissatisfaction, if they believe that they are compensated disproportionate to their contribution. Therefore, it is incumbent upon an organization that compensation system should not only be in proportion to performance, but also be managed in such a way that employees perceive it as equitable.

SWEENEY, MCFARLIN AND INDERRIEDEN'S PAY AND JOB SATISFACTION MODEL

This is a model developed by using relative deprivation theory for explaining relationship between pay and job satisfaction. According to this model, six factors cause pay dissatisfaction in employees. These are:

(i) Discrepancy between what employees want and what they receive
(ii) Discrepancy between a comparison outcome and what they get
(iii) Past expectations of receiving more rewards
(iv) Low expectations for future
(v) A feeling of deserving or being entitled to more than they are getting
(vi) A feeling that they are not personally responsible for poor results. This model is similar to Lawler's theory and focuses on equity principle, stressing on importance of employee perception of fairness in pay.

TYPES OF REWARDS

Non-monetary Reward

Non-monetary rewards include (i) conducive working conditions, (ii) job security, (iii) appreciation letter, (iv) felicitation of best performing employees, (v) providing challenging assignments, (vi) granting work freedom, (vii) opportunity to participate in policy making committees, etc.

Indirect Monetary Reward

This includes rewards like health insurance, leave salary, company sponsored family picnics, soft loans, cafeteria benefits, retirement benefits, club membership, so on and so forth.

COMPENSATION STRATEGIES

McNally's Compensation Strategies

According to Kathleen McNally, an organization must choose one of the three compensation strategies explained here. First is called *high pay strategy*. Basic philosophy of this strategy is: paying higher than industry average ensures superior performance, enables attraction of talented human resource to an organization, minimizes unwanted employee attrition and infuses high morale among employees and makes them believe that they are above average.

Second strategy is known as *low pay strategy*. Premise behind this strategy is twofold. Firstly, organizations may not be able to offer high or reasonable compensation because of external constraints like adverse market conditions and internal factors like poor financial performance and budget limitation. Secondly, a few organizations believe that lessening compensation enhances organization's competitiveness due to low labour costs. Third strategy is called *comparable pay strategy*. This is the most popularly applied strategy in organizations. It is based on conformist principle implying that pay is susceptible to cost of living index, compensation trends in industry, government legislation and bargaining power of collective bargaining forums. All these three strategies have their own merits and demerits.

Broadbanding

Broadbanding is a compensation strategy that originated in the 1970s but came into lime-light in 1980 by virtue of increasing emphasis on flattening organizational structures and creating organizational flexibility. Broadband is a simple concept but immensely hard to implement. *Broadband means collapsing or merging number of job grades into smaller number*. For example, transforming a 20 grades organizational structure into five grades for salary and job enrichment purposes. This gives opportunity for all employees to perform quality of tasks and also receive proportionate rewards without the hurdle of tall salary grades. Broadband system has assumed importance in the new economic era and is practiced worldwide.

Common Compensation Techniques

Organizations follow different techniques for implementing incentive schemes. Some of the commonly pursued techniques are:

(i) *Straight piecework:* This is a simple method of compensating for a measurable unit of production/result in defined time duration. For example, paying $50 for processing 10 customer calls in 60 minutes.

(ii) *Standard hour plan:* This is a commonly implemented method in most of organizations. This technique provides for paying compensation for unit of work time. For example, paying $50 for 48 hours of work in six days.

(iii) *Taylor plan:* This is a technique developed by Frederick Taylor and extensively used in manufacturing-based organizations. This plan consists of two types of compensation: basic pay assured to every employee for producing stipulated goods and additional reward for producing additional unit of goods over and above the stipulated.

(iv) *Productivity linked bonus:* This is identical to Taylor plan that gives scope for hourly compensation and bonus for above average performance monthly or yearly.

(v) *Team compensation:* In order to reward equitably wherever tasks are interdependent and performed by a group of employees, team compensation has become popular. There will be a common basic compensation structure that is applicable uniformly to all employees working in a particular team.

TECHNIQUES OF DESIGNING A REWARD SYSTEM

Job Evaluation

This is a popularly employed technique to establish relative worth of jobs in an organization for the purpose of determining pay. Job evaluation process identifies contribution of each job for organizational functioning and effectiveness. Job evaluation also determines (i) skills required to perform a job, (ii) degree of responsibility involved, (iii) effort required to perform the job and (iv) related working conditions. Information as obtained forms the basis for establishing compensation.

There are four techniques that are used as a part of job evaluation exercise. These are:

(i) Job ranking method
(ii) Classification
(iii) Factor comparison
(iv) Point system.

Application of one or more of these job evaluations techniques yields valuable information that can be effectively used to establish logical comparison and relative worth of jobs in order to determine compensation level correspondingly.

Hay Guide Chart Profile Method

This is one of the techniques used in evaluation of jobs. This is similar to the point method but a more reliable and sophisticated technique. Hay guide determines the worth of a job based on four vital parameters. These are:

(i) *Know-how:* Knowledge and skills required to perform job effectively

(ii) *Problem solving:* Abilities related to analyzing, reasoning, evaluating, developing solutions and making execution plans

(iii) *Accountability:* This refers to responsibility for a performance or action or decision taken

(iv) *Ability:* Additional compensable elements such as unique and exceptional conditions in which a job is to be performed.

These parameters are broken into further measurable elements. Points are accorded to each of these elements that form the basis for establishing said relative worth of a job.

Gain-sharing Techniques

Gain-sharing plans are primarily employed to distribute benefits of cost-cutting interventions, increased production, increased quality, etc. to employees organization-wide. However, gain-sharing techniques are more often used for enhancing production than anything else. Basically, there are four techniques in gain sharing. These are as follows:

Lincoln Electric Plan: This plan is named after its author John Lincoln. This technique comprises four fundamental principles such as (i) there is no basic pay and only piecework pay, (ii) no mandatory retirements implying that as long as an employee is producing he/she continues in employment, (iii) no prerequisites, leaves, bonus, and (iv) employees who have worked for more than two years cannot be laid off. In brief, this is a technique that provides for compensation in lump sum, proportionate to the service rendered. This means there will be a direct relationship between compensation and results.

Scanlon Plan: This is also named after its author Joe Scanlon. This technique comprises activities such as suggestion, group incentive and employee participation. Employees are organized into teams and whichever team invents and practices methods to reduce waste, save time and increase productivity, is rewarded. This is a comprehensive technique because it allows employees to participate and influence decision-making.

Rucker Plan: Like the Scanlon plan, this plan also promotes suggestions from employees and their participation in improving productivity. But this plan provides limited freedom to employees to participate in organizational decision-making. Here employees give suggestions, which are evaluated by a screening committee before they are adapted. Proportionate monetary reward is offered to employees if their suggestions result in profits to the organization.

Improshare: This technique is derived from consultative style of management. Here employees do not have scope for participation or involvement, but managers in the process of improving production and efficiency consult them. Employees are offered bonus compensation if that consultation process results in the organization making profits.

BEHAVIOURAL THEORIES OF COMPENSATION

In addition to motivational theories, some of the important behavioural theories of compensation are described as follows:

Employment Contract Theory: This refers to considering exchange of work for compensation or reward. Interesting issue in this theory is that each party makes an attempt to gain more than it spends, i.e. the employee tries to gain more compensation in comparison to the effort rendered, and the employer tries to obtain more work for less pay.

Job Characteristics Model: This model provides job autonomy, skill variety, task identity, task significance and feedback as stimulation and reward for higher performance. This means that employees tend to perceive these job enrichment elements as rewards in themselves.

Theory of Equitable Payment: This theory proposes that employees have an intuitive knowledge about their knowledge, skills and capacity to work, and compare them with their compensation to establish fairness.

Goal Setting Theory: This theory postulates that when employees are encouraged to participate in goal setting, determination of performance standards and defining performance evaluation methods themselves become motivational sources for higher performance. Linking pay for such activities can enhance involvement of employees in such activities also. However, in a goal setting activity, involvement itself becomes a bigger reward than monetary compensation.

FACTORS INFLUENCING REWARD SYSTEM

External Factors

Reward system of an organization is susceptible to pressures from external factors such as: (i) state legislation, (ii) market forces, (iii) cost of living, (iv) quality of living, (v) industry trends, (vi) labour supply and demand and (vii) geographical/location factor. For example, in India, Minimum Wages Act, 1948, Payment of Wages Act, 1936, Equal Remuneration Act, 1976 and social security legislation like Provident Fund Act 1952, Payment of Gratuity Act, 1972 have their own influence on organizational compensation management. Similarly, availability of a particular kind of workforce with particular skills also decides the rate of compensation for such positions. Inflation or cost of living index is considered as a primary factor in determination of basic pay. Generally, organizations located in a location tend to follow comparable compensation strategies regardless of the type of industry they belong to.

Internal Factors

Internal factors such as (i) financial health of organization, (ii) strength of collective bargaining forces, (iii) philosophy of organization and (iv) degree of skills required in organization influences reward structure. A profitable company can offer high compensation range and implement non-financial rewards that a loss-making company cannot afford. Similarly, an organization may have to agree to the collective bargaining demands if presence of unions is strong. As opposed to this, a green field venture, which means an organization free from trade unionism, can have freedom to adopt its own strategy in compensation and non-compensation management.

Individual Factors

There are individual factors that directly influence the reward system in an organization. These are: (i) performance of employees, (ii) competency of employees, (iii) skills and experience of employees, (iv) seniority and potential of employees. These factors are mainly taken into consideration for determining variable or performance linked compensation. These factors are also adopted as basic barometers for applying various non-financial and indirect financial rewards like best performance award or ESOPs (Employee Stock Ownership Plan).

LESSONS OF REWARD THEORIES

Reward theories as discussed in the foregoing content have significant implications for the design and implementation of the reward-based performance management. As already indicated some of them are theories, some are techniques, while others deal with the composition of reward. Nevertheless, the valuable insights these theories offer are briefly discussed in the forthcoming content. These insights are taken into consideration while suggesting twin interventions of the reward-based performance management strategy and relevant drivers.

Reward is Psychological

As opposed to the dominant belief of reward as a physical phenomenon, this is a psychological issue too. Behavioural theories, especially expectancy and exchange theories clearly highlight the role of employees' perception in obtaining effectiveness of the reward system. The reward system should not only be equitable in real sense, but also needs to be managed in such a way that all employees perceive it as fair. Many organizations lose talented employees to their competitors despite paying equivalent and sometimes more than their competitors, due to their inability to communicate to employees the real value of compensation. Theories in this regard sufficiently establish that management of employees' perceptions is a vital issue in reward management. Therefore, the lesson for the reward-based performance management strategy is that 'employees perceptions' must be given due consideration in its framework.

Contingent Reward Management

Broadly, there are three compensation strategies such as high compensation, low compensation and average compensation. Each of these strategies has its own merits and demerits. For example, a high compensation strategy advocates an idea that high compensation automatically attracts high talent while low compensation philosophy is built on labour cost factor, i.e.

incurring low employee cost becomes a competitive advantage. Therefore, what strategy is ideal for an organization depends upon the organizational philosophy and the internal and external context. Hence, the lesson is that organizational contextual factors must be considered while developing and executing a reward-based performance management strategy.

Reward is Susceptible to Multiple Forces

Management of reward is subject to consideration of many internal and external factors. Internal factors typically concern the organization's ability to pay and reward employees. Of course, strength of collective bargaining forces also influences the reward system. External forces include demand and supply forces, inflation and customers. These factors must be carefully analyzed and considered while designing a reward-based performance management strategy.

Reward is a Comprehensive System

Reward is not just equivalent to monetary compensation. Reward consists of monetary aspects such as basic pay, allowances, incentives and reimbursements, indirect monetary aspects like medical insurance, leave salary and retirement assurances and non-monetary aspects like recognition schemes. Each of these components is equally important to obtain the real impact. The reward system which is devoid of this comprehensiveness may not attain desired effectiveness in terms of employees' satisfaction and organizational performance. This variety in rewards has come into existence corresponding with hierarchical motivational structure. Therefore, reward-based performance management must comprise all these rewards variety and apply them to employees, depending upon their motivational profile.

Job Enrichment as Reward Strategy

Theories such as job characteristics, goal setting and need for achievement motivation emphasize on (i) challenging nature of work, (ii) opportunities for employees' involvement and participation, (iii) problem-solving opportunities. These can be effectively tapped as reward strategies. These theories are developed on the premise that employees are driven by higher-level of motivational needs once lower-level needs are gratified. Higher-level needs can be fulfilled only by providing opportunities for employees to participate in decision making and enriching their jobs through task autonomy and task variety. Higher-end strategies like this must be made a part of the reward-based performance management strategy.

Fairness of Reward is Dependent upon Measurement

Job evaluation techniques play an important role in creating fairness in reward system. These techniques also highlight that measurement is important in creating equity. Measurement must be reliable and transparent. Reward systems tend to gain wide acceptance if measurement used while evaluating jobs, performance, competency are approved by employees. Therefore, the lesson here is twofold. Firstly, efforts must be made to employ measurement techniques to create a fair reward system and secondly, such measurement must be approved by majority of employees.

Compensation is Multilayered

Compensation must be evolved through many layers. These layers are basic pay and variable pay. Both are equally important as theories prove. Basic compensation provides stability and is paid for basic aptitude and general job profile. Equally powerful and becoming more important is variable compensation that includes production incentives and gain sharing. This intends to take care of exceptional performances and also to motivate people to perform at their peak. Reward-based performance management strategy must consider both these components though more emphasis is accorded to variable compensation. Variable pay is an influential factor for obtaining superior performance of employees.

Reward-Motivation-Reward Cycle

Motivation theories almost assume the status of cardinal principles for reward management. There is direct and cyclical relationship between motivation and reward. An equitable and scientific reward structure leads to higher motivation, which drives superior performance and which results in obtaining rewards. Motivational theories are the foundation for design, implementation and renewal of the reward-based performance management strategy.

REWARD-BASED PERFORMANCE MANAGEMENT STRATEGY: INTERVENTIONS AND DRIVERS

Reward-based performance management strategy is a comprehensive principle which is evolved holistically. Reward as a strategy of performance management includes all three: financial, indirect financial and non-financial rewards. Objective of the strategy is twofold. Firstly, ensuring internal consistency within the framework of reward, thereby meaning there must be integration and cohesiveness among all reward-related policies and practices that prevail in an organization. A well-knit reward strategy creates a powerful positive impact and most importantly enhances performance of employees and improves bottom line of organizations. An integrated and performance driven reward strategy contributes to strengthen performance-oriented work and creates a path for institutionalization of performance management in organizations. Therefore, an effective deployment of a reward strategy for the institutionalization of performance management is the second objective.

The strategy of reward-based performance management can be designed, executed, evaluated, renewed and institutionalized with the help of two formidable interventions. These are as follows:

1. Nurturing Reward-Based Performance Management: An essential objective of this strategy is providing the base format to design and implement an integrated reward system that is most apt and compatible with internal and external environment of an organization. Deliverables of this intervention are of two types. First is application of this intervention must result in the organization having a well-crafted reward system. Secondly, such a reward system must enable employees to optimize their potential and the organization to achieve its goals including financial objectives. This intervention is developed consisting 10 tangible and pragmatic drivers. Adoption of these drivers makes organizations progress on their reward systems.

2. *Capitalizing on Reward Strategy in Institutionalization of Performance Management*: The second intervention is committed to the general cause of institutionalizing the policy and practice of performance management comprising seven performance management strategies discussed in this book. Reward as a strategy has an independent identity and also possesses a collective character. Collective character is reflected in its natural relationship with other strategies such as career, measurement, and team. For example, reward in order to be equitable must have a direct and positive relationship with the measurement-based performance management because rewards are contingent upon task fulfilment. In order to assess the extent of task fulfilment or non-fulfilment, application and usage of measurement-based management is desirable. This intervention is also designed to be implemented with the guidance of 10 drivers.

These twin interventions along with respective drivers are discussed in the following section.

INTERVENTION 1: NURTURING REWARD-BASED PERFORMANCE MANAGEMENT

Nurturing reward-based performance management is not only an immensely challenging task, but a task which has been rarely achieved in practice. There are instances where the best of the managers despite spending years of their effort are yet to realize an equitable, objective and integrated reward system that is performance-stimulated both in the perspective of employees and organizations. Reward is absolutely a dynamic issue and ought to be managed in both perceptual and realistic sense. Both perception and reality are complex. Nevertheless, present intervention makes an attempt to make it possible to realize reward-based performance management with the support of the following drivers. Each of these drivers contributes towards evolution and practice of an equitable, objective and integrated performance-stimulated reward system.

DRIVER 1: SETTING OBJECTIVES OF REWARD SYSTEM

In order to make any intervention systematic, successful and effective, it should ideally start with formulating and articulating objectives. An objective-less programme is like a radarless ship and also susceptible for mismanagement. Nurturing a reward-based performance management begins with setting realistic objectives. This driver is dedicated for evolving such objectives. Objectives must be compatible and dovetail with organizational history, objectives and also other human resource management systems. Importantly, an organization must decide the kind of reward system it intends to put in place. At the end of this driver, organization will have clearly stated objectives and a well-articulated reward strategy that is performance centric. The following steps are suggestive of what an organization needs to do in developing this statement of objectives for a reward system.

FIGURE 2.2 Drivers of the intervention nurturing reward-based performance management.

Step 1: Determine Reward Strategy

The first step in developing an objective statement is to determine the contours of reward strategy. Often organizations do not accord much importance to strategy-making of a reward system and simply leave it to supply and demand forces to decide the progress of events. Such adhoc and just situational fulfilment management can cause enormous damage to the overall reward structure of an organization. Also, lack of a clear strategy causes contradictions within the reward system. It is of paramount importance to organizations to articulate the strategy. In this process, there are three critical aspects that an organization must examine and decide. Firstly, it must decide 'volume of reward' as a strategy. This means organization must choose whether it intends to be in high reward category, average reward category or low reward category. There is no good or bad with any of these options. It is the organizational situation and overall philosophy that decides fitness and goodness of these options rather than options themselves. There are cases where organizations achieve performance excellence even with minimal rewards because their overall philosophy is oriented towards self-actualization like missionaries and other religious institutions. Therefore, it needs to be decided which option most suits an organization's reality the most.

Step 2: Articulate Objectives

Having developed a clear reward strategy, the next step is to develop objectives for the reward system. Objectives of a reward system can be manifold such as:

  (i) To ensure fair living of employees
 (ii) To reward equitably for work performed/services rendered
(iii) To share wealth generated by organization with collective effort
(iv) To enhance performance of employees
 (v) To increase employee commitment
(vi) To attract the best talent from labour market.

Objectives must be developed keeping in view the organizational objectives. There must be a high degree of integration between reward objectives and organizational objectives. Lack of this integration tapers off the impact of both organizational and reward objectives in influencing course of progress. Therefore, organizational objectives and business plans must form the basis for formulating reward objectives. There must be cohesiveness and homogeneity in these objectives. Objectives as set must be critically scrutinized in the light of their practicality and deliverables. Ultimately, every performance management system must result in value addition to both employees and the organization.

Step 3:   Balance Stakeholders

While setting the reward objectives, consideration must be given to balance interests of all stakeholders of the organization which include stockholders, employees, customers and distributors/marketing agencies. Reward, especially monetary, can have implications for others. Therefore, reward should not be managed in a way that costs others. However, it is also equally right that enhancement of reward need not always cost others. This only requires an act of balance. Effective balancing can be seen when no stakeholder perceives that the other stakeholder is getting more than they deserves and at the cost of organizational interest. The statement of objectives must ensure that there is harmony among all players as far as rewards system is concerned.

Step 4:   Focus on Superordinate Purpose

Mostly reward objectives must be derived from superordinate purpose of reward and reward strategy of an organization. For example, building competency and enhancing performance of employees can be a typical superordinate goal. This makes it abundantly clear that the major concern of a reward system in such a context is to manage reward to achieve performance excellence. Therefore, supplementary objectives must be made to endorse superordinate goal. This must be treated as a patent principle for all future purposes and for management of reward functions.

At the end of implementation of this driver, an organization must have reached to a stage where (i) it has a well-structured reward strategy clearly stating organization's reward philosophy and (ii) a statement of reward objectives.

DRIVER 2:   TRACK PAST AND PRESENT REWARD SYSTEM

Once an organization creates a reward vision mentioned here as reward objectives, the next macro level activity must be to make efforts to understand philosophy, underlying assumptions, policies and practices of the existing reward system. Every organization, whether it has a formal human resource system or not, must possess a reward system. This reward system will also have history that clarifies why an organization follows a particular pattern for management of reward. Therefore, in order to nurture a reward-based performance management strategy, it is essential that past and present is studied, analyzed and inferences are drawn. Apart from revealing interesting issues, it gives a perspective that helps while implementing the proposed performance centric reward system. Though every organization needs to adopt its own methods and steps to study this issue, a suggestive line of action is described here:

Step 1:   Understand Reward Approach

Firstly, the basic approach of an organization towards reward must be studied. This approach includes studying factors, which traditionally management considers to determine, composition and type of reward. Secondly, efforts must be made to identify the reward strategy, written or unwritten. Thirdly, most influential reasons for an organization preferring the kind of reward it is offering to employees must be analyzed. For example, an organization must not be implementing non-monetary reward practices or may be following an ad hoc approach. In contrast, some organizations may emphasize more on non-monetary rather than monetary reward. There must be some reason for such an approach, which need elaborate study to establish the basic underlying assumptions for the same. Once management's approach towards reward is understood, it becomes much easier to improve upon it in line with stated objectives or replace it with a more scientific reward system.

Step 2:   Study Prevailing Reward Framework

This step can also be combined with the first step. All reward-related documents, wage agreements, salary negotiations, compensation structure, reward methodology, policies related to indirect and non-monetary schemes must be studied and directional points must be generated. It is always useful to track the past as far back as possible. This effort must be supplemented with discussing and getting answers on some of the leading issues from the employees involved with preparation/implementation of such schemes. It is important to identify the overall focus of the prevailing reward system such as what it is contributing to, whether to maximize performance of employees, whether to just compensate for the work done, whether there is pressure of collective bargaining forces, whether to comply with state legislation provisions, so on and so forth. Further, alignment of such reward policy framework with organizational objectives must be studied.

Step 3:   Study Reward Mechanisms

Mechanisms mean techniques used in establishing relative worth of jobs/positions for determining monetary reward, techniques used for incentives, indirect monetary mechanisms like health insurance, social security and also instruments used for managing non-monetary and recognition-oriented reward practices. These are required to be studied and analyzed, particularly their role and relevance to the reward management that is in vogue in an organization.

Step 4: Understand Employee's Concerns

Efforts at the third step must be directed towards assessing employees' satisfaction and concerns with the existing reward system. Appropriate instruments and methods such as survey, interview and group discussion must be used with all or identified resource persons to gauge the satisfaction level of employees with the ongoing reward system. Based on the data obtained further course of action must be initiated to understand the reasons for satisfaction or dissatisfaction. Particularly, satisfaction of employees with the system per se must be assessed rather than only focusing on the type and level of rewards.

Step 5: Study Reward vs Profits

The final step in this driver is understanding the relationship between financials of an organization and its reward system. Whether reward, particularly monetary, is subject to fluctuations along with fortunes of the company or is it independent to financial health? This gives a perspective on how an organization treats profits and employee rewards. There are organizations which even at the cost of profits, extend handsome reward to employees and there are organizations who prefer that their employees sacrifice to keep the organization in the range of profits.

At the end of this driver, an organization must have developed comprehensive insight into its reward system, rationality and underlying philosophy. It also must have identified strengths and weaknesses of its existing system and the degree of cohesiveness among its various reward practices.

DRIVER 3: DETERMINE AND APPLY REWARD METHODOLOGY

When first two drivers are successfully implemented, an organization will own two important learnings. Firstly, it must have developed a reward strategy and planned a journey for realizing the same. That is called as setting reward objectives in the strategy of reward-based performance management. Secondly, the organization must have developed an in-depth understanding of prevailing reward system that is named as tracking the past and present of a reward system. Having made substantial progress, the organization must move to define and create a pragmatic method of designing a reward system which helps in achieving performance excellence both from employees' and organization's points of view. This is a critical driver in the intervention of nurturing reward-based performance management. Though, it is ideal for an organization to develop and execute a methodology that is most apt and compatible with its internal reality and context, a few vital steps that are commonly applicable are discussed here:

Step 1: Analyzing Gaps between Existing Reward System and Proposed Reward Objectives

The first step in this driver must be identifying gaps, similarities and differences between the prevailing reward system as studied at the level of Driver 2 and objectives as formulated at Driver 1. Many times, there can be a large gap between the proposed and the existing reward system. These gaps and differences must be systematically identified and analyzed. Higher the gap, more are the efforts required to streamline the reward system; lesser the gap, less are the efforts required for implementing new reward objectives. Gaps that are likely to surface can be of different types:

(i) Lack of integration between reward system and organizational objectives
(ii) Lack of internal consistency within the reward structure
(iii) Lack of judicious mix of monetary and non-monetary rewards
(iv) Lack of balance among various components of reward.

More resistance to the new reward system can be expected if gaps are sharp and severe. At the end of this step, data regarding gaps must be prepared in a meaningful fashion.

Step 2: Study of External Factors

As stated earlier, external factors such as (i) supply and demand factors of labour force, (ii) trends in the industry, (iii) reward system in similar organizations, (iv) location implications for reward and (v) cost of living index must be studied and their relevance and implications for the reward system, especially in the light of reward objectives, need to be analyzed. This step is expected to provide a pragmatic perspective and also enrich managers dealing with the reward system. Mere study of these aspects does not imply or make it mandatory on an organization either to follow or adhere to trends in the industry or succumb to supply and demand forces. However, it is imperative for effectiveness of the reward system that an organization's reward system is sensitive to external factors. This data also enables an organization to break the routine trend and make a fresh beginning in the reward system. Systematic efforts must be made to study, collect data, analyze it and draw inferences for designing a rational and purposeful reward system.

Step 3: Study of Internal Factors at Organizational Level

A careful study, analysis and due consideration of internal factors in order to design an appropriate reward system is of utmost importance. These internal factors include:

(i) Financial position, especially capacity to pay
(ii) Organizational structure/designations
(iii) Strength of collective bargaining forces
(iv) Technology employed in organization
(v) Working conditions
(vi) Nature of operations/activities

Depending upon the type of organization, these variables may vary. All efforts must be made to collect data and study these aspects in order to understand what kind of reward design and system suits an organization.

Step 4: Study of Internal Factors at Employee Focus

This step prescribes study of employee-related issues. These issues include: (i) employee aptitude profile, (ii) employee attitude profile and (iii) experience profile of employees. In order to understand these issues, this step must be executed in association with the competency-based performance management strategy. Competency strategy possesses rich data and analysis on competency profile of employees. This step primarily helps in designing person-based reward component. Data obtained by applying this step must be analyzed and relevant aspects that have implications for reward strategy must be drawn.

Step 5: Job Evaluation Data

An organization comprises many jobs to carry out different functions. These jobs vary in content, intensity and responsibility and, therefore, competency required to perform jobs. Study of these issues is necessary in order to determine quantum of formal reward for each job. In fact, most of the internal inequity arises due to the inability or wrong evaluation and misunderstanding of worth of a job. This misunderstanding contributes for inappropriately rewarding a job, which in turn becomes responsible for inequity. Organizations must implement job evaluation in an objective and scientific manner. A suitable job evaluation technique must be chosen. More often than not, it depends upon the volume and variety of jobs an organization carries. Job evaluation implementation requires spending formidable effort, time and resources. However, organizations intended to create a reward-based performance management have no choice but to implement job evaluation exercise. Data that job evaluation yields is immensely relevant, useful and imperative for design of an internally equitable reward system.

Effective application of this driver facilitates an organization not only to decide the methodology to be adopted to decide the reward structure, but also extends the same in practice. This driver emphasizes that an organization must carefully consider factors that directly or indirectly influence its reward system. Further, application of this driver obtains valuable data that forms the basis for design and execution of a world-class performance centric reward system. Once all these relevant factors are comprehensively studied and understood, the next macro-level action is deciding upon components of reward structure.

DRIVER 4: DETERMINING REWARD COMPONENTS

Driver 3 enables an organization to see the big picture of reward from multiple perspectives whereas the present driver encourages choosing components of reward. Reward can consist of several components as described in theoretical foundations of the reward system. These components include monetary, non-monetary and indirect monetary rewards. Challenge here is what is the judicious mix of these components, how much should be the ideal share for monetary, indirect monetary and non-monetary reward in the overall reward structure. Ultimately the effectiveness of a reward system is largely contingent upon the right blend of components. Type of reward components and their mix that an organization must choose depends upon the overall objective structure of the reward system. Following are some suggestive steps that ensure a performance-based reward component structure.

Step 1: Monetary Reward

Principle component in any reward structure is monetary reward. Studies and experiences have sufficiently established that it is the monetary reward that has supreme power to motivate employees to perform exceedingly. In a motivational structure also, monetary aspect forms the basic block as something that ensures physiological and security needs. Since middle and higher-level needs, which include social and self-esteem needs, can also be fulfilled through money, monetary reward component occupies a central place in the reward-based performance management strategy. However, the crux of the issue is how important is monetary reward in the overall reward structure. Important clarification that should be mentioned here is that monetary reward here means the monthly/weekly salary/compensation. Monetary compensation should not be less than 50 per cent and not more than 60 per cent in the overall reward sum. This helps in clearly projecting place of monetary reward in the overall structure.

Step 2: Indirect Monetary Reward

This is also a kind of monetary reward but not paid monthly and even many times directly to employees. Examples of indirect monetary reward include health insurance, gratuity and other social security measures. Indirect monetary component also has an important place in the overall reward structure. Especially, indirect monetary rewards possess an inherent capacity to instill employee commitment and consequently ensure higher employee performance. Indirect monetary reward also provides a kind of social security that presents itself as job security. Employees who are assured of a secure future tend to be stress free and focus on their performance. Therefore, this reward must be given due consideration in the reward structure. In fact, some organizations which choose a lump sum monetary strategy tend to realize the power and utility of indirect monetary reward when it comes to issues like innovation, quality and customer satisfaction. Indirect monetary mechanism provides for lasting relationship between employees and the organization. Latest entrant in the category of indirect monetary reward is employee stock ownership plans, which provide for issuance of stock share to employees at a predetermined price, usually significantly less than market price. Here also at the end of this step, an organization must clearly decide the percentage of indirect monetary component in the overall reward structure. Indirect monetary reward an organization prefers must also spell out with accompanying reasons/logic.

Step 3: Non-Monetary Reward

Reward that is devoid of financial implication or that is not in money form has gained popularity in today's organizations for more than one reason. Employees who are financially well rewarded look for some kind of recognition that fulfils their self-esteem and self-actualization needs. Employees who may not be financially very well rewarded, get stimulated for better performance through recognition-oriented rewards. This is a great opportunity for organizations to leverage on this recognition need in order to capture best performances. However, it is seen in organizations that managing non-monetary reward is more difficult than monetary reward. A badly managed recognition scheme loses on charm and can no longer work as a real recognition mechanism. Therefore, two aspects should be given high priority. Firstly, the organization must design and opt for the most appropriate recognition schemes ranging from appreciation letters to conferring annual awards to inviting on the board of company as special adviser. Secondly, such schemes must be administered with hard core sincerity and commitment. Criteria for identifying candidates for bestowing recognition must be foolproof, objective, measurable and transparent. Final aspect in this step is that the organization must decide the role and place of non-monetary reward in the overall reward strategy.

BEST PRACTICE
Non-Monetary Reward

Non-monetary reward can offer a wide range of opportunities and techniques to motivate employees. These include:

  (i) Feedback to an employee about his/her performance
 (ii) Congratulating good performance in public
(iii) Conferring social recognitions
 (iv) Publishing good performance acts in house journals and in public press
  (v) Felicitating high-performing employees on special occasions like annual day
 (vi) Recording about good performance in personal folders
(vii) Sending congratulatory letter to family members.

However, best practices in non-monetary reward indicate that the real impact of the non-monetary reward depends upon the right execution. The best execution is one that follows four principles:

- Recognition should be immediate
- Recognition should be delivered personally
- Recognition should be valuable
- Recognition should be a direct reinforcement of one desired behaviour.

An organization at the end of this driver must have determined composition of reward components and reward structure. The organization possesses on paper an integrated reward strategy that consists of all three vital components: monetary, indirect monetary and non-monetary rewards. Percentage that each of these components occupy in the overall reward structure also must have been decided with all substantiality and in consonance with the reward objectives as articulated at the Driver 1 level.

DRIVER 5: DETERMINE COMPONENTS IN MONETARY REWARD

This driver guides organizations in determining composition within the monetary reward component. This is very important for managing individual and collective employees, particularly from motivational point of view. It is a jigsaw puzzle: what shall be the composition of monetary reward in terms of three vital factors: position, person and performance. Again, what percentage must each one of these components be accorded in the overall monetary reward component? In this context, a few suggestive steps are indicated here:

Step 1: Pay for Position

Fundamental to any monetary compensation is determining the pay for position. Depending upon the placement of a position in the organizational hierarchical structure and worth of a position in the organization, compensation level, often called basic pay, must be decided. All similar positions will be getting similar base compensation because their positioning in organization and their worth are similar. Efforts must be made to practice broadbanding instead of creating several positions in organizations with an idea that such several positions provide career and pay increase opportunities to employees. In reality, many positions create confusion and dilute internal equity of a reward system. Ideally, an organization should not have more than six levels of base compensation. This number may appear arbitrary but in terms of manageability and ensuring equity, this can be the ideal maximum. Therefore, as a first step in this driver, organization must decide position-based pay.

Step 2: Pay for Person

It is equally important for an effective reward strategy to contain person-based compensation. Persons performing similar tasks and occupying same positions may be different in their competency and ability to ensure quality, timeliness, resource mobilization and ultimately delivering results. However, identifying such differences and proportionately rewarding on its basis is easier said than done due to complexities and presence of multiple variables in such a proposition. It is also true that reward may fall short of motivating employees to give peak performances if they feel that their distinct capabilities are not rewarded proportionately. In reality it is a double-edged sword. An ineffective management in defining and implementing person-based reward can cause large-scale frustration and a feeling of let down and grouse among employees. Professionally designed and managed person-based pay makes way for stimulating excellent performance. Therefore, as a part of this step, assistance of competency-based performance management strategy must be drawn to identify employees with distinction in competencies. Proportionate reward to such identified competencies must be decided. At the end of this step, the organization must ascertain competency profile of its employees together with the proposed reward provisions. Ideally, an organization must provide about 20 to 25 per cent of pay towards person orientation. This works as an assurance to employees that there is a system in the organization that is capable of identifying and rewarding distinct competencies, and every employee then perceives their importance through this person-based reward.

Step 3: Pay for Performance

This is a key element in monetary reward system. Pay for performance, also known as variable pay/performance-related reward/bonus/productivity incentive/commission, has gained immense popularity and is a widely preferred reward component in organizations across the world. Base pay is regarded as something which ensures stability and brings a semblance of work-reward exchange. Non-montarey compensation like recognition schemes are intended to reward exceptional performances. However, all these are not adequate to motivate employees to optimize their performance. This is to say that potential of employees cannot just be converted into performance with base pay. It is like expecting employees to provide base performance for base pay, but give superior or advanced performance only when there is advanced pay. Performance-related pay could fill this gap. Both position and person-based pay are constant and generally not flexible and not subject to fluctuations along the lines of performance. For example, regardless of actual performance, every employee by virtue of occupying a position is assured of a compensation amount and similarly a person's reward for possessing a competency is also seldom alterable. In such a scenario performance-related pay is the right solution that empowers organizations to manage employee performance and motivate employee to demonstrate their best and give results. However, realizing objective performance-related pay is a herculean task. The most critical step is to measure this performance in order to reward it. In some cases, (i) performance due to its very nature may be non-measurable, (ii) in some cases, tasks are highly interdependent therefore, individual measurement is not feasible and (iii) in still other cases, distinguishing an environmentally supported performance from adverse conditions is a great perplex.

Unless measures are defined beyond ambiguity, fine mechanisms are put in place to distinguish circumstantial factors and objective management is ensured, performance related pay may cause more damage to the reward fabric than good. Therefore, measurement-based performance management discussed in this book, and the principles prescribed for measurement need to be followed for crafting the performance-related reward. The other important issue that shall be addressed in this step is the share of performance-related pay in the overall reward structure. Different organizations prefer different formulas. In the reward, an average of 40 to 50 per cent share for performance is regarded as ideal. However, depending upon the organizational operations and profile of manpower this sharing formula can differ. Every organization, which is intending to implement reward-based performance management strategy, must provide provision for performance-related pay in a significant manner.

To conclude, the deliverable at the end of this driver is that, the organization must have reached a position where it has decided what shall be the composition of position-based pay, person-based pay and performance pay in the overall monetary reward structure. The organization must have also developed a framework for measurement based on the basic principle of competency and measurement-based performance management strategies, to enable pay for performance, person and position.

DRIVER 6: DESIGN REWARD SYSTEM

Leading objective of this driver is to assimilate all learning and information derived using the first five drivers to design an organizationally dovetailed, employee motivated and performance centric reward system. Work involved in this driver may appear as more academic and conceptual because everything is done with pencil-paper-based orientation. However, consolidating progress as achieved with the help of first five drivers, equips an organization to gain a powerful perspective in the design of a reward system. This driver also facilitates purposeful and rational alteration of the percentages drawn in various compensation components. Apart from this, this driver guides organizations to actually draft a reward policy for implementation. Following are few steps that are required to be taken at this stage:

Step 1: Assimilate Reward Data

Data obtained at various steps in the pursuit of creating the reward-based performance management strategy must be assimilated. For example, (i) data gathered and formulas developed for reward composition consisting of components and types of monetary, non-monetary and indirect monetary rewards, (ii) composition of monetary rewards like person, position and performance-based pay ratios, (iii) measurement methodologies, (iv) competency profile of employees and (v) data pertaining to organization's external and internal environment must be meaningfully organized at one place as single document. This acts as a basic document for all reward-related decisions. Any inconsistencies and disagreement within and among the data of different contexts must be resolved and reconciled. Major concerns, insights and inferences emerging from this data must be illustrated prominently and analyzed.

Step 2: Design of Reward Policy

The next logical step is to prepare the reward policy. This should have absolute conformity with reward objectives as set at the level of Driver 1. This reward policy must be derived from the above step of data assimilation. The assimilated document provides all levels of reward information that must be effectively used to develop this reward policy. A typical reward policy must consist of items that include:

(i) Objectives of reward
(ii) Reward structure comprising base pay, variable pay (performance-related pay) and indirect compensation details
(iii) Methodology of arriving at performance-related pay
(iv) Non-monetary reward types and methods of granting this reward.

The assimilation document must act as cardinal annexure to the policy document. Most importantly, the policy document must demonstrate how reward is linked to two vital aspects. Firstly, how reward is aligned with the organizational objectives and to what extent do reward objectives have conformity with the organizational objectives. Secondly, reward policy as a part of the performance management strategy must have special focus on how performance-related compensation together with a set of non-monetary rewards, is expected to raise performance levels resulting in tangible improvement of bottom line of the organization. Extra care must be taken to explain the measurement criteria for determining quantum of performance-related pay. In fact, success of the reward-based performance management is to a large extent contingent upon how well the measurement procedure is defined. Incorrect criteria or an ineffective measurement system can cause enormous damage to the reward structure and performance management of an organization. Therefore, absolute care is imperative. Many organizations with best of intentions could not ground performance-related compensation properly due to these ambiguities in measuring performance. Therefore, accurate measurement of performance is essential for a scientific reward system. Reward policy must also provide due explanation for cost of living index and how inflation is taken into account in order to protect real compensation.

One of the major portions of reward policy is non-monetary reward. Mostly, organizations separate recognition schemes from monetary reward policy. Whatever may be the reason for this, such independent handling or disintegration between monetary and non-monetary reward dilutes the impact of the reward system. In a reward-based performance management strategy both are taken as integral part of the reward system. Therefore, non-monetary reward must be given its due place in the policy document. At the end of this step, the organization must have a reward policy comprising monetary, indirect monetary and non-monetary reward schemes with all criteria and logic made self-explanatory.

Step 3: Determining Employee Compensation

This step involves translation of reward policy into employee-wise compensation package. After all, every employee ultimately looks at how he or she is going to be rewarded. This step only prescribes development of a model pay structure for a group of sample employees representing the universe. Also, how non-monetary reward is granted and for what kind of achievements, drawing instances of past breakthroughs attained by employees must be cited. This exercise helps primarily in two ways. Firstly, it enables to see how the policy translates into action as a trial run so that errors, if any, can be detected at this stage itself to initiate timely corrective measures. Secondly, it provides an operational picture at the individual employee level of how he/she is going to be rewarded. While designing a reward system it must be kept in mind that to achieve performance excellence in employees, base pay, indirect monetary reward and non-monetary reward are equal ·to and sometimes more important than performance-related pay. This is because all these are like foundations for performance-stimulated pay.

Efforts must also be made to create as few variables as possible in the reward package of employees. The recent trend of having innumerable variables in the reward structure adds to the confusion and therefore, obtaining the real impact becomes difficult. This multi-variable reward package also causes administrative inconvenience. Therefore, in a reward-based performance management strategy, components of rewards and variables are kept at manageable numbers and in a way that employees can easily understand why and how they are being rewarded. Effective execution of this driver positions the organization at an advantage with a well-designed reward system that is performance centric both in substance and style. Unique feature of such a reward system is that this would be tailor-made and organization specific since it is built after taking into consideration the internal and external organizational realities.

DRIVER 7: CONSULTATION AND COMMUNICATION ON REWARD-BASED PERFORMANCE MANAGEMENT STRATEGY

Many times organizations despite having an attractive reward package lose talented employees and fail to motivate employees to give their best performance. One of the most influential factors which is responsible for this state of failure is the lack of right consultation and communication regarding the reward structure and strategy. This issue assumes more importance in a unionized environment. Management may design a reward structure with best of intentions and with best of components, but the same would not see light of the day in reality if it were introduced unilaterally and without involving employees and unions.

Further, also from economic and management point of view, employees not being consulted and communicated about the reward for their work does not make sense. Therefore, prime objectives of this driver is to (i) consult with and communicate to employees about the premise behind reward, (ii) how it is designed, (iii) how it is planned to be implemented, (iv) how this system recognizes good work, (v) how this system fulfils employees' needs and (vi) how this system helps their organization to achieve its goals. However, communicating and consulting with unions/employees and gaining their endorsement involve a systematic and planned programme. Initial success of the reward-based performance management strategy depends upon how effectively this driver is applied. Following are some indicative actions for this driver.

Step 1: Publication of Reward Policy and Communication of Background Work

To start with, the reward policy must be published using house journal, intranet and other newsletters apart from bringing out an exclusive handbook on reward. Key managers must be communicated details at great length with an expectation that they disseminate this information among all employees. Efforts also must be made to gather views of managers as well as employees on reward policy and design. A minimum of three months to six months should be spent on this exercise to ensure that every employee in the organization is clear about the reward strategy. If possible, comparative analysis of proposed reward system with that of the prevailing reward structure and policy in other related organizations must be indicated, so that it works as a reference point and employees can realize advantages of the policy.

Step 2: Consultation with Unions

It is important that unions must be consulted on the proposed reward strategy. Generally, all unions, regardless of their ideology, tend to agree if they see through the merits of a scheme. However, care must be taken to present features on the proposed reward strategy in right earnest and it should be dealt in a manner that they have a major say in the whole strategy. In a nutshell, the whole issue must be approached with a positive mind and with respect for the unions' role in the reward strategy. If this is not done properly, it may contribute for distrust between management and unions. An environment of distrust can make any scheme, especially reward system ineffective, no matter how well it might have been conceived and developed. Maturity, perseverance and positive-minded management are prerequisites for successful application of this driver, i.e. consultation with unions in order to obtain their endorsement on the proposed reward strategy. Indication of effective application of this driver can be assessed (i) through awareness of employees about the proposed reward strategy and (ii) espousal by unions.

DRIVER 8: IMPLEMENTATION OF REWARD-BASED PERFORMANCE MANAGEMENT

As the title suggests, the core purpose of the present driver is putting performance focused reward strategy in action. Implementation must be carried out in a single shot unlike other strategies covered in this book, which are designed to be implemented in an evolutionary manner. Every employee is equally affected by reward practice and any difference in this context may be perceived as discriminatory. This perceived inequity could adversely affect principle of equity. Therefore, choose a right date and apply new reward strategy across the board. While applying, a few aspects should be given consideration. These include:

Step 1: Incorporation of Feedback of Unions and Employees

The feedback received at Driver 7 from unions and employees must be duly considered. All rational suggestions received from them must find place in the reward system in some form or the other. Communicating incorporation of these suggestions in the reward system to concerned employees in particular and to all employees in general helps in gaining acceptance of such a system. Further, it also must be communicated with reasons if some suggestions are not being included. The ultimate principle in this exercise must be to manage the reward system in a transparent manner.

Step 2: Opt for Strategic Launch

The new reward system should preferably be launched at the right time and in the right perspective. Right time means introducing new reward system when all employees are made psychologically ready for it. Commencement of the new reward system must also coincide with the start of the financial year, rather than during mid or end of the financial year. Work environment and relationships between management and employees must be harmonious and very conducive. Of course, as discussed in the above content, complete awareness and knowledge regarding the new reward system among employees is mandatory and a basic prerequisite for implementing the new system.

Step 3: Create an Exclusive Responsibility Centre

An organization is required to handle variety of activities arising out of the implementation of a new reward system. Further, many teething problems occur which should be resolved with contextual solutions within the overall framework of the new reward system. It is highly desirable that a separate functional cell is created to attend to these problems timely and wisely. This particular issue assumes more importance because real effectiveness and smooth execution of reward system happens only when initial problems are tackled effectively. Organization must define the responsibility centre clearly and communicate this to all employees in the organization.

Step 4: Notify Implementation Details

One to two months before launching the new reward system in a full-fledged manner, an organization must notify the implementation details. Time schedules and milestones for progress must also be notified. For example, notification must contain how the new system is going to be implemented and how long this system will be in operation without interruption. This notification must also be self-explanatory with regard to sources for resolution of grievances on the new reward system. Average duration of at least two years should be maintained for initial uninterrupted implementation. However, this duration is subject to change depending upon the size of the organization and the number of employees.

This driver stays in action as mentioned in the above paragraph for a period not less than two years. There can be many ups and downs during implementation. Execution is at least two times more difficult and requires more energy, time and money as compared to conceptualization and development of reward-based performance management. It is also a fact that number of organizations that suffered due to ineffective execution is twice as many as organizations which were found lagging behind in adapting a strategic reward system on account of lack of scientific policy framework. Therefore, organizations intending to realize reward-based performance management must attach great significance to this driver.

DRIVER 9: EVALUATION OF REWARD-BASED PERFORMANCE MANAGEMENT

Evaluation and continuous appraisal and renewal are part of performance management. Unless efficacy of a performance management strategy is established beyond doubt, same cannot be continued and called a strategy for performance management. Logical driver subsequent to implementation of a new reward system is evaluating the same at employee and organizational level. Apart from indicating efficacy levels, evaluation also presents some interesting insights into the whole issue that enables reward administrators to strengthen the system internally. Therefore, on completion of reasonable gestation period, i.e. the reward system in operation, evaluation exercise must be taken up. This initiative needs to be administered with an open mind. Individual managers should not be held responsible for failure or ineffectiveness of the system. This must be made very clear while launching the evaluation driver. Reason for this is that such an assurance can discourage individual interferences and some subtle manipulations with data. This evaluation as stated must be carried out at two levels as indicated here:

Step 1: Organizational Level

The first level of evaluation must be the organization. How the new reward system has contributed for improvement of organizational performance and effectiveness needs to be assessed. Organizational performance here means financial parameters that include sales, turnover, profits and earnings per share. Organizational effectiveness indicates the system level efficiency. System level efficiency includes (i) how the new reward system has been implemented and (ii) whether process followed is scientific or not is to be audited by experts. This audit exercise must specifically focus on contribution of each of the reward components such as monetary, non-monetary and indirect monetary to organization. Audit also helps to identify areas of improvement. In addition to it, critical comments and experiences of key managers also can be obtained on the implementation of the new reward system and its contribution to the organization. Methods followed in the measurement-based performance management have relevance for this evaluation exercise. Evaluation can be conducted in association with the measurement strategy of the organization.

Step 2: Employee Level

The second level of evaluation is employee centric. Satisfaction and morale levels of employees consequent upon introduction and implementation of the new reward system must be assessed. Methodology that includes survey, interview and open discussions can be used for this purpose. Ultimately, a good reward system is one that attains both employee satisfaction and organizational objectives. Unless employees are happy with the reward system in vogue, no matter what management pays it cannot bring in performance excellence. Employee level assessment must be given high emphasis and feedback must be effectively tapped.

DRIVER 10: REFINEMENT AND REINFORCEMENT OF REWARD SYSTEM

Last driver in the intervention of nurturing the reward-based performance management strategy is: (i) refining the reward system based on feedback and evaluation report obtained using Driver 9 and (ii) reinforcing the system with more consolidated effort. This driver mostly helps as a mechanism for wrapping up. In other words, it provides a final opportunity to plug the loopholes in the reward system and make the implementation strong and intensive. Broadly, two actions are required to be initiated as a part of this driver as indicated here:

Step 1: Refine Reward System

Based on the results of organization and employee level assessment/evaluation, reward system needs to be reviewed. Firstly, review must be done at the reward objectives level. This means examining whether feedback received from employees and organization as a unit of analysis is calling for any structural amendments. Secondly, component-wise feedback must be considered to refine the emphasis level, composition, criteria, methodology of conferring rewards etc. of each reward component such as monetary, non-monetary and indirect monetary. Thirdly, from the perspective of impact, implying that factors which are facilitating or constraining the new reward system from creating a tangible and contributory impact must be studied. This study must lead to refinement of the reward system. Dominant philosophy behind this driver is that no system can be perfect, especially when large-scale changes are initiated. There can be unanticipated predicaments, ambiguities, pitfalls and areas of concerned improvement and rejections. This driver insists that an organization should look at the whole system in a fresh perspective in the light of evaluation reports and make realistic improvements.

Step 2: Reinforce Reward System

Last step in this driver as well as in the present intervention, i.e. nurturing reward-based performance management strategy is reinforcing the refined reward system with military precision and religious commitment. This driver helps in making the reward system an integral part of the organization and a system that has a direct and strategic role in organizational and employee growth. Deliverable at the level of this driver is that the reward system must mature to achieve all its objectives as formulated at the level of the Driver 1. Reward system as reinforced must be continued without large-scale changes and system modifications at least for five years except when the same requires changes due to abrupt changes in the internal and external environment of an organization. At the end of this driver, an organization must be regarded as the best practicing organization as far as reward system is concerned, and many organizations must be tempted to consider it as a benchmark.

INTERVENTION 2: CAPITALIZING ON REWARD STRATEGY IN INSTITUTION-ALIZATION OF PERFORMANCE MANAGEMENT

Principal objective of present intervention is capitalizing on matured reward strategy to institutionalize practice of performance management in an organization. This can be achieved in two ways. Firstly by using reward strategy itself to promote other strategies like leadership-based performance management, competency-based performance management, career-based performance management and team-based performance management strategy. The second way is to draw synergy from other performance management strategies like measurement and culture. Ultimate success of reward strategy, like in the case of other strategies, is dependent upon the overall effectiveness of an integrated performance management framework (consisting of seven sub-strategies of performance management). Institutionalization of performance management as a part of reward strategy is also designed to be achieved with application of 10 drivers as discussed here:

FIGURE 2.3 Drivers of the intervention capitalizing on reward strategy in institutionalization of performance management.

DRIVER 1: REWARD FOR PERFORMANCE MANAGEMENT INSTITUTIONALIZATION

Reward can be used as a strategic tool for institutionalization of performance management. Ultimately, people are responsible for implementing each of the performance management strategies. There must be an appropriate reward for people contributing for institutionalization of performance management. This essentially means that employees who adhere to defined performance management systems are duly recognized. A reward strategy creates many sub-systems that are capable of identifying and distinguishing exceptional performances. Therefore, an employee who exhibits a high degree of organizational commitment by augmenting efforts of the organization for institutionalization of performance management must be rewarded. Such reward should be in the form of demonstration and preferably with a combination of monetary and non-monetary reward. Rewarding institutionalization behaviour works as a motivation for others to follow suit. Eventually, reward system contributes for cascading effect and serves to attain the objective of performance management institutionalization.

DRIVER 2: REWARD AS FOLLOW UP OF PERFORMANCE EXCELLENCE

Reward as discussed above is aligned with performance-oriented behaviour. This implies that mere job description and assigning an employee a particular responsibility itself cannot contribute for obtaining qualitative results. Often, employees identified to carry out certain functions do so in a manner that is devoid of spirit and involvement. However, this pattern of less involvement dramatically changes when the same is tied up with an appropriate reward. This means making reward contingent upon good performance. This performance-reward relation tends to get reinforced over a period of time and that eventually leads to inspire employees to aspire for fulfilment of higher-level motivational needs like self-actualization. Therefore, in order to institutionalize performance management, an organization without exception must pursue the link between performance and reward in a consistent and continuous manner.

DRIVER 3: REWARD AS CENTRE OF INSTITUTIONALIZATION

Undoubtedly, effectiveness of performance management strategies is largely subject to effectiveness of the reward strategy. If reward is ineffective and unsuccessful at any stage, the same dents the effectiveness of other performance management strategies. Therefore, reward must be given special attention. A good reward system can be deployed as a nerve centre for performance management institutionalization. Organization must exert efforts to manage other strategies of performance management through canons of reward strategy. An organization must create a fully equipped reward group that even after putting together a scientific reward system in operation, can continue to add value by sharpening implementation process of other performance management strategies discussed in this book. Institutionalization of performance management becomes a reality when the reward group grows beyond its traditional role to strengthen all performance management strategies. Therefore, an organization that intends to pursue institutionalization process must deploy a reward system and a reward group to sharpen execution of performance management.

DRIVER 4: INTEGRATING REWARD SYSTEM WITH MEASUREMENT MANAGEMENT

Reward is contingent upon performance and performance is contingent upon measurement. There must be total integration of reward-based performance management with that of measurement-based performance management. Lesser degree of integration between these two or any traces of mutual exclusivity can cause both strategies to become ineffective. This lessening of value goes against primary objectives of performance management. Further, dilution in value addition gradually becomes a potential source for de-institutionalization of performance management. Organization that chooses reward strategy must simultaneously opt for measurement-based performance management too. The overall administration of both these strategies must be pursued in tandem and with an objective to leverage each other. A well-integrated reward-cum-measurement system helps in performance management institutionalization. Together both can systematically ensure that both quantity and quality of an employee's performance is rightly measured and appropriately rewarded. This process of right measurement and right reward lays the basic foundation for institutionalization of performance management.

DRIVER 5: INTEGRATING REWARD SYSTEM WITH COMPETENCY MANAGEMENT

Competency at employee level must be aligned with reward and vice versa. Reward has the potential to motivate employees to sharpen their competency in line with changing technology, markets and internal organizational reality. Unless employees adapt themselves to emerging competency environments and continuously make endeavours to obtain contemporary competency set, matured and qualitative performance cannot be expected from them. Institutionalization of performance management remains as myth in such a scenario. Reward must be effectively used to enhance competency index of an organization. This can be achieved through defining specific reward structure for obtaining competencies. Competency possession automatically leads to great performance and increases innovation capabilities. Therefore, as a part and parcel of performance management institutionalization intervention, reward and competency relationship must be defined and used as mutual reinforcer.

DRIVER 6: MELDING REWARD WITH CULTURE STRATEGY

There can be a great synergy between reward-based performance management and culture-based performance management. There is no denying the fact that culture plays a significant role in making reward succeed on the shop floor. Unless culture-based support exists in absolute terms, reward strategy cannot obtain the desired impact. Any amount of systemic rules, procedures and monitoring mechanism cannot ensure implementation of reward in right spirit. On the other hand, building a mature, strong and positive work culture is subject to compatibility with the reward strategy. Mapped culture just can't be a reality when support of reward structure and strategy is absent. Employees, who see no reward in making themselves ready for continuous adaptations, withdraw from making such efforts. Reward and culture are both mutually dependent for attaining perfection and realizing their full impact. Such impact is imperative for performance management institutionalization. Hence, synergy between these two strategies must be ensured and special efforts need to be put into the process of institutionalization of performance management.

DRIVER 7: LEADERSHIP AS ULTIMATE FORM OF REWARD

Leadership itself can be effectively tapped as the finest reward. For example, the ultimate motivational need of any employee is to occupy the role of a leader. Every employee nurtures an ambition to lead an idea or a group or an organization. Leadership as a strategy illustrated in this book interestingly has no limitations and the organization can provide leadership opportunities for all employees. Leadership is treated as a dynamic and evolving concept rather than a physical role. In order to institutionalize performance management, an organization must leverage on leadership as the ultimate form of reward. An organization can certainly grow beyond conventional norms when all its employees aspire to be leaders. Performance institutionalization stays at the centre of such leadership ambitions.

DRIVER 8: CAREER AS FORM OF REWARD

Career is a multiple mechanism in reward strategy. This provides multiple opportunities to employees at one shot. An employee is graced with (i) job enrichment in the form of more responsibilities, authority and variety of tasks and also (ii) in monetary form since vertical career movement fetches more salary and perks. Career must be drawn as an important element of reward-based performance management. However, career strategy itself can be comprehensive and independent strategy, the same must be closely tied up with the reward strategy. Impact gets diluted and both strategies lose their motivational power if they differ in identifying deserving employees due to differences in their approach. There must be total agreement between these two systems. Such an agreement contributes to institutionalization of performance management. However, the organization must be conscious of this fact and make exclusive efforts to align both these strategies.

DRIVER 9: REWARD AS A SOURCE OF EMPLOYEE INVOLVEMENT

All performance management strategies lead to one common destination, i.e. merging identity of individual and collective employees with the organizational identity. Organization can achieve best performance only when all employees optimize their potential. This optimization can come only through involvement. In order to get such a high degree of involvement, employees need to be paid equitably and recognized well. All these aspects are inbuilt in the reward-based performance management strategy in the form of monetary, indirect monetary and non-monetary rewards. A reward strategy must be oriented and matured to inspire employees to voluntarily commit themselves and their identity with organizational identity, which they own. Institutionalization of performance management witnesses its finest moment when such merging of identity takes place. It is easier said than done. An organization must make its own share of sacrifice in order to expect such hard core institutionalization process. Nevertheless, this is not difficult to achieve. Reward is the best strategy for making such phenomenal progress. Hence, use reward for institutionalizing performance management through involvement.

DRIVER 10: USING PROCESS CENTRIC REWARD FOR PERFORMANCE MANAGEMENT INSTITUTIONALIZATION

All said and done, all performances do not result in results. Much time and effort is spent without yielding expected results because of unforeseen and environmental constraints. When a reward system becomes sensitive to performance, it becomes insensitive to effort. This approach of rewarding only performance of results and not efforts adversely affects genuine attempts and hard work. Genuine hard work is fundamental for breakthrough results. When genuine efforts are not rewarded properly, the same disappears as number of employees making such attempts evaporates. This needs to be remembered that breakthroughs do not occur on an every day basis. They happen once in a while when continuous efforts are made. Employees engaged in such efforts tend to get frustrated due to the very nature of the work. This frustration multiplies when reward is biased towards results. Such a behaviour is detrimental to institutionalization of performance management. Therefore, this driver prescribes reorientation of the reward system in favour of efforts once the same has matured into a performance centric reward.

SUMMARY

Reward is highly critical in management of employee performance. In fact, reward is the foundation for motivational behaviour of employees. An effective reward strategy can lead to high motivational levels, whereas an ineffective reward strategy contributes towards demotivation. This double-edged sword needs to be managed in a systematic and scientific manner. This chapter focuses on reward as the cardinal component of performance management. Similar to other chapters in this book, the chapter on reward strategy is also presented in five parts. What is reward-based performance management and what it is not discussed in part one. Significance of a reward strategy in attaining performance excellence of employees is illustrated in part two with the help of 10 principal factors such as:

   (i) Reward as a fertile source of organizational effectiveness
  (ii) Reward as medium between organization and employees
 (iii) Reward as an avenue for multiple motivational fulfilment
 (iv) Reward as factor of motivation
  (v) Reward as a performance guide
 (vi) Reward as a source of talent distinction

(vii) Reward as a source of employee involvement

(viii) Reward as a source of innovativeness

(ix) Reward as a source of competitiveness

(x) Reward as a source of organizational harmony.

Basic and application oriented reward theories that have practical implications for the architecture of reward-based performance management strategy are briefly described in part three of the chapter. These theories include:

(i) Lawler's reward and job satisfaction model

(ii) Sweeney, McFarlin and Inderrieden's pay and job satisfaction

(iii) McNally's three compensation strategies

(iv) Hay guide chart profile method

(v) Broadbanding

(vi) External and internal factors that influence reward system

(vii) Individual factors that influence reward system

(viii) Incentive techniques

(ix) Behavioural theories of reward

Eight practical lessons that have implications for design and execution of the reward-based performance management strategy are drawn from the following theories:

(i) Reward is more of a psychological phenomenon rather than physical

(ii) There is an element of contingency in reward strategy

(iii) Reward is susceptible to force of multiple factors

(iv) Reward is a comprehensive strategy

(v) Job enrichment is the higher end of reward strategy

(vi) Fairness of reward is dependent upon objective measurement

(vii) Compensation is a multilayered system

(viii) Reward-motivation-reward is a cyclical process.

Strategy, interventions and drivers of reward-based performance management are presented in part four and part five. Core objective of the first intervention, referred to as nurturing reward-based performance management, is enabling the organization to create a performance centric reward management. A set of 10 drivers assists in realization of this intervention. These are:

(i) Setting objectives of reward strategy

(ii) Tracking antecedents of past and present reward system

(iii) Determining and applying reward methodology

(iv) Determining reward components

(v) Determining components in monetary reward

(vi) Design of reward system

(vii) Consultation and communication on reward-based performance management

(viii) Implementation of reward-based performance management

(ix) Evaluation of reward-based performance management

(x) Refinement and reinforcement of reward-based performance management.

Second intervention, i.e., capitalizing on the reward strategy in institutionalization performance management as a way of organizational and employee work life is presented in part five of the chapter. This intervention also consists of 10 drivers which are:

   (i) Reward for institutionalization of performance management
  (ii) Reward as follow up of performance excellence
 (iii) Reward as centre of performance excellence
 (iv) Integrating reward system with measurement management
  (v) Integrating reward with competency management
 (vi) Melding reward with culture strategy
(vii) Leadership as ultimate form of reward
(viii) Career as a form of reward
 (ix) Reward as a source of employee involvement
  (x) Using process centric reward system for institutionalization of performance management.

KEY WORDS

Following are the key words discussed in this chapter:

- Monetary reward
- Non monetary reward
- Pay for person, position and performance
- Broadbanding
- Job evaluation
- Equity
- Reward and job satisfaction model
- Behavioural theories of motivation
- Hay chart profile method
- Melding reward with culture
- Nurturing reward-based performance management

- Indirect monetary reward
- ESOPs
- Gain sharing
- Balancing stakeholders
- Job enrichment
- Performance centric reward
- Three compensation strategies
- Contingent reward management
- Reward as medium
- Reward as avenue for multiple motivational fulfilment
- Institutionalization of performance management

DISCUSSION QUESTIONS

1. Define what is reward in the context of performance management and how is it different from a reward system that is not performance centric.

2. What is the significance of reward in performance management? Can reward contribute for enhancing performance of employees?

3. Discuss major theories of reward and their implications for design and application of reward-based performance management.

4. Reward is a psychological phenomenon. Substantiate this statement.

5. How and why is the principle of equity important in reward management?

6. What are the significant features of reward-based performance management strategy. Does this strategy enable organizations to create a performance centric reward system.

7. Write brief notes about monetary, indirect monetary and non-monetary reward?

8. Implementing a reward strategy is easier said than done. Discuss major challenges that an organization is likely to encounter while pursuing a reward-based performance management strategy.

9. How can reward-based performance management be nurtured? What are the steps an organization must initiate to drive performance.

10. Can a reward system that is prevailing in an organization be catapulted into institutionalizing performance management? What drivers assist in this process? What should an organization ideally do to institutionalize performance management?

CASE STUDIES

1. News Update Enterprises Ltd. is a private company that publishes daily newspaper in English and Hindi languages. Title of the newspaper is same in both the versions, i.e. News Update. The English version is ranked as largest circulated daily in India while the Hindi version as the third largest circulated. Conventionally reward, especially monetary component, is decided by a national wage board appointed by Government of India to determine the salary structure for employees working in the Fourth Estate. All newspaper organizations by law are required to implement recommendations of this national wage board. As a part of labour reform, Government has freed newspaper industry from mandatory adaptation of wage board recommendations and allowed freedom to individual organizations to form their compensation structures. News Update Ltd. intends to avail this opportunity. Board of directors of News Update has decided in principle to introduce a competitive and comprehensive reward structure consisting of all monetary and non-monetary components of reward. The core objective of proposed reward system is to enhance motivational levels and consequently performance levels of 215 journalists employed in the organization. Imagine that you are appointed as consultant to design and implement a reward structure for News Update in the background of this history. Discuss how you would progress on the issue.

2. Samson Electronics Ltd. is a public limited company engaged in the business of manufacturing long distance giant antennas. This organization employs about 900 engineers across the country. All of them are highly qualified and knowledge driven. The reward system of Samson is considered best. This reward system has all virtues of an ideal system and comprises monetary, non-monetary and indirect monetary reward system. In fact, 'Samson Champion' is a non-monetary reward

that is given annually to the best performing engineer, and is regarded as one of the best recognitions in the country. Many organizations in electronics industry follow principles and practices of Samson's reward system. Recently, an independent agency carried out a survey on 1000 organizations covering wide range of human resource management practices and found Samson's reward system as number one. Rakesh Malhotra, CEO of the company one day thought about using this best practice of reward to institutionalize performance culture in the organization. However, he is not quite clear how to go about it and what actions are to be taken for this. Therefore, he decided to hire services of a reward expert to advise and also to oversee the implementation of performance management institutionalization using existing reward practice. Discuss how, what and why a manager hired for this purpose must do to realize the task of capitalizing on reward system for institutionalization of performance.

SUGGESTED READING

Lawler, Edward E. (1971). *Pay and Organizational Effectiveness*. New York: McGraw-Hill.

Martocchio, Joseph J. (1998). *Strategic Compensation*. New Jersey: Prentice Hall Inc.

McNally, Kathleen (1992). "Compensation as a strategic Tool." *HR Magazine*, **37**(7), pp. 59–66.

Sweeney, Paul, Dean McFarlin and Edward Inderrieden (1990). "Using relative deprivation theory to explain satisfaction with income pay levels: A multi-study examination." *Academy of Management Journal*, **33**(2), pp. 423–436.

Chapter Three

STRATEGY 2: CAREER-BASED PERFORMANCE MANAGEMENT

Career is an age-old issue in management of people. However, recent spurt in attempts to leverage each and every system of human resource management has drawn a special attention to career management. Career planning and development can be a great opportunity as well as a great threat to organizational effectiveness. It is an opportunity since a good and systematic career management can motivate employees and enhance their performance. It can also be a threat especially when mismanaged, since the same leads to frustrated workforce with mismatch of skills and jobs. Distinction of career management lies in capturing interest of both: organization and its employees. Career management is a great source for employees to fulfil their career aspirations and to match their skills, interest and values with that of the organization. Career management is a vital instrument for organizations since it enables them to attain organizational objectives.

Career management has a special place in the overall framework and practice of performance management. In performance management, careers are used as avenues to gratify self-esteem and self-actualization needs of employees. This is also drawn as a pragmatic strategy in obtaining mutually integrated progress of organizations and their employees. Career as a strategy of performance management hinges on two broad but specific principles. First is that careers must be managed to (i) motivate employees to optimize their potential and (ii) attain peak performances apart from satisfying their individual hierarchical goals. Secondly, organizations must deploy career management as a sharp strategy to attain organizational growth and innovation by vertically and horizontally aligning the progress of employees with the organization. Formidable challenge in this context is what needs to be done to realize this twin principle of career-based performance management strategy in the face of emerging flat and thin organizational structures that provide meager opportunities for vertical growth of people. Forthcoming contents of this chapter unfold few solutions to overcome this issue and guides organizations and managers to draft career-based performance management strategy.

Similar to other chapters in this book, the present one is also organized into five parts. Part 1 focuses on what is career in the context of performance management and what it is not. The significance of career planning and development strategy in performance management is presented in part 2. Theoretical foundations in managing careers are captured in part 3. Career-based performance management strategy encompasses two interventions. The first intervention is *nurturing career-based performance management* is discussed in part 4. And the second intervention is *capitalizing on career planning and development in institutionalization of performance management,* as described in part 5.

CAREER STRATEGY IN PERFORMANCE MANAGEMENT

Career is described as a sequence of jobs occupied by a person in his/her professional life in the same or similar organizations. In the context of performance management, career strategy is defined as *a combined effort of an individual employee and an organization to nurture and mature aptitude and attitude of that employee in order to deliver results for both of them.* In other words, a career strategy consists of:

1. An organizational effort to identify aptitude and attitude profile of an employee.
2. An organizational effort to match identified employee aptitude and attitude profile with positions in the organization.
3. An organizational effort to address developmental needs of an employee in the identified area of aptitude and attitude.
4. An organizational effort to leverage the above three efforts to attain organizational objectives.
5. An employee effort to make self-assessment to identify strengths and weaknesses in terms of aptitude and attitude.
6. An employee effort to manage self to occupy an organizational position that is most compatible with self aptitude and attitude profile.
7. An employee effort to obtain the fundamental and advanced knowledge/skill/attitude in the career he/she is engaged in.
8. An employee effort to excel in the job in order to occupy the highest position in that field of work and fulfil the self-motivational needs.

What is Not Career Strategy

Career in the context of performance management is not mere hierarchical upgradation or vertical progression of an employee in the organizational hierarchical ladder. Career strategy in the context of performance management centres on the cardinal principle of an employee maturing in his/her own field and delivering results for both the organization and self. In this parlance, vertical movement in organizational hierarchy is incidental, and possessing advanced knowledge and competency is essential. Career as a part of performance management does not consist of:

1. Mere vertical movement from one position to the other without corresponding job enrichment.
2. Mere vertical movement in regular intervals as a part of organizational policy without obtaining/sharpening one's knowledge (aptitude and attitude).
3. Career progression of employees independent of organizational progression.
4. Career advancement as the sole responsibility of employees.
5. Career advancement of employees as a sole concern of the organization.
6. Planning and developing careers without matching employees profiles with profiles of the positions.
7. Inadequate effort in leveraging career management to obtain performance excellence.
8. Managing career planning and development as an isolated activity.

SIGNIFICANCE OF CAREER STRATEGY IN PERFORMANCE MANAGEMENT

Career planning and development has a prominent role in the grand strategy of performance management. This is one among the seven strategies of performance management that help to achieve twin objectives of employee and organizational progression. From the perspective of an organization, a well planned, developed and implemented career system can (i) enhance organizational performance, (ii) soar the pace of innovation, (iii) reduce employee attrition rate, (iv) enhance employee commitment and loyalty (v) optimize staffing and (vi) improve organizational adaptability.

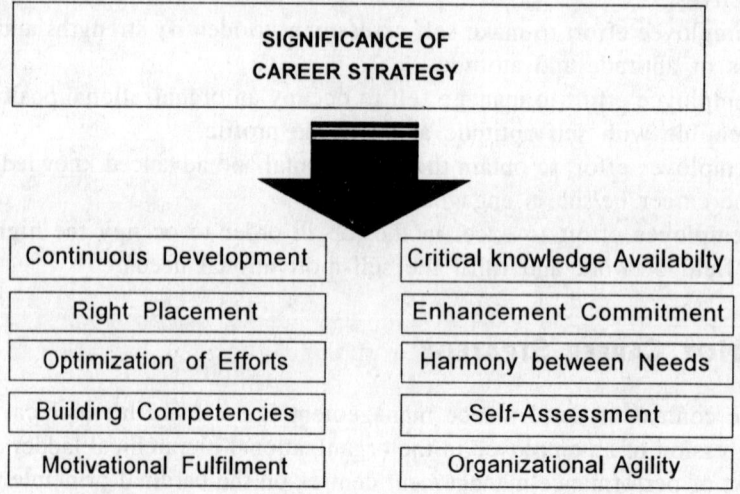

FIGURE 3.1 Significance of career-based performance management strategy.

From the perspective of employees, a good career system provides them with (i) avenues to fulfil higher motivational needs, (ii) addresses their developmental needs, (iii) assists in identifying and strengthening their professional forte, (iv) accelerates professional growth,

(v) makes career life meaningful and (vi) provides utmost job satisfaction and harmony in life. If a career system is left unmanaged or mismanaged, it can end up creating chaos not only in the sphere of performance management but organization-wide. Following are some of the most important issues that emphasize the significance of career strategy in performance management.

Continual Development

Development of people on continuous basis is possible when a systematically developed and implemented career strategy is in place. This development can occur in a logical and evolutionary sequence. For example, a career path for a software programmer position, if clearly laid down, is easy to develop into a meaningful developmental plan for career movement of that position. Aptitude and behavioural characteristics (attitude) required at each of the career movements of a software programmer can be mapped. In fact, in professional career planning system, mapping aptitude and attitude profile assumes more importance than the actual movement of positions in the ladder. In order to obtain effectiveness and the real impact, growth in employees' development is more important than just vertical movement. A systematic career strategy helps in creating conditions for continuous development, which is a strong pillar of performance management.

Right People to Right Positions

Ultimate success of performance management comes from people performing roles in which they can do their best and to which they are best suited. Career planning is a vital input and a critical step in placement of employees to right positions in the organization. Career planning involves assessing employee aptitude and attitude profile and matching them with the right positions/assignments in an organization. Automatically this process gives a fillip in placing right people to right positions.

Optimization of Efforts

Employees when placed on positions to which their profile best suits, do miracles with least of effort. It doesn't mean they are not required to work hard. Indeed, people put in more efforts and hard work when their profile matches with the job profile. Employees do not realize that they are putting in hard work or struggling to achieve something because work becomes very natural to them. People inspite of struggling hard and spending long hours/days/months/years of work, end up achieving something insignificant because of mismatch between their interest/skills/knowledge and the job they perform.

Building Competencies

As a logical sequence to the above issues, an organization can build distinctive human resource competencies through the means of a scientific career planning and development system. For a person to become master of an activity, two things must happen without fail. Firstly, a person must match his/her basic aptitude and attitude with the job/career that is intended to be pursued. Secondly, that person must make continual progress on that job/

career by acquiring knowledge, skills and attitude. Fulfilment of these two requirements can surely contribute towards people emerging with distinct competencies. Pursuing these two aspects is just an integral part of a good career system. As the chapter on competency-based performance management conclusively establishes, building competencies is one of the right strategies for achieving performance excellence.

Motivational Fulfilment

Career progression is one of the powerful sources to meet higher-level motivational needs such as self-esteem. This is a big issue with many present day organizations. Most of the employees are provided with avenues for fulfilment of lower-level motivational needs like physical, security and social, but opportunities to gratify higher-level needs remain scarce. Employees who do not find opportunities to satisfy this need within organizations look for chances outside the organization. A systematic career planning and development provides every individual clear opportunity to fulfil these needs. Peak performance in organizations can be derived by managing the higher-level motivational chemistry of employees.

Availability of Critical Knowledge

Effective performance of organizations is solely dependent upon its employees to a large extent. Effective performance of employees is proportionately contingent upon the degree of knowledge they possess. Career strategy when conceptualized and implemented in a scientific fashion, can lead to the creation of pools of knowledgeable employees. Cleverly crafted career-based performance strategy, each vertical or horizontal career movement of employees is closely tied to the upgradation and enrichment of knowledge base of employees. Career management has a significant place in the overall framework of performance management due to the knowledge creation role it performs.

Enhancement of Employee Commitment

Lack of a realistic and rational career system in organizations is cited as one of the most influential factors for a rise in employee attrition rate. Employees tend to look for opportunities outside when there is hardly any chance to grow within the organization. This results in employee turnover adversely affecting employee commitment and subsequently morale. Achieving even moderate levels of performance becomes a tough task where attrition is order of the day. Career planning and development can be used as a strategy not only to reduce employee attrition rate, but also to enhance the commitment rate. It is common sense that once employees' professional journey is clearly scripted, it is hard for them to abandon and pursue something else. A well-drafted career script strengthens employee commitment and loyalty to the organization.

Harmony between Mutual Needs

Harmony is the key that ensures great performance and accelerated innovation in organizations. Harmony is referred to here as the integration between needs of employees and of the organization. Inherent conflict of interests between employers and employees creates many speed breakers in the progress of innovativeness. Career planning and development can be used as a reliable vehicle in integrating mutual needs in harmonious conditions. In a simplistic vision, every organization aspires to grow and so does every individual employee. Career strategy helps in tying these two aspirations meaningfully. Growth of one is dependent on the other.

Provision of Self-Assessment

Career system encourages employees to indulge in self-assessment in order to understand and identify their own interests, professional competencies, skills and values. Career system also supports an employee's effort in matching self-profile with work profiles in an organization. Employees are assisted and guided in developing their own personal professional vision and mission statements. It is a hard reality that finally whatever organizations may or may not do, it is the individual effort of an employee that is very critical. And, for these efforts to be meaningful, effective and optimal, a systematic self-assessment is a prerequisite: a facility that career strategy provides.

Enhancement of Organizational and Employee Agility

Most organizations find it difficult to perform very well due to absence of professional zeal within employees and, therefore, in the organization. Great performances are natural to people and organizations when they are professionally agile. This agility comes from optimistic future they see together. Each individual employee has a career mission as that of the organization. Every employee is busy in attaining that mission and every time an employee reaches that mission, it gets revised upward. This is how professional life goes on in organizations where a scientifically made career strategy is in operation. This agility in turn strengthens organizational flexibility, enabling it to respond to environmental changes quickly.

THEORETICAL FOUNDATIONS OF CAREER-BASED PERFORMANCE MANAGEMENT STRATEGY

Some of the important and relevant theories of career management are briefly discussed in the following paragraphs. These theories chiefly explain and provide the basic understanding on (i) what makes a person choose a particular career over others, (ii) why it is important to assess congruence between an individual's personality type and career, (iii) what career stages does every individual has to pass through and (iv) different career paths for different situations/organizations among others. Apart from these theories, allmost all academicians, researchers, consultants and practitioners emphasize one common issue, i.e. aligning career management with organizational needs or integrating career needs/growth of employees with organizational needs/growth. Also insist that career planning is a responsibility of both: organization as well as every individual employee. A successful career strategy is one that is made and implemented with dual participation according to career management specialists.

SCHEIN'S CAREER ANCHORS

According to Edgar Schein, attitude that drives a person to choose a particular type of career forms in the early years of his/her life. A person's interaction with the environment during childhood and in the early years of personality formation decides the kind of career that person would most likely opt for. These attitudes which guide career choices become career motives as life progresses. Schein calls these motives *career anchors*. Further, he classified these career anchors into six types as indicated here:

Managerial Competence: People with this career anchor prefer leadership roles. They possess interpersonal relationship and problem solving skills and choose employment as vice-presidents, plant managers and administrative officers in Government offices, etc.

Technical/Functional Competence: People with this career anchor are excited by specialization and seek deeper knowledge in a given field. They are also disinterested in taking up administrative jobs and avoid generic jobs. These people can generally be found in research and consultancy organizations.

Security and Stability: The dominant motive here is to hang on to a job to derive stability in life. In order to satisfy this need, people adopt a conformist behaviour and are loyal to an organization. They dislike moving to other locations/organizations. These people are mostly found in government/large size organizations performing clerical and routine jobs.

Creativity and Entrepreneurship: These are the people who derive satisfaction launching and doing their own job/business. They make attempts to create something new even when they are employed in organization. They either set up their own business or prefer small and upcoming firms for employment so that they can get opportunities to do the kind of activities they wish to do.

Autonomy and Independence: This anchor is similar to the creativity. People of this type prefer self-employment and strive to have freedom from organizational constraints and code of conduct. They generally prefer professions like academics, and journalism where they can get freedom.

Technological Competence: All software workers and people who intend to engage themselves full-time on researching and developing new technology form this anchor. These people give technology a very high priority. This type of people are change friendly and extremely adaptable.

Schein's Stages in Career Cycle

Edgar H. Schein has also developed a framework for understanding how a person's career experience in turn influences the kind of profession/occupation that person prefers. According to this framework, any person's career life cycle consists of five stages as briefly described here:

Growth Stage: This stage constitutes mainly childhood, something like from birth to adolescence. Every individual develops a self-concept and gains an identity during this stage. The kinds of experiences an individual undergoes during this stage impact the career choices. During the growth stage, people experiment with many activities in a form of play and interaction with the world and draw their own lessons. These lessons mainly comprise their learning with regard to the activity/experience they like and dislike, and this ultimately forms a career anchor.

Exploration Stage: This stage occurs generally during the age of 18 to 25. People at this stage make serious experiments with a few careers in order to match their personal interests and skill profile. Generally, at this juncture, people choose very generic careers. Towards the end, they try to choose an occupation over the other that suits their interest and skills the most. This is also a stage in which people make realistic assessment and understanding of themselves and their competencies and interest.

Establishment Stage: This is a very critical and real stage in anybody's career cycle. This stage lasts for nearly 20 years. People who are fortunate find careers that suit them and are compatible with their profile, but for a few others it may not result in tapping of their potential. People during this stage make progress and advancements in their career. They also put before themselves certain career objectives to achieve in the forthcoming five to fifteen years. This is also the stage in which they face career crisis due to the environmental changes. Successful people are those who effectively manage this stage of their career by making realistic choices and having a clear career plan and progress accordingly.

Maintenance Stage: This is a stage in which people just put in efforts to maintain what they have already achieved in their profession/occupation. This stage generally occurs during the age group of 45 to 65. Even when people make significant career progress during this stage, it can be attributed to the efforts put in during the establishment stage.

Decline Stage: As the title suggests, this is the stage where the career recedes in full form. People lose power and responsibility apart from losing touch with the latest developments in their fields. During this stage, people seek retirement or are accorded compulsory retirement. This stage is also characterized by diminishing physical and mental energy.

HALL'S CAREER STAGE MODELS

D.T. Hall presented career stages model illustrating that every employee undergoes four stages in his/her total career as indicated below. He called these career cycles as career growth curve.

Exploration and Trial: This is the stage in which both employee and the organization explore and make trials of each other. Organization screens and selects an individual to a position with the belief that individual suits that position. Individual also chooses an offer of employment with an impression that position being offered is suitable. During this stage both make an assessment and evaluation and realize whether there is compatibility between the person and position or not.

Establishment and Advancement: Based on the experience gained at the first stage, both employee and the organization make efforts to place the employee suitably through transfers and promotions. Employees who find that positions offered to them are not appropriate in terms of skills, grades, responsibilities and roles may seek change or quit the organization. On the other side, same employees may make appropriate changes in order to fit themselves to right positions and start climbing the career ladder.

Mid-Career: This is a critical stage among other stages in the career cycle. Some employees may feel that they have almost made it and become contended, while others encounter a career crisis and make efforts to broaden their jobs. Organizations must make special efforts to enhance job content and provide more avenues for performance to employees who are at their mid-career stage. In the absence of special motivational programmes, employees may slip into doing something very routine and maintenance-oriented.

Disengagement: All employees face this situation subsequent to the stage of mid-career. The only difference is that some employees may reach this stage abruptly, like retirement, and for some it may happen gradually, particularly in case of people in consultancy, medical practice and engaged in offering professional service/self-employed persons. Organizations must gradually wean away the employee from taking larger responsibilities so that disengagement is gradual and systematic. Disengagement that occurs in a gradual fashion will have no adverse consequences to both employees and the organization.

MONDY, NOE AND PREMEAUX'S FOUR TYPES OF CAREER PATHS

Career path means how each job is related to other jobs and avenues for upward mobility in organizations. According to Mondy, Noe and Premeaux, there are four types in career paths as indicated here:

Traditional Career Path: Traditional type of career path is derived from the principle of bureaucracy. Here, employees progress vertically upward from one job to the other, which are well interconnected. Experience in lower position is regarded as essential training to occupy a higher position. However, this type of career path has lost relevance in the changing business environment dominated by flat and organic organizational structures.

Network Career Path: A distinct characteristic of this career path is that it provides opportunities for both horizontal and vertical movement. Jobs are described in broader terms and a group of jobs are also considered as interchangeable. Network career path lessens the problem of employee career progression that is generally encountered in traditional career path. However, defining career avenues precisely is comparatively difficult in the network system.

Lateral Skill Path: This career path is based on the approach of skill upgradation/learning itself as career enrichment. Here, employees are neither moved horizontally nor vertically in the organizational ladder. However, they are given opportunities to redefine their jobs and perform a bigger role. Employees are encouraged to (i) update themselves, (ii) obtain new knowledge and (iii) apply them in their jobs.

Dual Career Path: This career path has come into practice due to the increasing need for building technical specialists in organizations. Today, organizations need specialists as much as managerially competent people. Therefore, there must be a method through which these specialists can be rewarded from career point of view. Organizational structures are made to end with general management positions at the top. Specialists who like to spend their time and energies on technical issues dislike moving to general management positions. Dual career path provides opportunities for specialists to move upward in a similar manner as general management cadres.

HOLLAND'S FRAMEWORK OF CAREER CHOICE

John Holland proposed a framework that explains why and how people choose a particular kind of career. He emphasizes that people choose a career that is congruent with their basic personality. Therefore, according to him, it is important to understand personality types in order to offer suitable employment or make realistic career planning in this context, he identified six personality types as briefly indicated here:

Realistic: These are scientific-tempered people who like to work on machines, equipment, machinery, etc. They are mechanically skillful and prefer career in technical areas as technicians, engineers.

Investigative: These are analytical, critical, methodical and research-oriented persons. They are very curious to understand the process of cause and effect relationship, and are most likely to prefer career as researchers and analysts.

Artistic: These are unconventional, original, creative and non-conformists. They like to work in the fields such as beauty, fashion, interior decoration, entertainment and also professions like journalism.

Social: This type of people prefer to work for social cause, engage themselves in societal work and identify with social causes. They prefer to work among people and for the people. Even when they are employed in organizations, they are most likely to become trade union leaders and employees' representatives.

Enterprising: People of enterprising nature prefer to be self-employed as much as possible. They like to influence thinking and lead organizations. Professionals like doctors, lawyers, chartered accountants and businessmen fall in this category.

Conventional: These are system adherence people implying that they are very methodical, systematic, bound by procedures and customs. They are very good at clerical and accounting functions. They like to work in the areas of accountancy and data management.

ILEA'S RESOURCE-BASED CAREER APPROACH

Professor Paul Ilea advocates a resource-based career development approach that is derived from two principles. The first principle is based on environmentalism in which it is believed that all economic and social development should be sustainable, that is, it must not reduce options open to future generations. The second principle is based on strategic management literature or resource-based view, which promotes treating career development as a competitive advantage to both individuals and organizations.

PLATEAUING

This concept is as old as career management itself. It has assumed importance in the current environment in which organizations have no choice to move employees upward in organizational hierarchy. It means there will be no opportunities for promoting employees to higher levels. This also means that when people are moved to higher grades, they continue to perform the same job and functions, which they were doing due to job erosion. Promotions take place in some cases may just be ritualistic, and do not enrich job in any manner. In more or less measure, most organizations face this situation and carry employees with plateauing.

LESSONS OF CAREER MANAGEMENT THEORIES

The above discussed career management theories offer four vital and practical lessons in developing a career based performance management strategy. These are:

Integration of Career Planning with Organizational Objectives

First lesson is: career planning in an organization must be tightly integrated with organizational objectives. Practically every career plan must flow from organizational plans. Employees' growth and organizational growth must be made mutually inclusive. Strategic management literature also impresses upon the need to deploy career development as a mechanism of realizing corporate strategy. However, some theories particularly derived from ecological philosophy advocate that regardless of organizational growth, career advancement must be effected in a manner that avenues for career growth continue to exist even for future generations. This implies that promotions should not be made in an accelerated or decelerated manner in tune with growth fluctuations of organizations and instead, there must be stability in career movement of people.

Matching Career with Career Preferences of Employees

Career anchor and career choice theories establish two salient aspects: firstly, career choices originate and form within individuals during childhood and therefore they are very strong. Secondly, there must be absolute compatibility and congruence between preferences and personality types of individuals and their careers in order to be successful. In effect, every individual is most suitable to a particular type of career and can excel if provided with an opportunity to pursue career in that profession/occupation.

Career as Long-Term Learning Experience

Recent literature in career management is mainly tilted towards managing careers as long-term learning events than mere upward or vertical movement in organizational ladder. Traditional career development methods and approaches are losing their relevance and utility in the face of (i) collapsing traditional organizational structures and (ii) necessity to adapt flexible practices due to rapid technological and market changes. Therefore, alternative career strategies like the network model are gaining popularity.

Career Management as Dual Responsibility

Theories have also adequately emphasized the need for mutual participation, i.e. the organization and employees working together in developing a career plan for employees. Employees must share equal responsibility and put in equal efforts in developing an appropriate career plan and its implementation. Employees have a rich role to play in self-assessment and expressing self-preferences, interests, aptitude and values so that matching career avenues within an organization could be identified.

CAREER-BASED PERFORMANCE MANAGEMENT STRATEGY, INTERVENTIONS AND DRIVERS

Principal objective of career-based performance management strategy is to manage career development for twin purposes. First is to leverage career development to fulfil the higher motivational needs of employees such as self-esteem and self-actualization. Secondly, to use this motivational chemistry to pep up performance of employees so that organizational effectiveness and growth can be attained in a natural way. With this objective in view and based on theoretical foundations and benchmarking career development practices, two interventions are developed to realize career-based performance management strategy. These interventions are:

Nurturing Career-Based Performance Management: First intervention focuses on conceptualizing, developing, implementing and evaluating a tailor-made career development plan for organization-wide application. This intervention is designed to be realized through application of 10 drivers.

Capitalizing on Career Strategy in Institutionalization of Performance Management: This second intervention addresses the larger cause, i.e. using career development in institutionalization of performance management. Career development plans will be used as instruments in combination with six other performance management strategies discussed in this book to institutionalize performance management. This intervention is also made up of 10 drivers.

These interventions along with associated drivers are discussed in detail in the following sections.

INTERVENTION 1: NURTURING CAREER-BASED PERFORMANCE MANAGEMENT

Developing and executing an organization-wide career development programme is a highly challenging task. Often career development programmes, which are meant for motivating people as well as fulfilling their motivations, become sources of frustration. Ultimately, this demotivated behaviour leads to organizational ineffectiveness. Study and analysis of career development programmes in several organizations prove that it is certainly difficult to realize a balanced career development programme in which there is something for every employee in the organization, and which also contributes for organizational effectiveness. This challenge and limitation has arisen due to one major misconception, i.e. career development means upward mobility in organizational hierarchy possessing more power and authority.

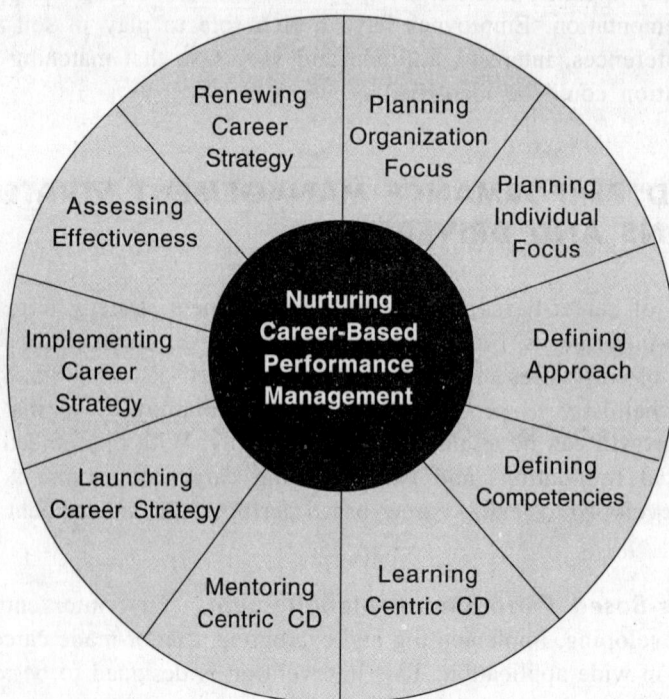

FIGURE 3.2   Drivers of intervention nurturing career-based performance management.

Obviously, every organization experiences limitation in delegating formal powers to people as well as moving them up in the ladder on continuous basis. People whose expectations are built around formal hierarchies and power, tend to get frustrated when they do not get opportunities to occupy positions at the top of the hierarchy. This misconception together with mismanagement of employee's career expectations and lack of a well-designed career development programme deprives organizations leverage on career management as a strategy to enhance performance and attain organizational effectiveness. This intervention of nurturing career-based performance management is developed keeping in view the existing maladies and also the best practices. This intervention comprises of 10 drivers application of which can contribute not only for the systematic practice of career management but also as the prime mover and harbinger of performance excellence.

DRIVER 1: PLANNING CAREER DEVELOPMENT PROGRAMME: ORGANIZATIONAL FOCUS

The maiden driver in nurturing career-based performance management intervention is planning for a career development programme that is comprehensive, balanced and strategy driven. A systematic career development effort is one which is well planned, can address motivational needs of employees and performance imperatives of an organization (*see best practice in career management*). Many organizations, both industrialized and information driven, have left career planning undefined and unmanaged in the realistic sense to a large extent. Industrial organizations have dominantly followed bureaucratic and tall organizational structures with some kind of socialistic career planning and development programme. *Socialistic career management means providing opportunities equally to both performers and non-performers, to climb up the organizational hierarchy at regular intervals.* This career progression lacks any substantive preparation like upgradation of competency and acquisition of new skills. It is assumed that experience in the lower positions is adequate for people to occupy higher positions. Organizations of information era have given birth to organizational structures like matrix, flat, strategic business units, network models, etc. in which career planning process and career movement of employees is hazy and not crystallized into specifics. A few organizations, however, continue to follow traditional organizational hierarchies in combination with project management structures. It is uncommon to come across organizations that have put in place a well-articulated career development plan. In many organizations, career planning is unsystematic, and it is not managed but exists on its own in some fashion. When career development is not managed deliberately, it neither contributes towards career enrichment of employees nor enables organizational effectiveness. Hence, developing a comprehensive, balanced and strategic career development programme is the first step in high-impact career management practice. The following steps are illustrative of what needs to go in developing such a programme.

BEST PRACTICE
Career Development at Corning Glass Works

Corning Glass Works is a fortune 500 company reputed for its glass and ceramic ware, and a leader in telecommunication, health and consumer products. It has successfully employed a career development system to develop a productive and effective workforce. Corning entrusted the responsibility of developing a career development system to a steering committee of divisional representatives, which would focus the employees' attention on the current job and how he/she could progress in the company. Before the introduction of the career development system, the workforce at Corning was a demoralized lot due to (i) lack of participation in appraisal, (ii) insufficient attention to appraisal interviews, (iii) lack of career information and (iv) lack of awareness about internal placement processes. The career development system was aimed at providing employees with information, skills and tools to help them take charge of their own career development. Interactive computer software, video booklets and personal counselling sessions were used as part of the system to help employees analyze their actions, goals and alternatives, and assess themselves.

Inputs provided to employees include (i) career planning at Corning, (ii) career planning for oneself, (iii) employees' role in career planning and (iv) career opportunities at Corning. Managers conducted career discussions with their employees to help them to do their own career planning. The efforts made by Corning paid dividends and the workforce became more productive, effective and efficient.

(Based on: Zandy, B. Leibowitz et al. April 1990. Career Development Works Overtime at Corning Inc., *Personnel*, 38–45).

Step 1: Study of Organizational Plans

Process involved in developing any organization-wide programme that includes career development is identical. Since, career development programme has to correspond with the organizational plan and growth, these plans must be studied carefully. Study is fundamental for developing an organizationally dovetailed career development programme. For example, an organization may have plans for introducing new technology, entering into new markets, to close some units or diversify or divest investments in areas of slack business. Each one of these organization plans has drastic implications for developing and executing career development programme. Therefore, organization plans must form the basis and building block for the career development programme. Therefore, organizational plans need to be studied and direction for the career development programme must be prepared as a first step.

Step 2: Study of Organizational Structure, Disciplines and Functions

The second step in developing a career development programme is studying carefully the organizational structure that is in vogue in the organization. Disciplines/departments and functions in organizations such as operations, marketing, production, finance, human resource management need to be studied, and how work flows through these departments and functions must be analyzed. This helps in understanding the key and supplementary functions of an organization.

Step 3: Study of Career Paths

Having studied organizational strategy, structure and functions: the next sequential step is understanding existing career paths in the organization. For example, how and why different grades, designations and positions exist in the organization. Most importantly, how an employee progresses from a position of induction to junior, middle and senior level in the organizational hierarchy. It is particularly to be studied whether the career path is same for all positions across the organization or is it different to different positions and functions. In many cases, positions in principle functions will have more career growth and more upward movement opportunities in comparison to positions in supplementary or staff functions.

Step 4: Study of Existing Career Development Policies

A detailed study of existing career development policies like promotion policies is very important. These policies ought to be studied and analyzed, especially their origin, linkages with organizational history, and growth. Theme underlying the promotion activity must be specifically identified.

Step 5: Study of Linkages between Career Development Policies with other Human Resource Functions

It is possible that the prevailing career development programme may not have strong linkage with other human resource functions such as human resource planning, performance appraisal, feedback system and training system. In quite a few organizations, all these functions of human resource management exist as independent entities sans any meaningful integration. A career development system that is weak in its relationship with other human resource functions tend to be weak too. An important element that is to be closely studied in the process of developing a career development programme is relationship of career system with other related human resource functions in particular and relevance to the overall human resource philosophy in general.

Step 6: Study of Human Resource Profile

In order to develop an effective career development programme that is capable of addressing real career needs of all sections of employees, it is imperative that profile of human resource in the organization must be studied and analyzed in detail. This profile study must cover academic qualifications, professional experience, professional competency and proficiency, managerial abilities, career movement of employees in past and attitudinal make up. This study comes handy while preparing a career development programme.

Step 7: Study of Human Resource Redundancies and Flexibilities

This is another factor that has significant implication for planning a career development programme. Organizations of industrial era and modern economy organizations such as information technology, financial services, hospitality, entertainment, transport, etc. are susceptible to human resource redundancies due to fast changing technological and market forces. These changes in turn cause organizational manpower redundancy. These redundancies can be managed effectively only when such manpower has flexibility within. Flexibility here means manpower should possess basic aptitude and attitude to learn and transform themselves on continuous basis in tandem with the changing organizational reality. Often, even a well-crafted career development programme ends up serving wrong people and wrong causes when it is not sensitive to the fact of redundancy.

Driver 2: Planning for Career Development Programme: Individual Focus

As discussed in the beginning of this chapter, developing a career development programme is the responsibility of both: organization and individual/teams of employees. First driver of nurturing career-based performance management intervention as described in the preceding content takes care of the organization side of effort. The present driver is dedicated to facilitating and encouraging employees to participate and put in their efforts in developing a career development programme that addresses their career needs. Though each and every employee is accountable for assessing his or her career needs, it should be the concern of the organization to provide them with a conducive environment, framework and platform. In other words, an organization must lead employees in identifying their career needs in line with the organizational focus. Among the 10 drivers in this intervention, this is the toughest driver to implement as well as highly crucial in attaining real benefits from a career development programme. Following steps are suggestive of the process involved in stimulating employees in developing a career development programme. However, kind of steps to be followed and their sequence is subject to change in consonance with the organizational context and type of group dynamics that exist apart from the total number of employees to be covered under the driver.

Step 1: Creating Awareness

The first action in involving employees in the development of a career development programme is generating awareness about the need and benefit of employee participation in such a programme. This initiative is required since many organizations might not have involved employees in career development effort in the past. Therefore, awareness initiative must be taken up by senior management and it must be launched in the right earnest. Initially, employees may be skeptical and may carry doubts why they need to participate in a career development programme that has been the domain of organization all these years. Effort at this stage must be restricted to warming up employees and drive the point that career development is principally meant not only for the organization, but also for employees. It must be effectively communicated that participation of employees is essential in mapping their realistic career needs.

Step 2: Providing Self-Career Assessment Tools

Once adequate awareness is generated to the extent that employees are also responsible in planning and implementing an organizationally relevant and individually rich career development, the next action to be taken up is enabling employees to assess their career needs. It is quite natural that most employees may not really know what their aptitude and attitude profile is and how these factors can be assessed. An organization must initiate a couple of actions. First action is developing tailor-made assessment tools that help in identifying employees' career interest and values apart from professional aptitude and attitude. For example, Campbell Skill Inventory Test (CSIT) is one such test that is used in assessing skill preference and proficiency of employees. Generally there must be minimum two tests for assessing each proficiency, i.e. aptitude and attitude. Aptitude tests range from assessing numerical, problem-solving skills, understanding of business environment, various functions that are cardinal and supplementary for managing organizations, operational and marketing issues, organizational economics and quality related issues. These issues assess macro level aptitude. In order to assess micro level issues such as managing inventory, there must be a separate testing format. This implies that to assess aptitude, there must be macro level as well as micro level assessment tool. In order to match organizational value system and attitude of employees (psychological/interpersonal abilities of employees), there must be generic tests like MBTI, FIRO-B, Killman's conflict management inventory, 16 Personality Factors test, Ennegram and a micro level test that need to be designed in the context of a particular organization. The critical issue here is that 'testing administration' must be left to individual employees instead of the organization deploying a team of people to administer and assess employees. This means two things here. Firstly, management/organization role is to identify/develop self-assessment instruments/tools and make them available to employees. Secondly, employees must be given absolute freedom to self-administer these instruments and identify their career interest. Assessment tends to be trust-based and is most likely to contribute to realistic assessment in comparison to the organization-led assessment that gives scope for apprehensions and misunderstandings.

Step 3: Providing Training for Effective Self-Assessment

Success and consequential effectiveness of career development planning is largely contingent upon how well self-assessment is implemented. Mere provision of few instruments and tools of self-assessment therefore, may fall short in achieving this effectiveness. Employees must be made capable of using these instruments and interpreting the results. Training employees on self-assessment becomes a necessity in this process. In proportion to the number of employees to be covered under the career planning and development, self-assessment orientation workshops must be held with the help of experts. Every employee needs to be fully equipped to use the instruments comfortably. This exercise may appear as elaborate and also cumbersome at the beginning stage but the same becomes manageable once initial progress is made. Positive aspect here is that this training offers repeated value to the organization;

once employees are trained on this, they will remain trained and can be used to train others. An organization can also employ the 'in-breeding strategy' in training employees. *In-breeding strategy means that an organization must take initiative in getting a few people trained and encouraging these trained people to train their co-employees in a phased manner*. Further, employees must be provided with detailed guidelines on the use of instruments, and particularly the scoring key and interpretation method. No standardized scores/benchmarks illustrating preferred/poor scores of these tests must be emphasized. Once benchmark/suggestive ideal and poor levels are provided, there is likelihood that such standards may dilute sincerity and alter the direction of self-assessment exercise.

Step 4: Self-Assessment Results to be Anonymous

Self-assessment results must be collected in a confidential and anonymous method. Employees can be advised (i) to assess themselves, (ii) interpret individual results and (iii) drop such interpreted statement along with raw results in a box that can be located at the entrance of the main office building or any such convenient and centrally accessible station. The logic here is that the employee-focused career assessment is required primarily (i) to gauge the kind of aptitude and attitude stock that exists in the organization, accompanied with (ii) data illustrating employees' wishes and perceptions regarding choices of careers. Performance managers must be made accountable to stimulate as many employees as possible to file their self-assessment results. In this context, a professional approach is one that notifies the complete schedule of providing instruments, training, self-administration of instruments/ tools and filing the reports/results well in advance. This serves as target dates for performance managers to monitor response rate at each stage and initiate remedial action to improve the same. Performance managers' behaviour also plays a pivotal role in succeeding self-assessment exercise. They must learn to practise an honest, straightforward and professional approach that sends right signals across to employees that this exercise is going to be very useful for them. In contrast, a threatening and non-personal business approach can minimize the self-assessment response rate.

DRIVER 3: ARTICULATING CAREER PLANNING AND DEVELOPMENT GOALS

Having gained clear understanding and deeper insight into the existing career management policies, practices and expectations from organizational and employees perspective, the next logical and sequential action must be oriented towards articulating a new career development plan. This new plan must be designed keeping in view data generated at the levels of Driver 1 and Driver 2. Core objective of present driver is setting operational objectives for career-based performance management strategy. Many organizations suffer due to lack of clearly defined career objectives, and most organizations also tend to believe that organizational structure itself forms the basis for career planning. This impression gains currency among organizations because of the popular misconception of careers as formal positional upgradations. Organizations are susceptible to mismanage and confuse career planning management in absence of predetermined direction in the form of career management goals. While first two drivers of this intervention enable organizations to gain and access holistic and relevant data, present driver facilitates them (i) to use this data in a rational perspective, (ii) come up with finer analysis and (iii) to articulate right career development goals. Following described actions are indicative of what organizations need to do for setting career development goals:

Step 1: Synthesize Data

Data collected with the help of Driver 1 and Driver 2 must be assimilated and synthesized in a meaningful fashion. For example, data can be arranged in the following classifications:

1. Implications of organization/business plans to career planning.
2. Implications of organizational structure to career planning.
3. Salient features and underlying assumptions of existing career planning, policies and practices.
4. Career paths in vogue.
5. Functional implications of career planning.
6. Integration of existing career management with other human resource functions.
7. Assessment of human resource profile as per organizational data.
8. Gravity of human resource redundancies, flexibilities and their implications for career planning.
9. Aptitude and attitude profile of employees as per self assessment.
10. Impressions of employees about their career goals.

Based on the actual yield of data and the nature of data, the above classification shall be done so that it is easy to obtain insights and reflections into the issue in an authentic way. Implementation of this exercise calls for research, analytical and consultancy skills. Organizations that do not possess adequate professional support in-house can draw help from outside management consultants. But this help from consultants must be restricted to data management and analysis. Career planning tends to be taken up seriously, especially at execution stage when organizations themselves steer the whole exercise on their own. Deep understanding of the organizational context, dynamics, history, present and future business plans is a basic necessity for drafting purposeful and pragmatic career management goals. Internal managers possess better knowledge on these issues than any consultant who can be very generic in competency. Such a generic approach dilutes the fitness of a career development programme.

Step 2: Deriving Inferences/Determining Focus

Based on the data as synthesized, chief inferences must be drawn and focus should be determined. For example, data analysis may reveal few contradictions between employees' expectations and organizational objectives. In some other cases, analysis may highlight how adequate/inadequate is the present career policy and practice in caring for interests of employees as well as the organization. This step must be availed as a great opportunity to resolve these contradictions. Once contradictions are resolved, consistency can be ensured in the existing set up itself. Secondly, efforts must be made to specifically figure out what this data indicates. For instance, data may indicate that organization has an immediate plan for diversification or forward integration in business, which requires corresponding competencies and experiences, but the existing human resource profile may not augment this. This issue can become a major focus in drafting the career development goals. Similarly, contradictions of a widening gap between employees' expectations about their own career growth and avenues an organization can provide, also exist. For example, employees may be nurturing dreams of fast upward movement like becoming managers/general managers/vice-presidents/ executive vice-presidents whereas the organization has plans to introduce flat organizational structure or to shrink hierarchical base in order to increase response rate. Due to this conflict between organizational plans and dreams, employees tend to be disappointed as they see hierarchical growth slowing down. In such a situation, one of the principal objectives of a career development plan should be managing expectations of employees, particularly making employees more realistic in their career aspirations. The end of this step must facilitate identification of focus areas of career development in the organization.

Step 3: Defining Approach to Career Development Plan

There are many approaches in managing career development in organizations. For example, as career management theories prescribe, there can be an ecological approach or strategic approach or a commitment approach in managing career development programs. Based on identified focus areas and keeping in view the chief inferences drawn as above, a superordinate goal to its career management must be evolved. At this stage, organization must clearly decide which approach is most suitable in order to fulfill organizational and employees' needs so that performance excellence can be attained. For example, an organization that intended to link career development program to organizational survival and growth sharply can choose strategic approach to the career planning and development program. Actual opportunities for employees career growth are absolutely contingent upon fortunes and well being of the company. To elaborate further, fluctuations in the organizational existence, how significant or insignificant they may be, will have direct and proportionate implications for career movement of employees. In contrast, a commitment model ensures that employees' career growth is not affected in any manner regardless of actual organizational growth. Similarly, organizations make efforts to preserve career growth opportunities for future generation employees even when the organization is growing much faster.

Step 4: Articulating Career Planning and Development Goals

Last step in this driver is articulating career planning and development goals in clear, specific, measurable and identifiable language. For example, a model statement can be as indicated below:

1. Focus: Strategic and business driven.
2. Superordinate goal: Mutual growth of organization and employees.
3. Operational goals:
    (i) Career planning as mechanism in enrichment of human resource competencies
    (ii) Current performance levels and potential to assume higher responsibilities as basic parameters in career movement of employees
    (iii) Career policy and practice as powerful motivational vehicle in driving performance excellence

(iv) Career policy and practice as objective, measurable and equitable human resource system

(v) Career planning and development that mitigates organization from manpower redundancy problem.

DRIVER 4: DEFINING JOB COMPETENCIES

Malady with career planning and development in a significant number of organizations is managing it as more of hierarchical mobility and less of competency enrichment. Therefore, as a part of the career planning programme, an organization requires to exert more effort with great intensity in expelling this misconception. Career planning and development programme must give a fillip to enhancement of job competencies in the organization. Ultimately, motivational fulfilment of employees and growth of organizations becomes a reality only when competencies are built. Obviously, this cannot be done through the presence of great designations and hierarchical legacies. It is very difficult to convince and make employees agree that competencies have priority over designations, especially in high power distance index countries like India. Delegation of powers and authority are centred on designations rather than competencies. Unless these fundamental blocks are dismantled and reorientation is done, it may not be feasible to put in place a real performance centric career planning and development programme in operation. In the absence of such systematic and structural readjustments, career-planning focus, superordinate and operational goals may remain on paper. Once career planning and development goals are articulated, the effort must be reinforced through system strengthening as illustrated below.

Step 1: Creating a Parallel Career Structure

Though it may appear as abstract and complex in the initial stage, one pragmatic strategy to deal with performance centric career planning programme is creating a parallel career structure based on competency approach. Parallel structure here means a substitute to traditional and hierarchy-based career planning programme. Many organizations at their best have a career planning programme but not a career development programme. This means, there is a basic policy that governs promotion of employees to higher grades and that does not address development issues associated with such promotions. Such policies only breed incompetence and become contributory factors for human resource redundancy and eventually organizational redundancies. Organizations can opt for creating a parallel career structure based on competencies. This structure enables a professional possessing a defined competency to be treated as equivalent to a particular position in the organization. This competency structure provides opportunities to all employees to acquire competencies and seek related assignment and grow in that career to be regarded as equivalent to any senior level executive in company. Objective of an organization must be to replace the traditional hierarchical career structure with competency-based career structure in a phased manner. Depending on the intensity of a problem and size of the organization, especially in terms of manpower strength, gestation period for this replacement/progression from traditional to competency-based structure differs.

The difference between hierarchical and competency-based structure is that a hierarchical structure indicates designations and levels in the same job. For example, human resource function. Hierarchical structure indicates junior HR executive, senior HR executive, human resource manager, senior human resource manager, deputy general manager-human resource and general manager-human resource so on and so forth. Whereas in a competency-based career structure, competencies such as fundamental competencies, intermediate competencies, advanced competencies for a discipline are defined and employees possessing competency proficiency at a particular level are identified accordingly. Distinct characteristic of competency-based structure is that it serves all types of organizations which intend to adopt matrix, flat and network model, and also provides unlimited opportunities to all employees for real performance stimulating career growth.

Step 2: Defining Job Competencies

Mostly organizations end up having job descriptions and specifications but with only rare job competencies. Absence of job competency framework can be the most influential factor leading to mismanagement of career function. Organizations must put in sincere efforts to define job competencies as comprehensively as possible. In this context, competency-based performance management offers great deal of help and data. Job competencies as identified and developed in the process of executing competency-based performance management, must be adopted here. To describe briefly, competencies required to perform each position must be defined. This description must contain aptitude and attitude specifications for each position. As stated earlier, each function can be classified into three or four levels depending upon the intensity and scope of knowledge, skills and attitudes. There can be fundamental level, intermediate level, master level and advanced level competencies required to perform a function effectively. These levels must be identified with the support of relevant content, experience and knowledge for each function and shall be notified. Eventually, these levels become career stages in an employee's career life in the place of formal designations. This exercise of defining job competencies also involves elaborate effort and requires input from different organizational functions and people. At the end of this driver, an organization that is working towards the career-based performance management strategy must have (i) created a parallel career structure and (ii) defined job competencies comprehensively that forms the basis for career growth of employees.

DRIVER 5: LEARNING CENTRIC CAREER DEVELOPMENT

Once career development needs are assessed at organizational and employee levels, career development goals are articulated and job competencies are defined, the next sequential driver is icing career management with learning flavour. Before a full-fledged career development plan is launched for implementation, learning required at all career stages must be specified accompanied by making available learning aids, systems and practices. This driver precisely facilitates such an action. Career-based performance management strategy is competency centric which implies the significance of learning. In fact, learning is the other side of competency driven career growth. Learning needs have to be managed with the same amount of faith as that of implementing employee legislative measures and with such regularity as that of running pay rolls. Unfortunately, organizations initiate development interventions like learning as optional and in a philosophical style. Rather, this must be done and followed up like a strategic issue with the belief that organizational existence and growth is contingent upon real enforcement of such systems. Great learning leads to great competencies and that leads to great careers which further lead to great performances. Following are indicative of steps to be taken by an organization in order to realize career-based performance management.

Step 1:   Building Learning Infrastructure

Having conceptualized a competency centric career development plan, facilities must be created to enable employees to acquire these competencies on the job as well as off the job. For example, there must be a good library, simulators, research and development facility, classroom environment and faculty/trainer resource. Objective of this action must be to create an infrastructure that helps people learn competencies in the minimum time possible and in a scientific manner.

Step 2:   Building Knowledge Depository

Every organization that is determined to create a career-based performance management must (i) build knowledge repository system and case studies providing insights into various business related issues/problems company encountered in the past together with (ii) strategies adopted to deal with them and how it succeeded/failed. There must be standardized reading material on each of these disciplines developed in-house, which particularly supports employees intending to acquire fundamental and intermediate knowledge in their field.

Step 3:   Building Testing Procedures

There must be either a certification or identification system through which proficiency of employees in the competency level can be assessed and certified. This certification serves twin purposes. Firstly, this enables an employee and organization to diagnose the proficiency level of an employee. Secondly, this helps to move an employee in career structure and utilize the services accordingly. The biggest challenge here is developing a very objective and high-class testing and certification system. In this context, measurement-based performance management can offer quite a few techniques that can be adopted here to develop the testing system.

DRIVER 6:   MENTORING CENTRIC CAREER DEVELOPMENT

Learning infrastructure, knowledge repository and testing procedures significantly help in creating learning-oriented career development programme. Such learning orientation undoubtedly lays foundation for nurturing career-based performance management. In order to reinforce the said learning orientation to career development, another development system that is required is mentoring. *Mentoring is a comprehensive tool that involves both personal and professional development of employees.* However, making mentoring succeed and deploying it as a career development tool calls for organization-wide involvement and an environment of trust and superb human and professional relationships among employees. It is also a hard fact that organizations that succeeded with mentoring are far less in number in comparison to those that have failed. This is mainly due to lack of commitment, inadequate effort and absence of sincerity on the part of top management coupled with lack of faith in the system among quite a few mentors and mentees. However, organizations whose innovativeness and competency is high attribute it to a formal or informal mentoring system that they practiced. Organizations planning for a career-based performance management must make mentoring an integral part and parcel of the career development plan. In this process, organization may be required to initiate a number of actions. Following steps are suggestive of such actions:

Step 1: Identify Mentors and Provide Orientation

Before launching a mentoring programme, an organization must make a mentoring strategy ready beforehand. Such strategy must consist of details like: how mentoring is linked to overall career development of employees and what is expected to be done to achieve good mentoring practice. Secondly, mentors in each field/function/discipline need to be identified and they should be given suitable orientation. Selection of mentors must be done keeping in view their aptitude and attitude profile. Sound attitude of mentors can motivate and inspire employees to achieve performance excellence. Mentors also must be very positive, optimistic and people with high patience and perseverance. Being outstanding in a given field is just not a sufficient qualification for assuming the role of a mentor, because it is more a process role than a functional one.

Step 2: Build Mentoring Culture

The second important issue in realizing mentoring as a career system is leveraging culture-based performance management strategy to build mentoring culture that is characterized by trust and healthy interpersonal relationships. Ultimately it is the trust between the mentor and mentee that contributes to the effectiveness of the mentoring system than the number of meetings and time spent by these players. Mentoring must be managed as a voluntary system in which all players have freedom within the overall spirit of mentoring system and as long as it strengthens the career development of employees.

Step 3: Allow Freedom to Mentees to Choose Mentors

As discussed above, mentoring as a career system is absolutely voluntary. Mentees must be given all freedom to identify and choose a mentor from organizational data bank of mentors. Mentoring tends to be effective when mentees identify and seek help of someone as mentor instead of organization formally allotting someone as a mentor. The organization must (i) confine itself to creating mentoring culture, (ii) training suitable number of senior employees as mentors and (iii) providing necessary mentoring infrastructure.

DRIVER 7: LAUNCHING TAILOR-MADE CAREER PLANNING AND DEVELOPMENT PROGRAMME

As organizations progress successfully from Driver 1 to Driver 6, they reach to a stage where they can launch a scientific and strategic career planning and development programme. When organizations reach to the level of current driver, they can launch career planning and development programme since all preparation and inputs required for such launch are in place. However, as a checkpoint, the following aspects must be revisited to ensure their inclusion/consideration while launching the career planning and development programme:

Step 1: Career Progression Plan

Career planning and development programme must clearly specify the progression procedure like how an individual employee progresses in his/her profession. This is like the typical promotion policy but possessing more professional and comprehensive treatment. Each and every trade/occupation/profession must be covered under the career progression scheme/policy/plan.

Step 2: Check Learning Provisions

Adequate role for learning must be ensured in the career progression plan. There must be exclusive provisions dealing with learning, as it is mandatory at each step of career progression.

Step 3: Check Mentoring Provisions

Mentoring must be given adequate emphasis in the career progression plan. Care must be taken that mentoring process and its linkage with career development is explained in the plan itself.

Step 4: Job Competency Provisions

Competencies required at each level of a profession/occupation/role as defined must be spelled out in the career progression plan.

Step 5: Career Path Provisions

This is cardinal to the career progression plan. How each career starts and ends in organizational network/organizational structure must be illustrated in plan.

Step 6: Check Integration of Career Progression Plan with Employee and Organizational Objective

Last but not the least, it must be ensured that the career progression plan has absolute compatibility with employee and organizational goals as assessed in Driver 1 and 2.

At the end of this driver, the organization should be having a well-prepared career planning and development plan that is ready for implementation. Such a plan is comprehensive and developed to address all concerns of employees and the organization. Most importantly, the plan must be designed to perform as a powerful instrument for motivating employees to give excellent performances. The said plan must highlight the superordinate goal of career management that will be taken as universal reference point/principle for clarifying any career-related issue.

DRIVER 8:   IMPLEMENTING CAREER PLANNING AND DEVELOPMENT PROGRAMME

Driver 8 guides organizations in executing the tailor-made and well-developed career planning and development programme in a systematic and less painful mode. Replacing existing career policy disturbs some employees and introduction of a new plan can also generate some confusion during the beginning. If this phase is not managed well and resistance is not tackled appropriately, career planning and development plan, no matter how good it may be, will be very difficult to push through in practice. It is advisable that organizations and managers responsible for career management must draft a pragmatic implementation strategy. As a part of this, organizations may be required to deal with collective bargaining agents and employee associations. The prime principle of career planning and development programme must be introduced in a positive, optimistic and equitable manner. Once employees perceive a human resource practice as positive, they pose no resistance and rather make endorsement of it. Following are few suggestive steps that help in this execution process:

Step 1:   Discuss with Employees before Implementation

It is very important that a detailed discussion with employees be held so that they are actively involved in designing and developing the career planning and development programme. This being a very sensitive issue among other human resource activities, top management must take due care and involve itself in the discussion. This must be a democratic process and be utilized as a forum through which greater awareness about the career plan may be created. This in no case should be conducted as a process of negotiation or collective bargaining activity.

Step 2:   Release Plan Document before Implementation

When organizations are big in size and operations are spread geographically, it may be prudent to circulate complete details of career planning and development plan together with the benefits the plan is expected to deliver when implemented. This effort can be supplemented by career managers and line managers addressing and making presentations to employees on the plan wherever and whenever possible.

Step 3:   Start with Soft Elements

Implementation must commence with soft aspects such as mentoring and learning, and cascade up to building competencies and moving employees through career paths/career progression. This strategy can effectively deal with resistance and it is also logical that employees are given opportunities to build their competencies before they are subjected to assessment for career progression. Once employees are put on to the mentoring and learning process, they tend to manifest less resistance to new career development programme.

Step 4: Replace Existing Positions with New Positions

On successful implementation of mentoring and learning in consonance with job competencies, the next step for implementation is replacing old designations/positions with new positions/ roles as envisaged in the new career planning and development programme. This step can be followed by regulating career in future as per the new plan. This means, steps followed in executing the career planning and development programme must be in the order given below:

1. Implementation of mentoring practice.
2. Implementation of learning process.
3. Matching existing career with job competency classification/career paths.
4. Replacing existing designations/positions with new ones as indicated in the career planning and development plan.
5. Transferring employees from old career positions/designations to new positions/ roles.
6. Implementing new career plan for career movement of employees.

Application of this driver contributes for execution of the new career planning and development plan successfully. Effective operation of the new plan becomes an output of this driver.

DRIVER 9: ASSESSING EFFICACY OF CAREER PLANNING AND DEVELOPMENT PROGRAMME

Assessing effectiveness of the career planning and development plan is last but one driver of nurturing career based performance management intervention. After executing career planning and development plan for a reasonable period, the same needs to be assessed in order to ascertain its efficacy in terms of fulfilling employees and organizational goals. Reasonable period means that it should be in proportion to the size and scale of the organization both in terms of operations and manpower. Larger the organization, more the gestation period and lesser the size of organization, shorter the incubation period. In any case assessment should not be done before completion of a minimum of two years of implementation. Assessment may be done on a criterion that is suitable to the organization and its career planning and development programme, and should cover the following levels:

Step 1: Organizational Level

Career planning and development assessment must indicate organizational level results. This result can be obtained in the form of organizational performance. Whether the new career plan has contributed for growth in production, services sales, turnover and profit and business performance as a whole or not. Assessment to identify the contribution of career management to profits, sales, turnover and other financial parameters must be conducted after about four to five years of implementation. The initial implementation preferably must be confined to assess production figures or quality of services and products and also the general impression/perceptions of internal stakeholders of organization. The second level of assessment with the organization as focus, can be ascertaining contribution of the new career plan for building competencies in the organization.

Step 2: Process Level

The second type of assessment is auditing whether the career plan is implemented as it was planned and whether this planning itself is technically and logically sound or not. Whole exercise of career planning and development must be documented and subjected to audit. This documentation can be forwarded to career management experts and consultants and other organizations known for best practices in this area, seeking their critical views on this. Essence of process level exercise is establishing how well this career planning and development plan is developed and implemented and whether such a plan is meeting the fundamental requirements of career management principles per se. This assessment can be taken up after a year of implementation of the new career planning and development programme.

Step 3: Employee Level

Assessing employees' satisfaction with the new career planning and development plan as implemented is the third type of assessment. Survey, interview and large-scale interaction techniques can be used to obtain the relevant data from employees. Assessment parameters must be confined to eliciting employee-related issues such as whether the new career programme has contributed to career enrichment and their overall satisfaction with the system or not. Suggestions for further improvement of the career programme can also be obtained from employees. This assessment can be taken up on implementing the new career programme.

DRIVER 10: RENEWING CAREER PLANNING AND DEVELOPMENT PROGRAMME

Last driver in nurturing career-based performance management is to make continuous efforts to renew career planning and development programme. Norms as devised, assumptions as made, career paths as developed, job competencies as identified, mentoring system as adopted and learning culture as cultivated: all subject to change in tune with changing realities. No matter how good and unique career planning system may be, it tends to become insensitive to organizational and employee requirements unless such system is refined from time to time. Renewal of career planning and development programme must be made as an essential step in the overall system itself. Following can serve as helpers in implementing this renewal exercise.

Step 1: Renewal in the Light of Process and Employee Level Assessment

Data obtained by conducting process and employee level assessment must be promptly used in refining career planning and development programme. These assessments provide wealth of information, particularly from execution point of view. Therefore, it is of utmost importance that such feedback be given due consideration and necessary alterations brought into effect immediately. No matter how best organizations may devise and implement career planning and development system, still there can be substantial opportunities for improvement. Hence, organizations must assimilate and analyze assessment data to draw inferences for ensuring greater effectiveness of the programme.

Step 2: Renewal in the Light of Organization Level Assessment

Using assessment data obtained by analyzing business data such as balance sheet calls for critical thinking. Care must be taken not to take any data on face value. Many times reasons for green balance sheet may not necessarily be because of introduction of new career planning and development programme, and similarly the same may not be responsible for red balance sheets. Various internal and external factors play a vital role in shaping business performance and particularly financial parameters like turnover, profits and sales. There is no doubt that a strategic career planning and development programme can have implications for financial health of an organization. Essence of argument here is that caution need to be taken in measuring contribution of a career planning and development programme to financial performance of an organization by controlling intervening factors. This control of other factors requires use of highly reliable and validated assessment instruments. Organizational level data may be utilized to improve structural factors of career planning and development programme.

At the end of this driver, organizations will have a highly refined, value added and strategic career planning and development programme in operation.

INTERVENTION 2: CAPITALIZING ON CAREER STRATEGY IN INSTITUTIONA-LIZATION OF PERFORMANCE MANAGEMENT

The second intervention in career-based performance management strategy is using career planning and development programme to institutionalize performance as a way of life. Career management once nurtured with the help of first intervention can make people perform meaningfully and exceedingly well. In the mature state of career strategy practice, it assumes the status of being capable to influence overall performance management of an organization. Career management must be effectively utilized to reinforce the performance excellence of employees in particular and organization in general. Leaving on its own, career management may progress well to attain self-objectives, but in order to utilize the same for performance system improvement, special efforts are solicited. This intervention is precisely to serve that purpose with the support of 10 drivers as forthcoming content unfolds. Each of these drivers guides the organization to initiate specific action that corroborates institutionalization process. These drivers are:

DRIVER 1: FOSTERING REALISTIC EXPECTATIONS

Process that is followed and work methods built in realization of career planning and development programme can be used to imbibe the habit of making realistic expectations. Self-assessment driver discussed in the first intervention is an example of this. Performance

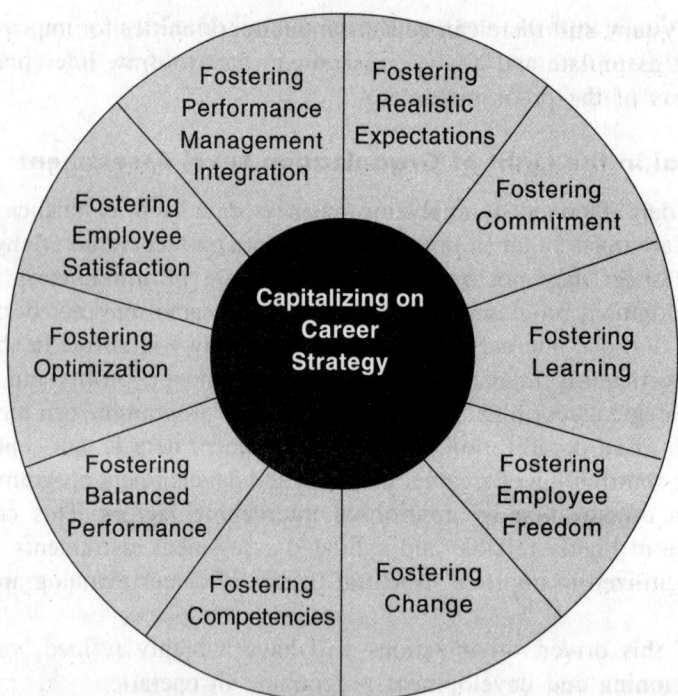

FIGURE 3.3 Drivers of the intervention capitalizing on career strategy in institutionalization of performance management.

excellence in many cases is contingent upon making right and real expectations. These expectations may be in the form of (i) understanding of self by employees, (ii) understanding their work, and (iii) understanding overall business and organizations. In other words, management is simply a game of expectations: What employees, management, customers and other stakeholders expect from each other. A career planning and development programme can work as a medium in moderating all expectations. Organizations must exploit the career planning and development system in institutionalization of performance management by fostering a culture of realistic expectations.

DRIVER 2: FOSTERING COMMITMENT

Although practising scientific career planning and development can create commitment, conscious efforts must be made to foster it further in order to achieve the goal of performance management institutionalization. A career planning and development programme provides for integrating organizational and employees' needs in a mutually acceptable manner. With this, serving one's own case becomes dependent on the health of other. Commitment comes from such mutually inclusive and well-blended system.

Performance excellence can be achieved when identity of organization and employees is one. Organizations must devote special efforts in emphasizing and leveraging this mutual culture for superordinate goal of transforming the organization into a competitive, innovative and agile machine. To conclude this driver briefly, organizations are required to transfer culture of mutuality to foster the commitment to a matured stage that eventually strengthens the case of performance management institutionalization.

DRIVER 3: FOSTERING LEARNING

Learning is an important ingredient of a career planning and development programme as vividly presented in the first intervention. Organizations can use this learning orientation to create a real learning organization. Ultimate goal of a performance management system is to create a powerful learning structure, processes and practices. A career planning and development programme therefore, can be effectively tapped to realize this learning orientation. Learning-based management is the matured state of performance excellence. A number of studies prove that learning is a soft dimension of performance management. Further, experience of organizations also highlights that maximum number of innovations and breakthroughs come from organizations that are learning-oriented. Building learning orientation among employees and the organization is one sure shot to attain performance institutionalization. This learning orientation can be created using embedded learning aspects within the career planning and development programme.

DRIVER 4: FOSTERING EMPLOYEE FREEDOM

A career planning and development programme firmly believes that employees should have absolute freedom to decide their destination and path of journey. Career programme also gets conceptualized with due inputs and self-assessment of employees. This environment of freedom created while implementing and pursuing a career planning and development programme works as the basic foundation for nurturing work freedom and ultimately employees' freedom. Humanistic and human relations' experiences attach importance to such freedom to employees for obtaining the best out of them. It is common observation that employees tend to perform well and often beyond expectations of anybody when they are given freedom to choose career, path, resources, conduct and time. Employees' performance dampens when there are restrictions imposed by someone at the top. Employees create tougher measures of self-discipline when given freedom to decide everything. This freedom that is extended to employees in career strategy should be leveraged to institutionalize performance management as a product of freedom.

DRIVER 5: FOSTERING CHANGE

As change management experts assert, change is the only permanent thing in ever changing world. Performance of organizations is largely influenced by their ability to adapt to changing environment. Organizations should enhance capabilities to influence the environment and lead the industry. A career planning and development programme is the best means to enable organizations to acquire these change management capabilities. A critical driver in the career planning and development programme is renewal of career strategy on continuous basis. This driver is basically drawn adhering to change management principles. Basic framework developed and steps followed while implementing renewal exercise can be of significant help for the change management strategy. Change management goals can be melded with renewal exercise and make careers accordingly. Career planning and development programme becomes an instrument for realizing changes, which can also be implemented without much effort and resistance. Employees tend to perceive changes as natural since subjects of change are part of their careers. Performance as a way of life gets institutionalized once change and career are managed as identical systems.

DRIVER 6: FOSTERING COMPETENCIES

Performance level of an organization is equivalent to the competencies it possesses. It is also a powerful fact that competencies need to be updated on a continuous basis. Continuous nurturing of competencies can contribute to institutionalization of performance management. Job competencies are regarded and practiced as a pivotal driver in the intervention of nurturing career-based performance management. Essence of this driver is that job competencies as discussed must be leveraged as a key input in performance management institutionalization. Modus operandi can be treating of competency updating as a part of position description. This implies that every employee in the organization, as matter of routine activity, must renew competencies in tune with changing reality of the organization that include technological, market and business changes apart from changes in one's own occupation/profession/trade.

DRIVER 7: FOSTERING BALANCED PERFORMANCE

Institutionalization of performance management can occur only when practice of performance management is built on a balanced approach. Balanced approach means, organizations should neither be obsessed with balance sheet exclusively nor short-term gains or excessive reliance on human relationships. However, this does not mean that financial parameters should not be a barometer for measuring effectiveness of performance management. In fact, balance sheet can be one of the factors in such an assessment. Central argument here is that equal attention should be paid to process, learning and innovation dimensions. System audit/ assessment can provide results on well being of performance management practice. In this context, career planning and development programme can be utilized to drive this balanced approach to performance management. A career planning and development programme is developed on the balanced approach where there is role for employee, organization and process health of both of them apart from the financial factor.

DRIVER 8: FOSTERING OPTIMIZATION

High performance work system is the result of optimization of human efforts. How much one can perform and how sincerely one is progressing can be assessed only by that individual.

An individual employee is the best judge of his/her own performance. Further, no matter how rigorously a system might have been conceived and followed to effectively tap human talent and utilize physical resources, it is the employee commitment to optimize efforts and resources that contribute to performance excellence. A career planning and development programme by nature provides enough space for employees to (i) assess and match themselves with career positions and (ii) to assess organizational needs and match them with their own assessment. This process motivates employees to optimize all resources including self-effort. This optimization behaviour should be effectively deployed for making all business decisions. Premise of this drive is that performance management institutionalization becomes a reality when such optimization is made to be an integral part of work in the organization.

DRIVER 9: FOSTERING EMPLOYEE SATISFACTION

Ultimately, all human resource related models emphasize two issues: human relations/commitment models advocate that any human resource system that includes performance management must serve cause of employees, i.e. employees' satisfaction. Business/strategic driven human resource models argue that organizational profit must be dominant motive of any human system. However, the fact is that both these are mutually inclusive. Employees' dissatisfaction can never lead to high performance and similarly a loss-making organization can never create employees' satisfaction. Career-based performance management is developed on the premise that employee satisfaction and organizational well-being are two sides of the same coin. This philosophy must be internalized within an organization through systematic efforts. Such internalization automatically leads to institutionalization of performance management.

DRIVER 10: FOSTERING INTEGRATION OF PERFORMANCE MANAGEMENT STRATEGIES

Career-based performance management strategy, particularly first intervention, i.e. nurturing career-based performance management, at various stages of its own development and practice draws support of other performance management strategies such as competency-based performance management, leadership-based performance management, culture-based performance management and measurement-based performance management. Career-based performance management can be effectively utilized as a focal point for attaining agreement among all these performance management strategies. Performance management institutionalization can come from such sharp integration and unified agreement. This driver prescribes that an organization must make efforts to deploy career-based performance management as a vehicle for such integration.

SUMMARY

Career management is nothing new to organizations managers and employees. However, career management has gained special attention in current decade as a sharp mechanism in fulfilling higher motivational needs like self-esteem and self-actualization. Career management is considered as a vital ingredient in the grand strategy of performance management. Within the overall framework of performance management, career planning and development has a special role because it can be an opportunity as well as a threat to performance-building efforts of organizations. A well-managed career system can enhance performance, whereas a mismanaged system can cause sagging morale and lowering of performance.

Career based performance management strategy, one of the seven performance management strategies, is presented in this chapter. This chapter is organized into five parts. What is career management and what it is not in the context of performance management is discussed in the first part while the significance of career management in overall performance management practice is presented in part two. The significance of career strategy is illustrated through the contributions it can make. This includes:

   (i) Continual development of human resource
  (ii) Ensuring right people to right positions
 (iii) Facilitating optimization of efforts
 (iv) Providing for competency building
  (v) Creating avenues for motivational fulfilment
 (vi) Making available critical knowledge for innovation
(vii) Enhancing employee commitment
(viii) Creating harmony between employee and organizational needs
 (ix) Creating provision for self-assessment
  (x) Enhancing organizational and employee agility.

Theoretical foundations of career management such as:

   (i) Schein's career anchors
  (ii) Schein's stages in career cycle
 (iii) Hall's career stage model
 (iv) Mondy, Noe and Premeaux's four types of career paths
  (v) Holland's framework of career choice and
 (vi) Ilea's resource-based career approach

are briefly presented in part three of the chapter. These theories provide valuable insights into issues such as congruence between career and employee personality, congruence between employee and organization, congruence between employee and environment, career stages, career anchors, etc.

Lessons derived from these seminal theories while building career-based performance management strategy include:

   (i) Need to integrate career planning with organizational objectives
  (ii) Need to match organizational careers with career choices of employees
 (iii) Career as long-term learning experience
 (iv) Career management as dual responsibility of employee and organization.

The strategy of career-based performance management is developed through two interventions. Nurturing career-based performance management is the first intervention and presented in the part four of the chapter. Career is proposed to be deployed as a prime force in achieving performance excellence in this intervention with the application of 10 drivers. These drivers are:

   (i) Planning career development plan: organizational focus
  (ii) Planning career development plan: individual focus
 (iii) Articulating career planning and development goals
 (iv) Defining job competencies
  (v) Creating learning centric career development
 (vi) Creating mentoring centric career development
(vii) Launching tailor-made career planning and development programme
(viii) Implementing career planning and development programme
 (ix) Analyzing efficacy of career planning and development programme
  (x) Renewing career planning and development programme.

The second intervention is referred to as capitalizing on career strategy in institutionalization of performance management as a way of organizational life. This is captured in the final part of the present chapter. This intervention is also envisaged to be realized through the execution of 10 drivers such as:

   (i) Fostering realistic expectations
  (ii) Fostering commitment
 (iii) Fostering learning
 (iv) Fostering employee freedom
  (v) Fostering change
 (vi) Fostering competencies
(vii) Fostering balanced performance
(viii) Fostering optimization
 (ix) Fostering employee satisfaction
  (x) Fostering integration of performance management strategies in practice.

KEY WORDS

Following are the key words discussed in this chapter:

- Career strategy
- Job competencies
- Mentoring centric career planning
- Career anchors
- Career stages
- Network careers
- Career choice
- Balanced performance

- Vertical career movement
- Learning centric career planning
- Self-assessment
- Career cycle
- Career paths
- Plateauing
- Resource-based career approach
- Realistic career expectations

DISCUSSION QUESTIONS

1. What is career-based performance management? Discuss salient features of career strategy.

2. Define career management in the context of performance management and also present what is not career management?

3. What is the significance of career planning and development in performance management?

4. How do you develop a career planning and development programme?

5. Can an organization leverage a career planning and development programme to institutionalize performance management? If yes, please discuss how it can be used and if no, discuss why it cannot be used?

6. Career management is the responsibility of both individual employee and organization. Substantiate the statement.

7. Does career planning and development programme need to be integrated with organizational goals? Discuss with supporting factors.

8. What is learning centric career development?

9. Discuss the role of mentoring in career development.

CASE STUDIES

1. Asian Insurance Company Ltd. is one of the largest insurance companies in India with significant market share. The company has been following hierarchical career planning. Employee development is a separate initiative and not linked to career movement of employees. Recently, the company has taken over Jumbo Insurance Ltd. and merged with its operations. Many human resources related issues have cropped up during and after the said merger. This has mainly arisen due to lack of parity in career policies and practices between Asian Insurance Company and Jumbo Insurance Ltd. Jumbo Insurance also has a hierarchical promotion system, but promotions are comparatively slow. This one issue has become a big hurdle in creating a unified work force. Top management of the insurance company has also realized that unless this issue is amicably resolved, it is difficult to attain real performance from employees. George Thomson, chief executive of Asian Insurance Company held a meeting of board of directors exclusively to discuss this career management problem. One of them suggested to extend Asian's career policy to erstwhile Jumbo employees also and another director disagreed saying the original Asian's employees are not ready to accept this equal treatment. On a detailed discussion, the board finally agreed to use this opportunity to revamp the career policies and create a contemporary, competency centric and organizationally dovetailed

career planning and development programme. Discuss how can a career policy and practice be built, which is most appropriate to Asian Insurance Company in the light of the above described background.

2. Oriental Oil Corporation Limited is a state undertaking engaged in petroleum products. The company owns two refineries, 32 LPG bottling plants and 367 retail outlets across India. The company has eight executive grades. First four grades are classified as junior management, fifth and sixth as middle and seven and eighth as top management. Due to unsystematic career management the company has landed in a peculiar problem of 70% of executive strength getting accumulated in the middle grades. For example, there are about 512 executives in the middle management category against the actual requirement of 84. Further, 245 out of these 512 are due to be promoted to top management category but vacancies are only 27. Due to this lack of adequate career upgradation opportunities, many in the middle level are frustrated and lack the motivation to perform. Discuss what strategy this company must adopt to overcome this situation.

3. Computer Incorporation is a software development company located in Bangalore, India. The company is facing serious problems in retaining employees, particularly newly recruited. Computer Incorporation has used all methods to minimize attrition rate. Mostly employees leave on completion of a year of service and in some cases even before that. Preliminary analysis points out that youngsters do not find any executive who takes interest in their activities and guides them. They also at times feel inhospitable in the company. To tide over this problem, company has decided to introduce mentoring system. Do you think this is the right solution for this problem? Discuss advantages and disadvantages in using mentoring as a career strategy to reduce attrition rate among employees.

SUGGESTED READING

Hall, Douglas, T. (1996). *The Career is Dead-Long Live the Career: A Relational Approach.* San Francisco: Jossey-Bass.

Holland, John (1996). "Exploring careers with a typology". *American Psychologist*, April, pp. 397–406.

Mondy, Wayne, Robert Noe and Shane Premeaux (1999). *Human Resource Management.* New Jersey: Prentice Hall Inc.

Schein, Edgar H. (1975). "How career anchors hold executives to their career paths". *Personnel*, 52, pp. 11–24.

Schein, Edgar H. (1978). *Career Dynamics: Matching Individual and Organizational Needs.* Massachusetts: Addison-Wesley.

Chapter Four

STRATEGY 3: TEAM-BASED PERFORMANCE MANAGEMENT

Teams and teamwork are not new to organizations. Philosophy and practice of teamwork continues to appear in different forms in tandem with changing organizational contexts. Participative management, co-determination, workers cooperation in management, quality circles, small group activity, so on and so forth are intended to infuse teamwork and team spirit in organizations. It is an undeniable fact that teams have assumed a new importance and acquired a new vigour with the advent of new economy organizations where work is more interdependent. Growing necessity to introduce flexibility, delegation, consensus, two way communication, collaborative effort and practices such as downsizing, flat structures, matrix structures, ESOPs (employee stock ownership plans), empowerment, just-in-time inventory, continuous improvement and more importantly, constantly changing work patterns have escalated role of teams in organizational life more than ever in the past. In brief, organizations of today have no choice but to implement teamwork.

Interestingly, teams are not always successful for a variety of reasons. The most influential factor that leads teams to fail is lack of clear expectation. Some organizations introduce teams as panacea to all organizational problems and some just to be in the bandwagon of team-based organizations and still others embrace teams without specifying why they are required. It may sound as paradox but history of teamwork consists of more failures than successes on the face of growing popularity of teamwork. However, organizations 33that introduced teams with a clear vision, purpose, commitment and alignment with organizational focus have been experiencing success. All these successful organizations have a commonality in their approach, i.e. their rational expectation of teams enhancing performance of people.

Teamwork and teams can be a natural source of improving performance. Teamwork is one of the critical pillars in the architecture of performance management. Forthcoming content reveals the strategy of team-based performance management in detail. This strategy like earlier ones is organized in five parts. Part 1 deals with what is team-based performance management and what it is not. The significance of teams in the context of performance management is discussed in part 2. Theoretical aspects of teams are presented in part 3. The first intervention of team-based performance management strategy, 'nurturing team-based performance management, is illustrated in part 4 while part 5 captures the second intervention called Capitalizing on teamwork in institutionalization of performance management.

TEAMWORK IN PERFORMANCE MANAGEMENT

Teamwork is an activity in which tasks are interdependent and performed by different individuals in a collaborative manner with distinct skills to produce a common goal with performance excellence. In this sense, team is a group of individuals who collaborate with their unique skills to achieve a common goal in the most efficient manner. Operationalization of this definition for teamwork and teams assume the following elements:

1. Tasks are interdependent.
2. Interdependent tasks are performed by different individuals with matching skills.
3. Matching skills are distinctive.
4. Interdependent tasks are performed in a collaborative manner to achieve a common goal.
5. Common goal is achieved in the most efficient manner.

WHAT IS NOT TEAMWORK

Misconceptions about teamwork are many. Prominent being:

1. Believing and practicing teamwork as mere group work carried out by collection of individuals.
2. Teamwork as duplication of efforts wherein more individuals indulge in the same task.
3. A group of individuals forced to collaborate to achieve a goal forced on them.
4. A group of individuals performing in independent mode to achieve a common goal.
5. A group of individuals working as a team on tasks that are not interdependent in nature.

Most of the troubles and failures of teamwork are attributable to the misunderstanding about teamwork. Merely collecting individuals together or expecting them to perform on a common goal is insufficient to create a team-based structure in organizations leave alone creating an impact over performance. It is more than that. This consists of many issues, many sacrifices and many commitments. When this happens, realizing a team-based management for performance excellence is much easier than anybody can imagine. In the context of performance management, teamwork that doesn't deliver excellence in performance of employees in attaining organizational and employee goals is not teamwork.

SIGNIFICANCE OF TEAMWORK IN PERFORMANCE MANAGEMENT

Teams possess unstinted capability to enhance performance level and optimize resources. Teams, therefore, have a special place in the practice of performance management. Team-based performance management strategy wields direct influence over the other six performance management strategies because teams are the basic building blocks as well as prime beneficiaries of these strategies. The significance of teams in performance management can be multifold. However, this significance varies from organization to organization depending upon the degree of teamwork required in an organization. The common benefits and significance of teams in the context of performance management to all organizations are described here briefly:

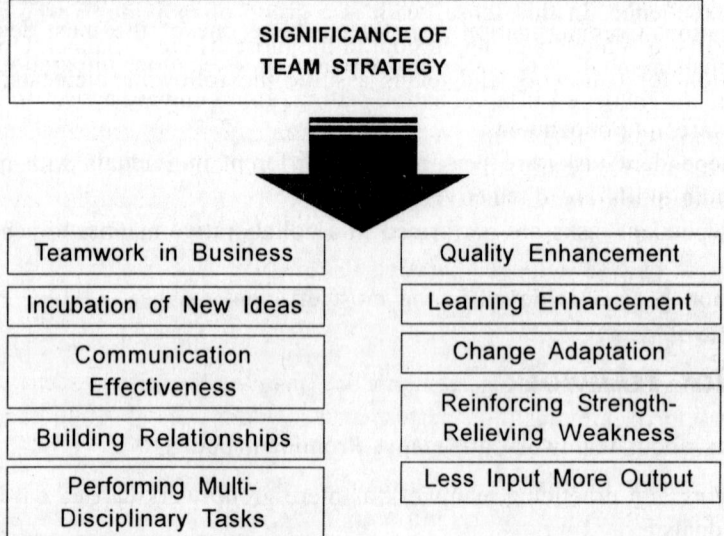

FIGURE 4.1   Significance of team-based performance management strategy.

Involvement of Employees in the Business

Teamwork is one sure shot and proper method to involve all employees in the business of an organization. In a situation where performance of an organization in particular and fortunes of business in general are susceptible to the effectiveness of people, there can be hardly any choice but to involve employees in management of the business. It is equally important that no single or a small portion of individuals or managers be allowed to exert control over the functioning of an organization. History of business performance indicates that performance goes down when few in the place of all are given opportunity to run organization. Every employee must be given an opportunity to participate in organizational business. Teamwork can ensure this equitable participation and involvement.

Implementation of New Ideas

Incubation and implementation of new ideas is central to great performances and consequential organizational successes in today's business environment. More often than not this generation of new ideas involves contribution of insights from more than one individual. This means vibrant exchange of ideas, information, knowledge and experimentation sharing is a prerequisite. Individuals of a loose group can't infuse such exchange culture. A well-woven team with a well-defined destiny is must. Teams possess inherent potential to create and implement new ideas through this formula of exchange. These new ideas infuse life into performance management.

Enhances Communication Effectiveness

The very nature of teamwork widens communication among all employees and stakeholders in an organization. Communication is believed to be one of the most decisive factors of performance management. When allocation, planning, execution, integration and evaluation of assignments are managed in a collective setting, communication rises to the level of real sharing. Several studies prove that lack of communication can create distrust, conflict and dysfunctional effects in the organizational working. Implementing a communication strategy on a stand-alone format may not yield anticipated results because communication itself is not an end. Therefore, making people come together can cause communication effectiveness. This togetherness can be achieved through teamwork.

Builds Relationships

Effectiveness of performance management practice stands on the salutary scenario of relationships in an organization. Achieving high performance of employees by building relationships is certainly a gentle practice. Good relationships can happen only when there is equity and a common goal among members of an organization. It is one of the toughest managerial challenges to ensure the said equity and a common destiny. Route to handle this challenge is obviously a team structure. Teamwork can provide equitable opportunities, equitable rewards, equitable disappointments and equitable growth. Teamwork has enormous potential in creating healthy human relations in an organization, which is a significant facilitator of performance management effectiveness.

Performs on Multi-Disciplinary Tasks

Emerging work systems are more of interdependent and multi-disciplinary in nature. This requires people with different skills collaborating to produce an outcome/result. Growing technological changes and corresponding complexity in tasks left us with no doubt that a single person can deal with all the processes or tasks independently. Fast developing knowledge base in all fields makes it extremely difficult for a person to work on a macro level issue independently. People in such an environment tend to choose a micro level specialization and make progress vertically. However, when it comes to resolving macro level problem, people with this micro level expertise need to come together. In brief, expanding knowledge dictates that people be specialists and at the same time solicit an integrated approach to problem solving. Hence, teams alone can handle multifaceted problems. More the interdisciplinary approach of an organization, higher the performance excellence in innovation.

Enhances Quality

Quality of products, services, operations, delivery, etc. are indicators of performance excellence. All quality theories, approaches, philosophies and principles of quality gurus invariably stress the importance of teamwork in achieving quality in practice. Quality can never be attained with the effort of a single individual or a group of individuals in the name of quality assurance function. Quality consciousness as a matter of value that should be embedded across the organization and internalized in the minds of people. Employees do not hesitate to supplement the efforts of others when they perceive and believe that quality is everyone's business. Teams are prime means through which quality agenda can be pushed successfully.

Enhances Learning

Teamwork has the potential to enhance learning of people. A good amount of learning happens in socialization process and when people work together on a common task. While supplementing each other's efforts with distinct capabilities, people also pass on that distinct knowledge to each other. It is well-established fact that colleagues in an organization or classmates in a school are the richest source of great learning. Teamwork formalizes that arrangement for learning and also encourages the creation of systems for learning in togetherness. Learning in reality is the other side of the coin of performance management. Excellent performance can come from people who are learners and not from those who are stagnant.

Enables Change Adaptation

Engineering a change and transforming an organization through change management is often a herculean task because most of the organizations comprise of individuals and departments rather than a well-cohesive force. There can be splinter groups and individuals conflicting each other. In such a scenario no matter, how laudable the objectives of a change programme and its expressed benefits to all the stakeholders might be, the programme faces stiff resistance. Implementing a change programme is much easier and success rate is much higher in any organization where teamwork and teams exist. Communicating with employees, with forming change management as a common objective, developing implementing plans and executing them is much easier. Teamwork imparts employees to consider rationality, overall objective and creates trust and openness. These characteristics are fundamental to launching a change management programme. Actual performance of employees and organizations is determined by their capability to accept change as natural.

Reinforces Strengths and Relieves Weakness

Every individual is blessed with strengths in few disciplines and constrained with few weaknesses. They continue to live with those weaknesses on one hand and on the other hand, strengths may not get exploited as long as performance is individual centric. Teamwork provides abundant opportunities for people to manifest, sharpen and fully utilize their strengths, and supports endeavours to overcome weaknesses. Excellence in performance is simply contingent upon this principle. For example, an individual with communication abilities can be utilized for variety of internal and external purposes of an organization thereby exposing him/her to a variety of situations. Likewise, an individual with low skill in quantitative aptitude can be coached and developed by his/her colleague in a work setting. This happens in a smooth manner if teamwork exists because reinforcing the strengths of co-members and supporting to relieve them of their weaknesses is considered everyone's concern.

Doing More with Less

Ultimate goal of any organization is to achieve more output with less input because competitive edge comes from that. How to achieve this is a million-dollar question to professionals, consultants and business managers. More or less, at least top organizations have the accessibility to same technology, capital, marketing network and other infrastructure resources. Theoretically speaking all such organizations must produce the same output for equivalent inputs. Puzzle is that this is not true. In fact, a few Japanese organizations with lesser inputs obtained much higher outputs. Secret behind this miracle was teams. Teamwork can make breakthrough achievements through collaboration of efforts. Success of performance management is measured by this principle of doing more with less, achievement of which is feasible only through teams.

Though teamwork offers valuable contribution, realizing effective teams is easier said than done. Teamwork is fraught with many challenges. For example, in the forming phase of teams, organizations must be willing to allow more time, show perseverance and be tolerant to inter and intra group conflicts, low productivity and low focus. Also team leadership can be a major issue. Managers must be very realistic about all these challenges because introducing team structure in the place of mechanistic organizational structures, at least in the beginning, can create formidable challenges. However, once the initial problems are handled successfully, teams can certainly create performance excellence.

THEORETICAL FOUNDATIONS OF TEAMWORK

Teams and teamwork have been well-researched. There are a number of theories and models that explain: (i) why people prefer teamwork, (ii) nature of teams, (iii) key behavioural patterns of teams, (iv) how teams influence a member, (v) emerging team structure such as work roles, norms, team size and team processes like communication and leadership, (vi) team dynamics like political process, conflicts and negotiations and conciliation, (vii) functions of teams, (viii) advantages and disadvantages with teams, (ix) implications of teamwork to work performance, etc. These team theories also perfectly capture the process of team formation and progress. A few such significant theories are described below:

TUCKMAN'S FOUR STAGE THEORY OF TEAMWORK

According to B.W. Tuckman who did pioneering work on teamwork, teams progress through four stages as presented here:

Forming: This is the beginning stage. It is also called the honeymoon phase. At this stage team structure tends to be loose, norms don't exist, members are not clear how to proceed, communication is fragmented, leadership is not formed and a few members start bidding for leadership. Unclear objective, a free and chaotic environment and a laisez faire attitude represents this phase. Productivity will be low and progress can be hampered with trial and error method of work unless special care is taken. Members get acquainted with each other and they tend to perceive an emerging powerful role for themselves.

Storming: Actual formation of team starts from this phase. Bidding for leadership hots up and some give up while a few intensify their effort. All members put in efforts to secure a clear role for them in the team. They also make attempts to define issues, the manner to solve problems, a code of conduct for members and the overall scope of the team. In this process, intra-team rivalries and differences in interests and approaches surface. Some members develop frustration and others come out openly with their views. End of this phase witnesses a remarkable progress in team formation and members' role.

Norming: This phase is characterized by a mutual understanding among members, setting of clear code of conduct, norms through which teams must perform, endorsement of leadership, and a realistic assessment of things to be done and embracing an overall objective. Substantive team structure with a clear focus can be seen in this phase.

Performing: Oneness of team members, working towards a common goal, performing on a task with clear purpose, leveraging on strengths of fellow members, helping and supporting each other, collaborating on multi-disciplinary issues and commitment to teamwork are prime characteristics of this phase. To put it briefly, teams actually start performing in this stage.

This theory helps performance managers in their mission to nurture team-based performance management in organizations. This seminal model presents an insight into how teams form, attain a shape and progress to accomplish tasks. Contribution of this theory is that it guides in planning and execution of the team-based performance management strategy.

THEODORE NEWCOMB'S BALANCE THEORY OF GROUP FORMATION

Based on intensive observation of group working, Newcomb proposed a theory called the Balance theory of group formation in 1961, explaining why people are attracted towards group. According to him, people are attracted towards one another as long as there is similarity in attitudes in pursuing a common goal. This similarity encourages people to share, form understanding and function as a team. If attitudes are not similar, balance is lost and a team can never be formed. Therefore, there must be balance in terms of attitudes among members.

THIBAUT AND KELLEY'S EXCHANGE THEORY OF GROUP FORMATION

This theory stipulates that formation of group is motivated and frustrated by twin factors of reward and cost outcome of the group interaction. Group becomes functional till members receive reward in excess of the cost factor. Members are likely to dissociate with groups if the cost factor is becoming much more than the reward. It implies that members tend to remain with group as long as there is benefit but group strength weakens the moment cost factor dominates.

GERSICK'S PUNCTUATED EQUILIBRIUM MODEL

C.J.G. Gersick's model argues that team formation does not happen in a universally applicable or expected mode of sequence. Rather this is decided by the time factor. According to the architect of this model, team formation is dominated by two critical phases: inertia and activation. When teams meet for the first time, there will be inertia and wastage of time. This is followed by an activity of giving a direction to team. Again, this is followed by a state of inertia. After this, teams renew their efforts and an intensified activity occurs. Teams perform through this process of inertia and activation.

ORSBURN, MORAN, WHITE AND ZENGER'S FIVE-STAGE MODEL OF TEAMS

Team formation and teamwork is an ongoing process according to this model. As the title suggests, typically teams undergo five stages as briefly indicated here:

Start-up: This phase involves training team members on teamwork and related aspects like team norms, interaction process and a few guidelines on team functioning.

State of Confusion: Despite training and familiarization of team concept, team members continue to reel under confusion. This ambiguity exists particularly in the shape of role clarity of members, leadership issues and the manner in which decisions are to be arrived at.

Leader-Centred Teamwork: This stage manifests visible signs of progress, especially in identifying leadership and deriving direction from it. Negative dimension of this stage is that members learn to depend on leadership for everything from identifying problems to resolving them.

Tightly Formed Teams: A remarkable achievement is made at this stage that teams become self-reliant. Leadership is assumed to perform the role of coordination only. Members wean away from excessively relying on leadership and commit themselves to attaining team objectives in the most efficient manner. They continue to depend upon the management for resource allocation and overall guidance. However, danger at this stage is that intensified cohesiveness within the team provides scope for inter-team conflicts.

Self-Directed Teams: Teams acquire maturity at this stage. They accord importance to the superordinate goals of organization and inter-team conflict recedes. Teams play a vibrant role in enhancing effectiveness of an organization in all respects.

BENNIS' TEN PRINCIPLES OF TEAMWORK

Management guru, Warren Bennis based on rigorous study of a number of teams, identified 10 essential principles that every effective team possesses. These are:

   (i) At the heart of every great group there is a shared dream
  (ii) Teams manage conflict by abandoning individual egos in the pursuit of the shared dream
 (iii) Teams protect themselves from corporate disdain
  (iv) Teams derive energy from a real or perceived enemy
   (v) Team members see themselves as winning underdogs
  (vi) Members prepare to pay a personal price in terms of emotional and personal disturbances in the mission of achieving team goals
 (vii) Teams make leaders strong
(viii) Team members are the products of meticulous recruitment
  (ix) Team members are usually young
   (x) Team members produce clear deliverables to organization that are more valuable than their personal gains.

SHAW'S THEORY OF DETERMINANTS OF TEAM COHESIVENESS

Credit for proposing a framework of determinants of group cohesiveness goes to M. Shaw. Degree of cohesiveness is correlated to seven factors. These are:

   (i) Team homogeneity
  (ii) Team maturity
 (iii) Size of team
  (iv) Communication among team members
   (v) Clarity of team goals
  (vi) Perception of threat and competition
 (vii) Processes like leadership.

Teams tend to be more cohesive when there is a state of idealness in these factors. Cohesiveness can never be attained in the absence or imbalance among these factors.

SUNDSTORM, DEMEUSE AND FUTRELL'S PURPOSE CLASSIFICATION OF TEAMS

Three experts on teamwork namely, Eric Sundstorm, Kenneth DeMeuse and David Futrell presented a classification of teams keeping in view their role and contribution to organizations. There are four types as described below:

Advice: This type of team is formed and developed to render advise to the decision-makers in organizations. Members of these teams are drawn based on their expertise in a given discipline. Examples of this are strategic advisers, policy making advisers, law advisers, defense advisers etc.,

Production: There can be multiple teams, each of the teams vested with the responsibility of producing a defined product. These mainly exist in the shape of shop floor teams, quality circles. The main task here is to schedule and implement production targets.

Project: Third kind is called project teams. These are formed for a specific purpose. For example, project teams are formed to implement a software project/to develop a drug formulation/to negotiate with suppliers to empanel agencies or a team of doctors is formed to carry .out a surgery. Essential characteristic here is that a team is formed for special purpose, completion of which sees disbanding of the team.

Action: These teams are also formed to carry out a special mission, but here responsibility of members is mainly confined to adhere to instruction and act accordingly. For example, deploying a special force to handle a terrorist attack or saving a hijacked airplane.

HACKMAN'S WORK GROUP NORMS THEORY

Theory of work group norms developed by J. Hackman has relevance to teamwork. Norms of work groups or teams in our context are evolved through five phases. In the first phase, norms are set in order to regulate behaviour of group members. The second phase sees maturity in this act of regulation. Regulation is defined as only seeking change in behaviour and alteration in an individual's thinking or feeling domain. In the third phase, members start appreciating importance of norms and begin adopting them. In the fourth phase, norms facilitate progress of groups and acquire the status of standards in practice. Members realize in the fifth phase that there must be some kind of discrimination in norms in order to protect interests of all members qualitatively. This leads to making concessions based on relevant factors. For example, extending concessions based on sex, economic class or health of an individual.

HOFFMAN'S WORK ROLES THEORY

Each team comprises different roles, and team members also prefer to play a role that is compatible with their aptitude and attitude. L. Hoffman on comprehensive study of team role structure, classified roles into three as described below:

Task-Oriented Roles: A few team members focus on achieving goals and fulfilment of tasks. They perform an active role in leading the team through planning and execution process of goal achievement. They spend their time, efforts and mobilize resources to attain tasks and functions.

Relations-Oriented Roles: The second type of team members is very relationship-oriented. They spend their energies to build relationships with other team members and advocate an emotional relationship among team members for achievement of goals. This group of people are also task-fulfilment-oriented but difference lies in their approach, i.e. task-oriented people are just functional and plan to achieve targets with sheer mechanical approach, whereas relationship-oriented people emphasize the route of relationship.

Self-Oriented Roles: Third type is built on the attitude of selfishness. People of this nature try to push their personal agenda at the cost of team. They find it difficult to commit themselves to the goals of team. Self-oriented people always concentrate on things that can bring personal recognition, rewards and benefits to them as individuals rather than as team members.

KATZ AND KAHN'S ROLE EXPECTATION THEORY

Katz and Kahn proposed a role expectation theory that explains the roles team members perform are equivalent to perception of their roles. This role expectation forms through a process of three phases as indicated here:

Group Expectation of a Position: What role a team member performs depends on the expectation of team about the role to be played by a particular team member.

Communication about Team Expectation: Teams generally communicate to team members about expectations of the team regarding role to be played by a member.

Perceived Expectation: A team member's expectation of the role to be played by him/ her gets influenced by his/her own perception and communication of the team about the role. However, this team's communication is also received in consonance with the perception of a team member about his/her own role.

LESSONS OF TEAMWORK THEORIES

The above discussed teamwork theories have quite a few implications and offer valuable lessons in developing the strategy of team-based performance management. Some of these important lessons are briefly indicated below:

People Prefer Teams to Fulfil Social and Esteem Needs

People in organizations prefer teams for a wide range of reasons which include: (i) to fulfil social needs by becoming part of a cohesive team and incidentally gratify the self-esteem need, and (ii) to learn and progress with the support of co-citizens. Lesson is that team nurturing must be done by a method which cares for and provides opportunities to team members to fulfil these needs.

Effectiveness of Teams Comes from Cohesiveness

More the tightness/maturity of team, greater the effectiveness. Studies establish that commitment and oneness are essential factors for team success. Vital learning is that team cohesiveness must be given a high priority and must be considered as a vital parameter in measuring effectiveness of a team.

Cohesiveness of Team Comes from Matching

Matching (homogeneity) of interests and attitudes among team members is a dominant factor in creating cohesiveness among team members. Further, size of the team and communication among team members are also factors that influence this cohesiveness. Hence, formation of teams must be done keeping in view these factors.

Teams Function through Norms

Teams regulate their own behaviour by setting and defining the norms from time to time depending upon situational demands. Teams must be given all freedom to form their own code of conduct instead of handing them a script such as rules, regulations and procedures.

Teams Influence Members through Expectations

Teams define roles and motivate members to perform through a process of expectation. Members perform in accordance with their understanding of team expectation regarding their roles.

Great Teams Follow a Set of Principles

Studies reveal that the most effective teams follow a set of principles. These include: dreaming to achieve, abandoning egos for the benefit of teams and making clear deliverables at each stage of team functioning. This is a significant lesson for the team-based performance management strategy. Teamwork must be promoted on these principles.

Teams Form in an Evolutionary Manner

Formation of teams, beginning from a state of confusion to the status of maturity, happens in an evolutionary manner. Progress of team building also occurs in a repeated twin sequence of inertia and activation. Introduction of teamwork must keep this aspect in view and expectations of team effectiveness must be made accordingly.

Unity in Diversity

Members of a team perform different roles that include performing specialized jobs wherein some members undertake managerial and coordination functions and others work in supporting services. Different roles contribute in different ways towards attainment of team objectives. Teams need to be built on diverse competencies for a unified objective.

Team Dynamics are Natural

Inter and intra team conflicts are natural in the progress of team formation. However, these conflicts disappear once teams reach the stage of maturity where all teams and all team members internalize and commit themselves to the superordinate goal.

Different Teams for Different Purposes

Studies on teams also identified and provided a classification of teams. There are different types of teams suiting to different tasks/goals and situations. Composition and processes also vary in tune with the nature of these teams. While launching the strategy of teamwork, teams must be introduced in tune with the purpose for which these are formed rather than with a generic focus.

TEAM-BASED PERFORMANCE MANAGEMENT STRATEGY, INTERVENTIONS AND DRIVERS

Strategy of team-based performance management comprises two interventions. These are:

Nurturing Team-based Performance Management: Objective of this intervention is to create, build, nurture and strengthen teamwork in an organization to attain performance excellence. This intervention is to be evolved and implemented with the help of 10 drivers. Forthcoming contents reveal the structure, content and purpose of these drivers in a detailed fashion.

Capitalizing on Teamwork in Institutionalizing Performance Management: The second intervention is drawn on the idea of capitalizing teamwork to institutionalize performance management in organizations. Here also like earlier, 10 drivers perform the instrumental role in catapulting the teamwork into realizing the institutionalization intervention successfully.

INTERVENTION 1: NURTURING TEAM-BASED PERFORMANCE MANAGEMENT

As stated above, the objective of this intervention is to introduce and grow the teamwork structure in organizations to enhance performance of people for their own and for organization's benefit. This intervention is deployed through the initiation of 10 drivers. These 5 drivers as described below enable the organization to effectively adopt teamwork and derive unparalleled benefits.

DRIVER 1: SETTING TEAMWORK OBJECTIVES

The primary driver in the journey of nurturing teamwork is meant to make organizations aware and question their own intention of introducing teamwork. This inquisition leads them to set realistic objectives and make rational expectations about teamwork. It may also

FIGURE 4.2   Drivers of the intervention nurturing team-based performance management.

happen that organizations can rightfully withdraw themselves from falling into the trap of teamwork if this work structure is incompatible to their organizational mission and work values. Inquiry, diagnosis and setting of objectives must be done in a systematic manner using relevant parameters. Following list of actions is indicative of the process:

Step 1: Why Teamwork

First concern that should be addressed as indicated above—is why teamwork? What benefits are expected as compared to the present pattern of work performance and at what cost? How organization and its people are anticipated to suffer if teamwork is not cultivated in the organization. What motivated the organization or a few people in the organization to propose the idea of teamwork and how valid is the rationality they offer? Most importantly, what can be the contribution of teamwork in improving bottom line of the organization? Following indicators may give reasons for preference to teamwork:

1. *Business:*   Reasons can be found within the business plans. Present and future business plans may seek a work structure that is team-based. For example, plans to develop and launch a new product may require people from multiple disciplines to perform together.

2. *Technology/Operations:*   Change in technology may demand change in work patterns. New technology implementation most of the times involves interdependence of tasks which

can be handled by a team only and not by a single individual or a mere collection of individuals.

3. *Productivity*: Organizations are also attracted to the idea of teamwork because experiences of similar companies show positive gains. There is ample evidence proving that teamwork increases performance of human resource, which contributes to the increase in productivity.

4. *Processes*: Continuous improvement, quality measures, just-in-time inventory process, cost reduction measures can be implemented to obtain greater results if teamwork is adopted. A number of organizations are attracted to the idea of teamwork because of these process reasons.

5. *Innovation*: Experiences of some organizations also point out that an organization's innovative capability depends upon the collaborative effort of employees. The best way to achieve this collaboration is to systematically pursue the teamwork concept. An organization intending to introduce teamwork must also verify whether it is seeking teamwork for increasing rate of innovation.

6. *Customer Satisfaction*: Organizations, particularly in service sector, which interface with customers day in and day out, can be enormously benefited with teamwork. All high-performing service organizations implement teamwork in one form or the other. It may be worth the effort to scrutinize reasons for preference to teamwork in the light of this fact.

7. *Employee Satisfaction*: Other important reason why organizations prefer teamwork is to gain employee satisfaction. Teamwork has an unlimited potential in providing abundant opportunities to people to fulfil their various motivational needs which in turn leads to improved employee satisfaction.

Step 2: Question Organizational Commitment

Though organizations want to implement teamwork, commitment for actual implementation may not be absolute. This occurs due to two reasons. Firstly, organizations may not be sure of the results teamwork can yield. This unsure attitude of results dilutes commitment to put in required efforts. Objectively speaking, any effort can be successful only when initiators carry complete faith in results. A skeptical attitude reflects in the efforts in a subtle manner. This phenomenon is a potential deterrent, especially because teamwork will not produce any magnificent results in the initial stage. This initial stage may last for at least two years. People who are unsure tend to abandon effort midway due to absence of magnificent results. Effort, which is likely to be left midway, adds more confusion and creates dysfunctional effects in the organization. Therefore, organizations must question this aspect before launching teamwork.

Second reason is organizations hurry up to implement teamwork without making requisite preparations. They hurry up because they see teamwork as one more management technique that should be implemented to gain image of a high profile organization. This attitude makes organizations initiate teamwork without understanding what it is. When the awareness is inadequate on the part of management, commitment also becomes inadequate. Organizations must question their commitment before thinking of teamwork implementation. This inquisitiveness about organizational commitment helps in setting realistic objectives for teamwork.

Step 3: Check Organizational Conditions

In order to set objectives, one more step that should be followed is to verify compatibility of the organizational conditions with the proposed teamwork strategy. Compatibility may differ from organization to organization. If compatibility is low, one of the teamwork objectives must be to create compatible conditions in organizations. Real effectiveness of teamwork comes from an integrated effort such as teamwork effort supplemented by associated system. For example, an individualistic compensation system is incompatible with teamwork initiative, whereas a compensation system that accommodates team compensation is a compatible system.

Step 4: State Expectations

Organizations must analyze and state clearly their expectations from the strategy of teamwork. In this process, reasons discussed at step 1 serve as the basis. Once expectations are well-defined, setting objectives becomes easier, methodical, realistic and also rational. Expectations must be realistic, achievable and also evolutionary. The logic is that results accrue to organizations in a phased manner; small gains in immediate future, medium and big gains in the long term.

Step 5: Set Objectives of Teamwork

Final step in the first driver of nurturing teamwork intervention is setting objectives of teamwork. The objectives should be drawn on consideration of all steps. Statement of objectives should be very clear, implementable and also measurable. This objective statement must be set in a manner that guides the teamwork strategy from beginning to end. Objective statement is not only like a road map, but also a patent document akin to constitutional document. It needs to be kept in mind that clearer the objectives statement easier is the execution. If this statement is ambiguous, greater will be the difficulty in implementation. Essence of this driver is encouraging organizations to develop a simple, clear and realistic statement of teamwork objectives.

DRIVER 2: FORMING TEAM STRUCTURE

The second crucial driver in the intervention of nurturing team-based performance management is to design and adopt a team-based organizational structure. Objective of team structure must be to ensure smooth and vigorous flow of work across organizational functions and roles. This is often a challenging task because it involves a structural reorientation. Every organization has some kind of structure. This may be a bureaucratic or a hierarchical structure, a process structure, or an ad hoc kind of arrangement. This needs to be altered in tune with objectives statement of teamwork. Degree of effort and scale of change an organization must put in to create a team structure is contingent upon the present state of organizational structure. Following steps are suggestive of actions to be taken in this context:

Step 1: Build Proposed Organizational Structure

First action is giving a shape to the team structure based on the statement of objectives of teamwork. Depending on the size and variety of functions in an organization, two or more team levels can be created. For example, there can be a strategic level team which guides and manages an organization through strategic planning, funds mobilization and resource management. Likewise, there can be multiple operational level teams that are responsible for transforming inputs into outputs. Secondly, there needs to be different kinds of teams suited to functional requirements. For example, there can be R&D team, HR team, finance team, project teams, virtual teams, etc. These structures must also clarify and explain how work is expected to flow through the teams. It means such an explanation must indicate how activities within the team, coordination among teams and linkage of each team with top-level team occur. Typically, the team structure must appear as one big team at organizational level that comprises many teams. It is like a nervous system in a human body.

Step 2: Study Existing Organizational Structure

The next step in forming a team structure is conducting a study on current organizational structure. More the bureaucratic features of an organizational structure, greater the changes required in order to build a team structure. Many big organizations follow a formal and relatively rigid organizational structure while medium and smaller ones might have created a semi-formal and loose structure. Workflow, reporting systems, designations, levels and hierarchical customs must be studied and analyzed.

Step 3: Assess Changes Required

Third step is making a comparative analysis of the proposed team structure with the existing organizational structure. This comparative analysis should be carried out to establish the degree of alterations and changes required to implement the team-based structure. This analysis can be again carried out at two or more levels. Firstly, figuring out changes required to introduce team at the top level. Secondly, creating middle level teams in the place of divisions/units in the organization. Thirdly, creating functional level teams in the place of departments.

Step 4: Refining Proposed Team Structure and Drafting Strategy for Implementation

Requirement of changes as assessed must be translated into action plans. This implies that a plan must be developed to replace the existing organizational structure with team-based structure. This plan must contain how and when the replacement progresses. Assessment exercise many times provides new insights into the proposed and existing organizational structure dynamics. These insights must be classified, analyzed and used effectively for refining the proposed team-based structure.

Step 5: Implementing Team Structure

Final and ultimate step in the driver of forming team structure is getting on to implementation of a refined team structure in an evolutionary manner. Execution often encounters with innumerable problems and also causes administrative and operational chaos in the organization at the beginning. This is a common symptom. This involves taking into consideration the gestation period until the team structure sinks well with all people in organization. There can be some amount of resistance also, particularly from those who are affected in terms of being deprived of their individual power and authority. This resistance should be managed appropriately. Common trap is that some organizations choose to pursue the team structure parallel with the existing old structure. This process adds more problems and team structure can never reach matured state. Therefore, the team structure must be initiated replacing the old structure, of course, in a phased manner allowing absorption of introductory shocks.

DRIVER 3: DEFINING TEAM GOALS AND ROLES

Next important action in nurturing teamwork is pushing a third driver into action. Objective of this driver is facilitating description and definition of teams and team roles based on team structure. Effectiveness of teamwork is largely the product of well-defined teamwork role. This basically involves motivating each team to set goals for itself and also clarify responsibilities and tasks each member in the team is expected to perform. During initial stages, support from teamwork experts and top management team may be necessary in order to help teams to make progress in the right direction in terms of this role clarification. Role definition also needs to be conducted levelwise, i.e. teamwise (top, middle and operational teams) and memberwise. This levelwise definition calls for an elaborate effort and generally consumes substantial time. Following are sub-steps in this driver that support an organization's effort in defining teamwork roles:

Step 1: Translating Team Structure into Teams

The maiden step in this phase is translating teamwork structure into teams. For example, creating strategic team, functional teams, audit teams. Important decision that shall be arrived here is how many teams should be there in each type. Workload factor is to be considered for this purpose. There can be a suitable number of operational teams; it implies that there can be more than one team in a function. For example, there can be three teams in finance function, each one catering to a specific requirement like funds mobilization, information technology applications in finance and finance audit and balance sheet preparation. There also may have to be cross-functional teams with members from different disciplines to work on specific projects. At the end of this exercise, there must be teams at top level (strategic team), middle level (functional and cross-functional level) and shop floor level (operational level).

Step 2: Defining Team Goals

Next step is broadly determining goals of each team. Though in due course, teams will start acting on their own and become self managing, the initial goal framework should be set up with initiation of top management, functional heads and shop floor managers for respective teams. However, this shall not be binding on teams once they are tightly formed. This step is to ensure a basic level work and create stability in the initial stage. Each of the teams must have a clear agenda in terms of short and long-term goals they are expected to achieve. Goals as tentatively defined must emanate from organizational goals. Also, there must be clear deliverables at the level of each team. Goals as set must possess absolute conformity with objectives of teamwork as developed at Driver 1.

Step 3: Defining Team Roles

The next critical step in sequence is defining roles in teams. Though it entirely depends upon the goals and functional nature of team, there must be mix of roles in terms of skills, competencies and deliverables. In this context, Belbin's nine team roles as shown in Table 4.1 can serve as specimen. Two aspects such as quality and quantity of roles need to be decided. Also, these definitions must be preliminary and subject to modification and replacement by teams themselves once they attain a proper shape. Roles as defined together with team goals must be documented.

TABLE 4.1   Belbin's Nine Team Roles

Plant	Devises creative solutions to problems.
Coordinator	Interprets objectives, encourages decisions and facilitates appropriate decisions.
Resource investigator	Finds useful contacts and resources outside the team.
Monitor evaluator	Discerns options and makes insightful judgements.
Implementer	Translates ideas into actions and organizes the process.
Team worker	Resolves disagreements and concentrates on diplomacy.
Completer finisher	Fixes errors, ensures work is complete and meets deadlines.
Specialist	Offers knowledge or skills that others may not have.
Shaper	Challenges other to overcome difficulties.

Step 4: Filling Teams and Team Role Slots with People

This step facilitates giving life to teams and team roles. Once the framework of teams and team roles is in place, task of filling up these with suitable people must be embarked upon. The strategy of competency-based performance management assists in the process of identifying the right people to right roles. Again, this would be a tentative action because finally people must be given the final option to join in a particular team and prefer a particular role. This is also a comprehensive exercise because redeploying people across organization is involved. This action leads to potential dangers such as disturbing work schedules and also causing low productivity till redeployment is complete and people settle down. Hence, utmost care is required to be taken. It is always better to initiate this action in a phased manner to dilute the adverse impact. Redeployment also causes heartburn and paves way for politicking. Teamwork initiators must be wary of these dynamics. Absolute objectiveness, rationality, openness, consensus and scientific method of deploying people to positions can lessen the adverse impact if any. At the end of this step, organizations can see a team-based structure in action.

DRIVER 4: COACHING TEAMS

Majority of team-building interventions do not succeed because of inadequate understanding of team members on the functioning of team and their own role in it. Immediate measure that shall be initiated on deploying the people to teams on temporary basis is enhancing their understanding about teamwork and imparting skills required to perform in a teamwork setting. Though coaching of teams is a continuous process, special efforts must be made just before launching teamwork in a full-fledged manner. This special effort can be in a form which is convenient and effective to an organization in its own context. Methods that can be used for coaching purpose are illustrated below as suggestive steps:

Step 1: Classroom Training

Offering formal training on teamwork using classroom situation is useful to increase conceptual knowledge of team members about teamwork. Classroom training should be done in a systematic method. Firstly, a standard curriculum on teamwork must be developed. Secondly, few people from different teams must be drawn using a voluntary choice to perform as resource persons for spreading awareness of teamwork and also to act as course coordinators/trainers. Thirdly, all people in the organization must be put through teamwork training based on this curriculum.

Curriculum must consist of aspects such as introduction to teamwork, objectives, benefits of teamwork to people and organization, challenges with teamwork, tools and techniques involved in teamwork, group problem-solving skills, work flow analysis, presentation skills, budgeting. Using silly techniques such as blind folding, rock climbing for teamwork, calling people by nickname must be avoided because teamwork training is a serious business, which cannot be achieved through lighter means.

Step 2: Case Study and Exercises

Team members must also be exposed to the real life success and failure stories of teamwork. Few case studies in hard copy version can be supplied to members, advising them to study and analyze them. This experience gives them an understanding of teamwork and enables them to appreciate practice of teamwork. A chart containing FAQT (Frequently Asked Questions on Teamwork) must be prepared and made available to all. There must be an awareness centre on teamwork within the organization whose function should be clarifying doubts and collecting views of employees on teamwork plan, structure, role definition and team coaching.

Step 3:　Mock Running of Teamwork

Third method is encouraging employees to conduct mock teamwork sessions. This can be done using normal work agenda, tasks and operations that employees perform as part of their duties. These mock performances of teams must be observed by resource persons and facilitators to identify strengths and areas of concern. Deficient areas as identified must be removed through either training or by imparting the necessary skills through suitable means.

Step 4:　Coaching Centre

An organization that puts in place an organization-wide network of teamwork will be required to establish a centre for continuous coaching on teams and teamwork. Above three steps serve the initial preparation of teams.

Teams will be needed to acquire the more advanced perspectives as they progress practicing teamwork. Therefore, this centre must be dedicated to cater to this requirement. This centre should be vested with the responsibility of developing customized solutions for building great teams and institutionalizing teamwork.

DRIVER 5:　DEVELOPING TEAM LEADERSHIP

The significant factor that can directly make or mar success chances of teamwork is quality of team leadership. Battle for mantle of leadership intensifies as the teamwork progresses. There can be a phase of inertia in which leadership issue reaches a state of deadlock. Teams normally possess an inherent capability to resolve this deadlock and progress. Choosing the leadership issue must be left to team members.

One issue believed religiously is that leadership is more a psychological phenomenon than physical. It means leadership is not necessarily leading people physically but more importantly influencing ideas and creating new pattern. These new ideas can emerge from any team member. Leadership in team setting often can be a rotational affair implying all members have equal opportunity to be in leadership position. Teams are expected to replace all supervisors and managers and perform these functions. These issues are discussed in a comprehensive manner in the strategy of leadership-based performance management. In essence, leadership training and development is necessary for all employees in teams. This team leadership development driver needs to be implemented with the help of leadership-based performance management strategy for effective results. In order to provide a generic map of how team leadership is to be built, following steps are presented to serve as suggestive framework:

Step 1:　Identifying Leadership Dimensions

Building leadership in teamwork context is different from traditional organizational setting. This is because of the variance in the role. Leaders in teamwork are expected to perform the role of coach, adviser, counsellor, facilitator and representative of team members. Leadership development also must happen with an aim to build these skills. First act in this step is identifying team leadership dimensions, based on which appropriate strategies for developing team members on such dimensions can be taken up.

Step 2: Defining Leadership Responsibilities

Training on identified leadership dimensions makes team members acquire generic leadership skills such as problem-solving, goal setting, communication, conflict management, progress assessment, resource mobilization. Equally important issue is making members aware of leadership responsibilities, which may include interfacing with other teams and coordination with strategic level team, enabling under-performers to enhance their performance, meeting agreed targets, managing resources and interpersonal problem-solving. This is a critical phase because effective performance of team leaders depends upon the level of awareness regarding responsibilities of leaders.

Step 3: Deploying Multiple Methods for Team Leadership Development

Development of leadership based on the identified dimensions and defined responsibility area must be achieved using multiple development methods. This may include classroom coaching, mentoring by experienced team leaders, visit to other team-based organizations, continuous coaching using Intranet/local area networks, experience sharing and case studies. There must be a balance in the content coverage such as (i) judicious mix of technical aptitude relevant to the organizational operations, (ii) functions to be handled by team leadership and (iii) attitudinal aspects like interpersonal relations, communication, group behaviour, and sensitivity training.

DRIVER 6: ALIGNING HUMAN RESOURCE SYSTEM

In order to make practice of teamwork a substantive and sustainable measure, the human resource practices also should be aligned. Various human resource practices like recruitment, training, performance appraisal, career planning, compensation, so on and so forth must have clear linkages and need to be oriented to strengthen teamwork intervention. Teamwork effort and investment runs danger of losing its impact and return on investment if human resource system is not aligned. For example, teamwork gets weakened if practices like compensation, appraisal, career planning are highly individual based. Unfortunately, in the past there were organizations that initiated team-building measure in a big way but could not accrue any benefits because of their inability to align human resource system. It is imperative for organizations intending to create team-based working to pursue the said linkages to their matured state, i.e. integrating human resource system with teamwork. It is an undeniable fact that reorienting human resource system to the needs of teamwork calls for a major revamp in the human resource policy and practice framework. Following steps are indicative of this driver in action:

Step 1: Redefining Human Resource Policies

Human resource policies must be reviewed in the context of teamwork. Aspects and elements that discourage teamwork specifically need to be identified and eliminated. Secondly, provisions that reinforce teamwork strategy must be introduced. For example, introducing a collective system of management by objectives in the place of individualized key results area system.

Thirdly, the new human resource system must be built on the overall objective of enhancing performance of people to attain individual, team and organizational objectives. Fourthly, the strategy of team-building is sculpted in association with six other performance management strategies like reward, career, culture, leadership, competency and measurement. Human resource system needs to consider the content and spirit of these strategies, though teamwork strategy itself is originated from the grand strategy of performance management.

TEAMWORK-BASED MANAGEMENT BY OBJECTIVES

Conventional system of management by objectives (MBO) is best suited to the situation where the tasks are individualized. A collaborative method of management by objectives is required when the tasks are interdependent. As opposed to what most people believe, this kind of MBO system to address teamwork needs is in existence at least conceptually for more than three decades. Organizational development experts, Wendell French and Robert Hallman developed a systematic framework for setting and managing teamwork-based objectives way back in 1975. This method of team-based MBO comprises nine phases as briefly indicated here:

1. *Diagnosis of organizational problems:* First phase prescribes use of data collection methods like group surveys, small group meetings, large-scale interactive process in order to identify the organizational problems.
2. *Information and dialogue:* Objective of this phase is to generate awareness about team-based MBO and the process involved in it. This is achieved through the training mechanism.
3. *Diagnosis of organizational readiness:* This phase is used to assess the readiness of organization through surveys, interviews and debates in adopting the team-based MBO system.
4. *Organizational level goal setting:* Based on the data obtained at phase 1 and with extensive interaction with all employees, goals are set at the organizational level to be achieved in a definite time frame.
5. *Unit level goal setting:* Unit level objectives are set in this phase. These objectives flow from organizational level objectives.
6. *Team level goal setting:* This phase is dedicated to defining the goals at team level and then at team member level based on the objectives of the unit.
7. *Performance review:* Teams prepare progress reports for their respective teams which are subject to review by neutral teams in reference to the defined goals.
8. *Re-diagnosis:* A review is undertaken at this phase to assess the tangible and intangible benefits obtained from the practice of team-based MBO.
9. *Recycle:* Process from phase 4 is to be repeated if the results obtained at phase 8 is positive and exercise from phase 2 is to be reimplemented with required modifications if results are not positively significant.

(*Source:* French, Wendell and Robert Hallman, 1975. "Management by objectives: The team approach". *California Management Review*, **17**(3), pp. 13–22).

Step 2: Training Human Resource Managers on New Policy Framework

Merely effecting changes in policy framework to address needs of teamwork business is not just adequate. Unless people who are responsible for implementation new policy framework are trained and well-informed, no realistic outcome can be expected. Immediate step should follow policy reorientation is training people on new policy framework. Training must ensure people possess full knowledge of the newly made team-oriented human resource policies.

Step 3: Delegation of Powers

Effectiveness and efficacy of teamwork is largely derived from delegation of powers. Unless, teams are clearly empowered in taking decisions and influence the organizational functioning, teams will remain on paper. It is herculean task for organizations to create altogether a different power equilibrium. It involves great deal of effort and the chief executive and other colleagues on board must agree to this. Studies reveal that teamwork delivered more results than expected wherever teams are empowered under well-defined framework. However, we come across very few organizations putting all efforts to create this empowerment to meet functional and administrative requirements of teamwork. Vital step in this driver is empowering the team in realistic sense.

DRIVER 7: ALIGNING WORK CULTURE/PROCESSES

Apart from notified/published organizational policies in different functional areas, organizations intending to infuse teamwork also must align cultural processes to support such teamwork. These practices are also physical entities, therefore effecting change in them is relatively easier and achievable in comparatively less time lag to that of ensuring change in culture. The strategy of culture-based performance management is highly relevant and useful in execution of this driver. Culture aspect wields enormous power over people in carrying out the tasks and on their work behavioural patterns. Aligning culture with teamwork involves months of effort and sacrifices of people. Following issues are presented as suggestive steps in planning and implementation of this driver.

Step 1: Top Management Commitment/Sacrifice

Although top management commitment is a common requirement for successful implementation of all performance management strategies, it is more so in the case of team-based performance management, especially in the cultural domain. Top management behaviour clinches cultural fabric of an organization. Whatever may be the intent, tone and objective of policy and practice framework, it is the top management's genuine commitment that makes things roll in a particular direction. Leadership research points out that in many cases managers become the biggest obstacles in progress like speed breakers. Managers expect their subordinates to perform at a level that is inferior to their level so it reassures and boosts their confidence. This happens more often in a latent fashion and not necessarily like an open expectation that comes from the bosses. Cultural augmentation for teamwork must come from senior management.

They must make sacrifices and give up arbitrary and authoritative power paving the way to a more functional democratic management. Mostly, teamwork efforts fail because of this lack of support from top management in spirit. When top management sets an example by themselves becoming members of a team, not only in style and but in content and spirit, the teamwork intervention can certainly deliver results.

Step 2: Managing Symbols and Artifacts

Cultural aspects are communicated through many symbols and artifacts in organizations. For example, reserving main portico of office building/for car parking of top bosses. Senior managers are given a separate enclosure in the canteen. Size of office table and type of chairs an employee is given depends upon his/her status in the company. All these are symbols conveying hierarchical culture existing in organizations. These symbols are required to be managed in a way that vouches for teamwork. There can be many types and varieties of symbols and artifacts; some are visible and other are invisible but powerful communicators of a particular kind of culture. Therefore, managing this driver involves identifying and smartly managing these symbols.

Step 3: Managing Organizational Norms

Potential area that can have implications for culture alignment is organizational norms. This is somewhat similar to symbols and artifacts with little difference. Organizational norms in this context refer to methods adopted by a group of employees in performing tasks and in order to have their way in organization. Some of them may be capable of causing dilution of teamwork effort. For example, there may be collective bargaining forums in organization, which puts in place particular code of conduct to its members. These need to be located and resolution must be found. There can be positive norms also which need to be catapulted to the advantage of teamwork. Norms in reality and in daily work life influence people to perform in a particular direction and in a specific mode. This direction and mode becomes more important than policies many a time. Driver of culture alignment must be engineered while taking into account factor of organizational norm. Once teamwork reaches a stabilized state, team itself can start and ferment norms that support collective work.

DRIVER 8: LAUNCHING TEAMWORK

Teamwork can be launched organization-wide once the first seven drivers are implemented. Setting objectives, creating a team structure, defining roles, coaching teams, building leadership, aligning human resource system and work culture with teamwork intervention are fundamental prerequisites for launching teamwork. Teamwork cannot succeed and may land organizations in great problems if teams are introduced without making these preparations in a systematic order. These preparations provide necessary platform and create salutary conditions for teamwork to thrive. There is also a philosophy that just forms a team structure and leaves it to teams to make their way. This is found to be a risky affair and is a highly philosophical argument. An organization and its employees who are used to a particular structure, practices, processes and mindset find it initially difficult to adjust to teamwork leave aside delivering results. Initial preparations as discussed must be made and management of organization is squarely responsible for creating these teamwork favourable conditions. Following are suggestive steps for launching teamwork:

Step 1: Launch Top Down

Teamwork must begin from the top. Unfortunately, most organizations prefer a partial teamwork structure. It means teamwork at operational level and a typical bureaucratic and hierarchical structure at the middle and top. Some organizations make progress up to middle level of the organization, leaving top untouched. This half teamwork produces halfhearted results. It is in the best interest of organizations they prefer organization-wide team structure and working. In such a scenario, teamwork introduction must start with top management block. Once implementation at the top is complete, it must be applied to middle and cascade down to the operating core.

Step 2: Implementation Must be Gradual

Implementation of teamwork must be taken up and progressed in an evolutionary manner. As stated above, implementation must be in a phased manner like starting from top and ending with operational level. Even within this block, particularly at operational level, implementation can be in a phased fashion like extending teamwork to a few departments and later to the remaining. This ensures absolute care in forming teams and leads to their growing in strength.

Step 3: Managing Conflicts and Contradictions

Despite all preparations, still there can be a possibility of teamwork encountering conflicts and contradictions. Conflicts are quite natural. Conflicts can be in the nature of intra and inter team differences and gap among the members regarding the norm creation. Whatever may be the cause for the conflict, largely it must be left to the teams to resolve it themselves. Exception can be resource persons and initiators of team structure, like top strategic team may interfere and enable teams to find a solution if conflict arises from structural issues like constitution of teams or objectives of teamwork.

DRIVER 9: EVALUATING TEAMWORK

Effectiveness of teamwork must be measured periodically. This needs to be carried out in two classes. First class is like a midterm audit of teamwork and the second is evaluation of teamwork after being in operation for more than one year. These actions help to establish utility and results of teamwork, and also help in identifying problems and taking necessary actions to rectify them timely and rightly. These two types of teamwork assessment are indicated below. Evaluation must be done with the help of organization specific evaluation methods and techniques and certainly not by using generic evaluation methods. Teamwork implementation tends to be unique for every organization not comparable with any other teamwork of any other organization. Such organization specific evaluation instruments must possess high reliability and validity. Evaluation must be conducted by people who are well trained, professional and capable and not by amateur evaluators.

Step 1: Midterm Audit

On completion of at least six months duration from implementation of teamwork organization-wide, a formal teamwork audit must be carried out with the help of resource persons and obtaining assistance from outside teamwork audit experts. Objectives of teamwork form the main basis for this audit. Exercise must focus on (i) whether teamwork is able to achieve the stated objectives of teams, (ii) what are the difficulties encountered by teamwork, (iii) what are the gains of teams so far and (iv) what is the perception of employees about teamwork. Audit aimed at eliciting these issues can provide organizations with vital inputs. Outcome of midterm audit can be used to initiate midterm correction that facilitates teamwork progress much faster.

Step 2: Evaluation of Teamwork

On completion of more than a year of teamwork in operation, evaluation of teamwork can be undertaken. This assessment must be executed at different levels such as at employee, team and organizational level. Employee level assessment can be done using survey and interview methods to capture individual employee's views and perceptions on positives and negatives of teamwork that organization adopted. Team level assessment is in the mode of evaluating performance of group of teams delivering and managing a function. For example, finding out performance of marketing teams in comparison with their achievements prior to introduction of teamwork. Organizational level assessment includes understanding the fulfilment of team objectives, which can be called process evaluation. Assessment is also about whether teamwork is implemented in accordance with team objectives and as per laid down plans or not; assessment in terms of attaining organizational objectives like organization plans in the short-term such as upgradation of technology, quality improvement, diversification, cost reductions, and measuring the effectiveness of teams at the bottom line of organizations through the indicators of turnover, sales, profits, earning per share and market capitalization.

DRIVER 10: CREATING STRONG TEAMS, OBJECTIVES AND METHODS

Evaluation often provides a mine of wealthy information on the effectiveness of teams. A logical action subsequent to evaluation and on obtaining results is to rejuvenate teams, objectives and methods. Teamwork needs to be reviewed and introspected in the light of evaluation report. Evaluation assumes greater importance because of one prime reason that by the time teams progress to Driver 10 they will be in an absolute position of competence to provide valuable inputs for bridging gaps and leveraging teamwork for competitive advantage. Information evaluation exercise yields must be gainfully utilized by taking expected actions as suggested below:

Step 1: Analyze Evaluation Report

First action on obtaining the evaluation report is to study it carefully, analyze and draw inferences. This must be done seeking help from resource persons, teamwork experts and facilitators. Evaluation report may throw light on some grey areas, which need to be addressed in order to strengthen teamwork. Evaluation report should be analyzed to ascertain the level of fulfilment at employee, team and organizational level requirements. Critical parameter and basis for measurement of course, remains the same as set at Driver 1 of this intervention.

Step 2: Plan Action on Inferences

Based on inferences drawn from the evaluation report, an action plan must be made to reorient and alter aspects required in the constitution of teams, objectives and methods. The strategic level team must take initiative in motivating other teams in the organization to effect these changes. At the best, the top level team, called in this context the strategic level team, can offer facilitation and guidance.

Step 3: Forming Strong Teams, Objectives and Methods

At this stage, there will be teams which are stronger with purposeful objectives and rationalistic methods. These teams can achieve miracles and keep the organization agile, efficient and innovative. Teams that progressed to this stage must be allowed to perform without interference and disturbances, as they themselves make changes at any level if required in the pursuit of excellence. Teams become self-managing in every respect at the end of this step and Driver 10.

INTERVENTION 2: CAPITALIZING ON TEAMWORK IN INSTITUTIONALIZATION OF PERFORMANCE MANAGEMENT

The second and final intervention of team-based performance management strategy is institutionalizing performance management practice in organizations using teamwork as a sharp instrument. Teams and teamwork can play the role of medium, objective and target of performance management. Teamwork can identify problems, concerns and solutions, bring consensus, execute, monitor and condition them to give real value results. There can be myriad ways through which teamwork can be driven to attain the ultimate objective of performance management, i.e. institutionalizing performance management practice effectively for attainment of individual, team and organizational goals. This intervention proposes a set of 10 drivers that can work as a road map to reach destiny of this institutionalization. To indicate tersely, matured form of teamwork itself can contribute for soaring performance in all fronts. Teamwork can hasten progress of performance management only if it is made responsible for it through focusing on a few vital issues. These issues become drivers of institutionalizing performance management.

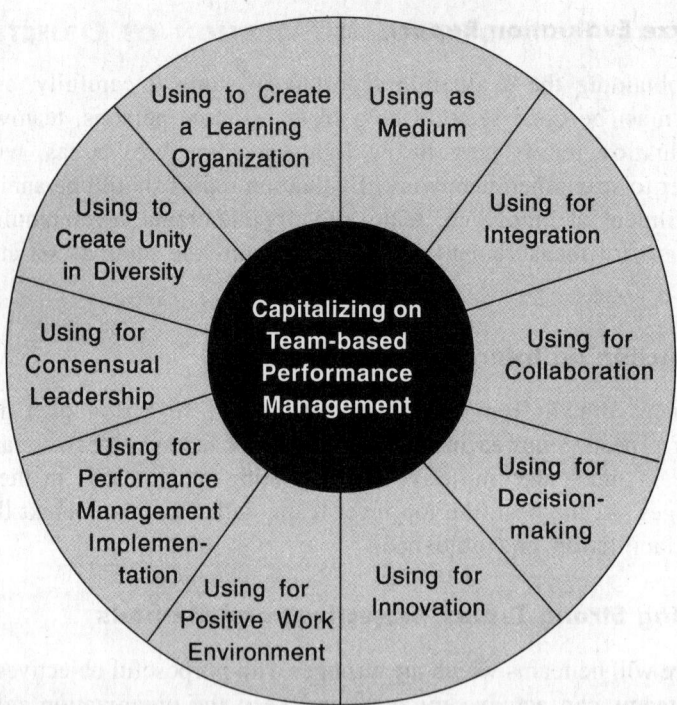

FIGURE 4.3 Drivers of the intervention capitalizing on team strategy in institutionalization of performance management.

DRIVER 1: USING TEAMWORK AS MEDIUM OF PERFORMANCE MANAGEMENT

Teams can perform multiple roles to drive performance management to a state of institutionalization. This can be achieved in three ways. Firstly, teams have infinite capability to spread awareness of an issue/subject/technology/change in the shortest time with minimum effort and cost. Teams can serve as competent medium to create rightful awareness about performance management practice. Secondly, teams can be a great source to improve general communication in organization. This is very critical to any organizational strategy particularly to the success of performance management because experiences of organizations indicate that they could not gain real benefit due to badly managed communication. Thirdly, teams are effective medium to institutionalize performance due to their status of self-management. This means teams are not only responsible for implementation of performance management strategies but they are planners and designers too.

The essence of this driver, therefore, is that teamwork should be pursued as an integral part of performance management to achieve high performance work practices as well as to institutionalize performance management practice. In order to achieve this objective, organizations must clearly bear in mind that teams are vehicles of performance management institutionalization.

DRIVER 2: USING TEAMWORK FOR INTEGRATION OF OBJECTIVES

Effective performance of organizations and people is largely contingent upon how well they work together on a common set of objectives. Ensuring commonality in objectives is an extremely difficult task because of inherent conflicts in the interest of stakeholders mainly between employees and management. This becomes easy if structure, systems and processes of an organization are team-based. In a team-based organization, there would be a functional and emotional synergy among objectives. Team-based work can present a unifocal objective in which individuals, team and organization as a whole can identify themselves. This happens mainly because defining organizational objectives is a bottom-up approach unlike in traditional organizations where it is top-down. Self-capable teams set objectives for each individual, these individual objectives are converged into team objectives and all objectives of teams transform into organizational level objectives. This process must be consciously used to institutionalize performance management in organizations. Objectives of performance management are integrated deploying same methodology. The typical performance indicators like key result areas (KRA) and management by objectives (MBO) are also drawn using this method.

A precious outcome of this driver is conscious integration of objectives through means of bottom-up approach resulting in institutionalization of performance management in which every individual has a lion's share of opportunity, contribution and reward.

DRIVER 3: USING TEAMWORK TO INSTILL COLLABORATION AND COOPERATIVE RELATIONSHIPS

Performance excellence is derived from collaborative relationships within the organization. Traditionally, relationships between employees and employers and within employees in the name of inter and intra union rivalries have been assumed to be conflictive with opposing interests. This kind of philosophy and practice built on such beliefs has led organizations to perform abnormally below their potential. Peak performance can occur only when collaboration exists. Collaborating with each other can help two persons to overcome their weaknesses and supplement and strengthen each other through reinforcement, whereas conflict between employees can weaken strength to a point of dysfunctionality. Teamwork is built on principle of collaborative relationships across the organization. Using teamwork to push this collaboration to their mature levels can automatically ensure institutionalization of performance management. This collaboration helps in every activity performed as a part and parcel of performance management. Key benefit of this driver is catapulting teamwork to mature collaborations. Collaborative working is a vital pillar of performance management. It means the driver of instilling collaboration can give a fillip to institutionalization of performance management.

DRIVER 4: USING TEAMWORK FOR EFFECTIVE DECISION-MAKING

Performance culture of an organization reflects in its decision-making pattern. As everybody knows, decision-making in most organizations is hierarchical and powers are centred at the top with little devolvement to middle and negligible to lower layers. In such circumstances, arrival at effective decisions is seldom. Therefore, such organizations perform at suboptimal level leave alone institutionalizing high-performance work practices. As opposed to this, teamwork creates conditions for effective decision-making. People in a team and different teams with different focus and with unique capabilities collaborate to produce business decisions that can be perfect for the situation. One of the objectives of performance management is to build an effective decision-making culture that realizes potential of every individual employee as a good decision-maker. This effective decision-making is reached through discussions, brainstorming, involving every employee to air views and providing opportunity to challenge everything. This pattern of decision-making paves a way for high-performance work practices.

Therefore, the pattern of decision-making apart from being a characteristic of performance management can create ideal conditions for institutionalization of performance management. Organizations, particularly at the top, i.e. strategic level team must be conscious of this and use it as a prime driver in institutionalizing performance management. How it achieves this can be found in its pattern of decision-making as stated above. The pattern of every employee (team member) becoming the decision-maker influences institutionalization of performance management positively.

DRIVE 5:   USING TEAMWORK FOR BUILDING INNOVATION

The indicator of high-performance management existence in any organization is its capacity to innovate. This comes only through systematic and integrated practice of performance management. Innovation culture also contributes for institutionalization of performance management. Innovation culture solicits teamwork in which collaboration, effective decision-making, communications are naturally inbuilt. Encouraging and building innovation can lead to institutionalization of performance management. These collaborative and efficient decision-making patterns are by-products of teamwork. Teamwork can be used for building innovation causing performance management institutionalization.

Traditional organizations despite huge investment in research and development facilities could not attain the kind of results the team-based Japanese organizations have achieved. It is because innovation is a part of the job description of every team member and there is no exclusive major research and development investment except for creating some basic facilities. These experiences prove that it is the teamwork which is more important than capitalistic investments. The same spirit plays a decisive role in institutionalizing performance management.

DRIVER 6:   USING TEAMWORK TO CREATE POSITIVE WORK ENVIRONMENT

Positive work environment is imperative for effective implementation of performance management. In fact, this is one factor that generates motivation and facilitates people to perform at their peak. Behavioural dimensions like openness, trust, collaboration, confrontation, authenticity, proactiveness, interpersonal relationships represent this positive work environment.

Outcome of such positive work environment is that employees feel emotionally healthy and happy. This happy environment contributes to higher performance. Teams and teamwork can be catalyst in creating such an environment. Teamwork process itself possesses unlimited potential in defining and generating a salutary work culture. Teamwork and positive work environment are mutually inclusive implying that success of teamwork in an organization automatically leads to positive work environment, and positive work environment contributes for effectiveness of teamwork. Conscious efforts must be made to use teams in creating a positive work environment, which in turn leads to institutionalization of performance management.

DRIVER 7: USING TEAMWORK FOR DEVELOPMENT AND IMPLEMENTATION OF PERFORMANCE MANAGEMENT STRATEGIES

Strategy of teamwork is conceived and implemented in close alignment with other performance management strategies like leadership, reward, culture, career, measurement and competency based. Teamwork also greatly helps in development and execution of these tailor-made strategies. Teamwork particularly plays a vital role in effectively pushing them from top echelons to bottom line of organizations using its extensive network of team structures. In more than one way, teamwork contributes for institutionalization of performance management through this implementation of performance management strategies. Therefore, all the remaining performance management strategies must be developed and executed effectively using team structures in existence.

DRIVER 8: USING TEAMWORK TO BUILD CONSENSUAL LEADERSHIP

Though the strategy of leadership-based performance management completely takes care of building an organization specific leadership development model and also creating pools of leadership competency at every level in the organization, practice of teamwork contributes for nurturing a different kind of leadership, i.e. consensual leadership style. Consensual leadership is a style that promotes consensual agreement on a variety of issues subsequent to comprehensive discussions and consideration of divergent perspectives. This method of reaching agreements (consensus) itself becomes a formidable agent in institutionalization of performance management. Teamwork must be consciously deployed as a medium of consensus, which in turn leads to institutionalization of performance management.

DRIVER 9: USING TEAMWORK TO CREATE UNITY IN DIVERSITY

Producing the best of performance and breeding a work culture that is highly functional and efficient calls for a highly divergent yet unified action. This means an organization must be capable enough to own people who together can present the most divergent perspective of an issue and still come together in choosing the most suited and appropriate solution. Traditional organizational structures do not accommodate divergence in the fear that such divergence results in conflicts or divergence makes people dysfunctional because of indecisiveness. Traditional organizations do not possess the capability to present divergence and choose the apt one. Therefore, there can be no unity in divergence in their management. Real practice of performance management emerges from unity in divergence. Teamwork by their very nature consists of this characteristic of divergence in unity. The matured state of teamwork functions in consonance with this principle. Again, this is the characteristic that contributes for effective institutionalization of performance management. Organizations must leverage this quality in their journey of institutionalizing performance management.

DRIVER 10: USING TEAMWORK TO CREATE A LEARNING ORGANIZATION

Teamwork ultimately contributes towards making an organization a learning organization because of its unique advantage of being positioned in association with the other six performance management strategies. Matured form of teamwork makes progress towards creating a learning structure in the organization. This learning is reflected in the way changes happen, decisions are arrived, innovations and availability of capabilities. Characteristics of a learning organization are absolutely identical to that of performance management. Teamwork that causes organizations to become learning entities would automatically lead them to the state of institutionalization of performance management. Hence, it is essential to leverage teamwork for this institutionalization through the reinforcement of learning organization characteristics in a systematic manner.

BEST PRACTICE
IBM's Communities of Practice

IBM's communities of practice is a right example for best practice in using teamwork model for building knowledge assets in organization. An estimated 60 knowledge network communities operate in IBM worldwide to institutionalize knowledge management practices. These knowledge teams are evolved through five phases as indicated here:

1. *Potential Stage:* Individuals explore among themselves in order to assess commonality in their interest and similarity in their professional disciplines.
2. *Building Stage:* Based on this exploration of similarity in interests and disciplines, employees form communities amongst themselves.
3. *Engaged Stage:* These communities which take shape at stage two begin to function. They create a common purpose, methods to progress and identify the goals. Sharing of thinking and ideas also occur at this stage.
4. *Active Stage:* Communities start to identify value addition activities, analyze and develop solutions. Their behaviour is dominated at this stage, by the characteristic of optimizing their efforts and attaining goals in the form of innovation/knowledge acquisition/problem-solving.
5. *Adaptive Stage:* Communities mature at this stage and become completely capable of executing solutions and also continuously explore the opportunities for growth.

The secret behind the super innovation competency of IBM is believed to be this best practice of 'communities of practice'. This case study reveals that teamwork can be effectively used as a vehicle to improve performance and this improved performance can be institutionalized by using teamwork as in this case, the communities of practice.

SUMMARY

Teamwork soared to the status of being a prime pillar in the architecture of performance management due to increasing interdependence of tasks. Practices like work flexibility, continuous improvement, just-in-time inventory, quality strategies, empowerment, downsizing, flat and matrix structures have given a fillip to the adoption of teamwork as a key strategy in enhancing performance. Teamwork is defined as a planned and nurtured cohesion of individuals who perform on tasks identified by them as critical for higher performance. The significance of teamwork in performance management can be found in teamwork outcomes such as:

  (i) Active involvement of employees in the business
  (ii) Implementation of new ideas effectively
 (iii) Increased communication
 (iv) Facilitating building relationships
  (v) Performing on multi-disciplinary tasks
 (vi) Enhanced quality in all aspects
(vii) Enhanced learning
(viii) Increased capability for change adaptation
 (ix) Reinforcing strengths and relieving of weaknesses
  (x) Ability to do more with less.

Teamwork is a well-researched and studied phenomenon. This chapter captures some of the important theories and concepts to derive insights for developing a team-based performance management strategy. These include:

  (i) Tuckman's four stage theory
  (ii) Newcomb's balance theory
 (iii) Thibaut and Kelley's exchange theory
 (iv) Gersick's punctuated equilibrium model
  (v) Orsburn, Moran, White and Zenger's five stage model
 (vi) Bennis's ten principles of teamwork
(vii) Shaw's team cohesiveness determinants
(viii) Sundstorm, DeMeuse and Futreu's classification of teams
 (ix) Hackman's workgroup norms
  (x) Hoffman's work role theory
 (xi) Katz and Kahn's role expectation theory.

These theories provide an inside view of how teams form, norms take shape, roles are defined, the kind of team dynamics arise, team behaviours, and how goals are set and achieved. Key lessons of the said theories to team-based performance management include aspects such as:

(i) People prefer teams dominantly to fulfil their social and esteem needs
(ii) Effectiveness of teams come from cohesiveness
(iii) Cohesiveness comes from matching of interests
(iv) Teams function through norms
(v) Teams influence members by placing expectations
(vi) Great teams follow a set of principles
(vii) Teams grow in an evolutionary manner
(viii) Teams generate unity in diversity
(ix) Team dynamics are natural to teamwork
(x) Different teams are formed for different purposes.

Team-based performance management strategy consists of two interventions. First intervention is: nurturing team-based performance management strategy. This intervention is proposed to be initiated and achieved with the help of 10 drivers. These drivers are:

(i) Setting team objectives
(ii) Forming team structures
(iii) Defining team roles and goals
(iv) Coaching teams
(v) Developing team leadership
(vi) Aligning human resource system with teamwork
(vii) Aligning work culture and processes with teamwork
(viii) Launching teamwork
(ix) Evaluating teamwork
(x) Creating strong teams, objectives and methods.

The second intervention is to use teamwork for institutionalizing performance management. This intervention is also proposed to be implemented with the support of 10 drivers such as:

(i) Using teamwork as a medium of performance management
(ii) Using teamwork for integration of objectives
(iii) Using teamwork to instill collaboration
(iv) Using teamwork for effective decision-making
(v) Using teamwork for cultivating innovation
(vi) Using teamwork to create a positive work environment
(vii) Using teamwork for the development and implementation of performance management strategy
(viii) Using teamwork to build consensual leadership
(ix) Using teamwork to create unity in diversity
(x) Using teamwork to create a learning organization.

Objective of this chapter is twofold. First is to present framework of team-based performance management strategy from a practitioner perspective. The second objective is to provide means (interventions and drivers) to achieve teamwork-based performance management in a systematic and result-oriented manner.

KEY WORDS

Following are the key words discussed in this chapter:

- Team
- Team-based performance management
- Team norms
- Team structure
- Teamwork as medium
- Consensual leadership
- Four stage theory
- Exchange theory
- Five stage team model
- Team-based MBO

- Teamwork
- Team cohesiveness
- Role effectiveness
- Coaching teams
- Positive work environment
- Unity in diversity
- Balance theory
- Punctuated equilibrium
- Communities of practice
- Learning organization

DISCUSSION QUESTIONS

1. What is teamwork and what is it not in the context of performance management?

2. What is the significance of teamwork in enhancing performance?

3. Discuss salient features of theoretical aspects of teamwork. What are the insights these theories provide for designing team-based performance management strategy?

4. How important is it to align human resource system and work culture with teamwork?

5. Describe how team-based performance management can be developed.

6. What is team-based management by objectives? How can team-based goals be reached?

7. How can team-based performance management be nurtured in an organization? Discuss drivers that facilitate conceptualization, development, implementation and evaluation of teamwork.

8. Institutionalizing performance management through teamwork involves attaching emphasis to a few factors. Substantiate this statement with supporting drivers.

9. Briefly present the framework of team-based performance management.

CASE STUDIES

1. Raju Labs is a Hyderabad-based pharmaceutical company ranked as the second most valuable pharma company in India, based on the market capitalization. The company's portfolio mainly includes both bulk drug manufacturing as well as formulation business. The company though presently performing very well, is expecting an intensive competition in both bulk drugs and formulations. This is due to the impending enforcement of intellectual property rights. This enforcement of new law implies that an organization must enhance its research and development capability to create new formulations and customize them. Raju labs has grown with the strength of manufacturing capability and is based on simple commercial principles that encouraged individualized working. Chief executive and her family members wield unlimited influence in decision-making. The company engaged a management consultant to suggest ways to develop research capabilities. Recommendation of the consultant is teamwork shall be promoted as the basic strategy to improve research capabilities apart from enhancing performance of the organization. Present working conditions of the company are individualistic, such as individual compensation, career and working.

   Now, imagine you are appointed as a performance management manager with the task of nurturing team-based performance management to build research and development capabilities. Discuss how do you progress on the issue in the backdrop of above mentioned case study.

2. Rajan Tyre Company as the title suggests is engaged in manufacturing tyres. The company is very progressive looking and known for best human resource practices particularly its teamwork. Recently, it is credited with the best team-based organization award. However, Rajan, chief team leader (equivalent to chief executive in traditional organizational structure) and promoter of teamwork in the organization is not satisfied with the progress they made with team-based performance management strategy. He feels that they couldn't leverage teamwork in institutionalizing performance management. He wonders what should be done and what are the factors to be given special focus to achieve this institutionalization.

   Discuss what Rajan must do and what factors need focus to catapult teamwork into an agent of performance management institutionalization.

SUGGESTED READING

Belbin, R.M. (1994). *The Belbin's Team Roles Package*. San Francisco: Jossey-Bass.

Bennis, Warren, (1997). "The secrets of great groups." *Leader to Leader*, Dallas: Journal Publishers.

Gersick, C.J.G. (1988). "Time and Transitions in Work Teams: Toward a new model of group development." *Academy of Management Journal*, March, pp. 9–41.

Hackman, J. (1976). "Group influences on individuals." In M.D. Dunnette (Ed.), *Handbook of Industrial and Organizational Psychology*. Chicago: Rand McNally.

Hoffman, L. (1979). "Applying Experimental Research on Group Problem Solving to Organizations." *Journal of Applied Behavioral Science*, **15**, pp. 375–391.

Katz, D. and R. Kahn (1978). *The Social Psychology of Organizations*. New York: Wiley.

Newcomb, Theodore (1961). *The Acquaintance Process*. New York: Holt.

Orsburn, Jack, Linda Moran, Ed Musselwhite and John Zenger (1990). *Self-Directed Work Teams: The New American Challenge*. Illinois: Irwin.

Shaw, M. (1981). *Group Dynamics*. New York: McGraw-Hill.

Sundstorm, Eric, Kenneth DeMeuse and David Futrell (1990). "Work teams applications and effectiveness." *American Psychologist*, February, pp. 120–133.

Thibaut, John and Harold Kelley (1959). *The Social Psychology of Groups*. New York: John Wiley.

Tuckman, B.W. (1965). "Developmental Sequences in Small Groups." *Psychologial Bulletin*, June, pp. 384–389.

Chapter Five

STRATEGY 4: CULTURE-BASED PERFORMANCE MANAGEMENT

Culture is the most powerful and intangible ingredient of performance management. It is accountable for an organization's great or poor performance to a large extent. Many organizational studies, including Peters and Waterman's *In Search of Excellence* and William Ouchi's *Z Theory,* have sufficiently pointed out that culture is the key factor in making an organization competitive, world-class and innovative. Culture management is a jigsaw puzzle for many because it may not be what it appears on the surface and it may be something that is not evident overtly. Therefore, culture means various things to various people. Difficulty in managing culture primarily arises due to its intangibility, but at the same time influence of culture is all pervasive. Each individual is affected by culture. Thinking, feeling, perceiving and consequently behaviour of people is influenced by the culture they live in. This difficulty grows when realization occurs that a particular culture very effective in the same organization in one location is proved to be the most ineffective in other location. This complexity can be dealt with adroitly when intricacies of culture management are understood and right interventions and drivers are adapted. In organizational context, culture wields enormous influence on decision-making, communication, interpersonal relationships, collaboration, trust and openness, and the way an organization behaves and interacts within and outside. This implies that culture is the strongest determinant of organizational performance. Organizations in their pursuit to achieve performance excellence must manage their culture professionally and in a scientific manner.

With this objective in view, this chapter presents the sixth strategy of performance management titled as culture-based performance management. This strategy also comprises five parts, each focusing on a specific issue of culture management. What is culture and what it is not in the context of performance management is discussed in part 1 and the significance of culture in performance management is presented in part 2. Theoretical foundations of organizational culture are captured in part 3. Twin interventions of culture-based performance management, i.e. nurturing culture-based performance management and capitalizing on culture management for institutionalization of performance management in organizations are discussed with the support of concerned drivers in part 4 and part 5 respectively.

ORGANIZATIONAL CULTURE

Culture means different things to different people. This is due to the intangibility of culture. In simple terms, culture means the way things are done. Culture also represents a common mind of an organization. Culture is defined, crystallized, operationalized, enforced and institutionalized by the people themselves to make progress and accomplish organizational objectives in a particular direction. This is achieved through the means of creating values, morals, customs, assumptions, traditions, ideologies, language, norms, legends, stories and anecdotes. People evolve this culture of doing things/behaving in a particular way drawing on the experience of success and failure. They transfer this to successor generation in the form of culture and monitor them to adopt this. This all happens in an implicit fashion. In the context of performance management, culture means *shared strong work assumptions and norms that facilitate the peak performance of employees and organization.* Groups themselves through experiences evolve these strong work assumptions and norms. Characteristics of performance driven culture are as indicated here:

1. Work assumptions that a set of things when dealt in combination or independently produce gainful results.
2. Work norms that determine performing activities in a particular method in order to deliver gainful results in the most efficient and cost-effective style.
3. These work assumptions and work norms are strong and, therefore, difficult to tamper with by an individual or subgroups.
4. Work assumptions and norms are shared.
5. Work assumptions and norms are evolved, developed and practiced religiously by groups in organizations in an experiential mode.

WHAT IS NOT ORGANIZATIONAL CULTURE

Differences in perspectives lead to multiple understanding of culture. Some of the perspectives have even contributed to misunderstanding of culture. For example, misunder-standing culture as same or similar to climate. In fact, climate is the peripheral feature of culture. Climate can present the feel factor much akin to weather, whereas culture is deep-rooted and determines this weather (feel) factor. Climate is perception-oriented and culture is fact-based. Similarly, culture is sometimes misunderstood as single dimensional. For example, a value/norm/assumption/language or a policy of an organization is reckoned as same that of culture. Some of these are antecedents and others are outcomes of culture and by any measure they cannot be equated as culture. Organizational culture also presupposes the virtue of sharing. Values, customs, norms and assumptions must be shared by a group of people for them to become integral part of culture. Such aspects cannot reach the level of culture if a group does not share them. Organizational change is also often thought to be identical to culture. Change is a physical phenomenon and culture is latent and represents the transition. Therefore, following are not similar to culture:

1. Organizational climate.
2. Organizational change.
3. Antecedents and outcomes of culture.
4. Values, norms and assumptions that are individualistic and not shared by majority of employees.

SIGNIFICANCE OF ORGANIZATIONAL CULTURE

A positive and strong culture is the key to good performance. It is the particular way of doing things that clinches success factor. For example, all possess the same computer hardware but it is the software that finally decides the utility and optimization of hardware. This software is the culture. In an era where most organizations have equal accessibility to resources that include human resource from same schools and institutes, it is this unique way of conceiving and engineering things that makes some organizations forerunners. For example, same strategies do not yield same results for two organizations in the same industry and in the same location because of variance in organizational culture. Culture has unstinted potential and power to influence the performance course of organizations in general and people in particular. A positive and strong culture can make even an average caliber individual perform and achieve magnificently, whereas a negative and weak culture can demotivate an outstanding employee to under perform and end up with no achievement. Culture has an active and direct role in performance management. Following discussion highlights such significantly positive relationship between culture and performance management:

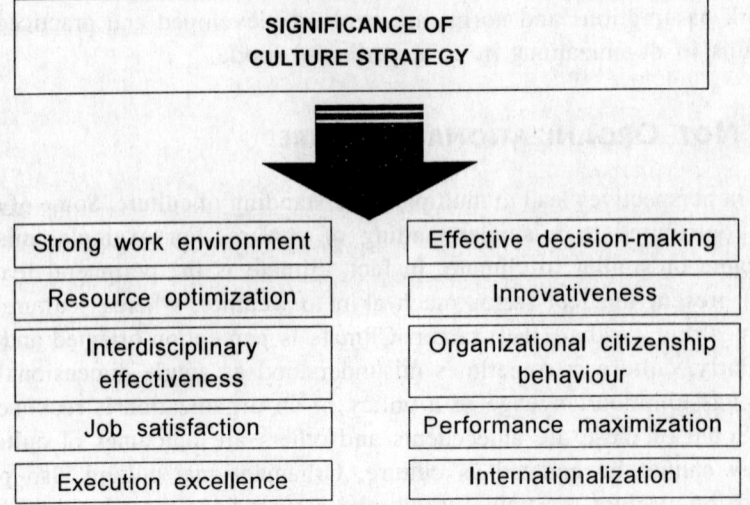

FIGURE 5.1 Significance of culture-based performance management strategy.

Work Environment

Strong and positive culture contributes to the installation of positive work environment in which every employee feels comfortable to work. Employees need not spend their energies on activities that are not directly related to their work output. In a sense, people in weak organizational culture or a culture that is not performance-oriented are expected to spend their time and energies to create protection covers around them. This happens when there are no well-defined values, customs and norms that guide people. Each individual's ultimate aim is to protect self-interest and ensure his or her existence in such a work environment. This we can find in organizations where group conflicts, authoritarianism, chaos in people systems and power politics are rampant. All such dysfunctionalities have serious implications for performance management.

Optimization of Resources

Performance orientation of people is reflected in the deployment of organizational resources. Often it is found that deploying resources optimally to produce goods and services is more a matter of organizational culture. A matured and strong culture guides people to demonstrate efficiency in exploitation of organizational resources both physical and intellectual. Therefore, some organizations are very cost-effective while others are cost ineffective due to overspending of resources. Secondly, using right resources at the right time is more a matter of subjective perception and situational acumen. No written rules and regulations can really help people in cleverly deploying resources. This happens only through subjective handling. Culture can condition this usage of subjectivity for objective purposes.

Interdisciplinary Effectiveness

Culture is at the centre of interdisciplinary work. Peak performance of people can be attained only through a collaborative and interdisciplinary effort as discussed in the team-based performance management strategy. Ultimate effectiveness of teams and interdisciplinary work is contingent upon the right culture. Human being by nature wants to live and perform in a collective manner, but it is the culture that motivates or demotivates people to be individualistic. Modern organizations require people to work in a collaborative manner due to increasing interdependence of tasks. Performance gets sharpened when people collaborate. But it is easier said than done. Interdisciplinary efforts of many organizations prove the formidable challenges in making people work together effectively. This happens due to non-espousal of the corresponding culture. Culture provides (i) unique language, (ii) guides interdisciplinary groups through customs and norms and (iii) governs them through values. Culture is the chief ingredient in performance management because it can enhance effectiveness of interdisciplinary work.

Job Satisfaction

Culture is one of the significant determinants of job satisfaction. People prefer organizations known as the best employers where opportunities for job satisfaction are fertile. This job satisfaction has wide implications for performance of people. It has been conclusively proven that organizational culture plays the decisive role in creating conditions for job satisfaction. An organizational culture that is positive and strong enables employees to transform to their potential into tangible performances through reinforcing the strengths and relieving the weaknesses. Functional, productive and emotional relationships are by-products of organizational culture. These by-products have a direct influence on the degree of job satisfaction people derive being members of an organization. Organizational culture oriented towards enhancement of performances creates norms and customs that facilitate job satisfaction.

Execution Excellence

Many organizations suffer not due to lack of systems, procedures, rules, regulations, vision, mission, objectives, strategies, so on and so forth, but they suffer due to poor or moderate execution abilities. Absence of cohesiveness among people is the chief reason for such poor execution abilities. An organization lacks cohesiveness because of weak organizational culture. This weakness results in people sharing divergent thinking, values and norms. It means there are subgroups in the organization sabotaging each other's efforts. Therefore, a positive and strong organizational culture that ensures commonality of mind is imperative for execution excellence.

A large portion of effectiveness of performance management comes from execution rather than from conception. For example, ineffectiveness of performance appraisal in many organizations is attributed to ineffective execution. This effectiveness cannot be brought about by adding some more procedures or by revamping the formats and systems. This can be attained only by tuning the minds of people. Organizational culture alone possesses magnificent power of conditioning people to be dexterous in execution.

Effective Decision-Making

This is an extension to the above discussion, specifically focusing on decision-making patterns. Organizational culture defines standards of decision-making. For example, two organizations following similar pattern of delegation of powers may not be similar in the decision making pattern of their employees because of the intervening force, i.e. the organizational culture. Decision-making is critical to performance excellence. A good number of organizations, particularly in service sector suffer due to bad or slow decision-making, adversely affecting the organizational performance. Few organizations make efforts to improve decision-making through the magic of empowerment. However, this magic of empowerment in practice only contributed for powerless empowerment. Mere change in systems cannot bring expected change in work behaviour as it involves transition in people. Reliable route for improving decision-making is to associate organizational culture to the newly evolved decision-making system.

Innovativeness

Survival, existence and growth of organizations in the changing times are contingent upon an organization's innovative capability. Innovation in this context means not necessarily breakthrough innovations achieved by research and development department, but the zeal of people to improve upon every activity and make progress in an evolutionary manner. This kind of attitude that makes people to look for improvements rather than accidental innovations is highly desirable for real innovation. Secret behind success of many Japanese companies is attributed to this all-pervasive innovation orientation. This orientation can be achieved only through organizational culture in which innovative behaviour is nurtured in every employee. Japanese innovation capabilities especially in electronic goods segment prove that it is the innovation culture that builds real innovation capability. This cannot be acquired simply by pumping more funds for research and development activity in a centralized manner. Matured state of performance management can be realized when innovative behaviour is evident in organization. There is no need to emphasize that organizational culture that is effectively managed can produce this innovative behaviour.

Employee Attrition, Commitment and Organizational Citizenship Behaviour

Employee turnover, commitment and organizational citizenship behaviour are consequences of culture that operates in organizations. These three to some extent can work as parameters to determine the strength of culture. For example, organizational culture can be considered as strong and positive where employee turnover is minimal in comparison to industry average and where good organizational citizenship behaviour exists. Organizational culture comprising of a unique set of values, customs, norms and language that is strong, makes people unadjustable in other environments. Similarly, an organizational culture that is weak cannot have any impact on the behaviour of the people and hence, it can easily contribute to employee turnover and also be unsuccessful in generating good organizational citizenship behaviour. Low levels of employee turnover and good organizational citizenship behaviour are highly desirable for performance improvement in organizations.

Performance Maximization

Maximization of performance on a continuous basis can come through a well-nurtured culture fabric. No managerial systems, monitoring techniques and extrinsic motivational tricks can maximize performance to the level of performance that is made natural to people as a matter of culture. Culture is a critical component in maximization of performance. Often organizations keep struggling to maximize performances by revamping systems, drawing new strategies, and indulging in creating new performance schedules without much success. Many a time an individual only knows how much he or she can perform and the bottom of performance potential is unknown to all. This complex phenomenon of potential can be effectively handled by equally complex phenomenon that is organizational culture.

Internalization

Real effectiveness is possible with any system if it is internalized with people. For example, let us take quality improvement initiative. All quality gurus and managers working in several hundred organizations across the world implementing quality management in the name of TQM, Kaizen, ISO certifications agree on one aspect, i.e. people processes are more important than statistical quality control or tools of quality assurance. This means that 'process', which is nothing but culture, can alone ensure the real quality. This process part should be internalized within the people to make a product/service with quality as natural as the basic product. Organizational culture undoubtedly has infinite power to push something to the state of internalization like a religious belief. This internalization phenomenon is very essential for effectiveness of performance management.

THEORETICAL FOUNDATIONS OF ORGANIZATIONAL CULTURE

Organizational culture is a well-studied, researched and documented subject. Culture is also one of the privileged subjects among humanities that received attention from a variety of disciplines which include Anthropology, Sociology and Social Psychology. In the following text, a few important theories that have relevance to culture in the context of performance management are briefly presented. These theories mainly explain levels, types and different perspectives on organizational culture. Factors that influence development of culture and aspects associating with evolving a strong culture are also discussed. These theories together provide a rich perspective on organizational culture. Such a perspective helps in developing strong and positive culture in organizations. These theories are:

SCHEIN'S THREE LEVELS OF CULTURE

The culture guru, Edgar Schein classified culture into three levels as:

Artifacts: This represents overt behaviour of people/organization/society. The way people dress, speak as well as their mannerisms demonstrate a culture that can be identified. Similarly, an organization's office layout, sitting arrangements, reception present cultural texture of an organization. These overt symbols are referred to as artifacts and considered as the most visible form of culture.

Values: Second level of culture is values that are built on beliefs. These are relatively demonstrable and visible. For example, decisions are taken in a particular pattern in an organization because value stipulates such a pattern. These values evolve over a period of time. For example, seniority is given priority in an organization for determining compensation and career-related matters. Priority for seniority becomes a value since organization sees positive gains for itself and its employees.

Underlying Assumptions: Third and most powerful dimension that explains culture more deeply are the underlying assumptions. For instance, in the above example, organization accords priority to seniority in compensation and career-related matters because there was an underlying assumption that age (experience/elderly) is an important criterion. Organizations, like in this case, in the first instance practice something which already exists in the larger society as a value. Organizations also learn these values unconsciously and practice them in daily routines. These underlying assumptions determine the above discussed artifacts and values too.

It is very important for an organization to analyze and adequately understand underlying assumptions of values and behaviours in order to manage culture effectively and meaningfully.

Egan's Overt and Covert Cultures

A meaningful classification of culture has come from Egan who describes culture as overt and covert. Overt culture is what we manifest and covert culture is what exists in latent and dormant fashion. Both are important but covert is the more intricate and complex between the two. Therefore, studying and understanding overt culture is much easier compared to covert. Covert culture is the key that comprises basic underlying assumptions, beliefs, values and norms. Overt culture is primarily manifestation of covert culture. Organization intending to manage culture building must accord great deal of attention to covert culture.

HANDY'S FOUR TYPES OF CULTURE

Charles Handy avers that history, technology, goals and objectives of organization, size, location and management and employees have their own influence on organizational culture and, therefore, understanding these aspects can provide real insights into culture.

According to him, there are four types of culture. These are:

Power Culture: This is a centralized system of administration where a single person or few selective persons wield all power in an organization. This type of culture is frequently found in new start ups and small organizations. There will be no rules, regulations and procedure. Words of key persons are considered as rules.

Role Culture: As the title suggests, this type of culture promotes specialization. Business of organization is conducted through these specializations like marketing, production, finance, operations, human resource, commercial, so on and so forth. All these departments perform through a set of rules, regulations and procedures.

Task Culture: Task culture represents issue-based administration. It is more like a project-oriented system where people form a group and work together to complete a task and disband on completion. Here, there will be no traditional dyadic relationships and rigid framework of rules. Business of organization is managed through situational acumen. Therefore, people who are knowledgeable and skillful wield more power and influence than others.

Person Culture: This represents person holding complete influence. It happens with professional bodies and associations where a person known for professional mettle is chosen to lead a group of co-professionals.

Understanding these four types helps performance managers (i) to identify type of culture that exist in their organizations and (ii) to analyze culture in order to understand to what extent it is conducive in the organizational context/nature of business.

DEAL AND KENNEDY CLASSIFICATION OF CORPORATE CULTURE

Corporate culture has been classified into four types based on T.E. Deal and A.A. Kennedy's twin criteria of risk taking ability and feedback system of organizations. These are:

Tough and Macho Culture: This type of culture can be found in organizations where risk taking is encouraged and people act on the feedback quickly: whether it is positive or negative. This kind of culture is more apt for an organization where professionals work and compete with each other.

Hard Work Culture: This is represented by tendency of organizations to take low risk but high on feedback system. It means organizations hesitate to take risks and touch untested waters. However, they are very sharp in obtaining the feedback on the actions and modify the proposed actions in accordance with the demands of this feedback. This can be generally found with sales and service organizations.

Bet the Company Culture: Organizations with this kind of culture are very high on risk taking and very slow in feedback implementation. This can be found with large-sized organizations like oil companies, financial institutions, civil construction companies. These are basically hierarchical and bureaucratic cultures.

Process Culture: This type represents government, municipal administration and service sector. Organizations of this kind are neither risk takers nor feedback seekers. The feedback obtained is unused since it is considered as a mere ritual.

KILLMAN, SAXTON AND SERPA'S DETERMINANTS OF CULTURE INFLUENCE

According to Killman et al., the following three factors determine the type and degree of culture influence in an organization:

Culture Direction: Direction of the culture (whether culture is facilitating or constraining performance of people and organization) decides the kind of influence culture has. The culture type that is facilitative is called positive organizational culture and culture that is constraining is called negative culture. This primarily reveals the type of influence.

Culture Pervasiveness: How widely spread is the culture is an important indicator of culture influence. For example, culture may be different in different units of the same organization and culture may not be the same in various departments in an organization. This means organizational culture is not pervasive. It is pervasive if the same organizational culture is evident in all units and departments. Influence of culture is intense if culture is pervasive.

Culture Strength: This indicates to what extent organizational culture is influencing the behaviour of employees. Culture is influential if it modifies behaviour and it is not if it has no impact on people's behaviour.

JOHNSON'S CULTURAL WEB

G. Johnson provided a more pragmatic description of organizational culture which says culture is susceptible as well as determinant of many aspects such as:

1. *Routines:* Daily activities and the way they are performed and the manner in which members exchange and interact.
2. *Rituals:* How an organization or groups in organizations treat and conduct special events and occasions.
3. *Stories:* Type of stories spread in organization regarding successes and failures of organization and individuals.
4. *Symbols:* Physical expressions such as office layout, public places in the office like canteen, toilets, car parking, language of particular type used.
5. *Power Equilibrium:* Delegation of powers, authority and the formal way of influencing the decision-making pattern.
6. *Reward:* Reward and punishment system clarifies such manners and actions that can lead to punishment or reward.
7. *Workflow:* This refers to how the business of organization is conducted and how workflow progresses.

MARTIN'S THREE PERSPECTIVES ON CULTURE

According to J. Martin, there are three perspectives on culture as described here:

Integrationist Perspective: This refers to an organizational culture that is pervasive organization-wide and guides people through well-internalized values and beliefs. This can be found in high-performing organizations.

Fragmentationist Perspective: This indicates that organizational culture is divergent and confuses people with contradictory values and beliefs. In effect, there will be no culture that can be identified. This can be found in poorly performing organizations.

Differentiationist Perspective: The third type represents organizational culture that has uniformity with minor deviations because of diverse background of people. This implies that there is an organization-wide culture that has its presence in a significant way but small groups simultaneously observe a different behaviour that is not in conflict with organization-wide culture.

PETERS AND WATERMAN'S EIGHT CULTURE CHARACTERISTICS

Tom Peters and Robert Waterman in their study of excellent organizations identified eight cultural characteristics that exist in all excellent organizations. These are:

  (i) Bias for action
 (ii) Staying close to the customer
(iii) Autonomy and entrepreneurship
 (iv) Productivity through people
  (v) Hands on management
 (vi) Sticking to the knitting

(vii) Lean organization with lesser people

(viii) Simultaneous loose-tight organization.

The premise of their argument is that the said cultural characteristics help these organizations to be excellent and competitive.

OUCHI'S CULTURE ANALYSIS

Management guru William Ouchi applying seven cultural parameters, has distinguished Japanese organizations from American Organizations and explained how these differences in culture accounted for success of some Japanese organizations over American companies. These cultural characteristics are:

   (i) Commitment to employees

  (ii) Evaluation of employees' performance

 (iii) Career planning practices

 (iv) Method of controlling employees

  (v) Decision-making patterns

 (vi) Centralization/decentralization of responsibility

(vii) Concern for people.

HOFSTEDE'S INTERNATIONAL CULTURE FRAMEWORK

Hofstede Geert conducted a multinational survey covering about one lakh sixty thousand employees with an objective to understand cultural variations. This international perspective on culture enables organizations and performance managers to draft culture compatible people policies and culture induced performance strategies. Geert presented these variations using four dimensions. These are:

Power Distance: This refers to equal or unequal power distribution among members of an organization. People in high power countries possess tolerance to unequal power distribution and low power countries are characterized by resistance to centralization of power.

Individualism-Collectivism: Some societies are highly individualized where personal rewards, personal recognition, personal challenges mot vate and people in collective societies are inspired by relationships.

Uncertainty Avoidance: Some societies are intolerant of uncertainty and, therefore, they put in efforts to avoid it while some others are tolerant and sustain the uncertainty.

Masculinity-Femininity: Masculinity is the indicator of materialism like money, power and positions. Femininity refers to relationships, cooperation, long-term understandings and emotional bondages. Geert again found that some nations are domin, ntly materialistic and some are non-materialistic.

FURNHAM AND GUNTER'S TWELVE TYPES OF CORPORATE CULTURE

According to corporate assessment experts Adrian Furnham and Barrie Gunter, corporate culture can be classified into 12 types such as:

  (i) Humanistic helpful culture
 (ii) Affiliative culture
(iii) Approval culture
 (iv) Conventional culture
  (v) Dependent culture
 (vi) Opposition culture
(vii) Power culture
(viii) Competitive culture
 (ix) Perfectionist culture
  (x) Achievement culture
 (xi) Avoidance culture
(xii) Self-actualization culture.

Nomenclature of these cultures themselves are self-explanatory as to what they represent and mean.

LESSONS OF CULTURE THEORIES

Above discussed culture theories have significant implications for the development of culture-based performance management strategy, interventions and drivers. These theories basically illustrate culture as a powerful mechanism in creating performance excellence. The precious lessons of these theories are:

Culture is Determinant and Susceptible

Organizational factors like history, technology, size, location and employees determine the cultural designs of an organization. At the same time culture also determines how an organization is managed, which includes technology, employees and size of an organization. This indicates that culture provides both, i.e. the mutual capacity to influence and for being influenced. Therefore, the lesson to performance managers is that organizational factors as afore-mentioned can be used to shape the kind of culture that is appropriate to their organizations in the pursuit of performance excellence.

Culture is Intangibly Tangible

Culture, as theories establish, is very intangible and complex, especially the issue of underlying assumptions. However, theories have also shown the tangible shape of culture such as artifacts, symbols, rituals, language, stories, jokes, power, rewards. Organizations by leveraging on tangible side of culture can map and cultivate desirable culture to enhance performance. Intangible culture can be attained in the long-term with sustained efforts by redefining the basic underlying assumptions. Grasping this tangibility and intangibility of culture is essential for the practice of culture-based performance management.

Culture is Peripheral and Deep-Rooted

Identifying two faces of culture, i.e. culture as overt and covert, is a significant contribution of culture theories that has practical implications for management of culture. Different approaches are required to manage these two faces of culture. Further, as already proved both are equally important for nurturing a strong and positive organizational culture. Such a culture is essential for soaring the performance to peak.

Culture is a Big Sum and Comprehensive System

Theories developed, particularly the works of culture guru, Edgar Schein presents the comprehensive view of culture that comprises artifacts, values and underlying assumptions. The important lesson for practice is that culture is a bigger sum than what practitioners are ready to believe. Real cultural roots lie in the underlying assumptions whose understanding and analysis is imperative for infusion of right culture in organizations. Success of performance management is dependent upon using this big sum of organizational culture to build the performance centric culture.

Culture is Multiple

Variants in the organizational culture are plenty. These include: power culture, role culture, person-based culture, task-oriented culture, a humanistic culture, dependent culture, approval and rejection culture. Based on the dominant culture characteristics of organizations, researchers have arrived at culture classifications. This classification helps performance management practitioners identify and slot their own organizational culture. Such identification is necessary for a meaningful understanding and evolving suitable culture development framework.

Culture Characteristics

Peters and Waterman and William Ouchi's organizational studies conclude that all excellent organizations follow a set of culture characteristics that motivate people to perform exceedingly well. This identification of culture characteristics that multiply the performance is like (i) providing practical principles with common sense and (ii) providing wisdom to practice performance management. These studies can serve as guidelines to develop a performance-oriented culture in organizations.

Cross Culture Perspective

Hofstede's international study on culture presents a very valuable insight into culture variations among different nations. This knowledge drives a vital issue, i.e. performance culture that is to be built must be compatible to that nation's superordinate culture. It means that performance management practice that is apt for a country may not be effective in some other country. Therefore, there must be a positive synergy between culture-based performance strategy and nation's culture paradigm.

Culture as Determinant of Business Behaviour

Contribution of culture studies as described in the foregoing text is that 'culture is a potential determinant of business behaviour of an organization'. For example, culture can either make an organization (i) a risk taker and (ii) sensitive to feedback system in improving response system or it can make organizations (i) intolerant to risk and (ii) insensitive to feedback. Performance managers can use this perspective as a strategy to deploy culture in shaping an organization either as risk taker or risk averse.

Culture as Strong and Weak

Organizational culture that is strong is expected to transform organizations into competitive, world-class, innovative and the best employers. Similarly, weak cultures tend to breed under performing organizations according to a few studies. Practical lesson to the strategy of culture-based performance management is that a strong organizational culture must be nurtured to enhance performance levels.

Culture as Integrative and Fragmental

Organizational culture is also classified as integrative and fragmantive, based on analytical culture studies. Effectiveness of culture is also found to be proportionate to the pervasiveness, i.e. integration of culture in an organization. Fragmented culture contributes for creation of subgroups that result in organizational ambiguities and ultimately leads to poor performance. Therefore, performance managers must evolve an organizational culture that is integrative.

CULTURE-BASED PERFORMANCE MANAGEMENT STRATEGY, INTERVENTIONS AND DRIVERS

Culture is like oxygen for performance management. This is one of the most challenging strategies among seven strategies of performance management discussed in this book. All the remaining six strategies need endorsement and complete support of culture. Execution effectiveness of performance management interventions and drivers is sheerly dependent upon the effectiveness of culture-based performance management strategy. This strategy akin to other strategies encompasses two interventions consisting of 10 drivers each. These interventions are:

Nurturing Culture-Based Performance Management: First intervention focuses on nurturing performance-oriented culture in organizations. This intervention comprises 10 drivers as discussed in the forthcoming contents. Application of these 10 drivers with each of them delivering tangible results can make organizations culturally mature, strong and positive.

Capitalizing on Culture in Institutionalization of Performance Management: The second intervention focuses on using this matured, strong and positive organizational culture to institutionalize performance management. Here also, 10 drivers form the structure and content of this intervention, application of which can drive institutionalization of performance management in a systematic and professional fashion.

These interventions along with relevant drivers are presented here.

INTERVENTION 1: NURTURING CULTURE-BASED PERFORMANCE MANAGEMENT

Nurturing the culture-based performance management involves organizations progressing through conceptualization and application of 10 drivers. Though each driver on its successful execution delivers tangible results to the organization, the real impact, i.e. creation of a matured, strong and positive culture can be achieved only when all the 10 drivers are diligently pursued. There is no denying the fact that each organization needs to follow its own course of action to evolve performance-induced culture. Following discussion helps and enriches performance managers in carving out their own strategy of culture-based performance management. It means drivers being presented here serve as specimen format for nurturing culture-based performance management. Incidentally, organizations may also find these drivers not only as drivers of guidance, but also as adaptable action plan. As opposed to what few organizations intended to disbelieve, culture is completely manageable. The case study of AT&T is a fine example in this context.

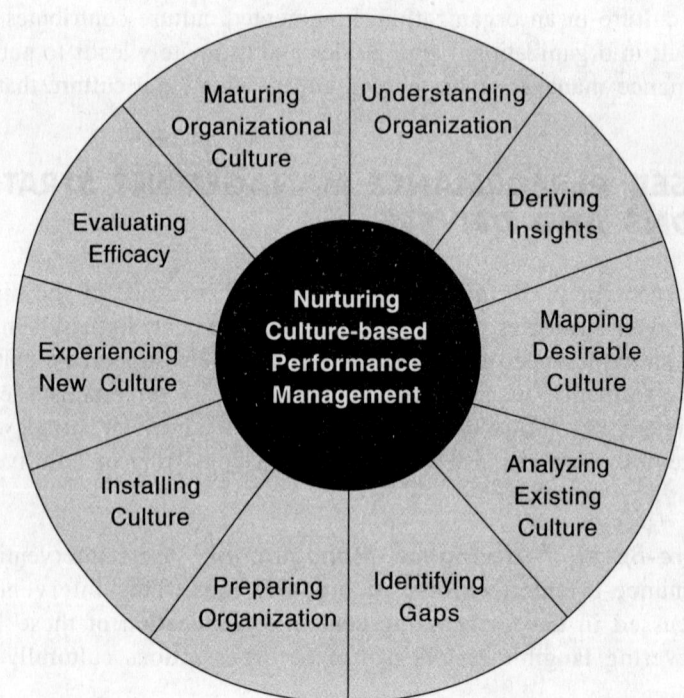

FIGURE 5.2 Drivers of the intervention nurturing culture-based performance management.

BEST PRACTICE
AT&T Model of Culture Management

The AT&T model of culture management can offer quite a few valuable lessons to organizations in their pursuit to cultivate an agile organizational culture. AT&T culture management in the context of its takeover of Bell Corporation is laudable. AT&T culture management comprises six vital steps as briefly discussed here:

1. *Setting example:* In the beginning, cultural change was not delegated. Instead, chief executive himself took the responsibility of conceptualizing, consulting all employees and mapping organizational culture. As a first step, chief executive adopted new behaviour and demonstrated it as an example. It means a top down approach was followed.

2. *Revamping management systems:* The second vital action initiated was revamping management systems and organizational structure in tune with planned culture norms, values and beliefs. As a result, AT&T changed the reward system, resource allocation process and decision-making pattern.

3. *Articulating value system explicitly:* New value system as a part of culture revolution was communicated and disseminated effectively to reach every individual employee effectively. This communication process involved distribution of documents, conduct of debates, usage of audio visual aids and large-scale consultation process.

4. *Training to support cultural values:* Training was used as key mechanism in imbibing the value system among employees. All training programmes invariably consisted of a module on new culture and its chemistry and relevance to the organization.

5. *Revising hiring methods:* In order to ensure harmony between cultural values of AT&T with individual value, hiring standards were revised to make best fit of person and job.

6. *Modifying symbols:* Explicit culture in the form of symbols is equally important to the implicit culture. This has been rightly recognized at AT&T. All members of top management availed every opportunity to communicate the new culture with the aid of symbols. New symbols that aptly illustrate the culture have been consciously developed and practiced.

Based on: Brooke, Tunstall, 1983. Culture Transition at AT&T. *Sloan Management Review*, Fall, **25**(1).

DRIVER 1: UNDERSTANDING ORGANIZATION

The maiden task in the journey of nurturing culture-based performance management is conceptualizing objectives of organizational culture. In order to make any intervention successful and yield valuable returns, the objectives must be made abundantly clear. This enables not only to express intentions of organization clearly, but also aids in charting course of progress. Organizations that are in a hurry and jump into action sans a systematic planning like drafting, operationalizing and disseminating objectives prior to acting can cause (i) tardy progress, (ii) multiple constraints due to unanticipated reactions and (iii) discourage organizations to continue with the intervention. Also, lack of planning can cost organizations substantially in terms of money, effort and time. Learning that occurs from such unplanned effort can be erratic and unscientific rather than insightful. In brief, setting objectives of organizational culture is a good beginning in the long journey of nurturing culture. Following steps are indicative of the process of setting up of performance centric culture objectives.

Step 1: Study of Organizational History

The first step in understanding organizational culture specific to an organization is getting to know a great deal about its history. Information relating to (i) in what circumstances the company came into existence, (ii) what efforts went into building such an organization, (iii) what was the dream of the promoters, (iv) the successes and failures in the past, (v) difficulties encountered, and (vi) sacrifices made, must be gathered to understand an organization better. This information will be useful to understand the basic issues/reasons for the kind of culture operating in an organization.

Step 2: Study of Business Vision and Mission

This may appear as common. Ironically, a cursory study reveals that culture being promoted in organizations is not compatible with their business vision and mission. The dominant reason for this is the psychological misconception that organizational vision and mission and evolving of culture are independent activities. Few organizations that make sincere efforts in drafting vision and mission statement, leave defining of culture objectives untouched. This is because sincerity as shown in developing vision statements is not shown in developing the culture. No vision and mission can be really successful unless organizational culture supplements them. The first and foremost task must be to carefully study and analyze intent and underlying assumptions of organizational vision and mission statements in order to derive the relevant lessons for defining desirable objectives of organizational culture.

Step 3: Study of Business Objectives and Plans

The next sequential step is to study and compare long, medium and short-term business objectives and plans of an organization with business vision and mission statements as indicated at step two above. This assumes the fact that in few cases the business objectives and plans may not match with organization's vision and mission statements due to some reasons. In such a conflicting scenario, conceptualizing culture objectives becomes a sticky job. Therefore, in the first instance, this lack of agreement among vision, mission, objectives and plans must be resolved with the participation of top management and drafters of these statements and plans. It will be impossible to derive logical and integrative culture framework if this issue is not clarified.

Step 4:   Study of Organizational Motives

Study of organizational vision, mission, objectives and plans contributes towards understanding of business motives of a company. The motives can be few or many revolving around (i) profit-making like corporate, (ii) service orientation like non-governmental organization/ missionaries and/or (iii) both the common motives can be to make organization world class, competitive, innovative and internationally most admired for its quality. These identified motives must be classified meaningfully.

Step 5:   Study of Organizational Technology

Culture is also susceptible to technology employed in an organization. For example, information technology company tends to possess a culture that is different from a financial services company or an automobile manufacturing company. Therefore, technological aspects must be studied in order to understand the picture of human interface. This human interface may be collective/individualistic/virtual.

Step 6:   Study of Organizational Structure and Delegation of Powers

Organizational structure and degree of delegation of power for decision-making also have their own share of participation in determining culture. Organizational structure must be analyzed in order to identify whether it is an organic or mechanistic structure. Likewise, power delegation indicates the intensity of centralization and decentralization of decision-making that reveals the preferred management style of top managers.

Step 7:   Study of Organizational Systems

This includes understanding various procedures, rules and regulations that govern and guide activities in organizations. These are: quality systems, financial policies, marketing policies, human resource policies and production manuals, so on and so forth.

Step 8:   Study of People

Employees working in the organization are major influences of organizational culture. Therefore, background of employees, which includes academic, professional, social, economic, geographical and personal culture of employees, must be studied. This involves accessing the demographical and emotional data of employees and mapping the same to derive realistic insights.

Step 9:   Study of External Environment

Once the pertinent inferences are drawn based on the study of organization's internal environment, external environment of the organization must be analyzed. This external environment encompasses socio-economic conditions of the surrounding society, customers and suppliers. This study provides an opportunity to clearly understand the type of culture surrounding the organization and factors responsible for the existence of such culture. Here also, significant inferences in the form of summary must be drawn.

Step 10: Study of State Systems

As a part of understanding the external environment of organizations, state systems like government legislation related to organization's business domain and workforce must be studied. This essentially gives an idea of what kind of culture the state administration is trying to enforce upon.

Step 11: Study of Competitors

Essential component of the external environment of an organization is its competitors. Therefore, organizational culture prevailing in competitors' and collaborators' organizations need to be studied. Learning obtained from such a study with analysis of how that particular organization is possibly facilitating or inhibiting performance must be well documented.

DRIVER 2: DERIVING INSIGHTS FOR CULTURE MANAGEMENT

Principal objective of the second driver is to (i) study data obtained using Driver 1, (ii) analyze data, (iii) draw inferences and (iv) build insights from such data in the light of organizational culture. This is a challenging task even to the best of culture specialized performance managers due to many gaps, contradictions, confusions and impossibilities that the data manifests. The ability to deal with these challenges is a testimony to an organization's commitment to nurture culture-based performance management. More the culture fragmentation in an organization, greater the intensity of these challenges. However, positive aspect in such a scenario is, more the challenges, brighter the chances for creating positive impact with culture management. Steps that are to be adapted in application of this driver are indicated below.

Step 1: Summarize Internal Environment Data

Data obtained for understanding the internal environment of an organization must be assimilated and meaningfully summarized. For example, summarized key issues can be like this:

- Organization having profit motive.
- Vision of organization is to emerge as leader in the world business segment.
- Mission is to expand business scope by fourfold every year.
- Objective to be cost and quality effective and innovative.
- Technology employed is new generation and sophisticated.
- Powers are centralized.
- Organizational structure is mechanistic.
- Organizational systems are bureaucratic and three decades old.
- Employees are highly educated and drawn from different parts of the nation.

The above summary clearly projects contradiction such that technology is sophisticated but organizational systems are outdated. Similarly, organization intends to emerge as a world leader and plan to expand operations rapidly, but the decision-making power is centralized. These contradictions being pointed here are just an illustration of the kind of conflicts that data can pose when analysis is done. All such analysis and inferences drawn must be well documented. These contradictions must be resolved with the help of top managers. Unless these contradictions are resolved, it will be difficult to precisely map the desirable culture.

STEP 2: SUMMARIZE EXTERNAL ENVIRONMENT DATA

Next action is to summarize the external environment data on the lines of the internal environment data analyzed. For example, it can be a cause of concern for an organization that employs new generation technology and intended to be world leader in its field, if state laws are regulatory and controlling in nature and the surrounding society is feudalistic. External environment is one of the key influencing factors in shaping an organization's culture. Inferences drawn from the external environment data also need to be well documented.

Step 3: Cross-Refer the Data

In order to ensure the correctness and reliability of data, cross-refer the data obtained for one dimension with the other dimension. For example, cross-refer the data of organizational systems with that of delegation of powers. This, of course, will be possible only when two dimensions are related or diametrically opposite in positions. Consequent upon cross-referring the data, create a document titled 'Understanding organization for culture management'.

Step 4: Present the Data for Critical Comment

The above mentioned document along with the raw data must be circulated among senior managers, resource persons and key decision-makers in order to (i) obtain a robust understanding of data and also to (ii) receive critical comments to enrich the document. This also serves the valuable purpose of preparing all these people for a large-scale change in the organizational culture. People in such positions are expected to compare data with physical reality and offer rich input. This kind of input is immensely helpful in understanding the organization in the context of organizational culture.

Step 5: Revise the Document

Last step in this driver is revising the document prepared for deriving insights into the organization and its culture. This revision must be carried out keeping in view the critical comments received from identified resource persons. This revision shall be attempted on careful analysis of the comments received. Comments and review arguments must not be incorporated to influence the inference drawn unless they are worthy, genuine and well thought out. If required, additional information must be sought from the person concerned prior to accepting or rejecting the comment. All efforts must be made to receive and consider comments in the right perspective with objectivity, sincerity and commitment. There shall be no place for political process or subjective considerations in this exercise. Effectiveness of the remaining drivers in this intervention is largely subject to the validity of the document 'Understanding Organization for culture management'.

Drivers 1 and 2 and the process of their application such as collecting and analyzing data may appear as an academic, cumbersome and never-ending task. This is partially true. Partial truth is, it is an elaborate exercise and persons managing this task must be conversant with data collection, analysis and documentation skills. It is untrue that it is never-ending and an academic exercise. Few managers and organizations may gather this kind of impression because many of us work in an unsystematic environment and performing just for the day. Endeavouring to be rationalistic and the drive to think in a logical manner makes the whole event abstract. Abstractness is natural when an issue like culture which is deep-rooted and invisible is to be managed. Therefore, performance managers must handle the total exercise as indicated in Driver 1 and 2 with perseverance and commitment.

DRIVER 3: MAPPING DESIRABLE CULTURE

Driver 3 makes a beginning by directly addressing the intervention of nurturing culture-based performance management. Essence of this driver is that a desirable culture is to be mapped keeping in view the inferences drawn at the stage of Driver 1 and 2. Desirable culture consists of both overt and covert culture strategies. The objective of mapped culture is to motivate employees to perform to their optimum levels and ultimately peak the performance of organization. Planning and execution of this driver is highly challenging, creative and involves participation of large section of employees across the organization. This is challenging because (i) issues that are taken into account, (ii) methods to be adapted while mapping the culture and (iii) the overall focus of the culture makes or mars the effectiveness of organizational culture as a vehicle of performance management. A suggestive process for mapping culture is given in the following steps that may assist organizations in their effort to map a strong, positive and matured culture or in reorienting the existing culture as performance-oriented.

Step 1: Setting Culture Objectives

Based on the document prepared at Driver 1 and 2, the macro and micro objectives of desirable organizational culture must be evolved. For example, a particular type of technology/people with a particular social background/customers with expectation of particular behaviour from organization solicits a particular culture. Internal and external environment of organization seeks a compatible culture. For example, managerial culture must be very dynamic if the internal data of organization reveals that the organization wishes to emerge as a world leader. Therefore, on careful consideration of the said consolidated document the objectives of culture must be defined in a meaningful, objective and measurable style. An example of how and what kind of culture objectives are to be set in alignment with understanding organization data is briefly described in Table 5.1.

Step 2: Operationalizing Culture Objectives

It is very important that culture objectives as formulated above be operationalized. Operationalization needs to be done in the form of actionable items. How the overt culture

TABLE 5.1 Setting Culture Objectives

Inferences drawn from understanding organization for culture management document about the organization	*Draft culture objectives*
1. Organization is in telecommunication industry. 2. Vision is to become world no. 1 in wireless telecommunication. 3. Mission is to enable connecting people worldwide. 4. Objective is to provide wireless communication facility cheaply and qualitatively. 5. Organization's operational motive is wealth maximization of employees, stock holders, distributors, suppliers and customers. 6. Organization is multi-unit and multi-locational. 7. Technology employed is new generation. 8. Professionals constitute the lion share of manpower and are drawn globally. 9. Organizational structure is organic and powers are decentralized. 10. Organizational systems are flexible, dynamic and ad hoc. 11. Interface with different governments in different nations having a high capitalistic perspective to socialistic perspective/philosophy. 12. Competitors are many but at global level there are three and at the local level (in particular segments) there are ten. 13. Organization was incorporated on ownership basis in USA and after three decades became a multinational with public stock holding.	*Macro objectives* 1. To evolve a positive, strong and mature organizational culture for attaining organization's vision, mission and objectives. 2. To evolve a humanistic-business organizational culture model that brings harmony in professional and personal lives of employees while attaining the organizational vision, mission and objectives. 3. To evolve an organizational culture that fermants sharing, sacrifice and optimization of wealth among all the stakeholders of organization. *Micro objectives* 1. To create and institutionalize a distinct and organization-wide overt culture that includes language, symbols, artifacts, rituals, stories, ideals and top management behaviour. 2. To integrate high technology, organic organizational structure, flexible systems and professional manpower to attain organizational vision, mission and objectives. 3. To create and institutionalize the covert culture such as values and beliefs in order to integrate the high technology, organic organizational structure, flexible systems and professional manpower to attain organizational vision, mission and objectives. 4. Optimization of human performance through overt and covert culture. 5. Culture to imbibe the aggression among stakeholders to achieve the organizational goal of emerging as world's no. 1.

TABLE 5.1 Setting Culture Objectives (Contd.)

Inferences drawn from understanding organization for culture management document about the organization	Draft culture objectives
	6. Culture to bring oneness/transformation of people working in different units at different locations as a single unified force.
	7. To insulate organizational culture in order to protect it from external culture that is controlled and regulatory in some nations.
	8. Culture to motivate and inculcate innovative behaviour.

is to be created, basically what kind of artifacts, symbols, language and stories are required to be used must be decided. For example, deciding that English will be adapted as a principal organizational language since organization's operations are spread across the globe and employees are drawn from different nations. Similarly, (i) how communications and interaction are expected to be held among employees, employees and customers, top management and shop floor employees and (ii) how common facilities like canteen, parking, toilets, etc. are to be provided in tune with the culture objectives ought to be pre-decided. For example, in a humanistic-business oriented culture like in the case of the organization indicated in Table 5.1, there must be equal and common rights for all employees for all the facilities. However, operationalizing overt organizational culture is much easier as compared to covert organizational culture. This comes from (i) consistent practice of overt culture, (ii) grooming employees on a set of values and beliefs over a period of time and (iii) through demonstration of these values and beliefs by members of an organization on all occasions and routines without exception. Further, operationalization involves redesigning following systems:

- *Organizational systems:* Organizational systems especially include human resource policy framework like compensation, reward, performance appraisal, career planning, welfare system must be scrutinized and redesigned. Systems may have to be redesigned to reinforce and realize the macro and micro cultural objectives.
- *Organizational structure:* In few cases, organizational structure which is expected to ensure smooth flow of work may itself be hampering the work or existing structure may not be compatible with the desirable culture as defined in the statement of culture objectives. Therefore, organizational structure must be reviewed and desirable structure must be mapped.
- *Decision making:* Delegation of powers and the manner in which decisions are arrived at also need to be critically examined in order to reorient the same in consonance with culture objectives. Many a time the issue of power equilibrium/ disequilibrium becomes a potential ground for weakening organizational culture.

Therefore, apt power distribution model must be mapped to strengthen the objectives of organizational culture.

- *Norms:* Norms here refer to unwritten rules and regulations that all members of an organization follow voluntarily in order to protect their status as a member of that group. These norms possess significant influence over the organizational culture. Though these norms are created and practiced by groups themselves, effort shall be made to create a framework of desirable norms.

- *Values:* Values play a guiding role in organizations. In real life, values work more powerfully than delegation of powers. Attempts must be made to map the desirable value system in the organization. Value of honesty, sacrifice, respecting other human beings, truthfulness, trust and openness must be made clear in demonstrable means.

- *Rituals:* Rituals remind people where the organization stands and what it stands for. It means, organizations create opportunities to reinforce the organizational culture and create impact over the people through these rituals. Therefore, desirable rituals that the organization must follow to attain the objectives of organizational culture must be mapped.

- *Symbols and artifacts:* As stated earlier symbols and artifacts are the most visible elements of organizational culture. Though they appear as superficial, they have inherent capacity to influence the formation of underlying assumptions in the people. Therefore, a great deal of attention must be given to this aspect. For example, chief executive sharing common facilities sends a message of organizational culture that is different from creating a separate lift, special chamber and special toilets to the chief executive. Based on these symbols, people tend to make wide scale interpretations about many things that have serious implications for culture management.

- *Key behaviours:* Work behaviours chiefly that of senior managers have an electrifying effect over the rest of the workforce. Therefore, these desirable work behaviours must be clearly described.

- *Basic assumptions:* This is the most complex exercise and calls for in-depth research and analysis before approaching on mapping the desirable basic assumptions index for an organization. For example, the respect of seniority over performance results in creating a set of assumptions that is different from valuing the immediate performance to that of seniority of an employee. Therefore, the contours of basic assumptions must be drawn in agreement with macro and micro objectives of organizational culture.

Step 3: Defining Superordinate Organizational Culture

An overall focus to organizational culture in tune with the objectives and mapped desirable culture needs to be drafted. It means that (i) there must be a superordinate symbol through which the kind of organizational culture that exists can be identified and (ii) this symbol must continuously remind members of the organization about their responsibilities and privileges in the revolution of organizational culture. For example, respecting humanity and revering innovation can be a superordinate symbol. This symbol must be developed not only in the form of a slogan, but also in various forms like representing through logo, celebrating festivals, and felicitating achievers in order to create an aura for superordinate organizational culture.

Step 4: Consolidation of Cultural Dimensions

Last step in this driver is to consolidate all mapped mechanisms, systems, behaviours and assumptions to create desirable organizational culture. Review must be conducted in order to remove any anomalies or lack of uniformity/disagreement among different parts of mapped desirable organizational culture. Integration of all aspects of desirable organizational culture needs to be ensured and clearly linked to superordinate focus of the culture. All such aspects as consolidated must be well documented in a consolidated form.

DRIVER 4: ANALYZING EXISTING CULTURE

It is most likely that once an organization successfully completes the execution of Driver 3, there will be a rejuvenated energy as first three drivers enable them to observe, study, analyze and experience their organization closely. Driver 3 also enables an organization to see the future through the experience of mapping desirable organizational culture. There will be a tendency to hurry up and jump on to implementing the mapped desirable organizational culture in the enthusiasm of realizing what is thought of. Such haste in trying to install the new culture system can lead the organization in trouble leave aside succeeding with new system. We need to understand the existing organizational culture before replacing it. Some organizations may think that the 'understanding organization for culture development' exercise done at the stage of Driver 1 and 2 is sufficient to understand the existing culture. This is partially correct. Definitely the document of 'understanding organization for culture development' and insights gained while studying an organization are highly relevant and useful. However, these studies are expected to be conducted with the objective to derive lessons for culture management. This study might have not captured the organizational culture that is directly affecting the daily work life of employees. Therefore, studying the aspects that are influencing the existing culture can help in installing the mapped desirable culture. Essence of this driver is to analyze the existing culture: (i) to identify match and mismatch between mapped desirable organizational culture and existing culture and (ii) to draw execution strategies for installing the mapped culture. Following steps are expected to facilitate this process:

Step 1: Adapting Mapping Parameters

Parameters adapted at Driver 3 for mapping the desirable organizational culture form the basis for analyzing existing culture. Factors such as language, symbols, artifacts, rituals, key behaviours, basic assumptions, values, beliefs, stories, top management style, delegation of powers, influencing patterns must be studied in the context of existing scenario. Following data collection methods can be used for this purpose.

- *Questionnaire:* Open ended/multiple options and structured/unstructured questionnaires must be designed to collect the perceptual as well as factual data. These questionnaires, depending on the issues being studied, can be administered covering a section or all. Prior to actually administering questionnaires for collection of data, reliability and content validity tests must be done.

- *Interviews:*   Key resource persons including shop floor employees may be interviewed to obtain the qualitative data about the existing culture, focusing on specific issues.
- *Observation:*   Internal personnel and external source duly trained on organizational culture diagnosis may be deployed to observe the organizational functioning and interaction over a period of time in order to identify the existing organizational culture.
- *Culture audit:*   Auditing existing decision-making style, policy papers and other relevant documents as secondary data is useful in identifying the culture that was built and currently operating in organization.
- *Small group brainstorming:*   Involving small groups based on issues, brainstorming sessions can be a good method to identify the existing culture. Results of brainstorming sessions must be systematically recorded.
- *Large scale interactions:*   All employees can be provided an opportunity to express themselves, discuss and deliberate on existing culture. This can throw up important issues that are dormant.

Step 2:   Identifying Culture Role in Organizational Objectives

The second step is to assess the extent to which the existing culture is facilitating or debilitating the attainment of organizational vision, mission and objectives. This is extremely important because the ultimate test of any culture is found in its role of making the organization successful. As indicated at the above step in this driver, questionnaires and interviews can be used to elicit views of employees about the type and role of organizational culture. In addition to this, instances where organization was not successful must be chosen to study and identify the role of culture in it. Data also must be obtained focusing on whether employees feel at times that (i) organization would have been more successful, (ii) more performing and (iii) more effective if organizational culture had been more facilitative than what it is now.

At the end of Driver 4, an organization is expected to possess data on existing culture and also on the desirable culture. Successful execution of the first four drivers is an indication of an organization's mammoth progress in nurturing culture-based performance management.

DRIVER 5:   IDENTIFYING GAPS AND PREPARING ACTION PLANS

Application of this driver contributes towards (i) identification of culture issues need to be given emphasis and (ii) preparation of action plans for implementing desirable organizational culture. This driver basically involves pursuing two steps in combination as illustrated here:

Step 1:   Identifying Gaps

First task is to identify agreements/disagreements and match/mismatch between desirable mapped organizational culture and the existing organizational culture. This comparative study is to be done adopting the same parameters that were followed while mapping organizational culture and analyzing the existing culture such as language, symbols, artifacts, organizational systems, key behaviours, values, beliefs, underlying assumptions. Comparative study leads to identification of the gaps. These gaps can be large, medium and negligible. This comparative study needs to be done with the help of internal key resource persons specifically chosen for the purpose and seeking external expertise wherever required. Gaps or no gaps as identified must be clearly documented with explanations, clarifications, illustrations and interpretations with the support of data. Document subsequently developed must be critically examined more than once by the resource group as well as neutral persons (not involved in the study) to make the report more robust and realistic.

Step 2: Preparing Action Plans

Next task subsequent to identification of culture gaps is translating these gaps into action plans. Depth, scope and intensity of this action plan are contingent upon how wide the gap is between existing and mapped desirable organizational culture. In few occasions, gaps are so huge that large preparation and planning might be required. While in some cases gaps may be specific. Whatever may be the case; the action plan must guide how to fill these gaps so that a positive, strong and matured culture can be placed in the organization. Action plan must consist of broad and specific strategies as described below. These actions as indicated below are just illustrative and organization can draw action plans and implementation strategies depending upon organizational context and internal reality.

Training as a Strategy: Action plan can propose training as a strategy for installing the new organizational culture. Organizational culture issues can be made part of all training programmes apart from designing specific programmes focusing on this issue exclusively.

Recruiting People: Inducting new people and orienting them on desirable organizational culture in order to spread it in the organization.

Reward System: Action plan can also suggest how the reward system can be used to encourage people to learn new culture and practice it.

Further, action plans can be built on long, medium and immediate term basis in consonance with the size of gap between existing and desirable organizational culture. Action plan must also indicate type of resources required in successfully installing the mapped organizational culture. Often installing organizational culture calls for substantial budgetary support apart from an unstinted commitment of the top management.

DRIVER 6: PREPARING ORGANIZATION FOR CULTURE SHOCK

Event after identifying cultural gaps and preparing action plans is: preparing organization for an organization-wide culture change. This is like applying spirit before injection is given to ensure smooth flow of medicine into the body. Similarly, organization needs to be physically and mentally prepared so that installation of new culture can be effective. Possible resistance to culture change must be assessed in advance so that remedial actions can also be planned proactively. Also, applying desirable organizational culture involves (i) training few resource persons as culture agents and (ii) mass education programs to disseminate knowledge about the new culture. Following steps are suggestive of what organization must do to prepare the organization for culture change.

Step 1: Communicating New Culture Plans

Top management, particularly the chief executive must make personal effort and take responsibility of organizing a special event with an aim to personally communicate to all employees about the plans to install new organizational culture. Salient features of this culture, such as how it is evolved, how various sections of employees participated in identifying existing culture and mapping desirable organizational culture must be shared in this public forum. Anticipated benefits to employees, organization and various stakeholders on implementation of mapped culture must also be shared. The chief executive also needs to communicate the plans of new culture to suppliers, contractors and important agencies associated with the organization. Apart from communication, suggestions from all must be invariably solicited for improving action plans as well as finalizing implementation methods.

Step 2: Training Resource Persons

Suitable number of employees representing all functions/departments from shop floor level to senior management category must be identified to impart training on new organizational culture in order to spread plans throughout the organization. Such identified people in addition to being given all information about mapped organizational culture must be trained in interpersonal and change agent skills.

Step 3: Release of Booklets and Publication on Intranet

Document containing all the information about new organizational culture must be released in the form of a booklet and displayed on the intranet if available. This can make information available round the clock.

Step 4: Debate Competitions/Essay Writings

Conducting debates and essay writing competitions on the new organizational culture vis-a-vis existing organizational culture can yield a lot of information that can be effectively utilized for improving the plans as well as sharpening implementation strategies.

Step 5: Discussions with Collective Bodies

Organizations having collective bargaining forums like trade unions must conduct detailed discussions with trade union office bearers to impress upon them the need to change. Unions' executives tend to have suspicions about new plans that these may affect unionism negatively. Therefore, these concerns need to be addressed adequately. Their suggestions also must be collected for improvement of plan and implementation methods.

Step 6: Prepare for Real Shock

Initially, experiencing some kind of shock in the form of chaos is natural, especially: (i) when new organizational culture is installed, (ii) when people are required to behave differently from past, and respect and believe in a different set of values. Organization as a whole needs to be prepared for this confusion. Otherwise, it may adversely affect the morale of people in particular and organizational performance in general.

Step 7: Look for Sabotages

Despite all preparations, chances of sabotage or manipulating the state of confusion to serve personal gains by a few individuals cannot be ruled out. It is utmost important that an eye should be kept on such people and a cautious approach must be adopted to deal with the situation. Any laxity in this respect can result in damaging the culture installation process.

DRIVER 7: INSTALLING MAPPED DESIRABLE ORGANIZATIONAL CULTURE

Objective of Driver 7 is to install the mapped desirable organizational culture in a systematic manner and in accordance with the plan developed for such execution. This is the toughest and most challenging driver. Conceptualizing, analyzing, developing desirable organizational culture and preparing organization for culture shock constitute only a quarter of the effort in the entire strategy. In that parlance, half of the effort goes in installing culture. Regardless of scientific planning and development of culture, still there will be umpteen chances for the culture getting derailed during the implementation stage. Culture is highly dynamic and its implementation is doubly dynamic, complex and intricate. Therefore, all strengths of the organization must be consolidated and channelized for effective execution. Implementation also must be progressed in an evolutionary manner with clear deliverables at each stage. Following need to be reckoned while installing new culture:

Step 1: Timing of Launching

It is important that mapped organizational culture must be introduced when conditions in organization are conducive. It means that the off-season for organizational operations must be used for rolling the plan. It is not desirable to introduce the new culture when the organization has many commitments to deliver products/services and meeting targets. As stated earlier, during the introduction phase the implementation is expected to cause some confusion, which may affect performance. Therefore, to avoid such a situation, soft time must be chosen for introduction.

Step 2: Start with Definite Success

Issues or parts of the new culture that are sure to succeed in implementation must be chosen to start with. Initial success is ten times more important than the success during mid-level progress. Everyone anxiously assesses the initial stage of implementation and is likely to follow up progress more at the beginning than in the later stages. Beginning must be made with items whose success is a sure shot. Initial success also encourages the organization to proceed with implementation with all optimism and confidence.

Step 3: Install One Item at a Time

Culture encompasses many aspects that are categorized as overt and covert cultures. During the initial stages, care must be exercised to implement one aspect at a time. Disadvantage in pursuing many aspects at a time is that efforts are spread and focus gets disintegrated, thus weakening the effect of implementation as well as presenting the change to penetrate deep into the organizational structure.

DRIVER 8: EXPERIENCING NEW ORGANIZATIONAL CULTURE

Consequent upon installing the mapped desirable organizational culture, new culture must be managed to ensure that it emerges strong and positive. Once implementation of new culture is over, it must be left like that for some time so that all employees can experience the system. It must be ensured that the new culture is spread across the organization and it reaches every individual employee. Two major issues that should be ensured as part of this driver are described below. These two issues are indicative of the process only and not exhaustive because finally it depends upon the organizational context and internal reality. However, the objective remains same to all organizations, i.e. ensure that employees, suppliers and customers experience the new culture.

Step 1: Implement Systems, Structure and Process in Letter and Spirit

Primary responsibility of management is to implement changes as agreed upon while installing the new culture in letter and spirit. In past, some experiments with managing organizational culture have failed in few organizations because of lack of commitment on the part of top management. This happens because top management tends to be the first segment that gets affected with the new culture because most of them have to forego the arbitrary power and authority. Therefore, some of them exhibit resistance in a subtle form in halting changes in systems, structure and process. Any non-implementation of changes as planned can cause dilution in experiencing the new culture.

Step 2: Deploy Resource Persons to Hasten Experiencing Process

Resource persons who were drawn and contributed while (i) analyzing existing organizational culture, (ii) mapping desirable culture and (iii) installing the new culture in the organization must be utilized to hasten the experiencing phase. Resource persons ensure that culture is spread, integrated and all stakeholders of organization experience the change in systems, structure, processes and key behaviours effectively.

Step 3: Allow New Culture to Exist Uninterrupted

New organizational culture as installed must be allowed to continue undisturbed at least for more than a year. This period may get longer in case of multi-unit and multi-locational large organizations. This period of one year is also just sufficient for overt culture but adoption of covert culture changes may require more time. Allowing organizational culture to exist and sustain the associated anxiety is very important for realizing the 'experience driver' in action. It is likely that a few organizations may make an attempt to postpone or differ implementation of some aspects under the guise of time not being ripe (things like that) due to their incapacity to sustain changes. These attitudes become stumbling blocks in experiencing new culture and transforming it as strong and positive. Implementers must be very careful of this aspect and must see that no compromises are made.

DRIVER 9: EVALUATING EFFICACY OF NEW ORGANIZATIONAL CULTURE

Once culture is installed successfully and managed in a way that all stakeholders experience the new culture fabric for a reasonable time, the next logical action must be assessing its efficacy in an objective manner. This assessment must be carried out at three levels as described below. The major objectives of this efficacy are twofold. First is understanding the contribution of new organizational culture in enhancing employee and organizational culture and secondly, identifying the areas of improvement/modification required so that they can be taken care of suitably.

Step 1: Auditing Processes of New Organizational Culture

First level of assessment must be conducted treating the new organizational culture as a subject of audit. It means that a paper-based audit must be carried out with the help of process audit expert to ascertain whether installation and experience phase of culture strategy is managed as per laid down plan or any deviations are made. Audit also must be made responsible to diagnosis in order to identify the reason for any laxity in implementation of cultural aspects and also to clearly figure out the issues of non-implementation. This must be an exhaustive audit covering all the related aspects in a detailed fashion. It also involves a minimum of three months time which can be the average duration for completion of audit in a medium size organization.

Step 2: Auditing Organizational Level Benefits

The second level assessment is to be conducted at the organizational level. This is precisely to identify the contribution of the new culture at the organizational level in terms of customer satisfaction, sales turnover, profits and earnings per share. New figures on these parameters can be compared with previous ones, i.e. figures obtained prior to introduction of new culture. However, in few cases, conduct of audit with references to company financials may not be appropriate unless new organizational culture is in force for a duration of at least three financial years. However, the audit in reference to customer satisfaction can be conducted after a year from the time the new culture is introduced. This audit helps in revealing contribution of the new organizational culture. Audit can also be conducted assessing the flow of work, speed and quality of decision-making and coordination among various departments and status of general organizational climate in the organization.

Step 3: Auditing Employee Level Benefits

The third and the most significant indicator of new culture efficacy is assessing its contribution at the employee level. This helps in assessing whether the new organizational culture is contributing for enhancement of employees' performance and utilizing their potential optimally or not. Data regarding this can be obtained using perceptual surveys, interview, discussions and comparing present performance levels of employees with previous ones.

DRIVER 10: MATURING ORGANIZATIONAL CULTURE

Last decisive action in the long journey of nurturing culture-based performance management is maturing the organizational culture. The first nine drivers contribute in creation of a positive and strong organizational culture. Objective of this last driver is to mature this organizational culture through a series of well-integrated and purposive steps as illustrated below.

Step 1: Revamping Organizational Culture

Results obtained with the help of Driver 9, i.e. the evaluation report must be utilized to make requisite changes for enhancing (i) effectiveness of organizational culture as well as (ii) to remove obstacles noticed at evaluation stage. Organization successful in installing organizational culture, generally will not require making any significant changes. Application of this driver helps to have a relook at the entire plan of organizational culture and implementation strategy. Organizations that require major changes have to move back to Driver 7 (installing mapped organizational culture) and Driver 8 (experiencing new organizational culture) and start a fresh from Driver 7. Organizations that require minor changes can go ahead with maturing organizational culture and need not start afresh from the level of Driver 7. This starting afresh may be frustrating but nurturing culture-based performance management as stated in the beginning of this chapter is full of challenges and success comes only from perseverance.

Step 2: Internalizing Organizational Culture

Critical action in this driver is internalizing strong and positive culture within people and organization. People must feel very natural and gain strength from organizational culture. At the organizational level, organizational culture must shape an organization as a distinct personality. This distinction comes from internalization of organizational culture. Internalization of culture can be achieved through consistent practice of a well-defined/revamped organizational culture for a longer period. This driver emphasizes that organizations must not be lax in the feeling of contentment that great deal of work has been done in this area. No matter how strongly culture may spread, efforts need to continue in order to fortify this culture beyond breaking up. Consistent and religious practice of organizational culture without abandonment of even a decimal of culture strategy can ensure matured organizational culture. Few may have apprehension that internalization or matured culture may itself become a big wall if culture is to be altered in future. But interestingly mature cultures are easiest to alter. Successful application of this driver ensures an organizational culture that is not only strong and positive, but also matured. However, it involves longer gestation period and series of consistent efforts as illustrated here. Organizations should not unduly expect a matured organizational culture within a short time and with few actions.

INTERVENTION 2: CAPITALIZING ON ORGANIZATIONAL CULTURE IN INSTITUTIONALIZATION OF PERFORMANCE MANAGEMENT

Second intervention in the strategy of culture-based performance management is capitalizing on the well-nurtured organizational culture for institutionalization of performance management. All performance management strategies discussed in this book such as reward, career, competency, measurement, team and leadership require the support of organizational culture for their own effectiveness. In fact, one side of each of these strategies encompasses cultural dimension. The how-to-do factor is totally influenced by operating organizational culture. Ultimately, how a strategy is implemented is more important than how it is conceived. Therefore, organizational culture occupies a significant place in execution of performance management. Intervention of deploying organizational culture as a vehicle in institutionalization of performance management is attained through implementation of 10 drivers. Each of these drivers makes it possible to leverage organizational culture in making an organization performance obsessed.

DRIVER 1: USING OVERT CULTURE TO DRIVE PERFORMANCE INSTITUTIONALIZATION

The maiden driver in this intervention is using organizational overt culture such as language, stories, symbols, artifacts, rituals, celebrations to make performance a focal point. Institutionalization of performance management strategies, interventions and drivers is greatly influenced by the kind of overt culture practices prevailing in an organization. Further, overt culture can be used to impress upon and remind employees about the need to excel in performance. For example, celebrating performance achievement religiously in a befitting manner reinforces the importance accorded to performance in organizations. This act of celebrating is an overt culture. Overt culture that is (i) mapped rightly, (ii) installed successfully, (iii) experienced fully and (iv) evaluated to make it mature must be fully leveraged to institutionalize performance by bringing sharp integration between overt culture and performance recognizing mechanism. Overt culture must be availed as a medium for institutionalization of performance management practice. Practice shall be followed here is simple: use well-nurtured overt culture agents such as stories, symbols, artifacts, rituals, celebrations and language to drive performance goals.

DRIVER 2: USING COVERT CULTURE TO DRIVE PERFORMANCE INSTITUTIONALIZATION

Both performance institutionalization and maturing covert culture in organization involve more or less the same process. This process is long drawn, and needs a consistent and integrated approach with perseverance. A medium size organization with three/four business units with employee strength of approximately 2000, takes about five to seven years to

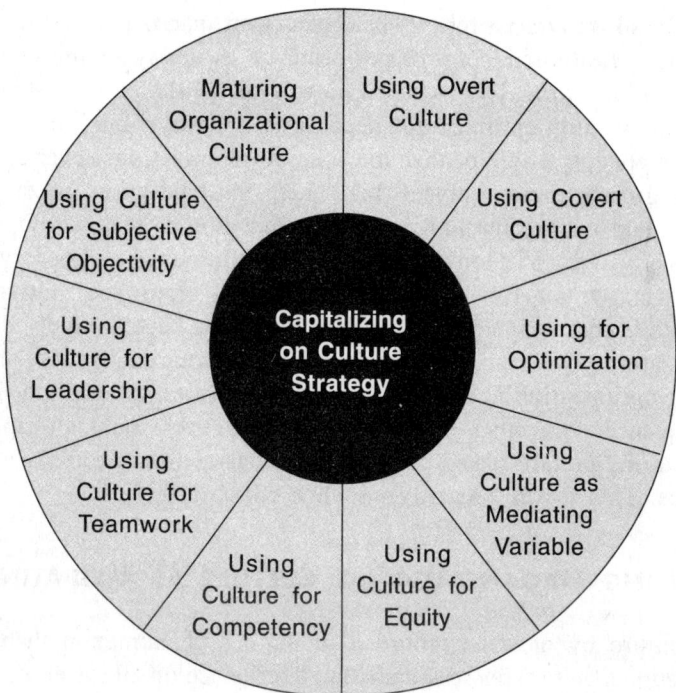

FIGURE 5.3 Drivers of the intervention capitalizing on culture strategy in institutionalization of performance management.

create a mature covert culture. Institutionalization of performance management also similarly involves five to seven years of effort that is well integrated and consistent. Integration here means coordination and strong relationships among various performance management strategies, interventions and drivers. When a covert culture that is positive, strong and mature is in place in organization, the same must be leveraged to institutionalize performance management. Time and effort required in institutionalization of performance management can be minimized when a mature covert culture is cleverly leveraged. Values, beliefs and basic underlying assumptions must be shaped as performance institutionalization agents. Culture-based performance management strategy must be used to build covert culture as a platform for institutionalization. Application of this driver can influence both conceptualization and application of culture in order to understand the task of institutionalization adequately.

DRIVER 3: USING ORGANIZATIONAL CULTURE FOR OPTIMIZATION

Institutionalization of performance management system as an integral part of an organization's life comes from the principle of optimization. There must be (i) a clear balance between potential and performance opportunities, (ii) balance between organizational and employee interests, (iii) balance between task and relationship orientation and (iv) balance between inputs and outputs, so on and so forth. This balance in macro perspective is referred to as optimization. Real institutionalization of performance as a way of life can be derived only from the state of optimization. There can be no rule or regulation or system framework that can ensure or facilitate this optimization because it is so dynamic and complex that none of these can have real control and manage the state of optimization. Several studies conducted on high performing organizations reveal this. There must be an organizational culture that is strong, positive and mature through which optimization is feasible. Optimization brings performance harmony. This harmony makes work, performance and achievement as natural and becomes a window for fulfilment of higher-level employee motives. Strategically, organizational culture that is systematically nurtured must be effectively deployed to reach a state of optimization. This optimization facilitates institutionalization of performance as a reality. State of optimization is nothing but state of institutionalization because each one is a natural consequence of the other. However, this relationship would not happen automatically or merely by nurturing culture-based performance management. It needs a conscious effort and specific focus. This driver prescribes such a conscious effort.

DRIVER 4: USING ORGANIZATIONAL CULTURE AS MEDIATING VARIABLE

Organizational culture by nature is more a mediating phenomenon than an independent variable. Organizational culture possesses unstinted influence on all systems in an organization. Often nature of this organizational culture makes a system work or fail no matter how well that system is crafted. Due to this, few organizations despite having a well-defined and articulated strategy fail to reach the top, while some other even in the absence of any system make it to the top. This is because having a well-defined framework is only one side of the story because the framework itself cannot perform to deliver results. This framework requires catalyzing agents like organizational culture that can provide medium, spirit, contextual relatedness and performance to translate framework into reality. Every strategy, system and plan needs to have full support of organizational culture. Organizational culture that is strong, positive and mature can provide a healthy platform for good system implementation. There must be compatibility between such strategy/system and the operating organizational culture. Application of this driver focuses on this issue, i.e. create system/strategy framework keeping in view the nature of operating organizational culture. Such compatibility gives a fillip in institutionalization of systems/strategy framework. Institutionalization of strategy/ system is nothing but institutionalization of performance management system.

DRIVER 5: USING ORGANIZATIONAL CULTURE TO GROUND EQUITABLE REWARD

There must be a positive and direct relationship between reward-based performance management strategy and culture-based performance management strategy for effective institutionalization of performance management practice. Successful application of reward strategy is largely the outcome of contributory role of organizational culture. In a considerable number of cases, rewards tend to create more frustrations and loss of equity than sense of accomplishment due to weak and fragmented organizational culture. This fragmentation in culture negatively affects the equilibrium of employee's perception. This lopsided perception results in every reward being perceived not a reward but somebody's generosity. Organizational culture that is nurtured as positive, strong and mature must be effectively used in conceptualization and implementation of reward strategy. Presence of a mature culture can provide opportunity for conceiving a reward as equitable and performance centric. A perfect reward system can be possible only when organizational culture is consciously capitalized to create equity. Institutionalization of performance management is not possible unless equity is ensured. Organizational culture can be a vehicle for institutionalization of performance through the route of equity in reward that again is dependent upon a positive relationship between reward and culture strategies.

DRIVER 6: USING ORGANIZATIONAL CULTURE TO CREATE COMPETENCY-BASED CAREERS

Performance excellence is a product of competencies. Competency-based performance management strategy makes this aspect abundantly clear. Institutionalization of performance excellence can be attained only through making competency, career and culture as well-coordinated and integrated strategies. Competency-based careers in the place of seniority/hierarchical/loyal and bureaucratic system often encounter insurmountable obstacles due to their non-acceptance by a few or more employees. These employees resist competency-based careers as they see such a system devoid of natural justice and mechanisms of arbitrary power. Organizational culture has the capacity to reverse this trend through a value and belief system that can create trust and respect for such competency-based career system. Unless, competency-based careers are pursued, it may not be possible to institutionalize performance management successfully. This driver prescribes that all three performance management strategies such as career, competency and culture must work together with common philosophy and objectives running through them. Institutionalization can take place automatically (i) when this integration is pursued systematically and (ii) competency-based careers are cultivated in an organizational culture context in which competency is considered as premium. Organizational culture must be used to create competency-based career environment before they are fully injected into the system.

DRIVER 7: USING ORGANIZATIONAL CULTURE TO INSTITUTIONALIZE TEAMWORK

Teamwork and culture strategies are dependent upon each other for their effectiveness. Organizational culture can be transformed into a mature stage with the help of teamwork and matured state of teamwork can be acquired only when organizational culture is contributory. Institutionalization of performance management is an easier task if culture and teamwork applications are tightly woven together. Teamwork is prime medium in shaping positive, strong and mature organizational culture through the means of mapping, installing, experiencing and evaluating. Teamwork can be made as perfect strategy when organizational culture completely supports it. Organization must specially focus on making culture and teamwork as mutually complimentary. Institutionalization of performance management is just the consequence of perfect teamwork driven by matured organizational culture.

DRIVER 8: USING ORGANIZATIONAL CULTURE TO DEVELOP LEADERSHIP

Organizational culture occupies a prominent role in leadership development efforts and leadership leads to the shaping up of organizational culture. It is difficult to know which starts first and exerts first influence. Both are dependable on each other. Organizational culture primarily contributes towards creating a culture centric leadership. Organizational culture contributes towards building leadership that is in conformity with deep-rooted organizational culture. In few instances such a matching may not happen, particularly when leadership is soured from outside. This adversely affects the institutionalization process of performance management due to the likelihood of conflict between leadership and operating organizational culture. This driver prescribes that an organization must focus on building culture centric leadership. Performance management can be successfully institutionalized through the leadership that is culture centric.

DRIVER 9: USING ORGANIZATIONAL CULTURE TO CREATE OBJECTIVITY IN SUBJECTIVITY

Despite well-articulated and quantifiable measures, parameters and barometers of performance, there still exists subjectivity factor as highlighted in the measurement-based performance management strategy. Reason for this is obvious. Human being cannot be controlled with measurable techniques all the time because performance is subject to many things. Measurement can ensure performance to a limit. Perfection and breakthroughs can come only through highly subjective observations and decisions. Many organizations and managers put their best efforts to create measures for performance because it is strongly believed that something that is not measurable is not manageable. This may be true but only partially. There is also a perception that subjectivity is the other side of arbitrariness. Subjectivity must be curbed in order to dispel arbitrariness. It is a jigsaw puzzle what to do in such a situation. Leaving performance completely to measurement can result in serious problems in institutionalization of performance management. In such a scenario, measurement becomes an end in itself and performance as incidental. Measurement-based performance must be integrated with emotional and subjective performance behaviour. Challenge here is how to ensure that this subjective and emotional behaviour is used judiciously and in the interest of the organization. There can be no tailor-made measurement formula for this. Organizational culture can ensure that people use subjective work behaviour for positive purposes through the value and belief system. An employee himself/herself becomes self-controller in the subjective work behaviour and uses only for good when organizational culture expects such a behaviour. Essence of this driver is that organizational culture must be used as a guide in subjective performance. This culture-subjective work behaviour relationship institutionalizes performance management in a salutary mode.

DRIVER 10: INSTITUTIONALIZATION OF PERFORMANCE THROUGH INTERNALIZATION

Institutionalization of performance management becomes a reality when it is internalized among employees. Institutionalization occurs when policies, processes and practices of an organization are internalized with working life of people. No audit, monitoring mechanism or incentive can make people adhere strictly to a practice except for the culture. Organizational culture must be effectively utilized to internalize performance philosophy among employees so that it leads to institutionalization of the same. This can be achieved through two prime means: Firstly, practicing top down approach implying that all senior managers must implement performance systems starting with them cascading down to lower levels. This helps spreading the system on a voluntary basis. Such a voluntary basis is essential for the institutionalization effort. Secondly, the organizational culture must be utilized by exposing all employees to performance system as a way of work in organization through formal and informal ways.

SUMMARY

This chapter unfolds the strategy of culture-based performance management in a step-by-step framework that enables (i) organizations to nurture performance driven organizational culture with the application of 10 most purposeful drivers and (ii) institutionalize performance management as a way of organizational functioning with the help of another set of 10 drivers. First part of the chapter discusses what is culture and what it is not in the context of performance management. A positive, strong and matured culture is a significant player in performance management because it can contribute to the creation of:

  (i) Positive work environment
 (ii) Optimization of resources
(iii) Interdisciplinary effectiveness
 (iv) Job satisfaction
  (v) Execution excellence
 (vi) Effective decision-making
(vii) Innovativeness
(viii) Organizational citizenship behaviour
 (ix) Performance maximization
  (x) Internalization of performance values.

Theoretical foundations of culture are captured in part three. A few important theories that have been briefly covered include:

  (i) Schein's three levels of culture
 (ii) Egan's overt and covert culture
(iii) Handy's four types of culture
 (iv) Killman, Saxton and Serpa's determinants of culture

 (v) Johnson's culture web
 (vi) Handy's culture framework
 (vii) Martin's three perspectives on culture
 (viii) Peter's and Waterman eight culture characteristics of excellent organizations
 (ix) Ouchi's culture analysis
 (x) Hofstede's internal culture perspective
 (xi) Furnham and Gunter's twelve types of corporate culture.

Each one of these theories have valuable lessons for building a culture-based performance management strategy such as:

 (i) Culture is determinant of organizational functioning as well as susceptible to organizational context
 (ii) Culture is intangibly tangible
 (iii) Culture is both: peripheral and deep rooted
 (iv) Culture is big sum
 (v) Culture is multiple
 (vi) Culture has definite characteristics
 (vii) Culture has cross perspectives
 (viii) Culture as determinant of business behaviour
 (ix) Culture can be strong or weak
 (x) Culture can be integrative and fragmented.

Culture-based performance management strategy encompasses two vital interventions. First intervention is discussed in part four of the chapter. Objective of the first intervention is to nurture culture-based performance management through the application of 10 drivers. These are:

 (i) Understanding organization
 (ii) Deriving insights for culture management
 (iii) Mapping desirable organizational culture
 (iv) Analyzing existing organizational culture
 (v) Identifying gaps and preparing action plans
 (vi) Preparing organization for culture shock
 (vii) Installing mapped desirable organizational culture
 (viii) Experiencing new culture
 (ix) Evaluating efficacy of new culture
 (x) Maturing organizational culture.

Second intervention of capitalizing on organizational culture for institutionalization of performance management is discussed in part five of the chapter. This intervention also comprises of 10 drivers application of which can result in performance management institutionalization. These drivers are:

 (i) Using overt culture in institutionalization of performance management
 (ii) Using covert culture in institutionalization of performance management
 (iii) Using organizational culture to attain optimization

(iv) Using organizational culture as mediating variable in institutionalization
 (v) Using organizational culture to ground equitable reward
 (vi) Using organizational culture to create competency-based careers
 (vii) Using organizational culture to institutionalize teamwork
(viii) Using organizational culture to nurture culture centric leadership
 (ix) Using organizational culture to create objectivity in subjectivity
 (x) Using organizational culture for performance internalization.

KEY WORDS

Following are the key words discussed in this chapter:

- Culture
- Shared assumptions
- Symbols and artifacts
- Strong and positive culture
- Work environment
- Optimization
- Mapping culture
- Culture shock
- Culture centric leadership

- Climate
- Values and beliefs
- Overt and covert culture
- Integrative and fragmented culture
- Internalization
- Cultural web
- Matured culture
- Culture as mediating variable
- Objectivity in subjectivity

DISCUSSION QUESTIONS

1. What is culture and what is it not in the context of performance management?

2. Culture as determinant of organizational behaviour vs. organizational behaviour as determinant of culture: Discuss the relationship.

3. What is the significance of culture in performance management?

4. Discuss important theories in culture.

5. What is overt and covert culture? Which is difficult to nurture between the two and why?

6. Describe the process involved in nurturing culture-based performance management.

7. Can culture be used as a vehicle in institutionalization of performance management. If yes, discuss how it can be done and if no, substantiate with supporting factors.

8. How can organizational culture be mapped? Discuss its salient features.

9. A positive, strong and matured organizational culture can enhance performance of employees and organizations to peak. How far is this statement correct?

10. How can culture theories help in understanding and managing culture in organizations?

CASE STUDIES

1. Chemtek Incorporation is a public limited company engaged in manufacturing and marketing of industrial chemicals. Chemtek has recently taken over two petrochemical companies namely, Hindustan Petrochemicals owned by Government of Maharashtra and Sindhwani Petrochemicals, a private sector company owned by Sindhwani family. On takeover Chemtek merged both these companies and named it as Chemtek Petrochemicals (India) Ltd. Though a year has passed since the merger, both the erstwhile units continued to work in their same styles as they used to. There is no uniformity in the culture. Erstwhile Hindustan Petrochemicals unit is very bureaucratic, formal and powers are decentralized. Seniority is given consideration in compensation and career-related matters. Employees are formal and reporting system is clear. In contrast, erstwhile Sindhwani company is highly centralized, informal and merit is given more importance in career-related issues. These differences have reflected in working of these units as well as the work behaviour of employees. Chemtek top management has decided to cultivate an organizational culture that is positive, strong, mature and uniform in both the units. The objective is to integrate both these units as one culturally. You are appointed as Manager (Culture Development-Performance Management) with mandate to realize this ambition of top management. Discuss what strategy, interventions and drivers would you adapt to progress on this.

2. Hotel Asia International, a five star hotel located in a metro city of India has a turnover of little over 100 crores with 420 rooms, five restaurants, six conference halls, golf club and other paraphernalia. The hotel is owned by a Rajasthan marwari business family. Currently, occupancy rate of the hotel is above 75 per cent, which a is remarkable achievement for any hotel. Financials of the hotel are sound with last financial year profit after tax standing at eighteen crore rupees. The hotel is known for its progressive human resource policies. Organizational culture is characterized by openness, commitment, risk taking, respect for individual and encourages employees to optimize their potential. Top management of the hotel takes keen interest in welfare, career growth and well being of employees. As a result, employee turnover of the hotel is far below than of average turnover of the hotel industry. Organizational culture across all departments in the hotel is uniform and employees take pride in working in such an environment. Management of the hotel has decided to capitalize on this rich organizational culture in institutionalization of performance of employees as a way of life. Discuss in your view what should the management of this hotel do to achieve this target of performance management institutionalization. How can a salutary organizational culture existing in the organization be of help in this process.

SUGGESTED READING

Deal, T.E. and A.A. Kennedy (1982). *Corporate Culture: The Rites and Rituals of Corporate Life*. Massachusetts: Addison-Wesley.

Furnham, A. and B. Gunter (1993). "Corporate Culture: Diagnosis and Change." In C.L. Cooper and I.T. Robertson (Eds.), *International Review of Industrial and Organizational Psychology*. Chichester: John Wiley.

Handy, Charles (1989). *The Age of Unreason*. London: Hutchinson.

Handy, Charles (1993). *Understanding Organizations*. Harmondsworth: Penguin.

Hofstede, Geert (1980). *Culture's Consequences: International Differences in Work-related Values*. Beverly Hills: Sage.

Johnson, G. (1982). "Managing Strategic Change—Strategy, Culture and Actions." *Long Range Planning*, **25**(1), p.31.

Killman, R.H., M.J. Saxton and R. Serpa (1985). *Gaining Control of the Corporate Culture*. San Francisco: Jossey-Bass.

Martin, J. (1992). *Cultures and Organizations: Three Perspectives*. Oxford: Oxford University Press.

Ouchi, William (1981). *Theory Z*. Massachusetts: Addison-Wesley.

Peters, T.J. and Robert Waterman (1982). *In Search of Excellence: Lessons from America's Best Run Companies*. New York: Harper & Row.

Schein, Edgar (1985). *Organizational Culture and Leadership*. San Francisco: Jossey-Bass.

Strategies
Interventions
Drivers

PERFORMANCE MANAGEMENT

Chapter Six

STRATEGY 5: MEASUREMENT-BASED PERFORMANCE MANAGEMENT

Measurement-based performance management proves that human element can be measured with accuracy and objectivity. There is a great myth surrounding human resource management that its contribution to business and effectiveness cannot be measured. This misplaced belief is squarely responsible for the sliding significance of human resource management in organizations. This is a single influential factor that is responsible for causing human resource managers to receive second grade treatment in organizations. Argument of managers who say human resource effectiveness cannot be measured is that (i) it is unethical to subject human talent and emotions to numerical assessment, (ii) management of human resource/performance is something very complex, intricate, intangible, (iii) there are too many variables that affect performance of performance management, (iv) measurement of performance creates more problems than it solves and attracts more criticism than brings credibility, (v) accuracy can never be attained in performance measurement because of the role environment plays and (vi) business-related indicators cannot be adapted for measurement of human resource performance, so on and so forth. This argument is not without its logic, but at best such argument can be used as an excuse for not doing or inability to apply measurement technique to performance management. As long as this gap between line managers and human resource/performance managers exists, performance management can never become an integral part of the organization. This gap can be seen in the language these two sets of managers use: line managers talk in the language of market capitalization: profits, sales, turnover, customers, costs, and performance/human resource managers talk in the language of feelings, emotions and employee job satisfaction.

Unless an activity is measurable, it is not manageable. No meaning can ever be achieved with any activity that is not manageable. Human management, especially performance management cannot be left to be managed under its own philosophy. It is fundamental for any function that includes performance management that it must be subordinate to the organizational vision, mission and objectives. Performance management must be run as an inseparable part of organizational operations. Adaptation of measurement philosophy is imperative not only for effectiveness of performance management as a strategy, but also for its survival. Unless, a function proves beyond doubt the kind of contribution it makes to the business, no budgetary support and appreciation to such function can be expected. An objective and scientific measurement-based performance management enhances the performance of employees and organizations. Measurement strategy has the capability to bring tangibility to other performance strategies discussed in this book. It is also an equally powerful fact that developing measures and applying them and analyzing them is an immensely complex task. This complexity scared many managers in the past to do away with measurement albeit they wish for it. This chapter is an attempt to make measurement of employees' performance and application of measurement philosophy as less complex as possible and make measurement as a simple common sense activity.

Similar to other chapters discussed in this book, this chapter too is organized into five parts to facilitate easy grasp and comprehension. First part of the chapter deals with what is measurement and what it is not in the context of performance management. The significance of measurement-based performance management is discussed in the second part, while a few concepts and practices that have implications for measurement-based performance management are presented in part three. Strategy of measurement-based performance management comprises two interventions. First intervention, i.e. nurturing measurement-based performance management is illustrated in part four and the second intervention namely, using measurement management in institutionalization of performance management is illustrated in part five.

MEASUREMENT-BASED PERFORMANCE MANAGEMENT

Measurement has a comprehensive meaning in the context of performance management. Measurement is defined as *a set of tools employed to establish the efficacy, utility and contribution of performance management in the enhancement of organizational and employees performance and also a vehicle that set standards of performance.* Chief characteristics of measurement-based performance management are:

1. It is comprehensive since it deploys a set of tools.
2. It is used to set standards/parameters/benchmarks for performance of employees.
3. It is used as a technique to present value addition role of performance management.
4. It is a technique that ensures and brings the factor of tangibility in performance management practice.
5. Measurement brings meaning and manageability in performance management activities.

WHAT IS NOT MEASUREMENT

Measurement in performance management is often understood as synonymous to defining key result areas and performance appraisals and use of 360-degree feedback system. As opposed to this misconception, measurement-based performance management is much more than all these as this chapter unfolds. Further, measurement management is also understood as simply using few statistical tools and use of numbers. This is a limited fact because measurement-based performance management uses subjective measures with equal frequency and proficiency to that of numbers. Measurement management is much more than simply illustrating contribution of performance management practice to the business progress of organization in terms of financial indicators. Measurement-based performance management does not represent:

1. A passion less statistical structure of employees performance.
2. Measurement is not simply financially oriented but multi-dimensional that reckon process, learning and other effectiveness targets and goals.
3. Measurement is not simply a tool that is used to present a positive picture of performance management for gaining appreciation of internal and external organizational forces.
4. Measurement is not unifocal in its approach such as focus on results and evaluation for mere identifying centre of accountability for poor performance.
5. Measurement is not a technique used to discard some activities and people but centres on optimization.

SIGNIFICANCE OF MEASUREMENT IN PERFORMANCE MANAGEMENT

Measurement is vital for establishing not only efficacy of performance management as an art and science of organizational management, but also as a comprehensive strategy that brings credibility. Measurement guides people and organization through the most effective ways in bringing best out of them. There is a widespread awareness and realization that individually perceived judgements and evaluations can cause organizational ineffectiveness.

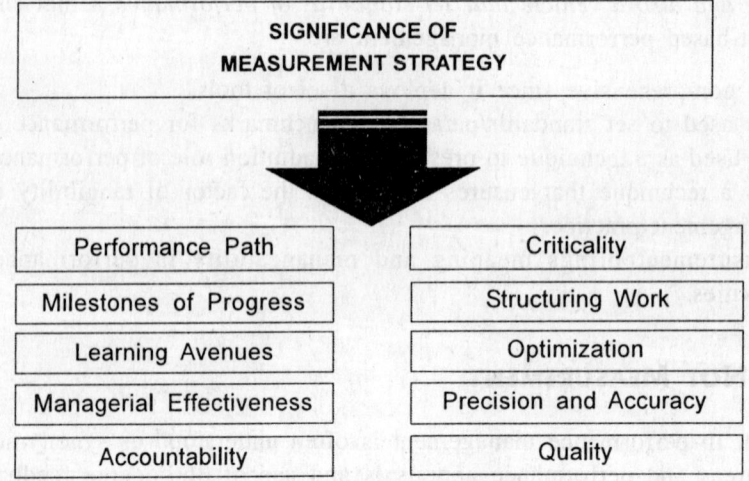

FIGURE 6.1　Significance of measurement-based performance management strategy.

Today's organizations realized the need to optimize resources, especially human resource and their performance with high precision. In a competitive environment where everything can be imitated and replicated, the distinction of non-imitable act can be created only through enhancing human performance. For this, exact understanding is a prerequisite. This prerequisite can be fulfilled only through the adaptation of measurement principles. Measurement has a special place in the overall framework and practice of performance management. Significance of measurement can be seen in the following aspects:

Measurement Provides Path of Performance

The biggest problem for managers as well as employees is what, how, where, when and why to perform. Traditionally, managers make their work and also their employees' so routine and in a conformist approach without asking answers for these questions. When answers for these questions are not explored and understood, employees do not know the basic premise of their work. Therefore, they cannot optimize their own potential. Managers also follow different paths to assess and guide performance of employees. This adds confusion and contributes for non-standardization in performance method of employees. Measurement possesses the capability to resolve this problem. Measurement by its sheer approach sets and clearly defines the path of performance for each employee.

Measurement Provides Milestones

Functions, tasks and activities especially in the new economy organizations, i.e. research and knowledge-based organizations and where an organizational success is dependent upon strength of innovation are complex, intricate and intangible. It becomes difficult for an organization to assess the real progress. This inability to identify progress can contribute in investing on value free activities and neglecting on value potential tasks. A few employees can take undue advantage under the disguise of non-accessibility of their work. Organization must know the real progress being made through each of the activities through identification of reliable milestones. Measurement management can provide such milestones for all functions, tasks and activities through its approach of backwards calculation. Measurement management prescribes that end outcome for any activity must be predefined and major stages should be identified in attaining such outcome. These major stages become milestones for performance of employees.

Measurement Provides Avenues for Learning

Measurement by virtue of its deep analysis and learning orientation suggests the kind of learning required in an organization in order to maximize performance of employees. Learning is imperative for enhancing performance of employees. Learning occurs when understanding of work and areas of performance are sharp. Measurement precisely provides for identifying learning elements in performance management. In addition, the indicators of measurement also provide the extent of learning existing in organizations. Measurement helps in twin aspects of identifying learning requirements and also enabling to understand the prevailing degree of learning.

Measurement Makes Management Effective

Effective management is cardinal to performance management. This effectiveness can be obtained only when management knows how to guide, motivate and monitor the progress of performance. Developing measures is fundamental for measurement management. These measures help management with their role as indicators of performance. Management knows where and when to monitor the progress and where special attention is required to be paid. Often managers become ineffective due to lack of or ignorance regarding real indicators of performance. Significance of measurement to management lies in providing the real indicators of performance.

Measurement Identifies Accountability

Accurately identifying the centre of accountability particularly in the generation of interdependent tasks and teamwork is certainly a difficult task. Unless the point of accountability is identified and defined, no meaningful monitoring and improvement can be attained. Measurement management by nature itself breaks any function into several tasks and activities and also identifies the accountability centre. Identification and definition of accountability greatly helps performance management in attaining its sole objective of maximizing performance through right accountability.

Measurement Identifies Criticality

In execution of any activity, especially the bigger ones, there will be areas where performing them is much easier in comparison to others on which performance is really challenging. There are instances where organizations simply adopt quantity principle to monitor and guide performance. This simple method can cause progress assessment to fail in detecting the real progress. The reason for this is simple. For example, manufacturing of one spare part takes equal amount of time and labour as that of other nine spare parts in an automobile component. In this case, simply monitoring by number misleads the management. Quality aspect is equally important in this context. Measurement when applied effectively identifies the areas of criticality that require special effort and resource in order to be completed/ executed. This ability of identifying critical areas undoubtedly helps in maximizing performance.

Measurement Provides Structure to the Work

Employees tend to give high performance and also perceive work as meaningful when they have the opportunity to visualize the whole assignment. It makes employees at ease when they have a clear understanding of what they will be doing at present and in immediate future. Also, their confidence gets enhanced when they are quite clear about why and what they are doing. This precisely implies that structure to the work must be created with the involvement of employees. Measurement in order to measure the performance contributes for crafting an efficient work structure. This work structure is a fertile source for stimulating great performance.

Measurement Helps in Optimization

Organizations can aspire for performance excellence only when they can optimize the resources. Human resource and their performance have a lion share in this act of optimization. Due to lack of this, few organizations often encounter shortage of skills, whereas others are saddled with surplus manpower. This surplus and shortage syndrome occurs when performance management is not optimized. Optimization certainly calls for measurement and assessment of real source requirement at various stages of organizational progress. Therefore, measurement can perform a catalytic role in enabling an organization to achieve the depth of optimization and consequently, great performance.

Measurement Provides for Objectivity, Precision and Accuracy

Fineness of management is largely dependent upon its ability or its usage as an instrument of objectivity, precision and accuracy. Organizations employ managers and practice the principles of management with an expectation of achieving precision in operations. Management per se cannot ensure this precision. This requires active association of measurement discipline. Measurement can ensure this objectivity, precision and accuracy through a combination of numerical and emotional aspects with judicious blend. These aspects are transformed into indices and measures that can be effectively deployed for a range of purposes in order to ensure this objectivity.

Measurement Enhances Quality

Indicator for superior performance is undoubtedly the quality of performance. Measurement is regarded as a reliable instrument in enhancing quality. This trend can be seen in any total quality management initiative. Statistical quality control has a significant role in quality management. Reason for this is that measurement by its sheer strength of objectivity, precision and scientific planning eliminates ineffectiveness and wastage. This approach of eliminating ineffectiveness particularly is very important for attaining smart performance in organizations. Measurement approach forms one of the foundations of performance excellence.

THEORETICAL FOUNDATIONS OF MEASUREMENT-BASED PERFORMANCE MANAGEMENT

Measurement-based performance management is yet to acquire a systematic theoretical body of knowledge of its own. Most of the methods, techniques and tools employed in human resource performance measurement management are borrowed from other disciplines like Social Research Methodology, Psychometrics, Generic Statistical Tools and of course, the self-adequate performance measurement techniques at the organizational level such as balanced scorecard, SMART, performance management questionnaire. Apart from these, there are also a few measurement-based human performance systems like human capital accounting, return on investment techniques that have relevance for measurement-based performance management. A few such relevant concepts and techniques are briefly discussed here:

FUNDAMENTALS OF RESEARCH METHODOLOGY AND STATISTICAL TOOLS

Fundamentals of research methodology like problem formulation, framing research questions, design of questionnaires, case study schedules, sampling techniques, reliability, validity testing, scaling methods and statistical tools like chi-square, partial correlation, analysis of variance, multi-variate analysis, regression, form basic theory for measurement management. Methodological books like *Research Methods in Social Science* by Fred Kerlinger can be significantly useful in this context.

KAPLAN AND NORTON'S BALANCED SCORECARD

Robert Kaplan and David Norton developed a balanced measurement approach called Balanced Scorecard in 1992 and it is considered one of the most popular and authentic techniques in monitoring, appraising and facilitating performance progress of an organization. In essence, balanced scorecard offers a combination of balanced measures in four areas. These are:

- Learning and growth perspective: This refers to employee training and corporate cultural attitudes related to both individual and corporate self-improvement.
- Business process perspective: This metric represents how well business is running and whether products and services conform to customer requirement.
- Customer perspective: This indicates the level of customer satisfaction having serious implications for business.
- Financial perspective: This metrics on one hand includes traditional finance data and critical financial data such as risk assessment and cost benefit on the other hand.

Balanced scorecard has brought an impressive attention to human element in the overall organizational performance index in the form of learning and growth perspective measures.

CROSS AND LYNCH'S STRATEGIC MEASUREMENT ANALYSIS AND REPORTING TECHNIQUES (SMART)

This is a comprehensive measurement technique developed by K.F. Cross and R.L. Lynch for measurement of an organization's performance. This is also known as SMART Pyramid. Special feature of this measurement system is that it emphasizes both internal and externally focused measures of performance. Human resource performance measurement is accorded significant place in the overall measurement pyramid.

DIXON, NANNI AND VOLLMANN'S PERFORMANCE MANAGEMENT QUESTIONNAIRE

Credit for developing an integrated and well spread questionnaire for measurement of performance goes to J.R. Dixon, A.J. Nanni and J.E. Vollman. This questionnaire is widely used measuring operations in world-class companies. A variety of measurement dimensions and items used in the questionnaire provide a practical perspective for measurement management.

MASKELL'S PERFORMANCE MEASUREMENT FOR MANUFACTURING

B. Maskell has developed a measurement framework suitable to manufacturing organizations. This framework consists of seven principles of performance measurement which have relevance to human performance measurement as well. These are:

- Measures should be directly related to the firm's manufacturing strategy.
- Non-financial measures should be adopted.
- One measure is not suitable to all departments/sites.
- Measures change with circumstances.
- Measures should be simple.
- Measures should provide fast feedback.
- Measures should be designed to stimulate continuous improvement rather than simply monitor performance.

GLOBERSON'S PERFORMANCE CRITERION SYSTEM

S. Globerson provides a detailed perspective of issues covered in designing a performance measurement system and approaches for design of performance measures. He prescribes a three tier criteria for designing a performance measurement system. These are:

- Performance criteria should be chosen from the company's objectives.
- Performance criteria must make possible the comparison of organizations that are in the same business.
- Purpose of each performance criteria must be clear.

Globerson's performance criterion helps in designing a human resource performance measurement substantially.

NEELY, GREGORY AND PLATTS' CAMBRIDGE PERFORMANCE MEASUREMENT DESIGN SYSTEM

Framework of Cambridge performance measurement design system prescribes the following as critical issues in measurement:

- What are the objectives of our business?
- What is our current strategy?
- Can current strategy achieve our objectives?
- Navigating towards our business objectives.
- Install an ongoing process of strategy making.
- Agreeing on performance measures for our business objectives.
- Signing off top level performance measures.
- Embedding top level performance measures.
- Identifying drivers of performance.
- Deciding key drivers of performance.

- Agreeing performance measures for key drivers.
- Signing off performance measures for key drivers.
- Embedding performance measures for key drivers.

These issues can be drafted as guidelines for developing an organization specific measurement-based performance management system.

ENZ'S HUMAN CAPITAL ACCOUNTING

Jack Fitz Enz has developed an enterprise level human metrics that enables gauging human costs and productivity at three levels. These are:

- *Organizational level:* This refers to human resource contribution to corporate goals.
- *Functional level:* This refers to impact on process improvement.
- *Human Resource Management value:* This intends to measure the value added by the human resource management function in an organization.

In order to make measurement and find out the impact of human capital, Enz suggests the following four steps:

- Perform through situation analysis.
- Determine a plan of action.
- Measure impact.
- Measure value.

Enz's human capital accounting system is not only a valuable basis for measurement-based performance management, but also an authentic source.

LESSONS OF MEASUREMENT TECHNIQUES

The above discussed measurement concepts/models/techniques offer some valuable lessons that having implications for developing measurement-based performance management. These are:

Balanced Measurement

Measurement frameworks like Balanced Scorecard and SMART especially emphasize the need to adopt a balanced approach in choosing the dimensions and metrics in a balanced way. This implies measuring the impact of human resource cannot be limited to its own area of functioning, but should be measured through the canons of customer satisfaction, financial indicators and process improvement. Measures also must include internal factors as well as external factors.

Approaches of Measurement Design

All these concepts and works suggest a similar approach for design of measurement system.

They suggest two criteria: firstly, to identify the critical factors affecting performance and secondly, translating these critical factors into measures for assessing the performance.

Measurement must be Aligned with Strategy

These concepts also highlight the importance and need to align the measurement system with the overall strategy and objectives of the organization. This implies that the measurement system should not be a standalone or an isolated activity, rather it must draw its meaning from the overall organizational goal.

Measurement as Means for Growth

Measurement exercise should have dual objectives. It should enable an organization to have a clear picture of its status. Secondly, it must enable an organization to redefine its strategy if required based on the measurement results and consequently, facilitate growth.

Balancing of Qualitative and Quantitative Methods

Measurement works also suggest that an ideal measurement system should consider both qualitative and quantitative methods for data collection and analysis. Combination of both can yield deep insights into organizational functioning. This also facilitates obtaining an exact picture as both these methods are complementary to each other.

Metrics must be Simple and Easy to Follow

There is a widespread agreement among measurement researchers that the metrics used in measurement must be clear, simple and easy to follow. They insist that any complexity in metrics can cause loss of the robust picture of reality.

Measurement must have Clear Framework

Unlike some of the activities, measurement needs to be pursued in a highly systematic and evolutionary manner. Any activity must start and end with a clear linkage with related activity. No deviation should be committed in the midway of measurement progress. Consistency and reliability are important features. Measurement must be first developed on paper, to be tested and established before the same is adopted.

Human Performance can be Measured

All the above mentioned performance measurement techniques though focusing at enterprise level, agree that human element can be measured and includes performance of human resource and contribution of human resource function as important dimensions of measurement. Framework like human capital accounting conclusively proves that human capital can be measured and its impact on the bottom line of an organization can be gauzed with accuracy.

MEASUREMENT-BASED PERFORMANCE MANAGEMENT STRATEGY, INTERVENTIONS AND DRIVERS

Strategy of measurement-based performance management is a holistic approach that guides organizations in assessing the progress made on several dimensions of organizational effectiveness and this process also suggests the most optimal ways of performing an activity. As the forthcoming contents unfold, measurement-based performance management is built on not a single principle of measurement such as statistical control and measurement but in a balanced perspective that reckons a wide range of approaches. This strategy consists of two interventions as indicated here:

1. *Nurturing measurement-based performance management:* Core objective of this intervention is enabling organizations to adopt an integrated and balanced measurement system with a view to maximize the performance of employees and organization. As a part of this intervention, an organization is encouraged to design and implement organization specific performance measurement techniques. This is achieved by application of 10 drivers with each one of them adding significant value to the organizational efforts. An organization can sport an objective and full-fledged measurement culture once execution of all these drivers is completed successfully.

2. *Capitalizing on measurement management in institutionalization of performance management:* This is the second intervention of the measurement-based performance management strategy. Purpose of this intervention is to encourage and guide organizations to capitalize on the strong measurement system that operates in organization as a result of successful implementation of first intervention. A combination of 10 drivers pushes the organization to extend the principles and practices of measurement strategy to other performance management strategies prevailing in the organization. This intervention also drives organization to ensure the integration of measurement strategy with other performance management strategies in order to leverage on each other's competence.

Following discussion provides greater details and text about these twin interventions.

INTERVENTION 1: NURTURING MEASUREMENT-BASED PERFORMANCE MANAGEMENT

As discussed earlier, the nurturing intervention consists of 10 drivers. Each one of them significantly contributes to organizations making progress in adaptation of measurement approach. All these drivers deliver tangible results at the end their application exercise. This intervention through enhancing organizational diagnostic and development capabilities in an objective, measurable and transparent manner contributes for achieving performance excellence. It is suggested that an organization that chooses to go through this intervention must be prepared to implement all the drivers for obtaining the real impact. Implementing a few drivers and neglecting others can dilute the process of measurement. It is holistic philosophy and emphasizes on balanced approach to measurement. Also, an organization must have and

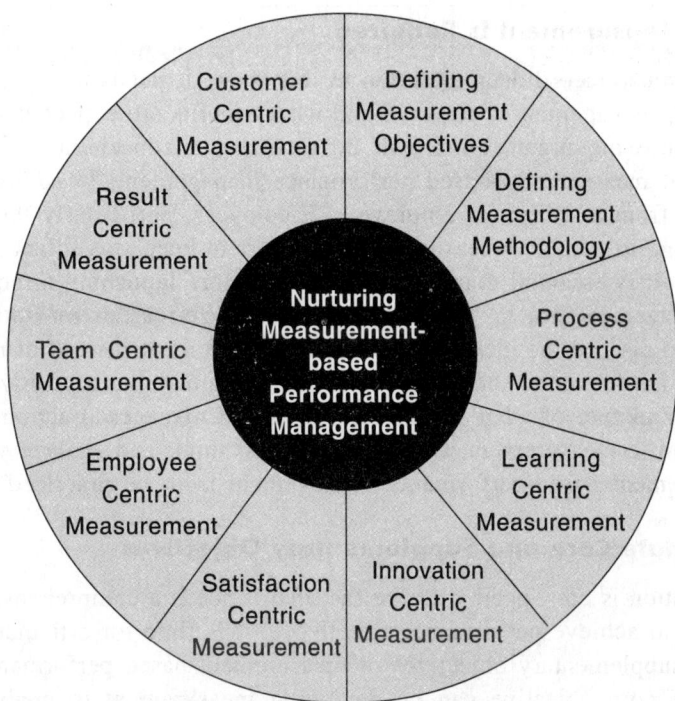

FIGURE 6.2   Drivers of the intervention nurturing measurement-based performance management.

demonstrate total commitment for grounding the measurement system. Commitment assumes special importance in the case of measurement management because this is a tough strategy that invokes high complexity in thinking patterns. After all it is an attempt to measure the soft performances of employees through some of the hardest measures.

DRIVER 1: DEFINING PERFORMANCE MEASUREMENT OBJECTIVES

First driver leads organizations through the setting of organization specific and performance centric measurement strategy objectives. Actions that are to be taken as a part of this driver are vital because quality of performance measurement strategy depends upon how well and professionally the objectives are set and how clearly they are articulated. Statement of performance measurement objectives also serve as a cardinal document that is drawn as a reference centre for clarifying any ambiguity and to take a leap in an uncertain position. In a tautological sense, the objective of this driver is facilitating organizations to have a statement of performance measurement objectives. Organizations require to take series of steps/actions that help in formulating these objectives. Such actions need to suit the organization's internal and external environment. Following are few model suggestive steps that provide an idea of how to go about implementing this driver in reality.

Step 1: Why Measurement is Required

An organization must accord deep attention to this issue. It needs to be reasoned out as to why measurement management is required and what benefits are expected. This justification is essential because the organization will be incurring a substantial cost on account of implementation of measurement-based performance management. In addition, there can be strong resistance from a section of employees. Employees, particularly those not in favour of this system, tend to perceive measurement as a ploy to keep surveillance over their work and performance. It is essential that an organization before launching a measurement-based performance management strategy must objectively analyze reasons for opting for the same. Often it is wise to discord the idea in the beginning stage itself instead of realizing midway that something is not feasible. Analyzing in the beginning also has a positive value addition. It presents a clear picture of what resources, efforts and managerial actions are required to achieve the scientific measurement. Organization must think and analyze what, when, why and how measurement based-performance management is to be practiced.

Step 2: Articulate Core and Supplementary Objectives

Once an organization is convinced with the fact that it needs a comprehensive measurement strategy in order to achieve performance excellence, it is time for articulating what should be the core and supplementary objectives of measurement-based performance management. For example, the core objective can be deploying measurement to enable employees to gauge and enhance their performance levels through the act of optimization. Also, enabling organization to attain effectiveness in all its spheres of performance management practice. Supplementary objectives can be to provide meaning to the employees' work and allocate appropriate resources and provide a learning and growth-oriented environment.

Objectives also must specify the outcomes at employee and organizational levels. For instance, the outcome at employees level can be to enrich and accomplish professional life and innovation, and customer satisfaction can be the organizational level outcome. These outcomes vary from organization to organization depending upon their vision, mission and corporate objectives. It is of utmost importance that objectives of measurement-based performance management should not only be in agreement with organizational objectives, but should also have absolute coherence and consistency with performance management strategies presented in this book. The chart of objectives should not exceed beyond a page, listing approximately one or two core objectives supported by 6 to 10 supplementary objectives. These objectives must be further defined in detail in annexure at length. There is no limit for this. Only criterion is that the annexure must specify in clear, tangible and simple terms the basic underlying premise behind these objectives. This is an operational explanation of objectives statement.

Step 3: Identify Areas of Measurement

Measurement-based performance management as stated in the beginning of this chapter is a comprehensive and integrated strategy and not an isolated activity. Measurement strategy also takes into account all dimensions that directly and indirectly affect the performance of employees and consequently, the organization. Measurement is neither confined to monitoring progress on the key result areas of performance or simply using one-shot techniques like 360-degree feedback system. This comprises a wide range of approaches and methods. These methods depend upon the kind of areas identified with in the performance management for measurement. Performance measurement strategy identifies eight measurement areas such as:

    (i) Process measurement
    (ii) Learning measurement
    (iii) Innovation measurement
    (iv) Employee satisfaction measurement
    (v) Organizational effectiveness measurement
    (vi) Employees' performance measurement
    (vii) Customer satisfaction measurement
    (viii) Financial measurement.

However, in reality these areas of measurement tend to differ from organization to organization depending upon the nature of operations and organizational environment. This step precisely suggests that an organization intending to apply measurement-based performance management must predetermine areas of measurement as a part of objective setting exercise.

Step 4: Identify Resource for Performance Measurement

It is also equally important for an organization to carry out an exercise to assess the kind of resource required to design and implement organization specific performance measurement strategy. Resource requirement typically involves investment of money (cost factor), expertise (resource persons), infrastructure (computers, labs, stationary, software package, telephones, etc.) and time (time with all employees have to allot for participating in measurement strategy). Actual resources required depend upon the areas of measurement, objectives of measurement and the size of organization in terms of units, location, and employees strength. This action enables an organization to have a clear picture of what efforts are involved in implementation of measurement-based performance management.

At the end of this driver, an organization must have developed a road map for design and implementation of measurement-based performance management. In particular, the organization must possess a composite document containing objectives of performance measurement, areas of performance measurement and resources required for application of measurement along with the rationality for embracing measurement technology in the organization.

DRIVER 2: DEFINING MEASUREMENT METHODOLOGY

Once an organization is through with the first driver successfully, it is time to enter into the nitty and gritty of measurement business. This driver focuses on methodological issues in measurement and enables organization to choose the most reliable route for design and implementation of measurement-based performance management. This is also the most difficult among the drivers due to some amount of methodological technicalities involved in it. Acceptance, and most importantly the effectiveness of measurement-based performance management is largely contingent upon the dependability, reliability and validity of measures. Application of this driver calls for expertise in psychometrics, especially in assessment and survey techniques. Efforts must be made to create this competency within the organization and in its absence the expertise needs to be outsourced. Every organization planning for measurement-based performance management has to create internal talent since this is a continuous activity. This driver primarily equips an organization with certain methodological facilities instead of facilitating the design of measurement methods. Measurement design differs depending upon the area of measurement. This design part is dealt individually in the respective measurement areas, i.e. how measurement design ought to be in financial measures is defined while discussing about such an area of measurement. Role of this driver is confined to preparing an organization with a few fundamental methodological issues. The most commonly used measurement methods are discussed in the following content.

Step 1: Qualitative Performance Measurement Methods

This is a well-known method in social research. Qualitative method has an important place in measurement-based performance management since assessing human performance involves soft issues. Depth of such soft issues can be captured only through qualitative measurement methods. Ensuring objectivity in data collection, analysis and drawing inferences in qualitative methods supposes high degree of commitment, sincerity and clarity on the part of performance measurement administrators, top management and other connected resource persons. A mature and professional qualitative method can provide rich insights than any other measurement method. Even in quantitative methods, some amount of qualitative judgement is involved. Success of this method is squarely influenced by removal of arbitrary and irrational subjectivity. Qualitative measurement methods are relevant to all areas of measurement such as process, learning, innovation, effectiveness. There are a number of techniques that are used in the qualitative measurement method. These are:

Interview Method: This is the most popular and commonly employed method of data collection and assessment in qualitative measurement. Measurement-based performance management prefers only structured interview method. Though unstructured interview methods can be a potential instrument in yielding some unusual and valuable information, the same is highly susceptible to misuse and in some cases tends to be abused. Therefore, only an interview that is highly structured finds place in performance measurement strategy. Common pitfalls such as halo effect must be avoided and safety measures should be inbuilt through cross-reference technique.

Critical Incident Technique: This technique is used to collect data that can be helpful in making predictions and extrapolations by understanding some particular incidents.

Repertory Grid Technique: This technique is used to capture the perceptions of employees and their world of work and their understanding of organizational events.

Projective Techniques: This is used to ascertain the hidden feelings and emotions of employees as well as to find out self-awareness and rationality.

Other methods include participant observation, action research, log book/diary recording, group discussions.

All above qualitative methods can be used in measuring effectiveness of areas of performance as mentioned in the above content such as learning, innovation, employee satisfaction, and employee performance. These methods are relevant for performance measurement because unlike in conventional performance assessment these methods are exhaustive and comprehensive that not only indicate results, but also guide through its diagnostic properties. There are different techniques such as content analysis, word processing packages, and grounded theory which may be used in analysis of data obtained through these qualitative methods.

Step 2: Quantitative Performance Measurement Methods

Quantitative methods are used in almost all the areas of performance measurement. Use of quantitative methods for the purpose of performance measurement is progressively rising. It is relatively easier to establish reliability of findings and modus operandi of measurement. Data obtained using quantitative methods can be analyzed in different combinations suited to the purpose and context. This is a highly structured method that has universal acceptance. Currently, many organizations are putting considerable efforts in extending quantitative methodology to all areas of performance measurement. Type of quantitative techniques that should be used is again contingent upon the purpose and area of performance measurement. There are many statistical techniques that are useful. These are known as descriptive statistics. Quantitative methods use surveys and questionnaires extensively for data collection. A few commonly used techniques that have relevance for performance measurement are illustrated below.

Questionnaire Method: These are of two types. First type is fact based. This means that questionnaires are developed and used to elicit factual information. Second is based on perception. Here, what people perceive and consequently believe is identified. Effectiveness of questionnaire method is largely dependent upon the reliability and validity of such questionnaires.

Surveys: Surveys are extensively used in quantitative method as a data collection instrument. The said questionnaires are used in the survey method. Appropriate sampling representing the universe plays an important role in the survey method.

Scaling: Scaling is a very critical issue in quantitative method.

Software packages like SPSS (Statistical Package for Social Sciences) offer great support in analysis of quantitative data.

Step 3: Specific Methodology and Measurement Tools

Methodology, data collection and analysis issues presented above are generic in nature but have universal applicability. There are specific measurement methodologies and techniques available in human resource management, especially in the context of human capital accounting and return on investment of human resource. There is a long way to go in transforming human resource management into an impeccably measurable discipline. Existing instruments help in understanding the intricacies and critical areas in measurement of human performance.

Step 4: Building Internal Expertise on Measurement

Performance measurement strategy is a continuous activity. This is not an annual affair, as most managers understand. Measurement in the context of performance management is not simply assessing and demonstrating results alone, but also acting as a source of authentic guidance for future action. It is imperative that a few people in the organization are identified and trained on measurement management or people with such competency be recruited. Expertise that is built in-house can contribute to the quality of measurement in addition to strengthening and evolving organization specific measurement techniques.

At the end of this driver an organization must have created adequate infrastructure, expertise and support systems apart from identification of a few methodological tools for launching performance measurement strategy. While defining and finalizing methodological issues in performance measurement, it is highly desirable that requirements of other performance management strategies discussed in this book be kept in view. Competency-based performance management also deals with few assessment and competency mapping techniques. As such these techniques can be considered and whichever seems relevant can be adapted.

DRIVER 3: PROCESS CENTRIC PERFORMANCE MEASUREMENT

Third driver makes a beginning for actually implementing measurement-based performance management. Process centric performance measurement is one of the areas that can be used to assess contribution of existing performance management in the organization. Process here means the extent to which work in the organization is done in an effective manner. To what extent factors such as work environment, relationships among employees, communication system, openness, trust, proactiveness are in a healthy shape on account of performance management practices. This driver needs to be associated with culture strategy, especially during the phase of culture evaluation and refinement. Reason for this is, ultimately it is the culture-based performance management that works towards creating a salutary processes in an organization. Objective as well as role of this driver is to bring rigorous structure into evaluation of such culture strategy elements to establish its contribution to highly functional processes. In addition to culture, other performance management strategies also perform a considerable role in shaping the fabric and texture of processes in the organization. Quantitative and qualitative measurement methods can be effectively used to measure effectiveness of process. Assumption is that an effective process ensures performance excellence of employees and organization. Such measurement at regular intervals helps not only to gauge the effectiveness, but also plugs the loopholes and strengthens the system in a systematic manner. Following are indicative measurement methods which can be used for this purpose:

Step 1: Reaction Surveys

Once in three months, reaction surveys on work environment and soft aspects such as communication, openness, freedom of work, trust can be conducted. Questionnaire method is suitable for this purpose. A standardized questionnaire covering all these processes elements must be developed. Usual reliability and content validity tests must be carried out and, once these are well-established such questionnaires can be customized. Efforts should be made to develop these questionnaires in-house in order to make them sharply organization specific. These questionnaires also need to be in a language that is easily understood by all employees. Wherever Internet/local area network facility is available the same must be utilized. Use of off the shelf generic questionnaires must be avoided.

Reaction surveys indicate the effectiveness of processes at a peripheral level. This would essentially facilitate in understanding the extent to which processess are conducive, however, but the same may not be able to explain reasons behind such a status. Still, reaction surveys are quick and reliable indicators for gaining feedback and understanding the status of processes.

Step 2: Processes Audit

Processes audit needs to be conducted once in a year. This is a comprehensive exercise involving a combination of qualitative and quantitative methods. Results obtained using reaction surveys must also be consolidated and plotted to identify trends and fluctuations. All line managers, key executives/employees and suppliers need to be actively involved as part of this audit. Two techniques that can be used in processes audit are:

(i) Soliciting descriptive feedback from all employees and suppliers on existing scenario of processes, their perceptions, to what extent efforts of management to create a salutary processes are successful and what needs to be done to further reinforce or improve the processes in the organization.

(ii) Carrying out an expert audit through interviews and discussion with employees on various dimensions of processes, making an effort to see the kind of relationship that exists between organizational effectiveness measures such as productivity/service efficiency and processes.

Audit must indicate whether progress achieved through improvement of processes has any positive implication for organizational effectiveness. This can also be done comparing the production/service quality figures prior to identification of process measurement initiative in the post measurement scenario.

All documents created using processes audit must be meaningfully classified. Appropriate data analysis tools must be used. Selection of data analysis tools depends upon the nature of data obtained. Apart from gaining insights into the issue, data also illustrates the grey areas that require managerial action. Methodological issues defined and crystallized at driver 2 above offers great help in developing tailor-made data collection and analysis instruments. At the end of this driver, an organization must have developed processes measurement instruments, and executed and evaluated the data in order to enable an organization to see itself where it stands in the development of processes management. There is no need to emphasize that good processes directly contribute for peak employees and organizational performance.

DRIVER 4: LEARNING CENTRIC PERFORMANCE MEASUREMENT

Learning is critical to excellent performance of employees. Learning not only ensures great performance, but also enhances organizational effectiveness. Recent studies and managerial thinking advocate that an organization in order to be competitive must become a learning organization. Various performance management strategies discussed in this book directly and indirectly contribute in imbibing and institutionalizing learning culture in an organization. Therefore, it needs to be measured, assessed and understood to what extent this learning environment exists in the organization and also, the relationship between learning and performance. Here also an organization is required to use a combination of measurement methods to create a learning centric performance measurement. Learning environment can be measured at three levels as indicated below:

Step 1: Individual Level

First level of measurement can be at individual level. Initially, perceptual data from employees can be obtained with an objective to find whether various performance management strategies that are in vogue in the organization have contributed for enhanced individual learning. This may be assessed on the dimension of improved work behaviour and effectiveness in performing one's responsibilities. Degree to which organizational environment is facilitating or hindering an individual's learning and growth needs to be measured, studied and analyzed. Learning here means functional knowledge, inquisitiveness and beliefs that are consistent with performance excellence. These traits are only illustrative of learning at the individual level. An organization in tune with its focus and context can have specific measures.

Step 2: Team Level

Teams are lifeline of organizational learning. This assumes more importance that team level measurement be carried out to understand existence of learning environment in an organization. This measurement needs to be associated with team-based performance measurement. Further, dimensions adopted for evaluation of team strategy must be kept in view while making team-based learning measurement. Issue here is the degree to which performance management strategies and practice are resulting in team level learning. Issues that are to be considered are: whether teamwork is effective, to what extent teams are collaborating to improve workflow, to what extent are productivity indices growing, commitment of individual employees to teamwork and how teams are helping members to update their knowledge base and efficiency in their areas of performance.

Step 3: Organizational Level

This is not just the total sum of individual learning and team learning as dealt with in the above steps. Organizational learning is something more than this entire sum. There are many methods through which organizational learning is measured. Primarily, there are three types of measurement. First is called *learning curve*. Philosophy behind this type of measurement is that cost decreases and volume increases due to enhanced organizational learning. The second type of organizational learning measurement is called *experience curve*. Premise behind this is that cost decreases as production increases due to strong organizational learning culture. Third type is *half-life curve* which says that quality and operational efficiency improves, as organizational learning is faster. Hence, one idea can be to adopt one of these curves as base measurement. Second idea can be following one of the standard organizational learning frameworks such as Peter Senge's five disciplines as dimensions for measurement of organizational learning. Here the dimensions include: systems thinking, personal mastery, mental models, shared vision and team learnings. Other standard dimensions are: knowledge acquisition, information distribution, information interpretation and organizational memory. These issues are to be probed in the context of performance management, that is, finding whether performance management strategies are contributing for creation of organizational learning or not. Such a measurement also invariably throws light on what needs to be done in order to improve it.

Measuring organizational learning is the most challenging function. Most of the organizational learning and its results are intangible. One can feel and experience these benefits but measuring them is like chasing a mirage. However, with improved techniques and sincere efforts some progress can be made. Initial runs of learning measurement must be confined to just understanding role of performance management in creating learning culture in the organization. These insights can be extended for managerial action once the measures are well grounded. It must be remembered that learning is a highly dynamic issue that keeps on changing and therefore, learning ratings also tend to change very fast. Therefore, learning centric measurement findings should be utilized in cross-reference with other measurement results discussed in this chapter. At the end of this driver, an organization must have made significant progress in developing a framework of learning centric measurement.

DRIVER 5: INNOVATION CENTRIC PERFORMANCE MEASUREMENT

This driver is in sequence with process and learning centric performance measurement systems. Process and learning must lead to enhancement of organizational innovation capability. It is logical that performance management once in its institutionalization stage must give fillip to culture of innovation. One of the core objectives of performance management practice must be to enhance the innovation capability of organizations because peak of employees' performance is reflected in finding new ways of doing things and developing new products. It makes absolute business sense to measure the performance of performance management strategies by measuring the innovation capability in the organization. Following are indicative measures for carrying out innovation centric performance measurement:

Step 1: Rate of Patents

One of the principal measures can be assessing the rate of patents an organization acquires on account of its research and development capability. Trends before and after introduction of performance management strategies also can be audited. This measure is based on factual data so that there can be no problem of reliability or ambiguity in it. If required, a survey can be administered on employees seeking their views on the extent to which performance management practices have contributed to the increasing or decreasing rate of patents of an organization. The same survey can be utilized to solicit employees's opinion on what needs to be done further to raise the level of organizational innovating competency.

Step 2: Research and Development Environment

The second level of measurement can be at research and development activity. Premise behind this measurement is that all innovation efforts do not necessarily lead to obtaining patents. Some efforts may be limited to ruling out certain possibilities and alternatives. This process is equally and sometimes more important than just obtaining patents for some innovation that can happen due to circumstantial help. Real innovation capability can be measured through research and development environment in the organization. This environment may include performance management strategies that work as support systems for stimulating research and development activity. For example, how a reward system prevailing in an organization supports research and development behaviour in employees or how competency-based performance management helps in enhancing research competency within employees so on and so forth. This data can be obtained using both qualitative and quantitative measures.

Step 3: Quality

This dimension is important for all organizations. In fact, most of the innovation currently is centred on how it can help in improving quality of products and services and reduce wastage. Here what it actually measures is how innovation capability of employees and the organization is resulting in enhancing the quality of goods and services. There are standard tools available to measure the degree of quality such as customer delight measurement, product dexterity measurement, service quality index. These instruments can be appropriately modified suiting to the organizational context. Rationality behind this measure is innovation means not simply generating a new product or a new process, but also improving/optimizing the existing product. In fact, most organizational efforts start with improving upon the existing products. It makes sense in evaluating efficacy of performance management measures through evaluating improvements in quality management.

Step 4: Assessing Innovative Behaviour

Risk taking capability of employees can be a good measure in evaluating the innovation capability. Innovation becomes a natural activity when organization gives employees freedom or tolerates their mistakes within a reasonable limit. This practice of risk taking enables employees to take a leap in the dark. This means organization supports and believes in their decision to make progress in an uncertain environment. Most of innovative work has to face this uncertain environment. Till something happens in value added manner even an employee putting efforts to innovate cannot be sure of the outcome. Innovation comes only through persistent efforts. Many times these efforts fail to produce anything worthy in monetary terms. Despite this, these risk taking efforts are foundations for innovation in organizations. Therefore, to assess the performance management effectiveness, it is desirable that innovative behaviour of employees should be measured.

At the end of this driver, an organization must have identified areas of measurement for innovation centric performance management and also developed appropriate measures. Innovation centric performance measurement once implemented in an organization, can contribute to not only providing insights on the role of performance management strategies in building innovation capabilities, but also can provide useful clues and ideas for sharpening performance management towards creating innovativeness.

DRIVER 6: EMPLOYEE SATISFACTION CENTRIC PERFORMANCE MEASUREMENT

Employee is an important stakeholder of an organization. Therefore, performance management strategies must lead to employee satisfaction. An effective performance management system must not only equip employees with all skills and support performance with relevant strategies, but also it must result in employee satisfaction. This satisfaction can be on account of a good reward strategy, career strategy, culture strategy, leadership development strategy. All performance strategies, interventions and drivers presented in this book are designed and patterned on the motivational structure of employees. Therefore, it is absolutely logical that such performance management system provides avenues for their satisfaction through adequate fulfilment of motivational needs at various stages. Measuring employee satisfaction can provide the efficacy status of performance management strategies. There are many standard tools available for measuring employee satisfaction. However, they cannot be borrowed and used as it is since the context and dimension used in such instruments would be entirely different. Such existing satisfaction assessment instruments can only provide an idea how to develop your own. Level of measurement can be here both: organization as a unit of analysis as well as employee as a unit of analysis. However, to start, an organization initially can confine this type of measurement with the organization as the unit of assessment. Though both methods of measurement, i.e. quantitative and qualitative can be used, for quick implementation quantitative measurement can be adopted. Once this measurement system is completely stabilized, qualitative measures also can be used for gaining sharper insights. Qualitative measurements call for allocating more time and involve deep analysis and interpretation skills. Following can be an indicative list of employee satisfaction measures:

Step 1: Employee Satisfaction Measures

All strategies used in this book can broadly form a dimension of employee satisfaction measures. For example, to what extent career-based performance management is contributing towards fulfilment of employee career aspirations and whether they are satisfied with career-related decisions in an organization. Similarly, how and with what intensity competency-based performance management is supporting employee efforts to acquire job-related competencies to perform the functions effectively. Measuring to what extent leadership strategy is providing opportunities to employee to grow as leader and grooming them to be effective leaders. These measures should not be confused with assessing the effectiveness of such measures per se. Such assessment is inbuilt in the strategy itself, i.e. one of the drivers of respective performance management stages provide for assessing effectiveness of these strategies as a performance management system. Here the objective is to measure to what extent, degree and intensity these strategies are contributing to employees' satisfaction.

Step 2: Employee's Professional and Personal Life

Objective here is to measure whether performance management strategies are contributing for giving meaning and happiness to an employee in personal and professional life. This can be measured by assessing how stress free the work life is, how meaningful it is, whether work is just a drudgery or joyful, how work life is matching with an employee's passion, and how due to working conditions employee is leading a contented and harmonious personal life so on and so forth. Premise behind this type of measurement is that ultimately all performance management strategies must facilitate an employee to lead a fruitful and meaningful life.

Step 3: Relationship Centred Measurement

There is one argument that employee satisfaction originates from the kind of relationship employees build with the organization as well as with their co-employees. This may be useful if an attempt is made to measure employees' satisfaction through the relationship measure. Performance management strategies, especially culture has an enormous potential to ensure the emotional bondage between an employee and his/her organization apart from cultivating salutary work relationships among employees. Questionnaire method can be used to assess this dimension. As in the case of earlier measures, this issue must be studied and assessed in the light of other performance management strategies.

Deliverable at the end of this driver is understanding the role and contribution of performance management strategies in employee satisfaction. It is one of the credible methods to establish both: efficacy of performance management strategies as well as its value addition at the employee level. Results gained out of such measurement must be effectively capitalized to improve performance management strategies. This issue will be dealt in a detailed fashion in the second intervention of measurement strategy.

DRIVER 7: EMPLOYEE CENTRIC PERFORMANCE MEASUREMENT

This is a critical driver in measurement-based performance management. This is also the most popular form of performance measurement employed by organizations. Every organization makes its own efforts to measure performance of each employee and in some cases performance of teams wherever teamwork is in vogue. Setting KRAs (key result areas) at the beginning of year/half-year/quarter and appraising them at the end of such stipulated period is a common sight. Performance management is also primarily known as this process of setting key result areas, appraising and rewarding accomplishment of key result areas. Even very conventional and traditional organizations have some form of employee performance measurement in the name of performance appraisal system. This performance appraisal system has taken a new shape as 360 degree feedback on performance with an objective to eliminate the subjectivity factor. There are different practices within this appraisal system. For example, a few organizations have quarterly performance appraisal system whereas others have it yearly and still some others conduct it half-yearly. Measurement of performance at employee level is a vexed subject and has been studied from different perspectives.

Measuring performance at individual employee level is very critical not only to employees, but also to the organization. From efficiency perspective, performance of every employee is important for organizational effectiveness. This employee level performance measurement is fraught with many challenges because often such measurement is linked to rewards and career growth. Due to this linkage, employee performance measurement is ultra sensitive to both the organization and employees. Objective of employee centric performance measurement is to provide the most reliable instruments through which employee performance is measured. As stated at the beginning of this driver, every organization must possess some kind of performance measurement system at employee level. This type of measurement is also very organization specific. A few instruments that can have common applicability are illustrated below as a suggestive framework.

Step 1: Performance Appraisal Techniques

Techniques such as graphic rating scale, forced choice, weighted checklist, behavioural anchored rating scale, behavioural observation scale, ranking method, paired comparison, forced distribution and performance tests are commonly used in measuring employees' performance. Each one of these techniques has their own advantages and disadvantages. Success and effectiveness of this type of measurement mostly depends upon commitment, sincerity, trust and honesty with which they are dealt with than these techniques themselves. It is a widely held criticism that all these techniques are subject to manipulation with varying degrees. Many times such appraisal, which is meant to facilitate an employee's development, ends up generating frustration and disillusionment. Therefore, these techniques must be used with extreme care and caution. No technique is superior to the other, rather it is the implementation strategy that makes a particular technique more effective than the other. Therefore, this kind of measurement must be planned well for flawless execution. There is no need to explain further that this measurement is carried out with the help of printed formats generally known as performance appraisal formats in conjunction with subordinate and superior discussion.

Step 2: MBO Type Performance Measurement

This is also one of the widely used methods in measuring performance of employees. This is known as *management by objectives*. Every organization implements this type of employee centric performance measurement in some form or the other. There are two principal activities followed in management by objectives. Firstly, setting key results areas for each employee. This is done with participation of concerned employee as well as his/her boss. Key result area that is generally identified and defined as a particular employee's responsibility flows from the overall objectives of the organization. Typically, at the beginning of the financial year, this system provides for discussion between a subordinate and superior regarding what is the key area of performance of the subordinate, what resources are required to accomplish such key result area, what are the various milestones of progress, what the superior has to do in order to facilitate the subordinate to carry out the responsibilities with effectiveness, so on and so forth. Second major step is appraising accomplishment of key results areas at the end of the financial year. This appraisal chiefly focuses on the extent to which an employee has achieved the targets and with what standards in reference to the key result areas as defined.

Setting key result areas can be toughest if an organization has just introduced such kind of performance measurement. Similarly, measurement also becomes a bit complex since effectiveness of key result areas measurement depends upon understanding the circumstantial factors. Circumstantial factors imply that there would be positive and negative conditions that an employee encounters while performing. Sometimes an employee requires to put in more efforts to achieve a simple task and sometimes even the toughest task can be attained with simple effort because of circumstantial support. Unless these dynamics are effectively scrutinized and incorporated while measuring the performance, real measurement remains far away from reality. Considering circumstantial factors can be a function of subjectivity. Utmost care needs to be exercised while doing so. It is also desirable for an organization to systematically document the defined key result areas of employees and make such document public to ensure transparency. Appraisal should be done strictly in reference to such document of employees' key result areas.

Step 3:   Multi-Rater Performance Measurement

This is also an employee centric performance measurement method. This is known as *360 degree appraisal system*, multi-rater assessment. Objective of this type of measurement is to eliminate the subjectivity factor by incorporating multi-level assessments and also to capture comprehensive perspective on performance of an employee. Increasing teamwork activity makes it difficult to measure performance of an employee through the traditional method of dyadic performance measurement system. In multi-level measurement, employee, employee's colleagues, employee's boss, employee's subordinate and employee's customers form as raters to measure his/her performance. Therefore, it is called 360-degree performance appraisal.

360 Degree Feedback/Performance Appraisal System

The term 360 degree feedback is actually a registered trademark of Team Inc., a company that did pioneering work on the theory and its application (Hurley 1998). Current survey research suggests that over 90 per cent of Fortune 1000 firms have used 360 degree feedback or some form of multi-source assessment. With the advent of service, marketing and software organizations, adoption of 360 degree feedback system has gained more acceptance and became a popular tool in feedback gathering and performance assessment.

The Backdrop of 360 Degree Feedback: Growth of 360 degree feedback systems can be attributed to flatter organizational structures, increased use of teams and problems with traditional performance systems. 360 degree feedback can be distinguished from other traditional types of performance feedback systems in several ways. Primarily, it utilizes multi-rater assessment, meaning that information on an individual and his or her performance is gathered from more than one source of person. Secondly, individual who performs rating (raters) have some degree of familiarity with the person being rated (ratee), that is, they know the ratee, interact with him/her frequently and are qualified to assess him and his performance. This provides more comprehensive feedback information than most traditional methods. According to Nowack (1993), some of the reasons for the increased use of 360 degree feedback in organizationa include:

- A need for a cost-effective alternative to assessment centres.
- Increased availability of assessment centre software capable of summarizing data from multiple sources into customized feedback reports.
- Need for continuous measurement of improvement efforts.
- Need for job-related feedback.
- Need to minimize employee potential in the face of technological change, competitive challenges and increased workforce diversity.

Benefits of 360 Degrees Feedback: Because the 360 degree feedback process actively involves managers, subordinates and peers by its very nature, it has an inbuilt impact within the organization. It offers an excellent tool for targeted performance feedback because multi-source assessment enhances the accuracy and credibility of performance information by enlarging the assessment pool from one supervisor acting alone. Organizations and employees could gain several benefits with the practice of 360 degree feedback as given in Table 6.1. 360 degree feedback is gaining acceptance not only as a developmental programme, but also as a comprehensive appraisal scheme. McCauley and Moxley's (1996) work in this context points to three prime aspects:

(i) People can learn, grow and change to become better leaders and managers. People are not simply born to be good leaders or managers; there is a lot of hard work and continuous learning that goes into the process

(ii) Self-awareness is the corner stone of development. Self-awareness means that a person understands his or her own personality, preferences and abilities and how these contribute to one's becoming skilled at some tasks and in some situations. Armed with this awareness, the leader can better apply and refine his or her situations where they are needed and work to improve in areas where he or she may be less naturally talented

(iii) Development is an ongoing process intricately related to work. Learning and working are not separate and distinct from each other, but too often, they are seen that way. Challenges in one's work force a person to learn and grow, and as the person learns, the work evolves. Thus, you cannot expect to send someone off to a single training programme and expect him/her return with developed, skills although such an event can play an important role in the development process if they are closely linked to the challenges and struggles of the work situations. All these three aspects are dependent upon multi-source feedback and can provide comprehensive and qualitative information to an individual enabling him/her to initiate constructive changes within himself/herself.

Challenges of 360 Degree Feedback. While it is accepted generally that feedback is invaluable within organizations, especially in managing employee behaviour, much research suggests that the flow of feedback in organizations is typically constrained (Ashford 1989). There are a few inherent difficulties and potential constraints with 360 degree feedback system. However, some of these difficulties are not unique and common with any appraisal and feedback system. The purpose of any appraisal is twofold: assessment and development. We need to recognize that inherent tensions exist between them. An appraisal interview is essentially concerned with (i) reviewing the year 2–5 target and assessing the performance of the appraisee and (ii) setting objectives for the coming year and considering how the appraisee might develop. It is the central divide which creates tension. O'reilly (1994) suggests that when 360 degree feedback is used for developmental purposes, things change. He found that friends pump up their scores and rivals become remarkably lukewarm. A summary of major challenges with the use of 360 degree feedback is given in Table 6.2. According to Barnardin et al. (1993), the significant constraints are:

- Managers may focus on pleasing subordinates in an effort to get higher appraisals.
- The authority of manager could be undermined by implications of low evaluations by reportees/subordinate.
- Subordinates may lack the ability, aptitude, training or necessary job information to provide valid ratings.
- Subordinates may be reluctant to be candid about their boss for fear of repercussions, or they inflate ratings in order to score points with the manager.
- Employees who are being pushed hardest by their supervisors may rate those supervisors more harshly.
- Managers may also be confused about how to interpret subordinate appraisal relative to ratings from other sources.

Solutions to 360 Degree Feedback: McCauley and Moxley (1996) observed that a number of factors are important for maximizing the developmental potential of 360 degree feedback, which include:

(i) *Good data from multiple perspectives:* Feedback from 360 degree instruments does grab the attention of the manager receiving it, having data that you can trust and that includes perspectives from all important working relationships. For good data, the instruments must be reliable and valid.

(ii) *Encouraging openness to feedback:* It includes the following steps:
   (a) Be clear about the purpose of the feedback process
   (b) Let managers choose who they want to distribute rating forms to
   (c) Ensure confidentiality of data
   (d) Set aside ample time for the manager to review and digest data
   (e) Allow the manager to work one-on-one with a skilled facilitator to understand and identify patterns in the feedback better.

TABLE 6.1 360 Degree Feedback: A Summary of Benefits

Author(s)/Researcher(s)	Views/Research Findings
Edwards, Mark R. (1996)	*360 degree feedback makes better performance possible because it:* • enhances performance quality • provides specific performance feedback • targets developmental areas • provides strong motivation • facilitates performance improvement • allows measurement of training effectiveness • enhances self-knowledge • supports continuous learning • improves the reliability and validity of performance information.
Garavan, Thomas, Michael Morley and Flynn (1997)	*Organizational perspective of benefits of 360 degree feedback* • It facilitates cultural change such as to accelerate a shift to teamwork and employee empowerment. • It can be used solely for developmental purpose. • The organization can use it as part of its succession planning systems. • It can be used for executive development. • It can reinforce the organization's desired core values and business strategies and provide feedback on how well managers are perceived to adhere to such core values. • It can be used by the organization as an input to the performance appraisal system. *Individual perspective of benefits of 360 degree feedback* • It can aid employees, thus improving weak or even unsatisfactory performance. • When weaknesses are pointed out, the process can be used to decrease employee's defensiveness about such weaknesses. • It can be used as a device to provide negative feedback. • It can be used to give employees a good understanding of their abilities.
Curtis, Derek (1996)	*The core benefits include:* • Increased awareness of strengths and weaknesses. • Enhanced management style/behaviour improvements. • Improved communication. • Recognition of value of good relationship skills. • Improved team working.
McCarthy, Alma M and Thomas Garavan (1999)	One of the characteristics of effective managerial career development is the creation of self-awareness in the learner. 360 degree feedback is considered as useful tool in this respect.

Table 6.2 360 Degree Feedback: A Summary of Challenges

Author(s)/Researcher(s)	Views/Research Findings
Edwards, Mark and Ann J. Ewen (1996)	• Insufficient communication • No training • Culture shock • Non-timely feedback • Data errors • Administrative overhead
McCauley, Cynthia and Russell Moxley (1996)	There will be some inconsistencies, particularly in rating which include: • One group may have more opportunities than others to observe certain managerial skills. • Manager may actually behave differently towards bosses, peers and direct reports. • One group may have different expectations than others of the manager.
Rowe, Christopher (1995)	360 degree feedback is clearly not an easy option and there is a final warning that must be added. Once you start down this path, it is extremely difficult to turn back. The stakes are high and no organization should embark on such a programme without carefully thinking it through.
Brutus, Stephane, Manuel London and Jennifer Martineau (1999)	Despite the popularity of 360 degree feedback and the high costs associated with its implementation, there exists very little research on how this process is linked to individual development.
Klugar and Denisi (1996)	360 degree feedback may not always have a positive effect. In most cases, the process does not affect the behaviour of the individual being assessed. The feedback can cause employees to feel vulnerable, uncomfortable, defensive or overly competitive.
Huggett, Marianne (1998)	How can you expect honest assessment from colleagues who are competing with you for limited promotion opportunities or from subordinates who may feel threatened by the very process of 360 degree feedback? The skeptical reaction may reflect natural anxiety about the process.The idea of being assessed in this way can be intimidating to even the most enlightened manager. However, the skepticism may be a clear signal that there is little trust within the organization and the 360 degree process is likely to be turned into a vicious weapon rather than a useful tool.

(iii) *A developmental plan:*   A development plan that gets managers to identify important improvement goals, and outlines multiple strategies for working towards those goals is a key follow-up component to the 360 degree feedback.

(iv) *Organization support for development:*   The best plans may fall short if the manager does not receive support in implementing them or if the organization in general does not have a developmental orientation. Following could be seen in a development-oriented organization:

- Senior managers participating in the 360 degree feedback process and actively pursuing their own developmental plans.
- Succession planning discussions that lead to managers being placed in jobs that will stretch and develop them.
- Bosses being held accountable for stimulating and supporting the development of their direct reports.
- Each employee having a development task within their job each year.
- Managers having easy access to others for coaching and mentoring.
- Mistakes being examined for potential learning rather than being fatal to a manager's career.

Following steps, if taken in design and implementation of 360 degree feedback system, can minimize difficulties:

- Design criteria that are specific and related to the jobs of the target groups.
- Ensure that skills are rated and relevant to the manager's jobs and also contribute to the strategic objectives of the firm.
- Avoid information overload in the reports by providing a general summary of rating followed by a detailed description of individual behaviour ratings so that gaps in skills can be traced down to specific behaviour.
- Use of goal planning, goal setting, follow-up meetings and learning contracts.
- Put processes in place for the development and achievement of plans and goals for task level behaviour change.
- If summaries of results are given back to raters, coach managers know how to deal with negative self-concept effects and to focus information session with raters on tangible actions and goals they will be taking.

The 360 degree feedback system as discussed above has its advantages and disadvantages. However, this has lesser limitations as performance management system in comparison to traditional top-down performance methods. There are more persons participating in appraisal and feedback of a single person instead of leaving it to the judgement of a single individual. This provides for more raiders and brings complexity in the system. No single individual at his/her discretion can mar or dilute the process. In order to reap full benefits, organizations need to nurture a value system wherein openness, trust and objectivity are given more emphasis. In the absence of such a value system, there is no doubt that even 360 degree feedback could be proved to be futile and may contribute for more problems in terms of bringing destructive group dynamics to the fore. Organizations, which are contemplating to introduce 360 degree feedback system, must start with critically questioning why it wants to have this system. Once decided to have the system, they shall use feedback for developmental purpose and once it is stabilized and constraints are removed in obtaining objective assessments, the same can be thought of extending to rewards.

Some organizations also adopted modified version of multi-rater measurement by removing certain levels such as colleagues or subordinates in order to make such a system compatible with their organizational reality. Ratings given by various raters on a set of performance parameters are to be aggregated in order to obtain a single score. This single score explains the performance level of an employee. This instrument also needs to be handled very carefully chiefly due to the fact that many people are involved in such performance measurement.

The above-explained three types of performance measurement have their own advantages and disadvantages. An organization can gain maximum advantage by introducing a particular type of performance measurement instrument suited to employees and organizational context. Same organization can also adopt all three techniques, applying them for different target group of employees. Further, on yearly basis the trend of performance of employees must be studied in the light of implementation of performance management strategies. Purpose is to study and understand to what extent and degree various performance management strategies that have direct link with performance of employees are contributing to the enhancement of their performances. This step is very critical and has a lot of significance to the practice of performance management strategies.

At the end of this driver, an organization must have achieved dual targets in the area of performance measurement. Firstly, it must have developed the most appropriate, simple, transparent and accurate performance measures to assess performance of employees. Secondly, it also must have developed mechanism to study the contribution of performance management strategies in performance enhancement of employees.

DRIVER 8: TEAM CENTRIC PERFORMANCE MEASUREMENT

Driver 6 provides for measuring employee satisfaction with performance management applications and Driver 7 for measuring performance of employees as well as contribution of performance management strategies for enhancing employees' performance. Current driver focuses on team performance. This driver needs to be administered in close association with team-based performance management strategy. The focus of the driver is the extent and degree of effectiveness of teams and their performance as results of performance management strategies prevailing in organization. There are many standard measures available to measure effectiveness of teams per se. These need to be adopted with suitable modifications. Both quantitative and qualitative measures can be adopted to identify contribution of performance management strategies for teams' effectiveness. There can be many methods and ways through which team measurement can be carried out. Here, a few methods are illustrated to serve as a suggestive framework:

Step 1: Survey on Teamwork

First level of assessment can be to conduct a broad-based survey seeking feedback from employees on effectiveness of teamwork and how performance management strategies facilitated or hindered the creation of a highly functional teamwork. Parameters for such measurement can be items like team spirit, collaboration among employees, participation, involvement, communication, problem-solving. Objective of this type of measurement is to assess (i) effectiveness of teams and (ii) role of performance management strategies in evolving the kind of teamwork that exists in the organization. Contribution of performance management strategies can be probed using parameters such as how they provided competencies, leadership, supporting culture, team centric reward and career.

Step 2: Teamwork-Performance Management Strategies Audit

This is dominantly a qualitative method of measurement. This involves using services of a few experts/resource persons to conduct an audit exercise with a view to identify relationship between teamwork and performance management strategies that are in force in the organization. A checklist containing a few measures centring on each performance strategy must be developed and relationship of these with teamwork can be studied. This audit provides deeper insights into why and why not performance management strategies reinforce teamwork in organization.

Step 3: Teamwork Achievement Report

This is a measurement of tracking tangible performance and achievements of teams. A yearly report containing significant achievements must be developed. In the second phase, contribution of performance management in these team achievements must be analyzed and areas of direct influence and hindrance must be clarified. This measurement apart from showing the contribution side of performance strategies also substantially helps to bring sharpness in strengthening team's achievements.

The deliverable at the end of this driver is twofold. An organization must have developed tailor-made and organization specifics steps to measure teamwork, and gained deeper insights into why and why not performance management strategies helped in making teamwork effective in attaining performance excellence.

DRIVER 9: RESULTS CENTRIC PERFORMANCE MEASUREMENT

This is commonly used measurement method in the area of people management. In fact, mostly business side of human resource measurement is known as Return on Investment (ROI) measurement. This measurement method is popularly used in the business context while evaluating investments vs profits. Every employer and organization would like to know return on the investment made in order to gauge commercial soundness of making such investments. Techniques such as human capital accounting, ROI of training, value audit analysis of performance management have come into existence to establish return on investment of human resource strategies. A few such techniques are illustrated here which can be used with right modifications in all types of organizations.

Step 1: Human Capital Accounting Techniques

There are various techniques that are used as part of human capital accounting. There are two methods such as monetary and non-monetary methods. Techniques in monetary method include replacement cost model, opportunity cost model, discounted value of salaries, adjacent present value model, stochastic process model and group level model. Non-monetary techniques include skill inventory, performance evaluation, assessment of potential, attitude measurement, subjective expected utility and group level model. All these techniques are developed to account for the value of human capital. Organization can employ the most appropriate monetary and non-monetary technique that is apt with respective measurement objectives and organizational context. Contribution of performance management strategies should be evaluated to find out trends of soft human capital value. For example, comparing value of current year human capital with the previous year's in the light of application of performance management strategies. This analysis helps to find out the monetary and non-monetary value of performance management applications.

Step 2: Study of Relationship between Performance Management and Organizational Performance

The second type of result-oriented performance management measurement is finding out the relationship between performance management applications and organizational performance. Organizational performance is defined here as market capitalization that includes parameters such as sales, turnover, profits and earning per share. Data on these parameters during pre and post performance management application must be obtained and both these data, if compared, can present the status of the said relationship. Both quantitative and qualitative methods can be applied for this purpose. Whatever may be the method; all performance management strategies must be covered in such a study. Also, such measurement must focus on finding out the contribution of each performance management strategy independently and jointly with other performance management strategies to organizational performance. Similar studies were conducted in the area of human resource management. These are known as *human resource scorecard* and *strategic human resource management*. Deriving some basis from these studies does help in the current context.

Step 3: ROI of Performance Management

The third type of measurement is return on investment. Models and techniques applied in return on investment for the purpose of training function are useful here. Among all human resource functions, training is one area where return on investment studies were conducted in detail. Therefore, referring to such studies provides a perspective. Methodology to be followed in the initial stage is simple. In the first phase of return on investment measurement, collect the data regarding total investment and expenses incurred on account of design and implementation of performance management strategies. This investment includes salaries of employees responsible for administration of performance management, infrastructure, consultants' fee, expenses incurred on implementation of various strategies. These expenses must be consolidated. In the second phase, calculate the value of competencies created, leadership training and motivational climate as a consequence of culture and reward strategies in terms of monetary value adhering to human capital accounting techniques. It is also a fact that all performance strategy outcomes cannot be translated into monetary values. Such items must be classified into facilities category. In the third phase, items for facilities category must be translated into hypothetical monetary value by way of conducting an assessment with the help of all employees. For example, seeking evaluation from employees as to what according to them is the monetary value of a motivational climate or implementation of performance management with reference to the investments made. Employees themselves on perusal of investments made and facilities created by performance management would ascribe a financial value in terms of profit and loss. This may appear as abstract and conceptual but this can be a powerful mechanism to establish the monetary value of performance management practice.

Step 4: Balanced Scorecard Approach

A comprehensive measurement method that many organizations intend to adopt is the balanced scorecard approach developed by Robert Kaplan and David Norton. This approach advocates a combination of methods to be included for establishing organizational results. According to them results do not mean financial results alone. This must include aspects such as customer knowledge, internal business learning and innovation. Though this is not strictly a method for return on investment measure, but can guide organizations in their efforts to measure the real results in the light of performance management adaptation.

Successful design and execution of the ninth driver as discussed above enables an organization to develop well-compatible measures to assess the organizational results on account of practice of performance management. It is suggested that an organization must confine results obtained by allowing this driver for internal consumption initially. Once the system is stabilized and measures withstand rigorous scrutiny, these can be made public and perhaps can be used in preparation of financial balance sheet too.

DRIVER 10: CUSTOMER SATISFACTION CENTRIC PERFORMANCE MEASUREMENT

Last but crucial driver is expanding the role of performance management outside the organization in the form of customer satisfaction measurement. Satisfaction of internal customer and the way to measure is discussed in Driver 6, Whereas this driver makes an attempt to measure the satisfaction of customers of an organization's products and services. This customer is an indirect customer of performance management. Rationality behind this measurement is the ultimate objective of any organizational system is, to attain customer satisfaction. Results and profits of organization are due to this satisfaction. Therefore, it makes an absolute sense for expanding measurement scope to customers too. There are many standardized techniques of customer satisfaction measurement that can be used in this context in conjunction with performance management strategies. Establishing a direct relationship between customer satisfaction and application of performance management may not be possible in absolute sense. Relationship between these two is neither linear nor a simple cause and effect relationship. A wide variety of factors/variables play mediating and intervening role between these two. This implies that a set of roles can intervene and facilitate or constrain the contribution of performance management strategies for higher or lower customer satisfaction. Nevertheless, an attempt shall be made to measure customer satisfaction in the light of performance because such an attempt leads to sharpening of performance strategies. Following twin techniques can be used as customer centric performance measurement:

Step 1:   Customer Satisfaction Survey

Measures such as overall satisfaction with product and service, likelihood of repurchasing the product/service, willingness to recommend the product to others, perception of product/ service as representing good value so on and so forth represent the dimensions of customer satisfaction. Every organization that is market driven generally develops and possesses a few customized instruments to collect data from customers on their satisfaction level. This needs to be obtained during post performance management period and compared with the pre performance management period in order to derive inferences. Also, after the implementation of performance management, trends can be analyzed by plotting it month and year wise.

Step 2:   Customer Satisfaction Audit

Using this method, customer satisfaction can be studied. Instead of collecting data from customers directly, reports from suppliers and franchises are invited. Suppliers' comments and views are solicited on the trends of customer satisfaction. They are specifically invited to focus on the reason for improvement or decline in the customer satisfaction with the products and services of organization. This is an open-ended report in which each supplier can provide a statement of actual figures together with an analysis.

Identifying customers, developing instruments of data collection and then linking them logically with the practice of performance management is definitely a complex exercise. However, organizations should not hesitate from launching such a measurement. This is because such an exercise has tremendous potential to enhance the value of performance management strategies. Deliverable at the end of this driver is that an organization by now must have made a beginning in measuring the effectiveness of performance management through canons of customer satisfaction.

INTERVENTION 2:   USING MEASUREMENT STRATEGY IN INSTITUTIONALIZATION OF PERFORMANCE MANAGEMENT

The core objective of second intervention of measurement-based performance management strategy is to capitalize on measurement in institutionalizing the practice of performance management. Its supplementary objectives include (i) to bring greater coherence among all methods of performance measurement as presented in first intervention and (ii) to assist in diagnosis and effectiveness assessment of performance management strategies such as reward, career, leadership, culture, competency and team-based as presented in this book. Measurement-based strategy is one that has relevance and direct relationship with all other performance management strategies. Similar to other strategies, here also a set of 10 drivers are developed that drive and support an organization's effort to institutionalize performance management as an integral part of organization and as a way of life for employees. Drivers presented

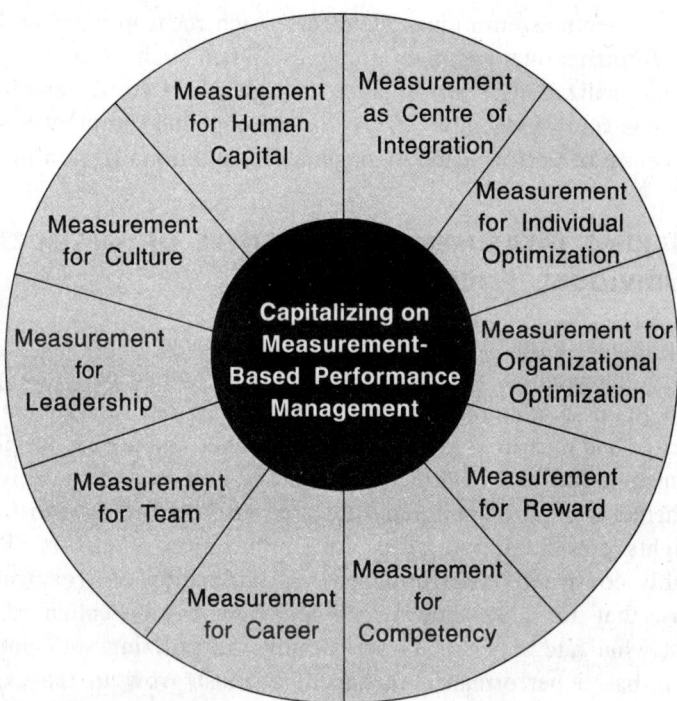

FIGURE 6.3 Drivers of the intervention capitalizing on measurement strategy in institutionalization of performance management.

are more illustrative in nature rather than as self-sufficient in themselves to lead an organization to launch institutionalization effort in a full-fledged fashion. Reason for this is that measurement strategy institutionalization depends upon the intensity of application of other performance management strategies. Depending on their enforcement and integration with the organization, measurement strategy can be tapped for institutionalization. With this in view, 10 drivers are presented as a suggestive framework. However, it doesn't mean that they cannot serve as drivers if organization adopts them with an intention of straightjacket implementation. These drivers are:

DRIVER 1: MAKING MEASUREMENT AS CENTRE OF INTEGRATION

Measurement-based performance management strategy can be effectively utilized as a centre as well as source for bringing tighter integration among all performance management strategies discussed in this book. Measurement application is required for all these functions at two levels. First level of measurement needs lies in assessing the effectiveness of existing scenario of performance management in an organization. The second level of need exists in order to measure effectiveness of the new performance management strategy. This means that all performance management strategies need to work in close collaboration with the measurement-based performance management strategy. Further, as discussed in the beginning of this chapter, measurement possesses enormous potential in providing structure to even an intangible aspect like feelings/emotions. Therefore, such measurement philosophy must be extended to all performance management strategies. When such extension is managed well, automatically institutionalization of performance management becomes a reality. Organizations must make conscious and systematic efforts in driving measurement-based performance management as a centre of performance management institutionalization in the organization.

DRIVER 2: MAKING MEASUREMENT AS CENTRE OF OPTIMIZATION: INDIVIDUAL FOCUS

The essence and principal objective of all performance management strategies in particular and human resource management in general is optimizing human potential, performance and efforts. In order to attain such an objective, it is imperative that such potential, performance and efforts be assessed and measured in an objective, accurate and precise fashion. Measurement provides deeper insights into the workflow, efforts and how particular activity/activities are performed and whether such flow and activities are performed in the most efficient manner or not. Such insights present opportunities for optimization of efforts. This optimization contributes to highly constructive performances and utilization of organizational resources. It is common sense that no value added work behaviour can be enhanced unless a person knows how and at what rate a person is performing and utilizing self- potential in precise form. Measurement-based performance management must grow to the extent that such a measurement is available at individual level so that optimization at this level becomes a natural process. Institutionalization of performance management as a way of life happens only when every individual employee is provided with tools and sources for measurement of self-potential, performance and efforts. No organization can aspire to attain high performance without enabling individual employees to optimize self. Therefore, organization in their journey of performance management institutionalization must extend principle and practice of measurement to individual employee level.

DRIVER 3: MAKING MEASUREMENT AS CENTRE OF OPTIMIZATION: ORGANIZATIONAL FOCUS

Having optimized the potential, performance and efforts of individual employees with the assistance of Driver 2 as above, the next sequential step is consolidating such individual efforts to produce organization level optimization. However, this is much more than simply consolidating the individual optimization index. This is complex because integration of individual optimization as an aggregate of organization level often encounters challenges in the form of difficulties in coordination and duplication. This duplication can be effectively removed when all individual performances are analyzed and codified with the help of measurement. Measurement also enables organizations to find out the blocks of coordination and tackle them effectively. Objective of this driver is to remove wastage and ensure that every effort put in the organization is a value added one. Measurement must be utilized as a tool for effective monitoring and keeping track of resource spending vis-à-vis progress. Such a process guarantees organizational level optimization. Performance management institutionalization is just the other side of the coin of organizational level optimization. Organization must capitalize on measurement-based performance management by according a special focus for institutionalization of performance through optimization.

DRIVER 4: MAKING MEASUREMENT AS CENTRE OF REWARD STRATEGY

Effective management of the reward-based performance management strategy is squarely contingent upon effective utilization of measurement principles. Measurement-based performance management offers support to reward strategy at multiple levels that include: (i) determining reward structure, especially monetary reward, (ii) determining the right reward for right position, performance and persons and (iii) assessing the motivational power of reward. All these assessments and determinations can be possible only when measurement is made part of reward strategy, especially at operational stage. This means effective coordination between reward and measurement is more a necessity than option if an organization is vying for institutionalization of performance management. It is imperative that organizations must make efforts in transforming the measurement strategy as centre of reward strategy. However, such finer integration is possible only when both these strategies are properly grounded in an organization. This means, at the first instance both these strategies must be initiated independently as illustrated in the respective chapters of this book. Once both these strategies are matured at operational level, they must be integrated at the strategic level. This integration at strategic level can be thought of as a part of institutionalization process. Hence, organization must focus on measurement as a key resource of effective reward management.

DRIVER 5: MAKING MEASUREMENT AS CENTRE OF COMPETENCY STRATEGY

Measurement and competency strategies as presented in this book play mutually complimentary roles. Much of the effectiveness for competency-based performance management comes from application of right measurement tools. Unless measurement is perfect, no competency modelling/mapping at any level can be executed. Therefore, it makes sense to adopt measurement not only as key ingredient in competency-based performance management, but also to borrow measurement as centre of competency. Here also like in the case of earlier drivers in this intervention, the prerequisite is that both measurement and competency strategies must be engineered independently which can be made collaborative once they attain a stage of maturity. Such collaboration surely results in institutionalization of performance management. Organizations need to make planned and deliberate efforts to ensure such collaboration as a part and parcel of performance management institutionalization endeavours.

DRIVER 6: MAKING MEASUREMENT AS CENTRE OF CAREER STRATEGY

Leveraging measurement strategy especially the measurement application is also important for effectiveness of career management and also in order to attain the institutionalization of performance management. Career planning involves measuring the required competencies such as aptitude and attitude profiles of employees vis-à-vis their job profiles in organizations.

Perfect matching and a rationalistic career planning are possible only when right measurement is done. Therefore, measurement has a definite role to play and substantial assistance to offer to the career-based performance management strategy. Careers in the context of performance management as discussed in the relevant chapter are more competency-based rather than hierarchy focused. This is the clinching factor for measurement influencing the career planning process. Hence, organizations must avail the presence and practice of the measurement-based performance management strategy to sharpen the career strategy and to give a fillip for institutionalization of performance management. This driver can be used to make the partnership between measurement-based performance management and career-based performance management strategy stronger. Such a mutually strong collaboration makes institutionalization of performance management, a natural process.

DRIVER 7: MAKING MEASUREMENT AS CENTRE OF TEAM STRATEGY

Continuous measurement contributes for effectiveness of team functioning. Unless teamwork is tightly structured, the same can remain as a passing fad. Sometimes teamwork introduced in organization without defining a clear structure and constitution, may create more performance-related problems than it serves. Team norms, targets, performance valuation, and refinement: all call for application of measurement principles. Measurement also helps in collecting and managing huge data related to team functioning. Especially in large sized organizations, there can be a large number of teams operating from operational level to strategic levels. Performance, processes and practices of such a large number of teams can be managed only through highly structured systems. These systems can be developed in a foolproof manner only through extension of the measurement-based performance management strategy. Every team-based strategy is a part of an overall framework which uses a few tools of measurement. Institutionalization of performance management process does solicit measurement playing a central role. Organizations need to travel that extra mile to capture the measurement management to meld with team strategy. Team-based performance management with the support of measurement can certainly drive institutionalization of performance management faster and smoother.

DRIVER 8: MEASUREMENT AS CENTRE OF LEADERSHIP STRATEGY

Leadership assessment, leadership training and development, leadership performance, leadership competency identification, leadership effectively managing people, so on and so forth requires understanding of right parameters, dimensions and results. Grooming leadership, as too many organizations tend to believe, is not a game of just naming a few individuals in whimsical fashion. Leadership identification, tracking and grooming involves hard core interventions based on undisputed and reliable data. Such data can be obtained and meaningfully analyzed only when right measurement techniques are used. Many leadership efforts end up without producing results of any worth due to organization's failure to make such efforts on measurable basis. It is essential that organizations use measurement as a principal driver in institutionalizing leadership development strategy. Measurement makes leadership development intervention more effective and also accurate. Unless leadership development is based on a sound footing, it is difficult to attain institutionalization of performance management. Competent leadership is imperative for steering the practice of performance management and gradually its institutionalization in a successful manner. Organizations need to focus on capitalizing measurement strategy in order to sharpen leadership development to attain the overall objective of performance management institutionalization. This driver prescribes that leadership development must be reinforced using measures and measurement principles.

DRIVER 9: MEASUREMENT AS CENTRE OF CULTURE STRATEGY

Measurement makes the culture strategy tangible, structured and manageable. Measurement has a special role and importance in the overall culture strategy. Many organizations and managers leave culture untouched and unmanaged due to the fact that they are not quite clear how to analyze, strategize, and operationally evaluate the culture. As a result, in organizations, culture forms on its own, influenced by all kinds of desirable and undesirable factors. In this kind of scenario, measurement is a strategy that enables organizations to see, feel, experience, analyze, manage and obtain stupendous results from the culture strategy. Measurement strategy facilitates identification of operating culture, culture dimensions, mapping desirable culture and launching it in organizations as a part of culture strategy. Institutionalization process takes this culture strategy further in terms of perfecting the measures and eventually managing culture completely through the canons of measurement. Such measurement-based objective and precise culture strategy supports institutionalization of performance management. This driver prescribes that organizations should not be complacent and rather must put efforts with more vigour in creating a measurement centric culture for institutionalization of performance management.

DRIVER 10: MEASUREMENT FOR HUMAN CAPITAL BALANCE SHEET

At the end of all strategies, interventions and drivers, all organizations commonly seek one thing, i.e. the value and liability of human asset in the organization, and whether the mammoth performance management architecture and sustained efforts that had been put in has any business wisdom or not. In precise, organizations would be definitely eager to assess whether the cost incurred on account of performance management practice has any financial results to offer or not. It makes absolute business sense that an organization must continuously assess to understand the value it has created on account of performance management. Further, the 7 performance management strategies, 14 interventions and 140 drivers are built on the premise of business value addition. Therefore, such an assessment would help in cutting down wastage and enhancing investment value of performance management. This assessment of performance management involves both financial and non-financial measures. Even non-financial measures can be attributed to hypothetical monetary value to gauge their value and contribution to the business process and growth of organization. In this process of measuring financial value of performance management practice, measurement strategy and principles help in a significant manner. It is highly desirable that measurement strategy be made the epicentre of this human capital assessment. This assessment can be a regular affair that happens once in a year in line with preparation of financial balance sheet of the company. This continuous financial appraisal of performance management not only creates a great accountability, but also strengthens institutionalization of performance management. Hence, it can be summed up here that the sole objective of this driver is to encourage organizations to adopt financial measurement of performance management practice through human capital accounting.

SUMMARY

This chapter focuses on the strategy of measurement-based performance management. Contents and discussion put forwarde clearly illustrates how human element can be measured with accuracy, precision and objectivity. Style adapted in the discussion is common sensical in order to dispel the myth of measurement meaning as more of numbers and less of insights.

Present chapter similar to others in this book, is organized into five parts. What is measurement and what it is not in the context of performance management is presented in part one. Measurement-based performance management is defined as a set of tools employed to establish efficacy, utility and contribution of performance management in the enhancement of organizational and employee performance and also a vehicle that set standards of performance. The significance of measurement strategy in the overall theory and practice of performance management is presented in part two of the chapter with the support of 10 salient features such as:

   (i) Measurement as an instrument for identifying path of performance
  (ii) Measurement facilitating to draw road map of performance
 (iii) Measurement providing unlimited avenues for exact learning
  (iv) Measurement contributing for effective management style
   (v) Measurement as an approach in identifying centre of accountability
  (vi) Measurement as an approach in identifying critical processes
 (vii) Measurement for structuring organizational and employees performance
(viii) Measurement causing optimization of employees effort
  (ix) Measurement enabling objectivity in performance management
   (x) Measurement enhancing quality in all walks of organizational life.

Theoretical framework of performance measurement consisting of few approaches such as balanced scorecard, SMART, performance management questionnaire, Cambridge performance management system and human capital accounting are briefly discussed in part three. The strategy of measurement-based performance management comprising 2 interventions and 20 drivers is illustrated in part four and five. The first intervention namely, nurturing measurement-based performance management and its 10 drivers are described in part four. These ten drivers are:

   (i) Defining objectives of performance measurement
  (ii) Defining measurement methodology

   (iii) Process centric performance measurement
   (iv) Learning centric performance measurement
   (v) Innovation centric performance measurement
   (vi) Employee satisfaction centric performance measurement
 (vii) Employee performance centric performance measurement
(viii) Team centric performance measurement
   (ix) Results centric performance measurement
   (x) Customer satisfaction centric performance measurement.

Second intervention of measurement-based performance management, i.e. using measurement strategy for institutionalization of performance management is described in part five of the chapter. This intervention too prescribes 10 drivers such as:

   (i) Making measurement as centre of integration
  (ii) Making measurement as centre of optimization: individual focus
 (iii) Making measurement as centre of optimization: organizational focus
 (iv) Making measurement as centre of reward strategy
  (v) Making measurement as centre of competency strategy
 (vi) Making measurement as centre of career strategy
 (vii) Making measurement as centre of team strategy
(viii) Making measurement as centre of leadership strategy
 (ix) Making measurement as centre of culture strategy
  (x) Leveraging measurement for establishing human capital balance sheet (value).

The strategy of measurement-based performance management is expected to add immense value to an organization and its people once the application of all the 20 drivers is complete.

KEY WORDS

Following are the key words discussed in this chapter:

- Market capitalization
- Measures
- Human capital accounting
- Quantitative methods
- Critical incident technique
- Projective techniques
- Scaling
- Statistical package for social sciences
- Learning centric measurement
- Employee satisfaction centric measurement
- Results centric measurement
- Centre of integration
- Process audit

- Numerical assessment
- Balanced scorecard
- Return on investment
- Qualitative methods
- Repertory grid technique
- Questionnaire
- Survey
- Process centric measurement
- Innovation centric measurement
- Team centric measurement
- Customer satisfaction centric measurement
- Reaction surveys
- Reliability

DISCUSSION QUESTIONS

1. Measurement of performance management is a dispassionate activity that is in conflict with the emotional fabric of people. Do you agree or disagree? Discuss with supporting factors.

2. Does measurement ensure objectivity, precision and accuracy in management of performance?

3. What is measurement strategy and what is it not in the context of performance management?

4. Measurement strategy has a significant role to play in the practice of performance management. Discuss.

5. Write short notes on balanced scorecard approach and how it helps in managing performance.

6. Performance measurement is much more than a simple return on investment calculation. Substantiate this statement.

7. How an organization nurture measurement-based performance management? What actions such an organization is required to take?

8. Can organizations leverage on measurement strategy to reinforce the practice of performance management?

9. Discuss the architecture of measurement-based performance management strategy.

CASE STUDIES

1. Knell International is a multinational corporation engaged in distribution and marketing of lifestyle products. There are about two thousand employees working in the organization, mainly posted in western part of India. The turnover of the company was standing at Rs. 280 cores in the last financial year with a profit of Rs. 31 crores. Knell is a progressive company that always makes efforts to adopt the best management systems. Kirk Paterson, till now working in Middle East operations is posted to India as chief executive of Knell. During the first month of his working, Paterson has understood that his company is implementing a variety of performance enhancement strategies. However, neither line managers nor human resource managers are quite certain about contribution and value addition happening as a consequence of such performance centric management systems. On the perusal of expenditure accounts on employees' head, he found that organization is investing substantial money in implementation of these strategies. Therefore, he is more eager to assess the returns the company is accruing on account of performance management practices. Imagine that your services are hired by Paterson for measuring the impact of performance management strategies both from bottom line and process point of view. Discuss

how you intend to proceed and how you would measure and present results for Paterson's perusal.

2. Indian Telematrix is a telecommunications company. This company has two divisions: one is in the business of manufacturing telephone, fax and PABX systems. The other is in the business of developing telecommunication software products. Mukesh Sagaria is the Director-Human Resource of the company. Telematrix has an in-house human resource development centre dedicated to implement surveys, assessments and measurements. This centre regularly conducts surveys and studies various human resource aspects by applying social science research methods. It has well developed data collection tools and administers learning, innovation, process, performance, employee, team and organization focused measurement and assessments. Both data collection instruments and measurement administration is well customized and efficacy is proved. Mukesh Sagaria intends to leverage on this measurement competency of the company to institutionalize the practice of performance management. In other words, he intends to apply measurement methodology to all performance management systems such as competency, reward, culture, leadership, career, etc. He called for a meeting of all assessors and performance managers in the company and shared with them his desire. Now discuss, in your opinion, what the team must do to capitalize on measurement competency in institutionalization of performance management.

3. Lalita Kashyap is working as human resource executive in a business process outsourcing company. Her job profile mainly includes taking care of training and development function in the company. There are about 800 employees working in the company in shift system. She reports to John Luthers, the human resource manager. Luther invited Lalita for a meeting to fix up her key result areas. Discuss, how do you go about the meeting and define key result areas of Lalita as if you are Luther.

SUGGESTED READING

Cross K.F. and R.L. Lynch (1989). "The smart way to define and sustain success." *National Productivity Review*, **9**(1), pp. 23–33.

Dixon, J.R. and A.J. Nanni and J.E. Vollmann (1990). *The New performance Challenge: Measuring Operations for World Class Companies.* Dow-Jones: Irwin Homewood.

Fitz Enz, Jack (2000). *ROI of Human Capital.* New York: AMACOM Books.

Globerson, S. (1985). "Issues in developing a performance criteria system for an organization." *International Journal of Production Research*, **23**(4).

Kaplan, Robert and David Norton (1996). *Balanced Scorecard: Translating Strategy into Action.* Massachusetts: HBS Press.

Maskell, B. (1989). "Performance measures for world class manufacturing." *Management Accounting*, May.

Neely, A., M. Gregory and K. Platts (1995). "Performance measurement system design: A Literature Review and Research Agenda." *IJOPM*, **15**(4).

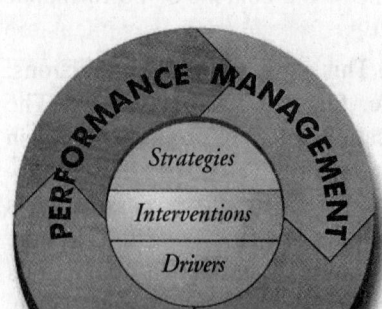

Chapter Seven

STRATEGY 6: COMPETENCY-BASED PERFORMANCE MANAGEMENT

Competency is a formidable weapon in the armour of organizations to create performance excellence. Level of human resource competency reflects in the core competence of an organization. To what extent and depth, an organization can optimize its physical resources like infrastructure, technology, capital, product lines, brand value, distribution and marketing network and to what length an organization can exploit emerging and existing markets, opportunities of business environment and leverage societal changes will be dependent upon the reservoir of human competency an organization builds. Fortunately, of late a good number of organizations have realized the strategic significance and unique advantage of competency-based management in attaining employee and organizational objectives. Recent studies however, establish that quite a few organizations are hesitant to adopt the competency-based management system due to complexity and intricacy of building the most relevant, pragmatic and business aligned competency models. Other apprehensions are: (i) evolving competency model is cost intensive and returns are not proportionate, (ii) life cycle of a competency model is either short or loses its relevance quickly, (iii) it generates more problems than it resolves and (iv) is required only in manufacturing organizations in the competitive sector. These apprehensions are more of suspicion in nature rather than doubts drawn from experiences or logical analysis of data. Benchmarking practices in the area of competency profiling and management highlights stupendous gains and positive results that organizations can receive. Study of competency management history, approaches, practices, and evaluation clearly points out that organizational inertia coupled with inadequate aptitude of managers is the dominant reason for their suspicious perception rather than realistic understanding and experience with competency-based management. An attempt is made to clarify all these issues apart from enabling managers to practice competency-based performance management in forthcoming contents.

This chapter on competency-based performance management strategy is organized into five parts. Part 1 is devoted to define competency-based performance management and its characteristics. The significance of competency management in the context of performance management is dealt in part 2, while theoretical aspects of competency management are discussed in Part 3. Strategy of competency management consists of two interventions: first intervention titled nurturing competency-based performance management is presented in part 4 and the second intervention, i.e. capitalizing on competency management in institutionalization of performance management' is presented in part 5.

COMPETENCY MANAGEMENT

Competency management, albeit yet to acquire a universally accepted definition, may be defined as *a comprehensive human resource strategy that identifies and builds the most relevant competencies to facilitate peak employee and organizational performance*. Competency management in the context of performance management encompasses six steps as indicated below:

1. Process of identifying critical, routine and supplementary knowledge, skills and characteristics required for performing a role effectively.
2. Process of identifying fundamental, medium and advanced level knowledge, skills and characteristics required by an employee to manage variety of functions/departments in an organization.
3. Process of identifying fundamental, medium and advanced knowledge, skills and characteristics required to lead an organization.
4. Grouping, classifying and defining steps 1, 2 and 3 into organization, function and role specific competency models.
5. Using articulated and customized competency model to nurture competency-based performance management.
6. Using competency-based performance management in institutionalization of performance management strategies like reward, career, leadership, measurement, culture, and team based.

A well-established and proven methodology can be used in execution of the above five steps. These are discussed in detail in the following text.

WHAT IS NOT COMPETENCY MANAGEMENT

Competency management is often confused with core competence. Competency management focuses on (i) identifying knowledge, skills and characteristics in order to perform a role, manage a function and lead an organization and (ii) converting such identified indices into competency models. In other words, it is centred on human resource competency whereas core competence model deals with distinct technological, product and business strengths of an organization. Often human resource competency leads to forming core competence of an organization.

Competency management is also understood as a mere improvement of job analysis or a sophisticated version of human resource planning study. Competency management as described above is a comprehensive and scientific process that paves a platform for building competencies at various levels of an organization, whereas job analysis is the process of studying and collecting information relating to operations and responsibilities of a specific job. Human resource planning is a function used in assessing the quality and quantity of human resource required in manning operations of an organization. Though there are some features and techniques that are commonly used in human resource planning and competency profiling, human resource planning is neither equivalent to nor a synonym with competency management.

SIGNIFICANCE OF COMPETENCY-BASED PERFORMANCE MANAGEMENT

Competency-based performance management helps organizations in accomplishment of their vision, mission and objectives. This achievement is possible because competency management enhances worth of human capital by evolving distinct and unimitable human competencies. Enriched human capital optimizes other organizational resources and leverages the existing strengths for organizational growth. Though competency management is potent enough to create indelible, positive and contributory impact on all organizational activities, a few of the essential advantages are indicated below. A renowned journal in the area of competency management, *Competency* identified the following 10 most significant reasons and purposes for adopting competency approach to their performance management:

1. Performance
2. Culture change
3. Training and development
4. Recruitment and selection
5. Business objectives/Competitiveness
6. Career/Succession planning
7. Skills analysis
8. Flexibility
9. Clarity of role
10. Integrating human resource strategy.

This identification was based on a survey of a number of organizations where competency management is in vogue.

Realization of Organizational Goal

Competency-based performance management facilitates contribution for achievement of organizational goals. This is done by aligning the role of every employee and functioning of every department with organizational goals in terms of competencies. For example, designations and formal positions form the basis for objectives realization in a hierarchical organization whereas competencies form the structure in competency-based performance

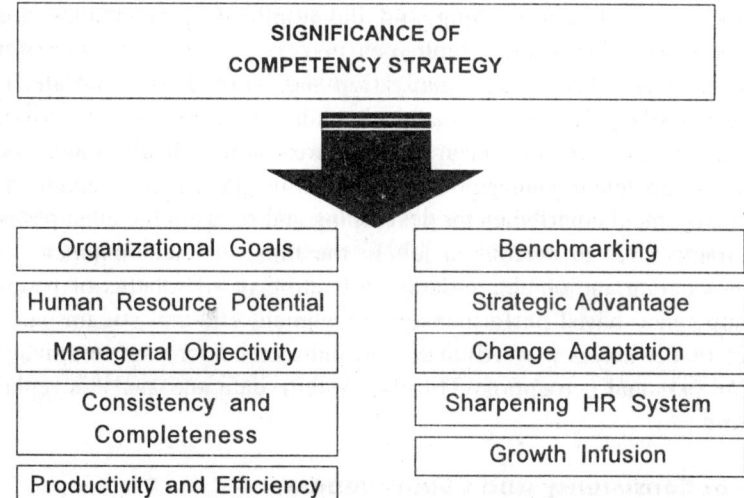

FIGURE 7.1 Significance of competency-based performance management strategy.

management strategy. Execution of competency strategy not only ensures availability of requisite human capabilities to perform various activities related to the said goal achievement in not just short and medium terms but also in long term. Employees individually and collectively will be able to see direct and clear linkage between competencies they hold and requirement of such competencies to attain organizational objectives. In a tautological sense, competencies are the means in realization of objectives. On the other hand, competency-based performance management augments the process of setting organizational objectives in a realistic manner. The stock of competencies themselves can influence an organization to adopt the kind of objectives that are in agreement with the available quality and quantity of competency resource.

Realization of Human Resource Potential

The structure of competency-based performance management is built on well-articulated model of achievement motivation. Competency profiling provides a direction for employee growth in a meaningful way. Firstly, it identifies the inner potential of an individual in terms of technical dexterity and attitudinal chemistry. Secondly, it matches the competency profile of this individual with a suitable role/position within the organization. Thirdly, it contributes in planning and development of professional growth of that individual. In this process, competency management enhances performance of employee and inspires to realize potential in the most efficient and fulfilling manner.

Realization of Objectivity and Accuracy

Essence of management, particularly people management lies in ensuring equity in decision-making. Unfortunately, subjectivity rules the decision-making pattern in most of the times, in most of the cases and in majority of organizations. This subjectivity occurs in management of recruitment and selection, training and development, performance appraisals, career planning and reward distribution. Employees perceive subjectivity as arbitrariness that in turn destroys the social fabric of an organization and causes loss of morale. This subjectivity occurs not necessarily because a manager intends to be biased or favours subjectivism. Often, absence of objective and accurate measures/indices leads managers to choose the intuitive way. Competency management bridges this gap in a scientific manner. Firstly, competency management contributes for developing and freezing the most pertinent knowledge, skills and characteristics to perform a job in the most efficient manner. This competency index helps in accurate and objective-decision making in all spheres of people management. Secondly, competency-based performance management strategy streamlines all activities in such a manner that it leaves proportionate and judicious discretion to managers to influence things based on personal perception. Thirdly, system, data and analysis replace personalized decision-making.

Realization of Consistency and Completeness

Logical consequence of objectivity and accuracy is consistency in decision-making. Consistency happens because competency-based performance management drives data and fact-based decision-making and expels subjective perceptions. Understanding of performance criterion and evaluation is uniform across organization, no matter how wide operations/activities of that organization are spread. Secondly, competency-based performance management develops parameters on extensive study of all directly and indirectly related aspects of performance. Parameters that exist are comprehensive in nature. Strategy of competency-based performance management realizes consistency and completeness in management of performance.

Maximizes Productivity, Performance and Efficiency

Developmental and growth role that competency-based performance management performs automatically enhances productivity, performance and efficiency levels. This occurs on account of three broad factors. Firstly, competency management plots right people with right skills to right roles. Such a match makes work as natural to people and they derive utmost esteem and satisfaction while working. It implies that competency management ensures that what people intend to do in life and what they actually do in the organization are same. Secondly, competency management aids in development efforts with result orientation. Thirdly, tangible measures that competency management evolves assist in self-monitoring of performance.

Creates Benchmarking

Possessing benchmarking culture is one of the real value advantage to organizations. Ultimate objective of competency-based performance management strategy is to create benchmarks in all areas of performance. The objective, measurable and well-articulated competency models not only contribute for peak performances and optimization of efforts, but also sets new standards in working and problem-solving methods. Breaking existing norms, revising, freezing new norms and again breaking these norms for perfection happens on continuous basis. Continuous improvement is thus the hallmark of competency management in the context of performance management.

Provides Strategic Advantage

In an ever changing and competitive business environment, organizations' search for gaining competitive advantage grows. Many a times past experiences of organizations in gaining supremacy with the support of state-of-the-art technology, heavy capital investments, economies of scale, large-scale mergers and acquisitions, have not been very encouraging. Technology, capital and other corporate strategies are equally available to all organization. All these resources are imitable and substitutable. In these circumstances, it is conclusively proved that the only resource that can provide a distinct competitive advantage to organizations is knowledge, skills and characteristics of human resource. Competency-based performance management puts organizations in a vantage position and gives precious strategic edge over competitors and rivals.

Enables Change Adaptation

Success of an organization is also largely influenced by its ability to adapt to environmental changes and also its capability to influence the direction and type of changes. Competency-based performance management builds organizational flexibility and agility through creation of relevant competencies. In competency-based management, people and organization acquire right competency profile. This enables them to lead organizations in the conditions of micro and macro level changes. The central issue is that competency management emphasizes attitudinal development in equal measures as that of technical/functional competencies. An organization with a wealth of competency stock can dominate the business scenario and precipitate changes in its own favour.

Sharpens Human Resource Management System

Competency management significantly contributes to systematic practice of human resource management in the areas of recruitment and selection, performance appraisal, training and development, career and succession planning. Each of these human resource management functions requires objective and measurable indices. For example, a recruitment manager must be clear with regard to what knowledge, skills and attitudinal characteristics are required to perform a job most efficiently in order to recruit the best talent. Similarly, data related to skills should be imparted to which person is of utmost importance to a training manager. Likewise, a career planning manager must possess accurate data regarding the potential profile of employees in order to decide their career movement in a systematic and purposeful fashion. Competency-based management provides all these data and assists all these managers with the competency models and indices. Strategy of competency-based performance management performs a central role in all human resource management functions in a direct and tangible manner.

Infuses Growth and Learning Optimism

The greatest advantage with competency-based performance management strategy is that due to its focus on identifying and building right blend of competencies on regular basis, it infuses tendency of growth and learning optimism. Employees can stay in a state of incorrigible optimism when they involve in learning, sharpening and adding competencies on a continuous basis. This optimism is precisely what many corporate organizations solicit in the environment of fluctuating business fortunes. Competency orientation also drives people and organizations to be growth focused, which is an excellent trait to make a steady progress.

THEORETICAL FOUNDATIONS OF COMPETENCY MANAGEMENT

History of competency management may be as old as human resource management because competency administration has already existed in one form or the other. However, it has gained a scientific shape and acquired systematically validated tools and techniques in recent past. Evolution of competency management and newly found magnificent advantages and benefits to organizations and people, made it to grow popular amongst other management strategies.

MCCLELLAND'S STUDY ON COMPETENCY

Credit for latest surge in the interest and practice of competency management goes to David McClelland. He brought competency management into limelight through application of competency mapping in a study conducted on US Information Agency in 1973. McClelland found that the following five competencies are critical for people to become successful managers:

- Specialized knowledge
- Intellectual maturity
- Entrepreneurial maturity
- Interpersonal maturity
- On-the-job maturity.

In order to identify these competencies, McClelland used a variety of data collection techniques such as interview, case study method and also deployed the conventional job analysis tools. This study contributed significantly for progress of job competency models.

BOYATZIS' 21 COMPETENCY FRAMEWORK

Richard Boyatzis is a researcher who made a significant progress in the development of competency management as a science. Based on a number of studies, Boyatzis identified 21 competencies that distinguish effective managers from average performers. These are called *Boyatzis' 21 competencies* organized into six competency clusters. These are illustrated in Table 7.1. Boyatzis's work is regarded as eloquent, blending persuasive economic argument with applied research.

TABLE 7.1   Boyatzis' 21 Competencies

1. Goal and action management cluster	1. Efficiency orientation
	2. Productivity
	3. Diagnostic use of concepts
	4. Concern with impact
2. Leadership cluster	5. Self-confidence
	6. Use of oral presentations
	7. Logical thought
	8. Conceptualization
3. Human resource cluster	9. Use of socialized power
	10. Positive regard
	11. Managing group processes
	12. Accurate self-assessment
4. Directing subordinates cluster	13. Developing others
	14. Use of unilateral power
	15. Spontaneity
5. Focus on customers	16. Self-control
	17. Perceptual objectivity
	18. Stamina and adaptability
	19. Concern with close relationships
6. Specialized knowledge	20. Memory
	21. Specialized knowledge

HENDRY AND MAGGIO'S STRATEGIC ORIENTATION TO COMPETENCY

I. Hendry and E. Maggio are credited for giving strategic orientation to competency management. They proposed a competency management framework linking to organizational goals through the following elements:

- Description of skills, attitudes, traits and behaviours that can be attached to pay, performance measurement, hiring criteria, training, organizational staffing, career development and succession planning.
- Clarification, communication, assessment and development of characteristics that focus individuals on core organizational goals.
- Identification of characteristics and behaviours that differentiate top performers from others in relation to their contribution to strategic objectives.

KANUNGO AND MISRA'S META COMPETENCY FRAMEWORK

Framework of R.N. Kanungo and S. Misra mainly focused on defining competencies and distinguishing them from meta competencies. These are described below:

- Competencies encompass ability to: (i) engage in overt behavioural sequence or systems, (ii) handle routine and programmed tasks and established procedures, (iii) cope with demands of the environment, (iv) perform specialized tasks and (v) engage in a behaviour that is contextually efficient.
- Meta competencies refer to the ability to: (i) engage in activities that require functional intelligence, (ii) engage in non-routine and un-programmed tasks, (iii) cope with complex and volatile aspects of environment, (iv) think analytically and capacity to engage in generalized and variety of tasks and (v) be non-specific and the capacity to lead.

LESSONS OF COMPETENCY FRAMEWORKS

Studies, research and development of competency management in general and competency models in particular are largely confined to the job level competency barring a few exceptions where studies focused on functional level competencies. Competency frameworks as discussed above contribute mainly to carving a path and showing direction for developing and practicing competency management. This is one of the areas of people management where practice is running ahead of theory. Chief lesson of the said competency works of early researchers of competency-based performance management is that utmost sanctity must be accorded to reliability and validity of competency development methodology. Competency models built on rigorous methods and in consonance with organizational reality yield real value and returns to organizations.

COMPETENCY-BASED PERFORMANCE MANAGEMENT STRATEGY, INTERVENTIONS AND DRIVERS

Competency-based performance management strategy is realized through a combination of two interventions as illustrated below:

1. *Nurturing competency-based management:* First initiative in planning and implementation of competency-based performance management strategy is nurturing a competency-based management in terms of systems, practices and people. This is popularly called building competency models. This intervention, in a state of matured practice, can transform an organization and its people into entities of competency. This is accomplished with the assistance of 10 drivers.
2. *Capitalizing on competency management in institutionalization of performance management:* Second intervention is concerned with institutionalization of performance management with the support of competency models. This is realized with the assistance of 10 most pragmatic and action-oriented drivers.

These interventions and associated drivers are discussed here in an illustrative manner. This illustration presents a model format that can facilitate organizations and managers intending to adopt competency-based performance management.

INTERVENTION 1: NURTURING COMPETENCY-BASED PERFORMANCE MANAGEMENT

Nurturing competency-based performance management is one of the biggest and challenging assignments a performance manager can ever dream of handling. This involves two critical aspects: (i) applying action-oriented-research-based analytical framework in building customized competency models and (ii) deploying contextually sensitive measures for effective execution of competency models. Both these critical activities, i.e. building competency models and executing them are continuous in nature like other performance management strategies discussed in this book rather than one time affair. This is because competency models and execution tactics are susceptible to change in tandem with changing internal and external realities of organizations. Intervention of nurturing competency-based performance management can be realized through initiation of 10 drivers as discussed below. Actual implementation and process can involve more elaborate and comprehensive efforts and hard work in consonance with size, nature, business dynamics and operational complexities, intricacies and competency poeple index of an organization.

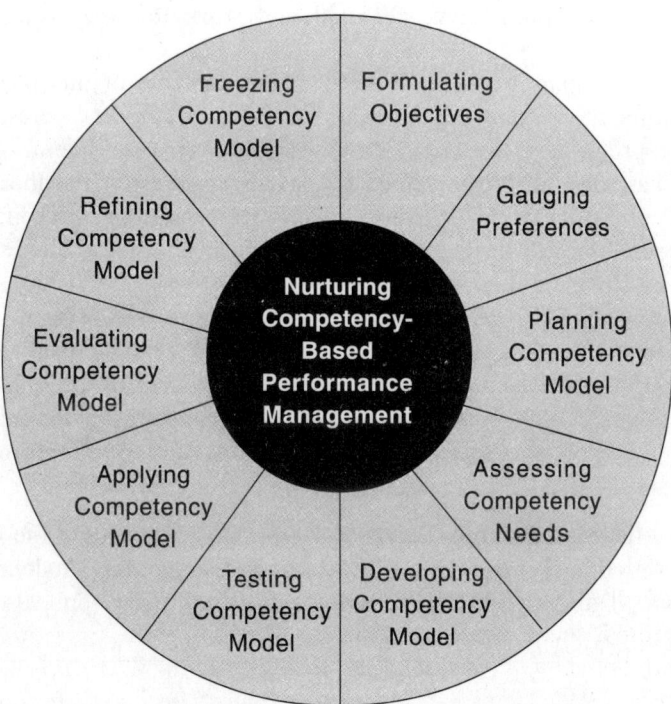

FIGURE 7.2 Drivers of the intervention nurturing competency-based performance management.

BEST PRACTICE
Competency-Based Integrated Human Resources System in Prudential Healthcare

Prudential Healthcare had embarked on creating a competency-based management system in 1994 with an objective to implement a competency-based human resources system that would complement Prudential Healthcare's efforts to produce a major change in compensation, performance planning and appraisal, training and development, selection processes and human resource planning. Before actually launching competency-building initiative, a comprehensive education and communication plan was executed using e-mails, newsletters, presentations in order to create awareness among employees about benefits the competency building initiative can provide.

This competency initiative which was developed with the assistance of Apple Consulting comprises of three phases:

- *Phase I: Identification of competencies*: 15 job families containing jobs held by almost all employees were selected for competency identification. Competencies were identified through a multiple step procedure consisting of (i) management meetings, (ii) focus groups and (iii) competency identification surveys. Based on this, competency statements were written for each family and grouped into categories. For example, core competencies that applied to all 15 job families were identified in four areas: communication, personal and work management, teamwork and customer focus.

- *Phase II: Competency assessment pilot*: The objective of this phase was to test the process for competency assessment. All pilot participants were given a special orientation programme to learn about competency assessment. All employees participated as ratees whose competencies have been assessed. Feedback was solicited on competency orientation sessions, selection procedure, rater education, content and completion process of the competency assessment survey. The overall feedback was very positive.

- *Phase III: Creating a competency-based human resources system*: Competencies were integrated into practices such as training and development, recruitment and selection, performance appraisal and compensation. For example, results of competency assessment were used in combination with performance results to determine overall basic pay for each employee. Similarly, training and development programmes were developed based on the results of competency assessment.

(Based on Bina, Michele and Juhlin Newkirk, 1998. "Competencies at the Rock: Creating a Competency Based Integrated Human Resources System for Prudential Healthcare Group". In David, Dubois (Ed.), *The Competency Case Book*, pp. 93–120, Amherst, MA: HRD Press.)

DRIVER 1: FORMULATION OF COMPETENCY DEVELOPMENT OBJECTIVES

It is of paramount importance that a competency development programme have clear objectives of (i) why competency development is required and (ii) what is the expectation from such a competency development intervention. This statement of objectives can guide and direct the competency development programme in a meaningful and effective mode. Exercise of building objectives can bring greater awareness and generate realistic expectations about competency-based performance management apart from preparing an organization for organizational, functional and role level change. Formulation stage especially assumes significance in organizations, as managers are attracted to competency management because this is the management strategy of the day or since some organizations that have implemented competency management are doing very well. A competency development programme must be attempted and seen as a critical business level issue and needs to originate from a hard core requirement rather than a ploy to generate good will or simply with an intention to join in the bandwagon of competency fashioned companies.

Competency development also must not be taken up with faith syndrome that doing it can provide some undefined fortunes to the company. A pragmatic understanding and clear expectation and purposes of competency development can produce (i) right allocation of resources, (ii) right combination of efforts and actions and (iii) right progress. In contrast, vague expectations and substandard understanding can cause (i) competency development efforts derailing, (ii) abandoning the programme midway (iii) not gaining any positive benefits and (iv) adding confusion in management of people and organization. In the past and at present, many organizations that experimented with competency mapping/ profiling/modelling/management have not experienced success. This is due to lack of clear objectives and consequential unsystematic plan in pushing through competency development programme. Therefore, the first driving force in the mammoth effort of building a competency-based performance management strategy is formulating a legible, realistic and implementable statement of competency development objectives. Preparing this statement involves considering all related aspects in management of an organization. Following steps are indicative of such aspects:

Step 1: Study of Organizational Vision, Mission and Environment

Effectiveness of a competency development strategy is contingent upon the extent to which such a strategy helps an organization to attain its vision, mission and business objectives. This mandates that objectives of a competency development must emanate from objectives of the company. This requires a competency manager to first study and understand vision, mission, objectives and business environment of an organization and draw lessons of importance. Intent of such organizational objectives and operational plans also must be studied. In order to make real progress on this, a wide range of discussions with strategic and corporate planning managers must be held and every aspect of company objective must be understood in the same spirit and wavelength as that of these managers and creators of business objectives. The second step in this process is understanding business environment of an organization. This includes aspects such as related governmental legislation, competitors and markets. This study contributes in grasping the background of business strategies and objectives apart from helping in drafting the organizational level competency.

Step 2: Study of Product Process/Product Knowledge

The second step in formulation of competency development objectives is to conduct a study of product process and product mix of an organization. Ultimately, a good competency development programme must strengthen efforts of product managers in creating a unique product range. In fact, competency development programme can wield a direct influence in improving product management. It is the human competency that creates products and enhances efficiency of product process. Concerns, plans, impending innovations, anticipated and intended developments in the area of product development and product process must be reckoned while setting up competency development objectives. A competency development statement that has no direct relevance with the said product/process will become irrelevant to an organization in general and product management in particular.

Step 3: Study of Organizational Systems

While formulating objectives of competency development programme, existing organizational systems need to be studied. Strengthening of organizational system is one of the objectives and consequences of competency-based performance management. For example, unless the philosophy and practice of quality management system are clearly understood, it will be difficult to apply and extend competency development intervention targeting at building quality competency. All such management systems at macro level must be studied and understood to derive the relevant insights to incorporate them into objectives statement of competency development.

Step 4: Study of Organizational Technology

Type of technology it employs determines the type of competency models that an organization requires. Competency is needed to be built in order to exploit the existing technology optimally and leveraging it for big gains. It is quite possible that no two organizations in the same industry may need and solicit the same competency models due to variance in technology. Competency models vary corresponding to the generation and sophistication of technology and the kind of techno-human interface that exists. Therefore, study of technology and its management is one of the compulsory steps in finalising the competency development objectives.

Step 5: Study of Competitors, Suppliers and Customers

In many occasions, valuable ideas and suggestions come forth from suppliers and customers in terms of improving functioning of an organization. Similarly, study of competitors and co-organizations help in gathering necessary information with regard to what is needed in building a unique and excellent competency framework. All this information can form a formidable base for developing the most relevant, contemporary and effective competency development objectives. A statement of competency development objectives that is sensitive to the world of customers and suppliers tends to contribute to create a customer focused competency development revolution. Study of competitors/co-organization efforts can motivate an organization to aim at a bigger set of competency models.

As discussed above, study of organizational objectives, product process, technology, the perceptions of suppliers and customers, organizational structure, strategy and systems provide the basic inputs to what kind of competency models an organization requires to build for survival and growth. Vision, mission and objectives and business plans set the backdrop in defining the purpose of competency models. Competency development objectives statement derived from these elements tend to be actionable and become a means to set the tone for marching towards competitive advantage.

DRIVER 2:   GAUGING CURRENT COMPETENCY PREFERENCES

All organizations perform and progress with the support and coordination of various functions like production, services, planning, marketing, materials, finance, human resource management, so on and so forth to deliver the goods and services. These functions are manned and handled by people occupying different positions in the organizational structure. Study and analysis of the role of these functional disciplines and also contribution of each job position provide a vital data with regard to the existing scenario of competency framework. Organization prior to creating a tailor-made organization specific competency models, must gather all information regarding functional disciplines and job positions in a scientific manner. Procedure and methodology should be adopted for undertaking this analysis varies from organization to organization due to their uniqueness. A model procedure is suggested below that can guide organizations in their effort to conduct such a study.

Step 1:   Study of Functions/Disciplines

In order to chart existing functional set up and workflow in an organization, a study must be done with the aim to gather information on how each of the functional disciplines contribute for organizational performance. Organizational set up and structure also must be studied in the context of competency-based performance management. This study hopefully assists in understanding how an organization presently meets the competency requirements and also what kind of competency models are sought.

Step 2:   Study of HR Planning Report

Some form of human resource planning, either systematic or unsystematic exists in all organizations. Some organizations call it manpower budgeting and others manpower planning. This manpower planning reports can be a good source to gather information regarding quality and quantity of manpower standardized to perform particular operations and to deliver stipulated results in a given set of framework. This data also provides quality part of manpower planning, throwing light on the solicited competencies in an organization. Perusal of manpower planning studies can lead to understanding internal competency standardization.

Step 3: Study of Delegation of Powers

Decision-making pattern is one of the good sources to figure out competency requirement at different levels of an organization. This especially provides a picture of managerial competencies distribution and intensity of knowledge and skills requirement.

Step 4: Study of Recruitment and Selection System

Recruitment and selection decisions are arrived for different position based on competencies required to perform such roles in most efficient, effective and innovative manner. A detailed study of all selection procedures and parameters adapted for selection of people can provide vital information regarding the relevant competency set for each position or family of positions.

Step 5: Study of Training System

Study and analysis of the training system in the context of competency-based performance management yields a mine of information. Basically, a training system provides data on (i) what kind of competencies are planned for being groomed, (ii) how these competency requirements are assessed and (iii) how the gap between competency requirement and availability is planned to be bridged. This also presents information on the competency profile of most of the employees in a language of training and development needs.

Study of training calendar/schedule itself gives the feel of competency position in an organization. These documents which include (i) training needs analysis at organizational and employee level, (ii) implementation of training programmes and (iii) evaluation methods of training, present wealth of information that immensely helps in assessing competency grooming endeavours.

Step 6: Study of Performance Appraisal System

Functions, responsibilities and roles that people perform in an organization can be accessed through the study of performance appraisal system. Dimensions/parameters/indicators adopted for assessing performance of employees present a picture of what is expected from employees. This also presents the scenario of competency in the shape of competencies that are expected from employees to perform their roles. The (i) key result areas (ii) rating people as star performers and (iii) substandard performers reveal the organizational preference for certain kind of knowledge, skills and attitudinal characteristics.

Step 7: Study of Career and Succession Planning System

Vertical growth plan of jobs and succession planning approaches of an organization also comprise relevant information that can be of significant utility in understanding the competency-related issues. The kind and level of competencies that are made mandatory for moving people to higher positions, and the kind of developmental activities people are exposed to as a part of succession planning, can point to the preferred competency model. Method an organization chooses to move its people on the upward ladder, i.e. merit or seniority, fast track careers or generic positions, specialist centred careers, etc. also gives a clue to the basic philosophy and orientation of an organization towards competencies.

Step 8:   Study of Job Evaluation

Few organizations implement job evaluation in order to assess the comparative worth of the job position for different purposes such as to (i) determine compensation, (ii) place the position at the appropriate level in the organizational hierarchy and (iii) delegate powers and formal authority. Reports generated using the job evaluation technique can be of potential utility to the competency development endeavour in terms of gauging the competency requirement with different positions.

Step 9:   Study of Benchmark Practices

It can also be useful in gaining a wider perspective if benchmarking practices in the area of competency development are studied. Web-based sites like www.bestpracticedatabase.com and annual survey of best practices like Hewitt-BT best HR practices survey results can provide the data regarding best practices in competency development. The study of such reports and their analysis helps in enhancing knowledge base and also comprehending the current preferences of competency models.

Step 10:   Study of Culture Preference

It is also important to understand the cultural preferences of employees as far as competency-based management are concerned. For example, collective cultures prefer seniority, experience and evolutionary growth whereas individualized culture favours fast track and performance-oriented careers. Though competency development can be successfully launched in both these settings with equal efficiency and results, understanding cultural issues have its own advantage in strategizing the competency development program.

DRIVER 3:   PLANNING FOR PERFORMANCE CENTRIC COMPETENCY DEVELOPMENT MODEL

Once the statement of competency development objectives are finalized and the existing scenario of competency development inside and outside an organization is understood, it is the right time to move to the third driver, i.e. planning an organization specific competency development programme. Planning with precision, diligence and pragmatism is a prerequisite for any corporate development strategy to be successful. This is more so in the case of a competency development intervention since it has implications for all stakeholders of an organization. Performance stimulated competency development programme must be planned to avoid any pitfalls because not having a competency development programme is much better for an organization rather than launching the one with loose reliability structure and weak foundation/fundamentals. Planning again has to be done in conformity with objectives of competency development programme and with high sensitivity to organizational reality. Though there is no universally applicable model that can be adapted for planning a competency development intervention, a suggestive process with a few tools and techniques are described as follows:

Step 1: Translate Drivers 1 and 2 into Action Plans

First step in planning for competency development intervention is translating the (i) statement of objectives of competency development, (ii) information gathered using a variety of techniques on the existing situation of competency development programme and (iii) competency preferences into operational and actionable plans. Actionable plan must particularly specify the type of competency development programme favoured to achieve the business objectives and performance excellence.

Step 2: Determine Competency Development Methodology

Based on the first step as discussed above, suitable methodology must be developed that fits well with the type of competency development methods sought for. Popularly used methods of competency identification with purpose are illustrated in Table 7.2. First level is choosing the competency method and the second level is choosing appropriate tools and techniques to be employed for data collection. These data collection methods include: (i) interviews with incumbents, (ii) interacting and conferencing with focus groups, (iii) surveys, (iv) 360 degree questionnaire surveys, (v) critical incident techniques and (vi) observation groups. These methods are discussed in detail in Driver 4, i.e. executing a competency development programme.

TABLE 7.2 Popular Methods of Identifying Competency

S.No.	Competency Method	Purpose
1.	Job competence method	• To identify differences between outstanding and average performers using interview and observation methods
2.	Modified job competence method	• To identify behavioural differences between top performers and average performers based on the written reports of interviewees
3.	Generic model overlay method	• To establish generic competencies required to perform a role or function with the help of an off-the-shelf generic competency model purchased from outside source
4.	Customized generic model method	• To develop a list of organization specific competencies using research-based methodology such as developing a tentative list of competencies and then validating them through application of these competencies.
5.	Flexible job competency model method	• To identify competencies that will be required to perform effectively under different conditions in future
6.	Systems method	• To identify what exemplary performers do not only at present and in overall scenario but also behaviours that may be important in future
7.	Accelerated competency systems method	• To identify competencies that specifically support the production of output such as an organization's products, services or information

Step 3: Allocation of Resources

Allocation of budget (money), creation of adequate infrastructure to conduct competency development programme and commitment of top management assumes greater importance in planning for competency building. Organizations require to allocate such resources depending upon size, operations, physical spread, technology, product range, services, and more importantly, number of employees expected to be covered and objectives of competency development initiative. Initially, a competency development programme attracts substantial investment in terms of money and effort. However, that should not be a discouraging factor since organization will be hugely benefited, may be in multiple times, to that of their investment from a systematically planned and executed competency development initiative. Therefore, resource allocation estimate is one necessary and logical step in this driver.

Step 4: Identification of Beneficiary Zones and Determination of Study Scope

Length and breadth of a competency development programme coverage, i.e. the functional areas and the people to be covered in the organization under this programme need to be identified and decided. For example, some organizations may like to identify competencies required to perform a few functional areas like operations, marketing only whereas some other organizations may like to cover all departments/functions. Likewise, some may wish to cover all positions and still others only selective positions like managerial posts. It is also not uncommon that some organizations plan to identify competencies required to perform a role only and not assessing people in references to these competencies. In other words, such a competency development programme will be confined to only establishing competencies required to manage departments and posts and not assessing the competency development profiles of employees. Complete and a scientific competency development programme must aim at both: (i) identifying competencies required to perform excellently various functions and roles and also (ii) mapping the existing scenario of people competencies in references to these identified functional and role competencies. Next sequential step can be to develop people in line with such identified competency models.

Step 5: Fixing up of Time Schedules

Competency development initiative must be launched with properly and realistically defined time schedules. For example, the time duration allocated for completion of competency identification for finance function and more specifically when it commences and concludes. This should comprise the entire break up of activities with time fixed for execution of each of these activities. Similar can be the case with assessing competency profile of employees.

Step 6: Identification of Resource Persons

To coordinate execution of competency development intervention, administrators and facilitators within an organization need to be identified. These resource persons must be drawn from all levels of organization and not only from managerial grades. This identification can be done with the help of external specialists also. Resource persons must be people with adequate knowledge in their own functional areas, with right attitude, communication abilities and must enjoy a neutral image in organization. These resource persons (i) must be trained in all aspects of a competency development programme and also (ii) should be motivated to realize competency-based performance culture in organization. Most importantly, resource persons must be exposed to data collection methodology and related techniques.

Step 7: Identify Deliverables

Entire competency development programme must be organized into well-connected parts. Each of these parts must deliver anticipated results on successful implementation. This helps in not only setting pace for progress, but also makes monitoring easy and meaningful. Fixing deliverables at each of these steps involves clear understanding of the process and making realistic expectations. This is also beneficial in diagnosing and carrying out midway corrections, timely and without much loss.

Step 8: Preventive and Contingent Actions

Good planning must have and leave scope for minor changes and modifications as and when required. Planning process should be specific, objective, well-defined and flexible within reasonable limits. It is difficult to prefix such limits because it is the sincerity and commitment with which competency development intervention is launched that decides such limits.

DRIVER 4: ASSESSMENT OF COMPETENCY NEEDS

Critical driver in nurturing performance centred competency management is actually developing customized competency models. The significant milestone in developing a competency model is assessing competency needs at multiple levels in an organization. This requires an organization (i) to set up a smooth communication system in place, (ii) determining levels of assessment, (iii) development of data collection instruments and (iv) their reliability and validity.

Step 1: Keeping Communicated

All employees likely to be affected in particular and all employees whether targeted to be covered or not must be clearly communicated (i) salient features of competency development intervention, (ii) methodology being planned, (iii) purpose of such initiative, (iv) benefits to individual and collective employees and, if possible, (v) time schedules fixed for implementation of the initiative. Discussions and special conferences shall be held with collective bargaining representatives if unionism exists in the organization. This communication process must be ongoing. Objective of communication must be to (i) generate awareness about competency development initiative and (ii) to dispel any apprehensions and misconceptions about such a competency development programme.

Step 2: Deciding Competency Assessment Levels

Developing competency assessment methods is a litmus test in the strategy of competency-based performance management. Competency requirements need to be assessed at different levels as indicated here:

- *Organizational level:*   Competency assessment must be conducted at organizational level. Identification of competencies that are necessary and strategic to lead organization towards excellence. This locating of organizational level competencies is a macro exercise. For example, it involves assessing the competency requirements in multi-disciplinary spheres like strategy, business economics, quality, finance, people management, operations, marketing, supply chain management, information technology application, analytical abilities, soft skills, leadership. As stated, this should be done at organizational level, meaning thereby that it shouldn't be extended to micro level knowledge and specifications of such disciplines.
- *Functional level:*   The second level of competency assessment must be conducted at functional/department level. This assessment provides data about the kind and depth of competencies necessary to manage functions effectively, efficiently and innovatively. This initiative covers all functions in an organization like finance, operations, marketing, materials, human resource management, corporate planning, etc.
- *Job level:*   Third level of assessment is job level. It helps identifying the type of competencies required to perform a job with excellence. There can be more than one kind of job in the same function. For example, operations department may comprise three jobs: managers, supervisors and technicians. This assessment, therefore, must be conducted at these three job levels. Competencies required to perform these jobs qualitatively can be different and hence, differences in competencies.

Step 3:   Developing Competency Assessment Instruments

Success of competency development intervention is largely dependent upon reliability and validity of competency assessment instruments. This is also called data collection method. It plays a vital role in developing realistic, credible and scientific competency models. Most commonly employed methods/instruments in such assessment are:

Questionnaire Method: The most popular and widely used technique in assessing competencies is questionnaire method. This method helps in all the three levels of competency assessment: organization, function and job. A few relevant variables need to be identified and developed. For example, competency variables for the job of human resource manager can be:

   (i) Knowledge of human resource management theoretical aspects
  (ii) Knowledge of best human resource management practices
 (iii) Knowledge of organization's human resource policies and procedures
 (iv) Knowledge about organization, it's business strategy and plans, operations, financials, competitors, various stakeholders.
  (v) Ability to use tools and techniques in human resource functions like recruitment, performance appraisal, training, and career planning systems
 (vi) Interpersonal relationship skills
(vii) Communication skills

(viii) Conflict management skills
(ix) Change management skills and
(x) Commitment to the organization.

These variables must be operationalized into measurable statements. These statements can be open-ended or in shape of checklist or with multiple choice or in a form of scale like strongly agree to strongly disagree. Similarly, this questionnaire method can be used for assessing competency profile at all levels.

Interview Method: Interviewing job incumbents to elicit what competencies are required to perform a job effectively reveals valuable information that helps in identifying the most relevant competencies of a job. Resource persons who are trained on interview method use both a standardized and contingency format to collect information. Format contains combination of structured and open-ended questions. Taking into account the scope of study, either all or representative sample of employees will be subjected to these interviews. Likewise, interviewing head of department, chief executive can reveal function and organizational level competencies.

Observation Method: Resource persons observe the top and average performers while working and taking decisions, interacting with people, leading co-employees, learning new aspects and applying them. Typically, the first part of such report contains record of observations and the second part observer's own interpretation and analysis of this record. This observation of extreme performers in action facilitates identification of the competencies required to carry out a task or job in the most efficient manner and also, what inadequacy in competencies result in average performance. However, effectiveness of this method depends upon the objectivity and neutrality of observers.

Story Writing Method: In this method, employees and their superiors will be asked to write in descriptive fashion, tasks they perform and knowledge, skills and behavioural characteristics required to perform such tasks with quality, precision and results. Writings from all employees and superiors will be collected and analyzed to assess competency requirements of various jobs, and functions and at the organizational level.

Critical Incident Technique: Major incidents either resulted in remarkable results or failures to organizations and individuals if studied can provide wealth of information on competencies required to handle such incidents. In this method, a few incidents happened in the past or situations likely to arise at present or future will be chosen for a special study. Both observers and incumbents of the jobs will write a descriptive version on the origin of incident, how this has been tackled, why a particular approach is used over others, what knowledge, skill or soft skills are used in resolving such an incident and what results are expected and actually what is achieved. Data collected using this method particularly helps in identifying critical competencies.

Repertory Grid: This method is somewhat similar to critical incident technique. Repertory grid is used to identify dimensions of good and poor standards of performance. These dimensions are developed through interviewing and surveying jobholders to explore what behaviours make some to perform exceedingly well while others give poor performance.

360 Degree Survey: Collecting views as well as perceptions of all stakeholders regarding what competencies are desirable and essential to lead an organization, manage departments and perform various jobs in an organization effectively, yields a lot of information. This data involving all stakeholders on all competency levels can be collected using questionnaires, essay writings, debates and conferences.

Focus Groups: In this method, employees (i) who are performing exceedingly well and (ii) whose innovation rate is far superior and who have the record of breaking status quo will be formed as a focus group. This group will work on identifying and suggesting the ideal competency model to put into practice at organizational, functional and job level for magnificent results.

Case study method: Highly successful performances which employees cherish and regard the best in their career in an organization and events of under performances must be studied in depth in order to understand circumstances in which performance goes to peak and conditions that cause below average performance. Skills required to successfully manage adverse conditions and skills required to create conducive conditions of superior performances can be identified. The case study method is used where a detailed study is required. Resource persons conduct the study with the help of a structured and unstructured information seeking formats.

Step 4: Establishing Validity of Competency Assessment Instruments

Quality of competency development effort tends to be equivalent to the standards of competency assessment methods. Standards can be ensured only through establishing reliability and validity of data collection methods and instruments. Reliability and content validity testing must be done once instruments such as questionnaires, interview schedules, structured statements/ measures are finalized. Unless, these instruments qualify standards of reliability and validity, they should not be used for data collection purposes. Similarly, methods for identifying samples, target groups, choice of incidents and selection of resource persons must be executed diligently, objectively and in a rigorous manner. Training of resource persons to carry out different functions as a part of competency assessment method must be given due importance.

DRIVER 5: DEVELOPING TENTATIVE COMPETENCY MODEL

Based on the knowledge acquired and progress made with the application of Drivers 1, 2, 3 and 4, a tentative competency model at organizational, function and job level must be developed. Competencies assessed and identified at Driver 4 and keeping in view objectives of competency development intervention at Driver 1 and considering the preferences for a particular kind of competency model, a tentative competency model must be built. Following discussion suggests steps involved in realizing a tentative competency model:

Step 1: Execution of Competency Assessment Methods

Appropriate data collection methods in relation to the target of assessment level must be implemented. Data collected using combination of instruments must be organized organization, function and jobwise. Actual classification of data will be dependent upon the type of data collection instruments used and target groups covered. Data must be processed with the aid of suitable statistical and methodological data analysis techniques. Statistical Package for Social Sciences (SPSS), software generally used for data analysis in social science research, can be of significant use in this context. Nature of data decides the type of statistical technique that should be applied for gaining robust understanding and insights.

Step 2: Managing Resistance

Resistance in the form of non-cooperation and blunt responses to competency assessment can be expected in some situations. Some employees carry a threat perception about such studies. Therefore, care must be exercised in handling these situations with tact and contextual behaviour. Communication plays a vital role in dispelling such misconceptions. In some cases of competency development efforts, resistance is experienced from even senior and middle level management. Resistance from such senior cadres can be very subtle, particularly in the form of creating suspicions regarding methodological issues of competency identification and profiling. Utmost care must be taken in effectively driving objectivity of methodology down the organization. Wholehearted support and commitment of all employees is a prerequisite for developing competency model that is realistic and business aligned.

Step 3: Compromisations

It has been the experience with some competency developing attempts that organizations make quite a few compromises at the data collection stage, i.e. while assessing and identifying competencies. This may be in order to (i) serve selfish interests of some influential people in the organization or (ii) on account of ignorance of competency development administrators or (iii) simply because of lack of perseverance. All compromises tend to dent quality of competency modelling. This dent will be proportionate to the compromises made. Therefore, while executing competency assessment, managers must commit themselves fully and manifest perseverance in good measure. This does not mean that midway corrections should not be carried out that are meant to improve execution clarity and sharpness.

Step 4: Self-Images

While administering assessment instruments like interview, case study, critical incident technique where resource persons as well as employees play an active role, caution must be taken to avoid self-images. This can happen in two ways. Firstly, resource persons may tend to see what they want to see instead of what actually exists. This attitude can lead to identification of competencies that resource person thinks most appropriate rather than the actual ones. Second is diagression relying excessively on perceptions of employees regarding type of competencies required for performance excellence. Important caution here is, not to depend on one method or one version beyond a limit and create as many speed breakers and filters as possible for capturing a robust picture of competency.

Step 5: Developing Tentative Competency Models

Based on data collected with the help of above discussed drivers and in sharp alignment with competency development objectives, tentative competency models at organizational level, functional level and job level must be developed with a clear description of knowledge, skills and attitudinal characteristics required to achieve performance excellence in all parts of an organization. Organizational-level competency model must comprise knowledge, skills and attitudinal characteristics at macro level and emphasize importance of wider perspective, strategic focus and futuristic mind. Competency modelling at functional level must stress the importance of fundamental, intermediate and advanced level of knowledge and skills in that functional area, and also associated behavioural characteristics that strengthen contribution of such functions to achieve performance excellence. Job-level competency, must depict knowledge, skills and characteristics required for performing a job in the most efficient, effective and innovative style. Job-level competency description essentially captures the micro perspective; in other words the nuts and bolts of performing a job, which in fact plays the core role on performance building.

DRIVER 6: TESTING TENTATIVE COMPETENCY MODELS

Developing competency model as discussed at Driver 5 tantamount to half the progress made in the journey of nurturing competency-based performance management strategy. A critical and logical step after developing tentative competency development models is testing their efficacy on the ground. Here also like in data collection stage, a combination of surgical and humanistic approach must be adopted for administering testing procedures. This testing should be done based on three prime criteria.

Step 1: Testing Competency Models against their Own Objectives

There is a need to verify whether competency models developed at job, functional and organizational level are in conformity with the objectives of competency-based management set at the phase of Driver 1 above or if there is any conflict or contradiction or any loose alignment. This is generally a paper-based audit through which logic, coherence and rationale of competency model design in the backdrop of objectives statement is critically examined.

Step 2: Testing Competency Models through the Means of Auditing Process

As discussed in Driver 3, competency effort involves planning for it in advance. Definition of deliverables at each stage in an operational language is part of such planning. Auditing process involved in development of such competency models like data collection methods, their reliability, analysis, interpretation, adoption of results for development of competency models, can be scrutinized and evaluated to establish whether actually execution is proceeded in adherence to this planning and fundamentals of competency mapping or not. Evaluating whether identified deliverables at each stage in fact are delivered or not. This is like the process followed in quality certification.

Step 3: Circulation of Competency Models

Competency models as tentatively developed must be circulated amongst employees inviting their suggestions and critical comments. It will also be very fruitful if special conference and workshops are held with the aim to involve all employees and gather views and perceptions on large scale. Likewise, views of experts on the subject with international standing and management consultants with exposure to that particular industry can also be invited. All these data can be used to refer and cross-refer to assess efficacy of competency models.

Organization must (i) collect views and comments on competency models as discussed above, (ii) carry out process audit, (iii) consolidate and analyze this data and (iv) start implementing models once the results obtained are positive.

DRIVER 7: APPLYING COMPETENCY MODELS TO ORGANIZATION

The most critical part in nurturing competency-based performance management intervention is the successful launch and sustenance of Driver 7, that is, application of competency models to real life situations. This means grooming an organization on the curriculum and structure of competency models. This involves organization-wide revolution in terms of change in systems, practices and people. Following steps are indicated as suggestive of this process:

Step 1: Applying Competency Model to Systems

Application phase must begin with reorienting systems requirements and standards that include altering policies and procedures in organization in line with competency models. For example, human resource policies covering compensation, training, performance appraisal system, must be transformed to reinforce competency-based management strategy. However, an organization which initiates implementation of all the seven strategies of performance management discussed in this book just needs to check whether systems are correlating with conditions of competency models.

Step 2: Applying Competency Models to Practices

Every organization follows a distinct way of carrying out tasks and running organization and functions. This method of working pattern vary depending on the nature of organization and its perceived and real environment. This pattern of working also gets internalized in some organizations because of decades of practicing it. One of the biggest challenges to bring change in practices. It is much easier to make change in system in comparison to practices. Persistent approach must be adopted in realizing changes in practices to make them competency model friendly and as catalysts of competency-based performance management.

Step 3: Applying Competency Models to People

Next important step which needs to be implemented simultaneously along with applying competency models to practices is imparting or developing people drawing competency models as basis. This needs elaborate assessment strengths and weaknesses of people performing different roles in reference to job competency models. This initiative may provide different results. Firstly, it helps in mapping competency profile of people. This mapping paves a way for matching right people with right jobs. There are instances where applying competency models to people led to re-engineering of human resource placements within. It means there is a feasibility that people may be performing roles in which they are neither comfortable nor their competency profile matches with demands of the role. Secondly, as pointed out, competency models application highlights areas of concern, i.e. in what areas people need to be made competent through developmental intervention. This can be the most significant contribution of job competency models to people in particular and organization in general. Application of competency models can be complete only when the competency profile of people exactly matches with that of competency model of jobs.

Application of competency models as discussed above is an integrated activity which involves systems, practices and people. It possesses a systemic effect implying successful application of competency model to one sphere leads to positive gains not only to that segment, but also for other two segments. For example, effective application of competency models to systems automatically tends to strengthen the practices. Likewise, practices built on competency models called in this context functional competency, automatically contributes for enhancement of people competencies while competent people give a fillip to competency-based practices. There must be equal emphasis and balance in applying competency models to these three spheres of organization.

DRIVER 8: EVALUATION OF COMPETENCY MODELS

Efficacy and contribution of competency-based performance management must be evaluated at three levels such as organizational, functional and employee level. This can be initiated only when execution of competency models at job, functional and organizational levels through the means of systems, practices and people is complete. Some of the methods and approaches followed in this context can have similarity with approaches and methods adopted in Driver 6 while pilot testing competency models. Basic difference between these two drivers is that testing as discussed in Driver 6 is basically to establish content validity and reliability of measures, whereas the basic objective of the evaluation driver is to measure contribution of competency models to organization, functional areas and people in specific terms.

Step 1: Organizational Level Evaluation

Evaluation at organizational level can be done in many ways suiting to organizational context in which competency-based performance management strategy is introduced. Most popular among them are indicated below:

Competency Index Assessment: Efficacy of competency model application can be checked through the assessment of competency stock in organization. This can be measured by assessing and accounting the quantity and quality of competencies available in organization prior to application of competency models and repeating the same study after implementation of competency models for a period of two consecutive years. The difference obtained can express the contribution of competency management. For example, a pharmaceutical company came up with a result that the implementation of competency models has contributed to enhance the competency stock by 45 per cent. In other words, it created 45 new pharmacists for every hundred, without physically adding any manpower. This happened because existing pharmacists acquired competencies in the area of formulation at the advanced level, which they were not possessing earlier.

Customer Satisfaction: This refers to measuring internal and external customer satisfaction in the context of competency models application. Customer satisfaction figures obtained prior to implementation of competency models must form the basis for the analysis of gain.

Financial Perspective: Evaluation of competency models in financial perspective involves verifying the turnover, sales, profits, earnings per share prior and after the execution of competency models. This evaluation must be carried out implementing the competency-based performance management at least for a period of four to five financial years.

Productivity: This involves checking whether competency models have contributed for improvement in efficiency, utilization of physical resources, growth rate of production figures.

Organizational Health/Effectiveness: Efficacy of competency models can also be examined through perceptual study of organizational effectiveness. This assessment can be conducted through questionnaire survey method, collecting perceptions of people on competency models and their contribution to organization.

Step 2: Functional Level Assessment

The second type of assessment is to understand contribution of competency models in functional improvement. For example, measuring the extent to which competency models have improved the contribution of functions like operations, marketing, finance, human resource management, research and development, in attaining organizational objectives. Second level of measurement is understanding how competency models have helped to improve its own working and performance. For example, (i) two people may be producing the same results, both in terms of quantity and quality in the place of three people earlier or (ii) there may a possible change or (iii) value addition to functional excellence. Another example can be measuring whether competency models lead to finding out any new ways of performing function. Third level of functional assessment is collecting perceptions of people regarding improvements or non-improvements of a function and their role in the post competency model scenario.

Step 3: Employee/Job Level Assessment

Third type of competency evaluation model is assessing the utility and contribution of competency models in enhancing knowledge, skills and attitudinal characteristics of individual employees performing on different roles/jobs. This can be done using the usual assessment centre method customized to the requirements of organization in the context of competency-based performance management. Second level of assessment is measuring actual performance of employees after the application of competency models and referring these results with that of pre-competency model period. Third level of assessment is measuring work satisfaction through survey of employees' views and perceptions. It is also useful if the audit is conducted to find out the degree of fulfilment of developmental needs of employees.

Developing right measures, instruments and administering them scientifically is the most essential feature in the assessment of competency models. Expertise built at the stage of testing competency models and trained resource persons can be of good support in the assessment exercise. An objective, sincere and systematic assessment provides great insights and learning into competency management as an art and science of new generation people management.

DRIVER 9: REFINING COMPETENCY MODELS

In a few instances, a need arises to refine the structure, content and direction of competency models based on the results of competency models assessment at organizational, functional and job levels. Lessons learned while applying competency models also provide the necessary learnings impetus for refining competency models for greater gains. Type of actions required for this purpose will be dependent upon the type of refinement solicited. In some cases, this refinement involves the change of mix of knowledge, skills and attitudinal characteristics required to perform a job and in other cases, new skills may require to be added at functional level and still in others competencies identified at organizational level may warrant a new orientation. Whatever may be this requirement, the following course must be adhered while doing so:

Step 1: Cross-Verify Results

Assessment results obtained using various instruments, measures and schedules at three levels, i.e. organizational, functional and job levels must be cross-verified before acting on the new information. These three levels assessment many times comprise quite a few commonalties. Cross-reference of findings gives proper picture of semblance apart from presenting realistic results.

Step 2: Fix Causes of Barriers

It is utmost important that factors that are causing barriers in the progress of competency models yielding expected results at various levels must be clearly and accurately identified. It means that there should be no (i) confusion, (ii) improper diagnosis and (iii) identifying a cause which is not responsible for sluggish progress or ineffective contribution of competency models. More often a cause that appeared to be responsible for inefficiency may not be the real cause. Complexity and dynamics involved in design and implementation of competency models produce a mixed scenario that at times make wrong diagnosis of the problem. Therefore, nothing should be taken on face value or on cursory examination. Careful and detailed analysis is hence a necessity.

Step 3: Verify Genuineness of Expectations and Duration

Few experts of competency management have experienced that organizations sometimes keep irrational expectations or expect big gains in short time. Practice of competency management cannot produce magnificent results either to organizations or people in short time. This essentially supposes a reasonable time of implementation before accruing big gains to organizations. When an organization manifests impatience and indulges in assessment without completing adequate incubation time, it can only present a picture that is immature and far from perfect. Before launching refining exercise, care must be taken to establish genuineness of expectations and time duration of implementation.

Based on the above-illustrated criteria, refining process must be initiated. Teething problems are bound to occur initially either with contents part or with implementation process. Design and implementation of competency models is a dynamic process and therefore, conditions predicted may undergo a change. Refinement driver is meant to take care of these situations.

DRIVER 10: FREEZING COMPETENCY MODELS

The last driver and step in nurturing of competency-based performance management intervention is standardizing competency models as benchmarks. This is a sequential step on refining competency models. It essentially means that competency models that organization adopted should be followed in all spheres of functioning. These benchmark competency models also must be subjected to revision and review based on the experience and results that these models produce from time to time. However, a clearly laid down procedure must be clamped for such reviews and revisions. Employees can be invited to make suggestions for further improvement of competency models on regular basis. These suggestions can be scrutinized periodically by a committee of experts and valuable suggestions need to be shortlisted. Once in six months or so a high level committee of experts can peruse these shortlisted suggestions and decision for applying them must be determined.

This exercise is desirable because of two reasons. Firstly, the freezed models must form the basic foundations of competency management and no deviation or aberration must be tolerated. Any tolerance to such deviations and dilution of commitment in implementation of competency models can cause large-scale loss to the organization and users of competency models. There must be a firm administration. Such strict form of competency management should not discourage and constrain continuous improvement of competency models. Inherent philosophy of competency is that there will be always scope for improvement and nobody can believe what they have done is ultimate or peak of the activity. Therefore, there must be suitable windows for carrying out improvement. Above-discussed procedure acts as this window. Raider on the driver of freezing competency models is that (i) in reality competency modelling is a dynamic activity and not static, which requires (ii) continuous appraisals and revitalization must not be forgotten.

INTERVENTION 2: CAPITALIZING ON COMPETENCY MANAGEMENT IN INSTITUTIONALIZATION OF PERFORMANCE MANAGEMENT

The second intervention of competency-based performance management strategy is to use competency management as a critical mechanism in realization of performance management in organizations. Competencies built at organizational, functional and job levels must be capitalized to institutionalize performance management through means of reinforcing other six performance management strategies such as reward, career, culture, measurement, leadership and team-based performance management. Competency management achieves institutionalization through (i) internalizing competencies with people, (ii) driving people to move from middle order motivational levels to higher order, (iii) enabling people to exploit their infinite potential to create benchmarks and (iv) tuning people to link every activity with performance management. As such this second intervention of competency-based performance management also comprises 10 drivers, pursuing of which can strengthen the practice of performance management to its perfect shape. All these drivers are derived from the strategy of competency-based performance management. Though application of competency management, particularly the intervention of nurturing competency-based management comprises all drivers within it which cause performance management institutionalization, most of them are latent and implicit. Therefore, they should be aroused with specific focus. Drivers that instigate this

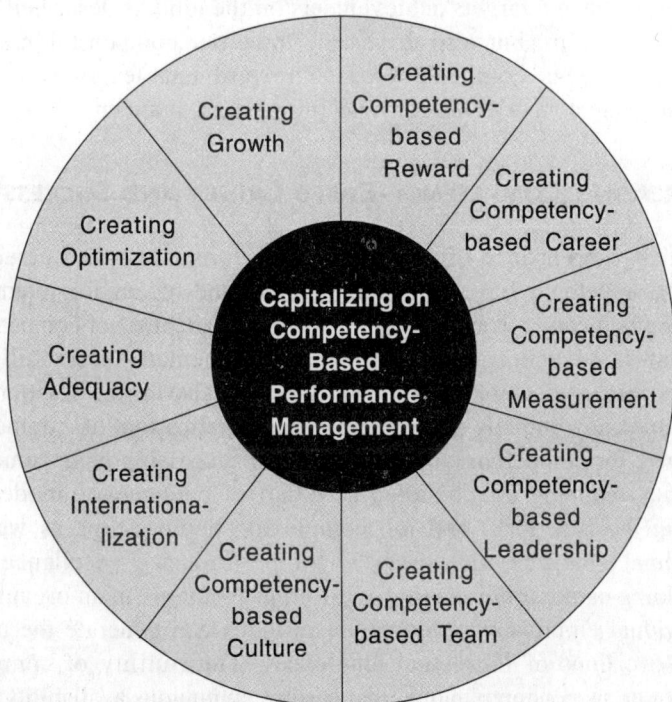

FIGURE 7.3 Drivers of the intervention capitalizing on competency strategy in institutionalization of performance management.

arousal are included as drivers in the second intervention of competency management. These drivers are discussed in forthcoming content:

DRIVER 1: CREATING COMPETENCY-BASED REWARD MANAGEMENT

Competency models conceived, developed, freezed and practiced as a part of competency-based performance management assists in creating a reward system that is performance centred. Basically, this can be achieved through three principal ways. Firstly, competency models help in deciding position-based compensation. Knowledge, skills and attitudinal characteristics identified for performing a role with excellence form one foundation for determination of compensation structure of different jobs in an organization. This is called adopting job level competency model for creating the structure of basic compensation for a job or a family of jobs. Secondly, competency management also builds a huge data regarding competency profile of employees together with their professional strengths and weaknesses. This data can be used to determine person-based compensation. Employee competency profile is beneficial in equitably rewarding an employee for his/her superior knowledge, skill and characteristics. Third use of competency models is supplementing data for determining performance-based compensation structure. Performance related data of individual employee also get collected while evaluating job-based competency models. This data can be used to cross-verify and validate the performance-based incentives depending upon actual performance and targets achievements on the job. As described here, competency management not only helps, but also drives the three-tier compensation system to become performance focused. This competency-based reward enables in institutionalization of performance management in a scientific and progressive manner.

DRIVER 2: CREATING COMPETENCY-BASED CAREER AND SUCCESSION PLANNING

Competency models can enhance effectiveness of performance-based career and succession planning system. Competency lies at the core of career and succession planning. Competency management can support career designs, progression and availability of competent managerialism in adequate measures. While doing so, competency management successfully institutionalizes performance management not only in its own area, but also in the segments of careers and successions. Competency models in particular and application of competency models in general paves a way for competency-based career and succession management in three ways. Firstly, competency mapping administered as a part of competency modelling can provide the data regarding the functional and job complexity, depth, scope as well as knowledge, skills and attitudinal characteristics required for performance excellence in various jobs. This helps in building career architecture for different functions in an organization. Secondly, profiling of individual employees on competency index can generate the data that is useful in career-related decisions of individual employees. Third utility of competency is that it can contribute towards succession planning that ensures continuous availability of managerailship in an organization by facilitating identification of people who can succeed as well as the method in which they should succeed.

DRIVER 3: CREATING COMPETENCY-BASED MEASUREMENT MANAGEMENT

Competency models are enormously beneficial to measurement-based management in innumerable contexts. Fundamentally, competency management pushes measurable indices and indicators while building competency models in organizations. This approach helps measurement-based performance management in its superordinate goal of transforming all management functions of people into measurable form. For example, competency index and data obtained using competency assessment and mapping helps in identifying key result areas and also fixing up performance targets. The role of measurement-based management becomes easier and meaningful when it is juxtaposed with competency-based management. Secondly, competency-based work culture makes the case of measurement-based management easier in terms of its acceptability and encouraging its adaptation. Competency culture seeks measures for managing various aspects, particularly people-related issues. Thirdly, respective competency models can ensure introduction and success of measurement management. One of the competencies identified for the purpose such as operations research or strategic planning will be finally responsible for developing measures. Accurate measures can be developed only when competency capable of developing it exists in an organization.

DRIVER 4: CREATING COMPETENCY-BASED LEADERSHIP

As discussed in the strategy of leadership-based performance management, an important step in developing performance stimulated leadership is identifying knowledge, skills and attitudinal characteristics required for performing the role of a leader in the most effective mode. Further, development of leadership competency dictionary in the context of organization, i.e. organization specific leadership development index and customizing it to build pools of talent at various levels in organization, is another basic function. In both these objectives of leadership-based performance management strategy, competency management plays a key role. Competency management performs catalyst role in creating leadership effectiveness through identifying (i) what needs to be done, (ii) how it is to be done, (iii) what needs to be developed and (iv) how it is to be developed. To put it simply, competency management identifies, defines, tests, refines and standardizes the competency model of leadership. This mutual inclusiveness of competency management and leadership development when strengthened in the backdrop of performance management creates an organization that is par excellence.

DRIVER 5: CREATING COMPETENCY-BASED TEAM MANAGEMENT

Effectiveness and successful deployment of team-based performance management strategy is contingent upon creation of distinct interpersonal competencies. Ever increasing interdependence of work in organizations solicits collective effort. Usually, available competency profile becomes short in making teamwork progress. Chief reason for this is team competency profile is different in content and structure to that of individual based competency profiles. Competency-based management supports team-based performance management in identifying the nature of social and interpersonal competency model that is essential for teams' functioning. Individual competency profiles apart from providing fitness for employees to participate in teams, also maps their developmental journey in attaining social competency.

DRIVER 6: CREATING COMPETENCY-BASED CULTURE MANAGEMENT

Culture has become an intriguing concept and operationalization of the same is viewed as an arduous task for more than one reason. Dominant among them are: (i) what kind of culture an organization must nurture, (ii) how this nurturing or imparting culture to people can be done, (iii) how to measure progress of this nurturing and (iv) to what extent culture needs to be made inbuilt in the job profile of people. Competency management by virtue of its objectives, tangible and measurable approach helps culture management to emerge from an intangible and a climatic managerial feature to that of a very visible management system apart from clarifying all aspects of complexity. Important dimension in competency modelling at all levels, i.e. organizational, functional and job is that culture is its integral part. This is expressed in a language of soft skills, positive work environment such as openness, trust, collaboration, pro-activeness, customer satisfaction, so and so forth. Competency models standardized at different levels of an organization work as a collaborating agent in creating a competency driven culture-based performance management. Sharp alignment between competency and culture management ensures institutionalization of performance management in a substantive mode.

DRIVER 7: CREATING INTERNALIZATION OF COMPETENCIES

Competency management leads institutionalization of performance management through internalization process of competencies. Every individual possesses raw competency in one or more areas. Competency management helps to identify the raw competencies and sharpens them. In order to channelize these competencies into products of performance in the context of an organization, a few characteristics of that product must be imparted to people. Competency management not only prescribes these product specific characteristics, but also provides the road map for their internalization within that individual. Unless this internalization takes place, psychological integration of an individual with an organization may not happen. This integration is the basic necessity for obtaining superior performance. In tautological sense, competency management leads institutionalization of performance management by facilitating people to internalize competencies.

DRIVER 8: CREATING CONDITIONS FOR MOTIVATIONAL GROWTH

Competency-based management in vogue provides abundant opportunities for people to move from a motivational level of middle to higher echelons. Structure of competency management as illustrated in the first chapter is patterned and designed after the motivational pyramid of Maslow, locating competency as the level of self-esteem and self-actualization. Therefore, one of the fundamental functions of competency management is to escalate people to the higher level of motivational behaviour. Once competency has become the basic foundation for people management in all its spheres of activities, people automatically look up for fulfilment of higher-level needs like achievement, performing exceedingly, taking risks, seeking challenges, asking for formidable tasks and urge to innovate. Performance management institutionalization precisely is relied on this kind of professional and work behaviour. Performance managers must utilize the driver of motivational growth through the practice of competency management for the broad goal of performance management institutionalization.

DRIVER 9: CREATING CONDITIONS FOR OPTIMIZATION

Performance management institutionalization is also driven by the phenomenon of optimization of human efforts. No institutionalization can be attained when performance management efforts are nor optimized. Optimization is like doing more with less. A competency case study conducted in one of the world-class companies engaged in computer chip development reveals that nearly 35 per cent of human efforts are superfluous because either there is duplication of efforts or more efforts are put in than required because of competency gap. Therefore, competency models that are sensitive to the element of optimization certainly contribute for good methods of work. When these methods are spread across organization as the way of performing, performance management institutionalization becomes a reality. Therefore, the optimization driver must be accorded due appreciation within the gamut of competency management.

DRIVER 10: CREATING CONDITIONS FOR ADEQUACY

Effectiveness of performance management is largely influenced by the state of adequacy of systems, practices and people. This effectiveness reflected in the state of adequacy leads institutionalization process. Competency management ensures adequacy in the life of an organization because of its focus on, systems, practices and people. For example, competency management application creates competency-based systems, competency-based work practices and people with competency orientation. When competency runs through all these parts like a single thread and when people witness and experience the quality of performance because of their competency, they tend to feel adequate. This feeling of adequacy like incurable infection seeks institutionalization of performance management. Competency management, particularly the driver of adequacy must be fully exploited in order to achieve the benchmark practice of performance management institutionalization.

SUMMARY

Competency management is a comprehensive performance management strategy that identifies and builds the most relevant competencies to facilitate peak employee and organizational performance. Competency management is a formidable instrument that supports performance management revolution in innumerable forms. Competency-based performance management maximizes performance of organization through optimization of all resources like infrastructure, capital, technology, products, markets. However, quite a few organizations are yet to realize the significant contribution that competency-based management can make by transforming them as competent entities. Hesitation of organizations to embrace competency approach is due to few apprehensions that include (i) practice of competency management as cost intensive activity, (ii) life cycle of organizations being short, (iii) developing and executing competency models as a complex intellectual activity than a managerial function and (iv) competency models are required only in few industrial sectors like manufacturing or knowledge driven organizations. Experience of organizations implementing competency-based management proves that these apprehensions are misconceptions. Studies establish that competency management provides big gains to organizations and people.

This chapter focusing on the strategy of competency-based performance management is organized into five parts. First part deals with competency management and its characteristics. Theoretical base of competency management is briefly discussed in part two while part three captures the significance of competency-based performance management to organizations such as:

(i) Realization of organizational objectives
(ii) Realization of human resource potential
(iii) Realization of objectivity and accuracy in managerial decisions
(iv) Realization of consistency and completeness in decision-making
(v) Maximization of productivity, performance and efficiency
(vi) Creation of benchmarking
(vii) Provision of strategic advantage
(viii) Enabling change adaptation
(ix) Sharpening human resource system
(x) Infusing growth and learning optimizm.

Strategy of competency-based performance management comprises two interventions. First intervention is presented in part four. Objective of this intervention is nurturing competency-based performance management in organizations through application of 10 drivers such as:

(i) Formulation of competency development objectives
(ii) Gauging current competency preferences
(iii) Planning for developing performance centred competency development model
(iv) Assessing competency needs
(v) Developing tentative competency models
(vi) Testing tentative competency models
(vii) Applying competency models
(viii) Evaluating the efficiency of competency models
(ix) Refining the competency models
(x) Freezing competency models for practice.

Second intervention titled as capitalizing on competency models in institutionalization of performance management is presented in the final part. As the title suggests, objective of this intervention is to institutionalize practice of performance management leveraging competency models. This intervention consists of 10 drivers. These are:

  (i) Creating competency-based reward management
 (ii) Creating competency-based career and succession planning
(iii) Creating competency-based measurement management
 (iv) Creating competency-based leadership
  (v) Creating competency-based team management
 (vi) Creating competency-based culture management
(vii) Creating internalization of competencies
(viii) Creating conditions for motivational growth
 (ix) Creating conditions for optimization
  (x) Creating conditions for adequacy.

KEY WORDS

Following are the key terms discussed in this chapter:

- Competency
- Competency model
- Human resource planning
- Gauging current competency
- Generic model overlay competency method
- Accelerated competency method
- Tentative competency model
- Refining competency models
- Internalization of competencies
- Repertory grid

- Core competence
- Job analysis
- Nurturing competency
- Job competence
- Systems competency
- Assessing competency needs
- Applying competency models
- Freezing competency models
- Critical incident technique
- Competency development methodology

DISCUSSION QUESTIONS

1. How can competency management benefit organizations? Discuss organizational level implications in adopting competency-based performance management?

2. Briefly discuss what is and what is not competency management.

3. Competency-based people management is not a new approach but techniques and usages are newly found. Justify this statement with relevant theoretical aspects and history of competency management.

4. How can competency-based performance management be developed? Discuss salient features of nurturing competency in organizations with the support of relevant drivers.

5. How can competency-based management be used in institutionalization of performance management?

6. Does competency management contribute for professional growth of individuals? If yes, how and if no, why not?

7. What are various steps involved in development of organizational, functional and job level competency models? How important are these steps?

8. Briefly discuss methodological aspects of competency needs assessment?

CASE STUDIES

1. National Merchant Bank is a private sector bank with head quarters in Mumbai. The bank has operations across the country with significant presence in the states of Maharashtra, Gujarat and Madhya Pradesh. Majority of customers constitute small and medium size business people. Financials of the bank are moderate. Bank in its board meeting has decided to improve quality of services in view of growing competition and mushrooming of private sector banks. One of the areas identified for improving this service is toning up performance management system in order to build distinct competencies. As a part of creating competencies, bank has recruited Sheila Parker, a human resource professional as General Manager—performance Management. Parker on preliminary study of recruitment and selection procedure, performance appraisal and training systems of the Bank found that none of these are competency based. For example, most of the questions used to test the aptitude of candidates for selection as officers are generic in nature like asking what is the capital city of Brazil, Hari Prasad Chaurasia who plays flute is from which _gharana_, the name of the sport Pullela Gopichand is associated with, etc. Basic observation she has made is that none of these questions can measure banking aptitude of candidates. In your view, what must Parker do now? How can competency-based performance management strategy help to build competencies to improve service quality? What competency interventions and drivers are required to be initiated for this purpose?

2. Genius Minds is a business process outsourcing company engaged in back office operations. The company serves multinational clients through voice-based customer support, electronic accounting transactions and technical backup service. Presently, the company employs about 3,000 people. Due to its early entry into the call center business, the company had gained big contracts and grabbed lucrative business deals. It is also a fact that pressure on the company is mounting to scale down rates since quite a few companies in the business are willing to offer same services at much lower rates. The Company is in nascent stages as far as performance management practice is concerned. Neither there is a systematic human resource framework nor professionalism in managing human resource issues. Top management of the company has decided that there must be a competency base depending on which training and

development, appraisals, promotions and compensation issues can be handled. They are hopeful that practice of human resource management can be improved through competency model. This improvement is expected to save millions of rupees by way of employee costs since competency-based management can lead to reduction of manpower.

Based on the above case history, discuss (i) how competency-based performance management can help this company to stay ahead in the business, (ii) what actions should the company initiate to nurture competency-based management, and (iii) whether competency-based management contributes for rationalistic decisions in the areas of selection, performance appraisals, training and compensation as expected by the top management of this company? If yes, elaborate how it contributes, if no, substantiate the viewpoint why competency management doesn't help.

3. Vikram is employed as operations manager in a telecom company. This company offers both basic and cellular telecom services. Vikram is in-charge of technical operations for Delhi circle. Over one hundred employees in the category of technicians and supervisors report to him. It means his job involves not only ensuring availability of bandwidth and its maintenance but also managing these employees to produce best of the results. You are invited as a competency manager (i) to map competency profile of Vikram and (ii) match his competency profile with competency model of operations manager job. Discuss how do you go about it.

_____ **SUGGESTED READING** _____

Boyatzis, Richard E., (1982). *The Competent Manager: A Model for Effective Performance.* New York: John Wiley.

Matthewman, J., (1996). "Trends and developments in the use of competency frameworks." *Competency*, **4**(1), pp. 2–11.

McClelland, D.C., (1973). "Testing for competence rather than for intelligence." *American Psychologist*, **28**, pp. 1–14.

Chapter Eight

STRATEGY 7: LEADERSHIP-BASED PERFORMANCE MANAGEMENT

Essence of leadership in organizations is achieving performance excellence in all spheres of organizational activities. Leadership is the engine of performance management. Leadership is the most vital and influential strategy among the seven strategies of performance management for more than one reason. Firstly, leadership is the key means in conceptualization, facilitation, execution and evaluation of the other six performance management strategies such as reward, career, competency, culture, measurement and team. Secondly, leadership still can make performance management work at least for certain time in the absence of one or more other strategies of performance management. But all six strategies even in their togetherness may not obtain the desired impact if leadership strategy is absent or ineffective. Thirdly, leadership is not only a factor of performance management, but more importantly, it is the objective of performance management. A successful performance management programme builds leadership internally through tailor-made initiatives. In a nutshell, leadership is at the heart of performance management.

This chapter is organized into five parts: Part 1 deals with fundamentals of leadership in the context of performance management. Part 2 focuses on the significance of leadership in performance management. Basic theories of leadership are dealt in part 3. Strategy of leadership-based performance management comprises two interventions: each consisting of 10 critical drivers. First intervention, i.e. nurturing leadership is discussed in part 4, and the second intervention, i.e. role of leadership in institutionalization of performance management is discussed in part 5.

LEADERSHIP IN PERFORMANCE MANAGEMENT

It is tough to provide a working definition of leadership because of its infinite role, application and understanding. There is no single pattern or universally applicable style and content of leadership ever made in the theory and practice of leadership. Leadership can be understood as a process of influencing in the form and way that is sensitive to human and organizational factors with an objective to maximize benefits of internal and external stake holders. In the context of performance management, leadership is defined as *a process that maximizes performance of employees and organizations in all types of business environments and situations by (i) sharply aligning objectives of performance management strategies with business strategies, (ii) nurturing leadership at all levels of organization and (iii) developing, integrating, executing and evaluating six performance management strategies such as reward-based performance management, career and succession planning-based performance management, measurement-based performance management, competency-based performance management, team-based performance management and culture-based performance management to deliver the best of the human and organizational results.*

WHAT IS NOT LEADERSHIP

Leadership as a concept and practice is mostly misunderstood. These misconceptions include:

   (i) Treating leadership only as a domain of top echelons of organizations
  (ii) Leadership as merely leading a collection of individuals
 (iii) Considering all managers like chief executives of organizations as leaders
  (iv) Believing leadership as something that can be inherited due to positional advantage
   (v) Leadership means a democratic form of managing
  (vi) Leadership as form of technical/professional knowledge alone
 (vii) Leadership as merely humanitarian, sentimental and emotional role
(viii) Belief that leadership can be totally imparted
  (ix) Perception of leadership as a mechanism of control
   (x) Thinking leadership is applicable only to lead people but not ideas/knowledge and only applicable to some groups/societies and not to all.

Leadership and its origin is a little more complex than what most of us are ready to believe. Oversimplification of leadership by a few led to the situation in which leadership is understood in a way which it is not. People who know life in organizations can be certain that leadership is required at all levels of organization and in each individual. People disagree to this view by advancing an argument that who will be the followers if all are leaders. They make this point because they think leadership as a fixed and static role. Leadership in reality is dynamic since every time someone brings a new perspective, that person is leading and the rest of the organization is following. This person can be at any level in hierarchical ladder of the organization. Leadership means it is not simply leading people but it can be influencing ideas for which one need not have any formal or direct control over people. Similarly, leadership qualities c̲a̲n̲ ̲ ̲ ̲mparted to a large extent but not in its entirety because an individual's personalit̲ ̲ ̲ ̲ ̲compatible with such training/acquisition of competencies. Leadership is not entirel̲ ̲ ̲ ̲ talent but nurturing it is essential. Good leadership represents both profound tech̲ ̲ ̲ ̲ssional knowledge in one's own field and a tremendous sense of socialization. ̲ ̲ ̲ ribute can be adequate on its own. Most importantly, a chief executive need not necessarily be a leader though that position provides plenty of opportunities for it, a shop floor employee need not necessarily be a follower though most of the organizational circumstances demand so. Leadership can be independent to formal organizational norms and it rises above all such hierarchical blocks by the sheer will of people.

SIGNIFICANCE OF LEADERSHIP STRATEGY

Leadership as discussed above occupies prominent position because after all, leaders have to lead the other six performance management strategies. Salient reasons for its supremacy are:

Setting Direction

Leadership helps in giving direction to the practice of performance management in organizations. Leaders analyze and set direction for organizations and then adopt a suitable performance management system for leading organizations through the direction so chosen. Lack of competent leadership can cause superficial performance management practice and each performance management strategy progressing in its own direction and at some times even grossly conflicting with the other strategies.

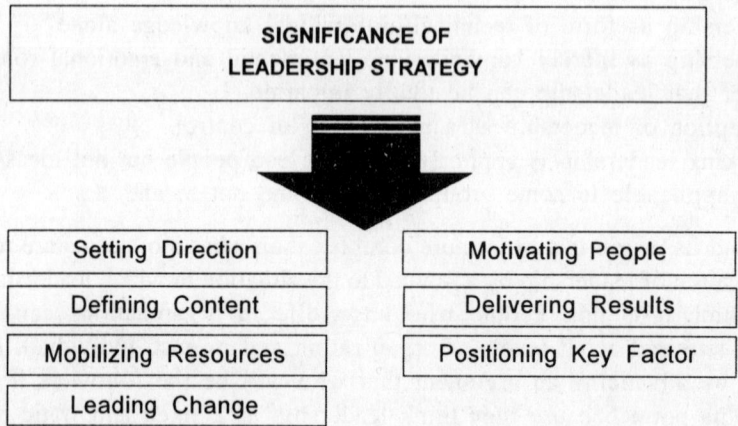

FIGURE 8.1 Significance of leadership-based performance management strategy.

Defining Content

Leading organizations through performance management revolution is the responsibility of leaders. They develop strategies, interventions and drivers that are compatible with ever changing organizational reality. No performance management system is static but dynamic that presupposes continuous appraisal and renewal in tandem with changing internal and external reality of organizations. Sound leadership is the basic necessity that is capable of guiding and making organizations adaptable with right performance management content.

Mobilizing Resources

Leaders are capable of mobilizing resources to push through performance management strategies. In the beginning, organizations will be required to make substantial resource allocations to introduce and consolidate performance management strategies. In the absence of such resource allocation, performance management will be a dream rather than a reality.

Positioning of Leadership as Key Factor

Leadership is the key factor in determining success of performance management strategies. Ultimately it is the leadership quality that decides quality of performance management system. Poor leadership leads to substandard performance management practice and a poor performance management results in ineffective leadership.

Leading Change

Often introducing or formalizing performance management system calls for organization-wide change in terms of systems, structure and processes. Effective leadership in such an eventuality is more a necessity than an option. Leadership can remove formidable obstacles that come in the way of this change. In the absence of an effective leadership, organizations compromise with change and tend to engineer piece-meal performance management practices, which eventually creates more harm than help to people and organizations.

Motivating People

Leadership plays a unique and unparalleled role in attracting, developing, motivating and retaining talent in organizations. All these are prerequisites for a successful performance management system. No other strategy will possess even half of the power that leadership can have in motivating people. Leadership can make people to commit themselves even in the scenario of low compensation and gloomy careers, as it has the capability to paint lack of such things as an attractive scenario.

Delivering Results

Leadership can strengthen efficacy of other performance management strategies and make them deliver results to an organization and its employees at every level. Apart from focus on results, leadership also ensures that each of the strategies create the desired impact and reinforce each other to achieve superordinate objective of performance management.

THEORETICAL FOUNDATIONS OF LEADERSHIP

Understanding leadership chemistry is fundamental before moving to (i) build performance centred leadership, (ii) obtaining its benefits and (iii) catalyzing its role in deploying other performance management strategies. Basic theories of leadership present this chemistry and facets of leading like:

  (i) Forms of leadership
 (ii) Range of leadership
(iii) Conditions for effectiveness of leadership
(iv) Orientation of leadership
 (v) Skills of leadership
(vi) Attributes of leadership
(vii) Charisma of leadership.

Wisdom of basic principles and fundamental structure of leadership is imperative for shaping it as a formidable strategy of performance management. These theories and their relevance to performance management is discussed below:

LIKERT'S LEADERSHIP THEORY

This theory is also known as *four systems of management leadership*. Rensis Likert is the author of this theory who vividly described it in his book *The Human Organization*, published in 1967. Essence of this theory is that leadership can exist in four forms such as:

Exploitative-Autocratic: As the title suggests, this style of leadership believes in using people as much as possible and coercing them to obey instructions and fulfil directions of leaders without question and deviation. People are untrustworthy, incapable of deciding course of action, and limited in brains are some of the premises here. Therefore, people will have no work freedom including over their own work.

Benevolent-Autocratic: Leaders of this category are also autocratic who expect their employees to follow their instructions with blind faith and reverence. Loyalty is given paramount importance and it is rewarded. It is assumed that people are not competent and able enough to decide their methods, ways and discipline of functioning. Therefore, they should be programmed and strictly monitored. The only concession of this style of leadership is little sympathy to loyal people.

Participative: This style is practiced when leadership believes in competence and abilities of people to a great extent. People are treated as capable of understanding and handling things and need only guidance. Their participation is solicited and contributions are invited in the decision-making process. However, leaders retain control over decision-making and people will have only opportunity to present their views and influence course of action. In other words, they can participate in decision-making but decision power will remain with the leaders.

Democratic: This style represents confidence, mutual respect and absolute belief in the knowledge, wisdom, competence and intention of people. Leaders here treat people as equally competent like themselves. Involvement of people in decision-making is complete. Their views determine the course of action and they are masters of their own role, work and methods within a broad framework of mutual convenience. They are only subordinate to issues, goals and objectives of the group and not to individuals. Leaders here are considered more as teachers, guides and facilitators.

These four styles provide wide range and forms of leadership. All these four styles are equally important for managing performance of employees. Suitability of particular leadership style is contingent upon people and organizational environment. Therefore, in the leadership-based performance management strategy, employees are exposed to all these styles of leadership with varied emphasis.

BLAKE AND MOUTON'S MANAGERIAL GRID

The grid model presents five different styles of leadership that ranges from extreme concern for people to extreme concern for results. These styles are:

Deserter: This style is also termed as *1, 1 leadership* and *impoverished management* style. Leaders of this category neither bother about results nor about people. Their concern is only to keep their continuance or membership sustainable and undisturbed. They perform and make people perform to the extent of maintaining themselves.

Autocrat: *9, 1* is other title for this leadership style. Leaders of this mode are excessively concerned about results and show no care for people. Machines are considered more dependable, efficient and result oriented than people. They make efforts to eliminate human role and their interference in work as much as possible. They look for opportunities to substitute people with machines.

Missionary: This is also called as *1, 9* or *country club management* style. Leaders in this form are excessively concerned about people, their well-being and comfort. They create conditions that are very favourable to people even if they do not produce results. Leaders here present themselves as humanitarian, sympathetic, emotional, sentimental, empathetic and sociable. They give least importance for other resources of organization as they put people welfare before the results.

Compromiser: This *5, 5 style*, as title suggests, tries to balance the result and people factors. Leaders of this type perceive results and people in opposite and conflicting roles. Therefore, they function as conciliators with a belief that such a conciliatory/mediator role can make things better. Incremental improvement is the root characteristic of this style.

Executive: *9, 9/team manager* are other popular labels of this style. Leaders here see results and people as mutually inclusive and dependent on each other. Therefore, they believe in optimizing both of them. They build systems, process and structure to motivate people to produce the greatest results. They practice in a manner that greatest results are possible only through accomplishments of people and breakthrough achievements are possible only with people of great morale. This great morale can be built only with great results.

Robert Blake and Jane Mouton detailed the grid leadership in their book *The Managerial Grid*, published in 1964. According to Blake and Mouton, executive leadership is the most effective among the five styles. This theory provides a practical platform for grooming performance management.

FIELDER'S COGNITIVE THEORY OF LEADERSHIP

This is a contingency style of leadership. Central argument of this theory is twofold:

Firstly, effectiveness of leadership is equal to the degree of control a leader has over a situation. Effectiveness of leadership is high where leader has control over the situation. It will be ineffective when a situation controls the leader. Following three factors will determine the degree of leader's control over a situation:

(i) *Leader-member relations:* This is characterized by trust, confidence and respect the followers have towards the leader. It also refers to whether the leadership is accepted voluntarily/willfully or it is forced/thrusted upon.

(ii) *Position power:* This indicates competency of the leader to wield and exercise power in terms of rewarding or punishing group members. More the powerlessness of the leader, greater the leadership ineffectiveness.

(iii) *Task structure:* This indicates how clear group members are about their tasks and goals. Better the clarity, higher the leadership effectiveness and higher the ambiguity, lesser the effectiveness.

Leadership tends to be very effective when a leader (i) maintains positive relations with subordinates, (ii) is able to exercise power and (iii) defines the task clearly.

Second principle of this theory is that effectiveness of leadership is dependent upon the compatibility between a particular style of leadership and the situation. There is no standard leadership style that can handle all situations. Different styles suit different situations. Leadership can be very effective wherever it suits to that situation and unsuitability to situation results in ineffectiveness of leadership. Practicing a type of leadership should be contingent upon the situation.

Implication of this theory to leadership-based performance management is that performance driven leadership should be built around aptitude and attitude that enables them to understand situations and behave in consonance with the reality, and also to obtain complete acceptance and respect of employees collectively. Fred Fielder who developed this theory in 1971 had brought international recognition through publication of a book titled *Leadership*.

HERSEY AND BLANCHARD'S SITUATIONAL THEORY OF LEADERSHIP

Paul Hersey and Kenneth Blanchard had developed this theory, which is close to contingency theory of leadership. This theory also establishes that effectiveness of leadership is dependent upon situational factors and acceptance of followers. They point out that aptitude and attitude of followers also play an important role in leadership effectiveness. Situational theory identifies four styles of leadership. These are:

Telling: This style of leadership is appropriate when quality of followers is substandard. Activities of people are required to be planned, directed and monitored by leaders since their aptitude and attitude are below average. Leadership of this form is also more concerned about task and results than caring people. People are considered as immature and therefore their roles are rigidly defined. This style of leadership is also known as *high task-low relationship management*.

Selling: This is a high task and high relationship model of leadership, which emphasizes that people need to be guided as well as directed. Here people are perceived as intelligent, possessing abilities to perform with the help of leader. Role of a leader here is setting goals, targets, methods and parameters of performance and monitor the performance based on these parameters.

Participating: People are given priority over task and results. Leaders will have complete trust and confidence in abilities and commitment of followers. Therefore, leaders of this type believe that effectiveness comes from their relationships and interactions with people than exclusive focus on task. They invite and encourage participation of people in decision-making.

Delegating: Leaders in this mode abdicate their responsibility both for task fulfilment and concern for people. Hence, this style represents low task and low relationship leadership. People are provided with little direction and guidance to perform. Leaders here are very non-serious in their approach, indecisive and non-existent. They will be unclear about the task to be fulfilled and the role of people.

These four styles present complete picture of leadership. These styles are not conceptual, rather identified by authors based on their years of research and consultancy experience. This theory also has drawn wide acceptance from leadership trainers and developers. Insights of this theory can be supportive in developing the structure for building performance-oriented leadership.

EVANS AND HOUSE'S PATH-GOAL THEORY OF LEADERSHIP

This theory developed and popularized by Martin Evans and Robert House is derived from expectancy framework of motivation. Path-goal theory explains the impact of leadership on subordinate's motivation, satisfaction and consequential performance. It proposes four different styles of leadership. These are:

Directive Leadership: Followers are expected to merely follow direction set by the leader. They will have no participation in decision-making or role in influencing events. Leaders use authority and formal power to control people.

Supportive Leadership: Leadership here cares for people and supportive of their activities. Followers expect support in all forms that include resources, direction, and guidance and also seek control of their activities. Though leaders possess control and authority over people, they manifest it in the form of support.

Participative Leadership: Leaders exhibit confidence in abilities of people. They seek participation of people and allow influencing course of progress. This is mainly in the mode of seeking suggestions, asking followers to make proposals, inviting them to generate alternatives and making them part of the decision-making and implementation process.

Achievement-Oriented Leadership: Leaders strongly believe that people are competent to direct themselves, arrange resources on their own, make plans and execute them to achieve progress. Role of leadership is viewed as one that defines and set formidable goals before people. These goals themselves must be structured in such a way that they act as motivators for higher performance.

The path-goal theory of leadership provides a pragmatic direction for grooming leaders who can cultivate people of high achievement genre. This theory amply proves that performance management should be derived largely from a leadership of achievement orientation. Other leadership styles are also relevant as alternatives, which need to be adopted at times in relation to the quality of people who are to be managed for performance enhancement.

House's Charismatic Theory of Leadership

Though charismatic leadership is as old as human history, credit for building a theory around this style goes to Robert House. This theory originated from the analysis of political and religious leadership. Essence of this leadership style is that some leaders wield enormous personal influence on followers. This influence is also voluntary and more informal in nature. It means power they attain is mostly earned by them rather than borrowed, inherited or delegated to them. This type of leaders exhibit superior confidence in themselves as well as in their followers. Their ability to influence and motivate people is extraordinary. Followers see in leaders a great vision and mission and identify themselves with the leader fully. Charismatic leaders possess excellent communication, persuasive, behavioural, emotional skills as well as technical competence and proficiency. Followers derive fulfilment of their needs by following leaders and they draw satisfaction and esteem in their interactions with leaders. Charismatic leadership is capable of bringing revolution and changing the course of future.

Most importantly, in the context of performance management, charismatic leadership can be a powerful vehicle for transforming the potential of followers into great performance. This style can obtain unstinted commitment from people and motivates them to excel in their performances.

BURNS AND BASS'S TRANSFORMATIONAL THEORY OF LEADERSHIP

This is an important leadership theory that guides development of strategy, interventions and drivers of leadership-based performance management. J.M. Burns in his seminal work titled *Leadership* published in 1978 classified leadership into two types: transactional and transformational. Bernard Bass further explained distinction between these two styles in his paper titled "From Transactional to Transformational Leadership: Learning to Share the Vision" published in 1990. *Transactional leadership* is more a maintenance kind of role that involves protecting the status quo, managing formal boss-subordinate relationships, acting in accordance with prescribed procedures and customs, managing people through secondary sources like auditing their work, advising to make corrections wherever deviations are found, and formally rewarding good performance. In brief, performing a formal role within well-defined framework. This style may be suitable in situations of high certainty, and in a stable and static environment. In contrast, *transformational leadership* is vibrant. It precipitates change, does not work within a fixed framework and with formal methods, it stimulates subordinates with charisma, intellectual competence, knowledge power and engages prudent personal considerations in handling people. This leadership is very apt for high velocity environments and in conditions of uncertainty and when nothing is predictable.

SINHA'S THEORY OF LEADERSHIP

This is called *nurturant task leadership* style. Based on years of leadership studies in India, Jai B.P. Sinha proposed this theory. Essence of this theory is that leaders need to nurture followers and be task-oriented in order to obtain superior performance from people. Nurture characteristic is defined in the leader's role such as caring for subordinates, showing affection, taking personal interest in the well-being of employees and family, and focusing on professional growth of subordinates. Task orientation involves defining role of subordinates, setting guidelines for performance, monitoring progress, correcting substandard performance, rewarding and recognizing good performance and controlling work behaviour of subordinates. Architect of this theory firmly believes that this is the most appropriate style of leadership in Indian context given the socio-cultural contours in which followers expect their leaders to not only care for their personal and professional life, but also control them.

This theory also presents two prime dimensions of leadership, i.e. results orientation (task) and also relationship importance. Both these perspectives are equally important for leadership that is meant to drive employee and organizational performance. This theory has a special place in this discussion of leadership-based performance management since it is founded on the Indian cultural ethos.

VICERE AND FULMER'S STRATEGIC LEADERSHIP THEORY

Modern leadership gurus Albert Vicere and Robert Fulmer proposed a leadership framework through the typical organizational evolution cycle. This framework captures six different types of leadership of which each one of them suits to an organization depending on its life stage. These are:

Prophet: Values, ideals, a vision and sheer commitment characterize this style of leadership. Followers are also motivated by the ideals and vision rather than any materialistic rewards and corporate mechanisms of motivation. Leaders here lead by example and often cause mammoth revolution and change. They wield enormous influence over their subordinates in their presence as well as in absence. This style of leadership is the most appropriate in emergence of organizations like building institutions of excellence.

Crusader: This style of leadership succeeds and is required when organization is in the growth stage. Motive of this leadership style is to define role of people, bring structure to informal organization, introduce control mechanisms, and translate ideals and values into actionable plans. In short, regulation, implementation, evaluation and improved regulation are chief concerns of this leadership.

Explorer: Improving managerial systems, motivating people to excel in their performances, revamping corporate strategy in tune with changes in market, upgrading technology, recasting product lines, leveraging competencies are the key result areas of explorer. This style of leadership is most preferable when organization is established, grown and reached to a stage of stability. Leadership helps to reorient this stage to another direction that facilitates further consolidation and growth. Therefore, as title suggests, leadership explores opportunities for greater growth.

Administrator: Ruthlessness is the synonym for this leadership style. Leaders are obsessed with greater internal efficiency through compliance to processes and procedures. When an organization is completely established internally and externally, this mode of leadership helps in maintaining status quo. Leaders use carrot and stick in equal proportions and emphasize optimization in all fronts. Therefore, it is ruthless. For example, GE is obsessive about its six-sigma implementation. Unknowingly, this obsessive style as a reaction discourages breakthrough innovations.

Bureaucrat: This style of leadership can be found in organizations in their decline stage. Leaders here don't do anything worthwhile either to revive or direct organization towards a purposeful destiny. Leadership is ignorant of organization's vision, values and ideals on one side and is incapable to drive organization through competition on the other side. Employees under this leadership tend to detach themselves psychologically from the organization and its goals.

Aristocrat: This is opposite to the prophet style of leadership. Leaders behave in complete selfishness and live in a make believe world. They keep themselves away from reality. Followers tend to be disillusioned, frustrated and go wary. This style causes organization to die or reach to a point of no return.

    This is a pragmatic framework and presents the most efficient and inefficient leadership in the context of life cycle of organization. Implication of this work to the strategy of leadership-based performance management is that leaders must adopt a corresponding leadership style to attain effective performances.

FARKAS, BACKER AND SHEPPARD'S APPROACH THEORY OF LEADERSHIP

Charles Farkas, Phillipe de Backer and Allen Sheppard based on their study of nearly 200 chief executives, proposed a new generation framework of leadership. There are five approaches that modern chief executives adopt in attaining organizational effectiveness. These are:

Strategic Approach: This approach involves systematically envisioning future, planning for long-term goals and their achievement. Leaders of this approach spent their energy on determining how their company can be market leader of tomorrow and structure the organization around it. They prefer (i) compatible human resource policies and practices, (ii) believe in delegation, (iii) involve all employees, (iv) share with them organization's vision, mission and strategies to realize this vision and mission.

Human Assets Approach: Attracting the best of talent, grooming it through systematic competency enhancement programmes, motivating through cutting edge human resource policies and programmes and empowering people to laid down path of growth is the central philosophy of this approach. Leaders in this style spend lion share of their time and energy in shaping people for organizational excellence.

Expert Approach: Building specific competencies, motivating, rewarding and recognizing expert knowledge applications is the core principle of this approach. Leaders encourage people to attain competency and build business based on these competencies. They see competency as the route in gaining competitive advantage. They prefer any policy, programme and practice that directly and indirectly augment efforts for competency development.

Box Approach: Leaders of this type focus on creating a rigid framework of rules and regulations and monitor and control their compliance. They also institutionalize organization specific culture to attain consistency as well as identity for organizational existence.

Change Approach: Change, transformation, revolution, breakthrough, breaking the past are right words that can explain this approach. This style is suitable when organizations are in crisis and encountering extreme competition. Whether there is crisis or no crisis, leaders here will be restless and always intend to rewrite and change rules of the game. Likewise, they seek change agent behaviour from their followers without exception.

Leaders are required to practice all five types of approaches depending upon context and purpose. Leadership is more a dynamic process than a type cast or a role of rigidity that supposes them to behave in a particular manner. This means, leaders must behave in a flexible manner but at the same time they must be firm in their behaviour. This is the real challenge for leaders. Cardinal argument of leadership-based performance management is that leaders not only should be able to adopt, but also are influential to make environment adaptable to their approach.

LESSONS OF LEADERSHIP THEORIES

Basic, contemporary and emerging theoretical aspects of leadership offer quite a few valuable lessons and guidelines for developing a leadership model in the context of performance management. Commonalties and features of these leadership theories are summarized below. These commonalties are adapted as basic structure for mapping leadership in the context of performance management. These are:

Focus on Results with People Orientation

Leadership theories identified both relationships (interpersonal skills) and task orientation (focused on organizational achievement) as important for leaders. In order to motivate people to optimize their potential and drive performance excellence, leaders need to be trained on both dimensions, i.e. enhancing their social and emotional skills and equipping them with business competencies. Leadership with either competency will be ineffective and neither of these will be disastrous. Therefore, first lesson for leadership-based performance management strategy is to nurture complete leadership.

Consistent Personality with Flexible Orientation

The second most important finding of the research and contribution of theories is that leadership requires both flexibility and rigidity. Unless a leader is rigid, he will not be in a position to remove obstacles and sustain pressures and resistance to change. Quality of rigidity also helps to commit oneself to an ideology and to a set of values. This also provides consistency and ensures progress. However, rigidity alone can create complications in terms of making a leader prisoner to self-ideas and can keep the person away from reality. In order to gain different perspectives and sense variances in reality, leadership should be flexible enough. Flexibility helps a leader to adapt himself/herself to changing reality very quickly. Flexibility alone can lead to ineffective leadership because a flexible leader instead of influencing followers and influencing the course of action becomes subject of influence all the time. Therefore, any one skill alone will be inadequate for driving performance in organizations. Both these are two sides of the coin of performance management. Therefore, the lesson of leadership theories for building performance management leadership is consistent personality with flexible orientation.

SKILLED INCOMPETENCE OF LEADERSHIP

Competence of leaders (i.e. ability to conceptualize, communicate and lead people towards a direction which they believe perfect) can be a potential incompetence. This is because a competence when it reaches its stagnation and extreme end becomes a constraint for effective leadership. Pioneer of many behavioural and learning models, Chris Argyris based on his years of study, research and experience with leadership development found that skills that leaders possess are factors that make them incompetent. In his seminal work titled *A Leadership Dilemma: Skilled Incompetence*, he observes that:

- Key leaders in an organization agree with their CEO that they must develop a vision and make some strategic decisions. They hold several meetings. Unfortunately, meetings end up in no agreement and no choice. This is a group of executives who are at the top, who respect each other, who are highly committed, and who agree that developing a viable vision and strategy is long overdue. Yet, whenever they meet, they repeatedly fail to create a vision and strategy they desire. The reason is all of them have string egos. These egos are essential for leaders to be effective but same are inhibitors because they are hurdles in the way of even functional compromises. This rigidity fuelled by egos prevents them from thinking about changing their behaviour, because it understandably makes little sense for them to undergo some kind of therapy. It implies that skill, which enables leaders to function effectively, makes them incompetent to sense the reality.

- Executives turned leaders demonstrate a behaviour that is laden with safety and security in their communication. They say 'yes' in such a way that it can be proved as 'no' later if they wish or circumstances lead them to shift their stand. These communications are very generic in nature. For example, exhorting subordinates 'to be innovative, take risks but be careful'. This communication can be labelled as intelligent and cleverly expressed. Leaders are expected to make such communications since simple communication is regarded as business of ordinary people. Yet, this leader's competence confuses subordinates and the leader stature discourages them to seek clarification of this ambiguity. To put the observation straight, intellectual skills of leaders at times become their incompetence.

Multifaceted Orientation

Leadership needs to be built on a structure of multiple-platform. For example, approach theory of leadership proposes five varieties of approaches in leading an organization. These are identified from a study involving a number of organizational heads. In modern organizational context that is dominated by technology and service industries, leadership with multifaceted approach is fundamental. Leadership lacking in any of these approaches may encounter difficulties in leading organizations, importantly in obtaining superior performance from people with relevant interventions and drivers. Hence, a lesson for strategy of leadership-based performance management is that leadership competency should be developed *on multifaceted approach*.

Aptitude with Attitude

Intellectual competence, understanding business environment, operational and general management skills, quantitative background and ability to analyze, interpret and draw rational inferences is equally important to that of possessing a positive attitude. Recent research and studies on leadership support the truth highlighted by early theories of leadership that necessity of having and demonstrating attitudes is double in its importance to that of aptitude. However, attitude alone may create country club leadership as indicated in the above discussed leadership theories. Leadership with judicious blend of aptitude and attitude can certainly be capable of institutionalizing performance-laden workflow and performance- oriented workforce. Fourth lesson for leadership-based performance-management is that leadership must be built around twin necessities: Leadership with aptitude and attitude.

Charisma

This style has outstanding potential in motivating people to excel themselves and inculcate corporate citizenship behaviour culminating in great performances. However, training leaders to be charismatic or imparting charismatic characteristics may be possible infrequently. Still, in view of the benefits it ensures, efforts should be made to generate awareness and encourage people to acquire the traits of charismatic leadership. This style has gained popularity in recent past due to increased competition, uncertain business environment, changing demographics of people and cultural fabric. Building charismatic leadership is essential lesson for a performance management strategy that intends to thrive with the fuel of leadership.

Situational Sensitiveness

Situational and contingency leadership theories emphasize the importance of context, reference, environment, circumstances, roles and backdrops in attaining effectiveness of leadership. No matter how competent the leader might be, situational insensitiveness can cause a demoralizing effect and lead to inappropriate conclusions and incorrect decisions. There can be neither rulebook nor a set of do's and don'ts that can ensure situational sensitiveness. This comes only through repeated exposure to similar situations and constant practice. Using simulation case studies and hypothetical situations, people can be trained and made situational sensitive. This training also enables them to be confident in conditions of high contingency, adhoc and temporary. Therefore, a critical lesson is that situational sensitive leadership is necessary for performance management.

SOMATIC MARKERS

Gut feeling is a popular name for Somatic Markers. Leaders, whether in personal or professional life, take decisions out of intuitions. These may appear to be intuition on surface but they are generally well-processed and thought out decisions. Somatic marker is a kind of automatic alarm that alerts people to choose a course of action. These markers are formed in subconscious of people through repeated experience and reflection of events/incidents/circumstances. Bjorn Johnson, head of a Zurich search firm specializing in placing top level executives, states that business is intuition from A to Z (as quoted by Daniel Goleman in his book *Working with Emotional Intelligence*). Successful leaders possess an ability to sense, smell and predict consequences of an event and act upon accordingly. Success of leadership is attributed to this ability of sensing and predicting largely rather than arriving at a decision based on sheer data and numbers. The reason is that every decision will be unique in a way and if decision is drawn based on data alone, it can be an act of dispassion. Therefore, such a decision may appear as rational and logical but it fails to deliver results often because of this associated dispassion. When leaders act on intuition, they do so with passion that makes perfect match of situations. Situational leadership quality comes from sensing and smelling situations. Leadership-based performance management strategy accords intuition as an essential quality in nurturing performance stimulated leadership.

Managing Expectations of People

Leadership theories based on valence-instrumentality-expectation framework establish that managing expectations of employees is the key to obtain super performance from them. Leaders must be able to construct links between fulfilment of people needs and task achievement. This process presupposes that leaders must be capable of understanding the need structure of people in order to reward them appropriately for work performances. This also mandates them to be knowledgeable in design and application of powerful reward interventions and drivers. An important lesson of leadership theories to leadership-based performance management is that leaders should be masters in managing employees' expectations and also influencing their expectation process.

Organizational Leadership Synchrony

Leadership models built on life cycle theory of organizations prescribe that leaders must be capable of adapting themselves and use a leadership style in synchrony with life cycle stage of organization. Based on the growth stage of organizations, a leader has to be a prophet or crusader or administrator. Leaders must be trained to be competent of practicing any of these styles depending upon the organizational demand. Exposure of leaders to all these styles also helps them to appreciate value of each of these styles apart from making them dynamic leaders. Lesson is leadership-organizational synchrony is practical path for building high performance organizations.

Master in Mechanics of Organizational Business

All leadership theories in various forms emphasize that leaders must be capable of not only understanding present objectives of an organization, but also able to redefine and if required change the course. This is a strategic role and long-term. Secondly, they also must be competent to work on medium-term goals and direct various departments, functions and people on them. Thirdly, they must have good grasp of routine affairs in the organization. All these three steps involve leaders mastering mechanics of organization at all levels. They should have knowledge of all functions, both operational and managerial. Therefore, leadership with hands-on competency is critical for creating a leadership that is performance-oriented.

Definition of Roles: Leadership and Followers

Though leadership and its process basically are more informal and unstructured than formal and well-defined, leadership theories prove positive effects of structured roles. This means that leadership will be effective if leaders are given formal authority, powers and an organizational role of influence. However, this clarity of roles and delegation of powers should be within limitations. Otherwise, it may provide little flexibility to leadership apart from making it more a managerial role than leadership plays. Likewise, followers' quality and their commitment is a cardinal issue in effectiveness of leadership. There must be a meaningful interaction between approaches of leadership and followers' preference for such approach. Largely it is the able leadership that facilitates enhancement of quality and commitment attitude in leaders. Leadership that provides structure for leader-followers interface is a significant factor in performance effectiveness.

LEADERSHIP-BASED PERFORMANCE MANAGEMENT STRATEGY, INTERVENTIONS AND DRIVERS

The strategy of leadership-based performance management embodies two prime interventions such as:

Nurturing Leadership: Building leadership competencies is the primary strategy of leadership-based performance management. This is achieved through conceptualization and application of organization specific leadership development interventions and drivers.

Leading Institutionalization of Performance Management: The second strategy of leadership-based performance management is leaders adopting a set of behavioural and managerial strategies that help institutionalizing performance management strategies in the areas of reward, career, culture, competency mapping, team and measurement-based management.

The said interventions of leadership-based performance management strategy are deployed with the support of suitable customized drivers as described here:

INTERVENTION 1:   NURTURING PERFORMANCE CENTRIC LEADERSHIP

Architecture of performance centred leadership is built on 10 most powerful and pragmatic drivers. Each one of these drivers pave way for creating formidable leadership and pools of talent in organizations that enable an organization to be competitive and successful in its area of business. These drivers are discussed below and illustrated in Figure 8.2.

Adoption of these drivers facilitates managers and their organizations in developing a road map for nurturing performance-centred leadership.

DRIVER 1:   SETTING OBJECTIVES OF LEADERSHIP

Objectives of leadership development should be clearly defined in conceptual and operational terms. In order to set objectives, we must understand dimensions of organization as discussed below. This understanding helps in setting and defining objectives in a systematic and rationalistic manner.

Step 1:   Understanding Organization's Vision, Mission and Objectives

Leadership development must start with understanding essential and ancillary features of vision, mission and objectives of an organization. This is mainly for three reasons. Firstly, leadership competency and strategy should be in tune with these aspects and secondly, leadership will be responsible for leading the organization through these vision, mission and

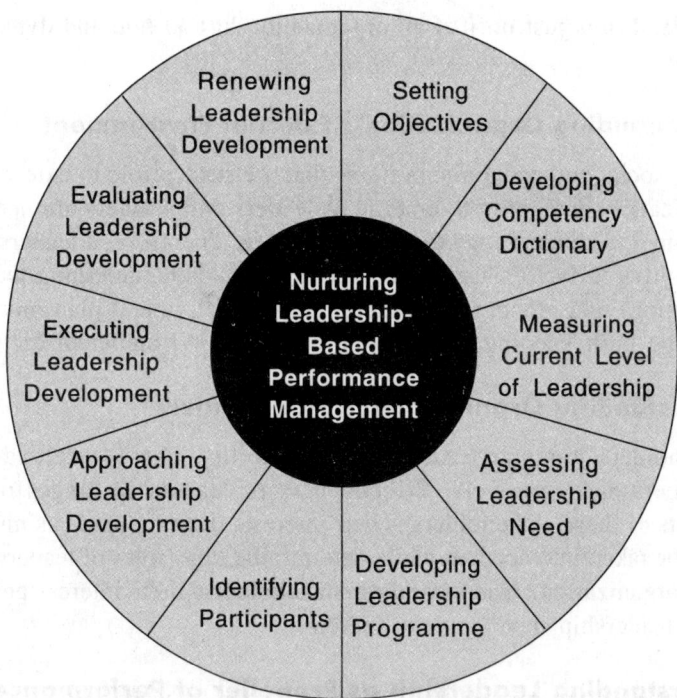

FIGURE 8.2   Drivers of the intervention nurturing leadership-based performance management.

organizational objectives. Thirdly and most importantly, the nature of organizational vision will have implications for the type of leadership that will be sought.

Step 2:   Understanding Organization's Long, Medium and Short-Term Strategies

Development of leadership should be sharply aligned with the organizational strategy for all time spans. Pursuant to this, leadership development also needs to be classified into different phases in order to impart relevant skills in corresponding to these periods/terms and make available the right leadership to realize these strategies. For example, if short-term strategy of an organization is to generate funds from capital markets, leadership development plan must focus on this issue in its initial schedule itself and address it on priority basis.

Step 3:   Understanding Organization's Internal Environment

Organizational history, structure, systems, processes, technology and product lines are like raw material in envisioning a leadership development plan. These are the instruments for driving performance of organizations. Leaders depend on them as well as use them to attain organizational progress and ensure competitiveness. Leadership must be compatible with existing structure, systems, processes and technology. Leadership development plan must take into consideration existing and envisaged systems. There must be a complete agreement between leadership and systems and structure. For example, a plan to infuse bureaucratic type of leadership gets into conflict if structure of organization is organic. Likewise, a transactional leadership is just unfit if an organization has ad hoc and dynamic systems and structure in place.

Step 4: Understanding Organization's External Environment

Organizations are social and economic systems that are susceptible to external environmental pressures. Organizations intending to emerge as leaders and winners are needed to influence external environment to shape things to their advantage. Therefore, a leadership development plan must be sensitive to factors such as competitors, markets, emerging technologies in the field, state regulations and global trends. Leadership development plan must comprise these issues and must be built keeping in view the external environmental factors.

Step 5: Understanding Organization's Stakeholders

Interests of stakeholders dominate leadership responsibility. These stakeholders are investors, employees, suppliers and customers. Effectiveness of leadership hinges on balancing and protecting interests of these stakeholders. Their interests must be made as mutually inclusive. This aspect must be taken into account while determining objectives of leadership development initiative in any organization. Understanding stakeholders, their interest and concerns is an essential part of leadership development exercise.

Step 6: Understanding Leadership as Propeller of Performance and Growth

Understanding theory and practice, both best and inferior leadership development practices strengthen efforts of organizations in creating valuable objectives for development of performance-oriented leadership. This requires a group of managers and experts (vested with the responsibility of setting leadership objectives) must refer relevant literature, peruse the best practices database, visit organizations, hold discussions and consultations with successful leaders and trendsetters. Data and insights obtained through such exercise will be of significant assistance in setting objectives.

Step 7: Understanding Expert's Views

It may also become a necessity to seek the help of an expert who can guide the organization through setting objectives of leadership development. A fresh and different perspective can emerge when an outsider who is well-versed with leadership development participates.

The above steps are more illustrative and indicative in nature than comprehensive because each organization needs to develop its own approach and follow some or more steps depending upon its position and situation. Motive for explaining the above steps is to present essential aspects that directly or indirectly influence leadership development process in organizations as well as to underline that these are subject to be influenced by the quality of leadership.

In order to study the issues discussed at previous steps, a multiple method of study may be required to be used. For example, the survey technique may be useful in understanding followers' preference of leadership objectives. Similar may be the case with suppliers and customers. Secondary sources such as industry statistics, competitor strategy, existing organizational policy framework, systems, may be studied in order to draw some relevant inferences. Employees within an organization are required to be identified and trained in leadership development process to perform as facilitators. It may also be possible that some organizations may not yet have an articulated vision, mission and objectives statement. However, an undefined image must be existing in the minds of top management, which should be taken into consideration. In brief, while setting leadership development objectives, macro and micro level factors should be accorded due attention and appreciation in order to obtain a meaningful and purposeful mandate for performance-oriented leadership development.

DRIVER 2: DEVELOPING LEADERSHIP COMPETENCY DICTIONARY

The next sequential action in nurturing performance-oriented leadership is developing a competency dictionary of leadership. This is the most challenging task in leadership development intervention. Competency dictionary must be as comprehensive, self-explanatory, realistic, measurable, actionable and purposeful as possible. Competency dictionary is similar to that of developing a curriculum for advanced studies. Quality of leadership talent is largely contingent upon standards and methodology followed in creation of leadership competency dictionary. Following steps are suggestive of the process of developing this dictionary:

Step 1: Translating Leadership Development Objectives into Functional/Competency Areas

Leadership objectives as set in Driver 1 should be converted into specific areas of competency. For example, one of the objectives of leadership development is to make people technology savvy. This objective solicits people of leadership potential to be well-versed and possess appreciable aptitude in technological issues of organization. Similarly, each of the objectives must be spelt out in functional/competencywise areas like finance, human resource, operations, commercial, marketing, quality, corporate planning, project management, information technology, research and development, so on and so forth. Each of these functional/competency areas as identified must be classified into suitable levels. For example, competency in human resource management can be classified into essential, desirable, intermediate, advanced, and mastery likewise. This classification of levels must be done in relation to complexity of skills/knowledge. Levels so set for each discipline can provide vertical structure for competency.

Step 2: Identification of Leadership Attributes

The second step calls for identification of leadership traits that enable leaders to achieve objectives of performance management. Lessons/insights offered by leadership theories can be one authentic source for developing this attribute checklist. For example, 10 prime lessons of leadership theories were presented in foregoing content. These are:

   (i) Focus on results with people orientation
  (ii) Fixed personality with flexible orientation
 (iii) Multifaceted approach orientation
 (iv) Aptitude with attitude

(v) Charismatic leadership
(vi) Situational sensitiveness
(vii) Managing expectation of people
(viii) Organizational leadership synchrony
(ix) Mastery in mechanics of organization
(x) Leadership and followers' role clarity.

The second source can be studying the generic leadership attributes developed by academicians, consultants and leadership development institutes based on leadership studies and research as shown in Table 8.1.

Step 3: Translating Leadership Attributes into Individual Competencies

Competency areas and leadership attributes as identified will be required to be translated into actionable micro level individual competencies. For example, finance competence needs to be structured as corporate finance, budget making, balance sheet preparation, finance-related state laws, information technology applications in finance management, managing public issue. Similarly, soft human resource skills can be defined as interpersonal relationship skills, communication skills, conflict management skills, team building skills, etc. Model checklist of such generic individual competencies is given in Table 8.2.

DRIVER 3: MEASURING CURRENT LEVEL OF LEADERSHIP DEVELOPMENT

Establishment of leadership development objectives and leadership competency dictionary provides a scientific platform and format for leadership development plan. However, to decide on the nuts and bolts of leadership development programme and their levels, we must understand the current level of leadership as well as current leadership development efforts (programmes) within the organization. Following steps are involved in such an effort:

Step 1: Understanding Current Level of Leadership

First step involves assessing the current leadership level in terms of its competencies and performance on various fronts in the manner as indicated below:

- Individual competencies as identified in Driver 2 will be used as parameters for developing leadership effectiveness indices. These indices must be converted into data collection instruments like questionnaires, checklists, study schedules, simulation games, role-plays and business cases. All such data collection methods must revolve around the identified indices. These indices representing competencies can also be used in interview and group discussion methods. Development of leadership effectiveness index is the most complex and multi-disciplinary in nature and calls for deployment of both qualitative and quantitative techniques. The parameters thus identified and variables, items and statements drawn to measure these parameters must be statistically tested and empirically proved. Reliability and validity of such indices and data collection instruments are critical in measurement of the current leadership level, performance and potential.

TABLE 8.1 Inventory of Performance-Oriented Leadership Attributes

Attribute	Operational Definition
1. Focus on external environment	• Networking, customer orientation, setting direction and managing external environment.
2. Focus on future	• Creating vision, setting mission, objectives, defining core values, ideas and strategies thinking.
3. Focus on action	• Operationalizing vision into action plans, translate mission, objectives, values and ideas into results and enlist people in attaining the vision.
4. Focus on collective relationships	• Affectionate towards people, ability to live alone, empathic, set co-operative goals and ensure collaboration.
5. Focus on sharing	• Encouraging participation and involvement, hear before act, share power and authority and control only when necessary.
6. Focus on confidence	• Reach to people's heart, energize people, involve their emotions, use strategies to increase follower's confidence, remove anxieties and generate optimism.
7. Focus on organizational resources	• Coordinating, facilitating, resourcing, mobilizing, directing and integrating various activities, aligning organizational strategy, structure and processes.
8. Focus on diversity	• Encouragement to diversity in people, plans, practices, culture, and in operations and product integration.
9. Focus on teams	• Manage with teams, build team culture, team system, and support team processes.
10. Focus on human resource	• Instil development and strategic-oriented human resource system to attract, motivate and retain best of the talent to achieve organizational objectives.
11. Focus on change	• Perform as catalyst of change, critically evaluate the status quo, experiment, rewrite the organizational script, look for opportunities to change the direction, make the organization agile, flexible and contemporary.
12. Focus on self-demonstration	• Setting self as an example, practice the values and ideals preached, demonstrate confidence in the self and others, possess analytical, intellectual and emotional abilities, learn constantly, admit failures and improve continuously and exhibit an open mind.

TABLE 8.2   Model Checklist of Leadership Competencies

• Set vision and strategy	• Build organization and inspire people	• Know the business
• Drive for results	• Make the difficult decisions	• Encourage open communication and knowledge sharing
• Think strategically	• Champion of change	• Establish plans
• Manage execution	• Influence others	
• Improve systems and processes	• Commitment to quality	• Focus on customer needs
• Foster enthusiasm and teamwork	• Reward and celebrate achievement	• Attract and develop talent
• Build relationships	• Lead courageously	• Foster open communication
• Act with integrity	• Use sound judgement	• Convey information
• Adapt and develop oneself	• Know the organization and its business	• Culture development

- The second task in this process is to consider various generic leadership competencies/ attributes, assessment instruments and techniques in use in order to decide whether some of them can be adopted. This will also provide an opportunity to cross-verify the developed leadership effectiveness index, parameters and data collection items/ statements in references to these generic sources. For example, to assess interpersonal relationship orientation, we may need to consider and derive contours from FIRO-B instrument (Fundamental Interpersonal Relationship Orientation Behaviour).
- Managers/employees at different levels in an organization will be assessed against this leadership effectiveness index by administering pertinent data collection instruments. Later, mapping will be carried out accordingly.

Step 2: Understanding Current Level of Leadership Development Efforts

Most of the organizations make efforts in their own way in developing leadership. This may be as simple as nominating people to undergo leadership training modules/programmes offered by external agencies or annual general management development programmes organized internally or it may be as elaborate as using combination of competency mapping, assessment centres, training and development interventions, and on-the-job rotations. Whatever may be the intensity and coverage of this effort, this process must be evaluated in order to establish the current status of such efforts and their utility in building leadership talents in required quality and quantity. This assessment can be done at multiple levels. For example:

Content Level: Content part of the current leadership development efforts such as competencies focused and curriculum followed in building these competencies must be scrutinized in relation to the leadership development index.

Customer Level: Feedback from participants and beneficiaries of the ongoing leadership development efforts of an organization must be obtained and analyzed. Questionnaire and interview techniques can be used in this context. Descriptive feedback in the form of essay writing collected from participants can also be a good source.

Administrators Level: Feedback and views of people associated with design and implementation of leadership development efforts, if obtained, can significantly serve in analysis of such development efforts and their background.

Competencies Level: An audit of available competencies inventory versus demand for such competencies within an organization can be a vital indicator of benefits and pitfalls of the current leadership development effort.

General Level: It will be a potential benefit to collect perceptions of all members of an organization on leadership development efforts vis-à-vis their views and experience of implications of such leadership efforts to organization and to employees.

Results Level: Most crucial is measuring utility and role of leadership development efforts in assessing contribution of the same in attaining organizational goals and results.

DRIVER 4: ASSESSING NEED FOR LEADERSHIP DEVELOPMENT

Implementation of drivers 1, 2 and 3 enables (i) to draft objectives of the leadership development programme, (ii) development of competency development dictionary and (iii) analysis of current leadership development efforts. Based on results obtained with the help of these three drivers, current leadership development needs must be determined. In other words, results of current leadership development level and efforts must be compared with leadership development objectives in reference to the competency dictionary. Unified concerns can be identified through this exercise. Following steps are suggestive of such process:

Step 1: Perceived Need for Leadership Development

Though comparative analysis of data derived with the help of drivers 1, 2 and 3, can be great source in establishing the leadership development need, perceptions of all members of an organization should be gathered in order to understand their perceived level of need. This is important because after all they will be the prime beneficiaries and customers of the leadership development programme. Their involvement, hard work, sincerity and contribution will be tantamount to their belief of the need. In few instances, it can also happen that though there is an acute need for leadership development, members of organization may not share this perception. This mismatch of perception with dormant reality may pose challenges. If this mismatch is diagnosed at early stages, leadership development effort can commence with removing this mismatch between perception and reality.

Step 2: Establishing Quality and Quantity of Organizational Leadership Demand

Leadership, as discussed earlier, is required at every level of an organization. For example, leadership is required at operational level to ensure happening of routine operations as per prescribed standards and procedures. It is required at micro planning and execution level to ensure attainment of various functional targets and in mobilization of resources. Leadership is required at organizational level to lead and integrate different departments and functions to deliver results. It is also required at macro level to steer the strategy process in long-term and position the organization as competitive and formidable in ever changing business environment. Size of these different levels of leadership demand within an organization must also be assessed. For example, all employees of an organization will be required to be trained in the first level of leadership, i.e. operational level. In contrast, a few identified and selected employees will be required to undergo the leadership development programme at higher stage, i.e. the strategy level. Human resource planning system if already existing in the organization must be used and linked to this exercise.

DRIVER 5: DEVELOPING LEADERSHIP DEVELOPMENT PROGRAMME

Having articulated objectives of leadership development, measured the efficacy of ongoing leadership development effort, assessed the need for leadership development and having created the competency dictionary, the next sequential driver is evolving the action plan for performance-oriented leadership development. This involves a series of actions as briefly presented here:

Step 1: Developing Organization Level Specific Leadership Development Programme

Based on the results obtained with the assistance of above-mentioned drivers, the leadership development programme specific to the organization must be developed. Programmes specific to each level such as operational, middle and strategic levels must be developed. Each of these programmes consist of many phases and modules as shown in Table 8.3. Content, coverage, methodology, duration, frequency is to be determined in accordance with the level of leadership development programme.

Step 2: Considering External Leadership Development Programmes

Management schools around the world offer comprehensive executive development/education programmes. Michigan Business School, Harvard Business School, Cornell University, Stanford University situated in United States and Richard Ivey School of Business in Canada are examples of this. Their management development programmes aim at strategic leadership, are comprehensive in coverage, case based instructions and rigorous in their approach.

However, consideration of external programmes must be limited to understanding content and structure of the programme rather than seeking it as the only route for leadership development. Leadership development in order to be effective, particularly in the context of performance management, should be developed, implemented, evaluated and managed in-house.

TABLE 8.3 Model Leadership Development Programme

	Interpersonal skills	*Functional/product skills*	*Operational skills*
• Individual Contributor	• Build effective communication and relationship skills	• Develop specific functional skills • Learn roles and relationships within the function/product unit • Develop work planning, program and performance assessment skills	• Synthesize personal values with organizational value system • Understand how his/her function and business relates to the entire company • Grasp the role of company in the global market • Learn about customers and suppliers
• New Manager	• Learn to delegate work and get things done through other people • Learn to effectively appraise the performance of subordinates and secure their improved performance • Acquire and effectively apply team-building skills • Learn to share insights and values with others so that effect is multiplied	• Acquire basic managerial skills, such as budgeting or programme planning	• Reconcile personal values with company's shared values • Learn to integrate work of a unit with related units
• Experienced Manager	• Develop negotiation skills and effectiveness in dealing with conflicting situations • Gain executive communication skills	• Gain deep, well grounded understanding of all related functional skills in the area of prime assignment	• Develop strategic thinking and the capacity to use both inductive and deductive problem solving

TABLE 8.3 Model Leadership Development Programme (Contd.)

	Interpersonal skills	Functional/product skills	Operational skills
	• Increase ability to deal with ambiguity, paradox and situations where there is no right or wrong answers		• Learn how to effectively implement organizational change • Understand the difference between what is best for the customers and what is easy for the business • Maximize understanding of global business dynamics and inter-functional relationships
• General Manager	• Gain capacity to deal with multiple issues of increasing complexity and ambiguity • Develop a recognition that he/she cannot and should not try to solve all problems personally • Build skills in framing problems for others to solve • Understand how to maximize contributions of individual, team and staff • Develop an attitude where asking for help is a sign of maturity rather than weakness • Develop sensitivity to respond to the needs of others, based on limited stimulus or cues		• Refine broad perspective that includes the well-being of the entire organization • Sharpen analytical and critical thinking for solving organizational problem solving • Play an active role in the development of the vision for his/her business

TABLE 8.3 Model Leadership Development Programme (Contd.)

	Interpersonal skills	Functional/product skills	Operational skills
• Business Leader	• Learn to effectively exercise power in making those decisions that only the leader can make • Develop projection and extrapolation skills to deal with situations where he/she has no first hand knowledge • Develop sensitivity to the forces that motivate people to behave as they do		• Develop multifunctional integration skills to manage a business based on profit and loss • Develop and effectively articulate vision for the business • Develop the capacity to conceive, not just adopt, change • Develop an effective understanding of the dynamics of the industry • Develop a balances posture between leadership of the business and integration/cooperation among the functions or other business in the industry • Develop the capacity to effectively manage community relations.

Step 3: Developing Internal Learning Providers

Special effort should be made to identify people with knowledge, experience and teaching capabilities to be groomed as leaders for grooming leadership. This process of selection of resource persons can be carried out in association with other relevant drivers focused on competency identification/mapping. There will certainly be a few people with such aptitude suitable to anchor and lead the leadership development effort in all organizations. However, they are required to be exposed to leadership development technology and methodology and nuances of implementing the leadership development strategy, interventions and drivers. They must be specifically earmarked for this role and their job descriptions should be written accordingly.

DRIVER 6: IDENTIFICATION AND SELECTION OF PARTICIPANTS FOR LEADERSHIP DEVELOPMENT

Employees must be identified for leadership development participation. All employees must be exposed and should undergo the basic level leadership development programme since leadership is essential at every level of the organization. This also helps in encouraging people to notice and realize their inner potential. People with moderate aptitude and attitude potential must be identified for middle-rung leadership. Similarly, people with capabilities to assume higher responsibilities need to be selected for strategic level leadership. This identification of people for middle and higher-level leadership must be a continuous process and therefore, leadership development also should be an ongoing rather than a single shot affair.

In order to identify and select people for leadership development, techniques deployed while developing competency dictionary (Driver 2), measuring current level of leadership (Driver 3) and assessing the need for leadership development (Driver 4) can be used with minor modifications if required. Data obtained using these drivers will also be relevant and significantly useful. Exercising objectiveness, equity in providing opportunities, use of multiple approaches in the place of excessive reliance on a single technique, current performance levels and achievements, and formal educational background must be accorded their due consideration in such selections. To summarize, all employees should have supreme confidence and trust in this selection criterion apart from its direct alignment with business objectives in general and with leadership objectives in particular. Running assessment centre and individual competency mapping are some of the well-established techniques which can be drafted for this purpose.

DRIVER 7: APPROACH AND METHOD OF LEADERSHIP DEVELOPMENT

It is beneficial and also result-oriented if a multiple approach is adopted in leadership development. Most common and popular among the approaches is classroom training. It is empirically proved that classroom training alone cannot contribute for building formidable leadership. This ideally can be used in combination with other approaches. Other leadership development techniques are:

    (i) Job rotation
    (ii) On-the-job training
    (iii) Coaching
    (iv) Mentoring
    (v) Special project work
    (vii) Feedback
   (viii) Business games
    (ix) On-line long-term instruction
    (x) Sharing experiences
    (xi) Visits to other organizations
    (xii) Mock performance.

Leadership development as popularly believed is not a short-term or one time activity, but a long drawn process that is continuous, consistent and logical in the sequence.

Method adopted in imparting leadership competence needs to be in congruity with the nature of skill so targeted. Methodology also may differ according to the level of leadership development programme. Simultaneously, there must be a common theme and spirit across all levels of leadership development programmes. In a sense, there must be unity in diversity in leadership development efforts.

DRIVER 8: EXECUTION OF LEADERSHIP DEVELOPMENT PROGRAMME

Execution is the key in leadership development effort. This demands spirited cooperation and participation of all members of an organization. Execution must be led akin to an organizational revolution and the mission of such effort should be internalized in people. Although implementation is a process specific to an organization and its context, a suggestive process is illustrated here:

Step 1: Demonstration of Top Management Commitment

Most crucial action in implementation of a leadership development programme is that top management not only need to be committed internally, but also externally. It means top management must avail every opportunity that comes in their way or create context by which their unstinted commitment must be declared openly and loudly. They must also prove their involvement in their decisions and managerial actions. Point of caution is that the leadership development programme should in no case be attempted on ad hoc basis or to gain good will or as a matter of faith rather than as an issue of necessity. In such eventualities, the development programmes not only fail to yield any positive results, but also adds chaos to organizational functioning and generate sarcasm and distrust among employees.

Step 2: Resource Allocation

The next step in this phase is resource allocation. It means creation of physical infrastructure suitable to the scale of leadership development programme. This encompasses building, teaching aids, library, computers, database and proportionate annual budget. Budget allocation must be corresponding to demands of the programme and as per the approved plan rather than subject to fluctuations of company fortunes. Because it is neither an item of luxury nor a programme that is ancillary in nature to receive the budget cuts in first instance.

Step 3: Leadership Development Planner

Leadership development programme needs to be transformed into modules and schedules with dates, coverage, and preparation indications on the part of participants. This will be made available to all people in the organization. This is more like a typical training calendar that exists in organizations. This is not necessarily a classroom kind of training programme calendar but covers all on-the-job and critical incident observation schedules.

Step 4: Registration Procedure

Freedom must be given to participants themselves for self-nomination based on their current year selection for different levels of leadership development programme and as per the convenience to their work and personal schedules. Care needs to be taken to mix participant profiles and create a heterogeneous group as much as possible in formal leadership development programme because the mix itself ensures a cross perspective learning. Non-classroom programmes could be used for homogenous group learning. This helps them to work on common problem/issues of concern.

Step 5: Leadership Development Workbook

Every employee/participant of leadership development should be given a leadership development workbook. This book contains leadership objectives, details of leadership development programme, methodology, planner, evaluation and conceptual input on leadership in general and in the context of organization in particular. The second part of the workbook deals with guidelines on how a participant should proceed and progress with self-efforts/direction and with the help of leadership development programme. Third part of the book must be devoted to writing insights/reflections of the participant on daily basis. This part demonstrates how a participant is growing as a leader in his/her own stride. This book also helps to keep the record of development in a systematic manner. Workbook underlines the basic principle of leadership development, i.e. development must be continuous and it happens every second.

Step 6: Every Employee as Participant

As stated earlier in different contexts, no one must be an exception to the leadership development effort. Each and every employee needs to be a participant. It means from chief executive to the shop floor employee, everyone must be a participant and be given a leadership development workbook in which progress must be recorded on daily basis. All employees, irrespective of their position must be exposed to the operational level leadership development programme. The selected group on completion of this phase will be placed on to undergo the middle/specific competence level programme and to the strategic level programme as per laid down procedures and on qualifying the evaluation at every stage.

Step 7: Leadership Development Agreement

There must be a tripartite leadership development agreement among participant, leadership development programme administrator and the chief executive officer describing the responsibilities, duties and role of each of them in building performance-oriented leadership in the organization. This will form a declaration of inspiration that can stimulate the leadership development endeavour in a substantive fashion.

DRIVER 9: EVALUATION OF LEADERSHIP DEVELOPMENT PROGRAMME

Evaluation provides a perspective on results, establishes the utility and success, and gauges satisfaction of employees with the leadership development programme. Cycle and approaches followed at Driver 3 and Driver 4 are immensely beneficial and relevant here. The same methodology can be adopted with suitable modifications. Evaluation of efficacy of the programme must be carried out at (i) reaction level of participants, (ii) functional fulfilment level, and (iii) at the level of business results. In addition, the midterm audit of programme implementation, if followed, can be helpful for instant corrections and bridging the gaps. An essential factor in evaluation is that the process adopted should be highly objective and purposeful to the extent that critical inferences can be gained.

DRIVER 10: RENEWAL OF LEADERSHIP DEVELOPMENT PROGRAMME

Based on results of the evaluation as derived by applying Driver 9, and to tone up the leadership development programme in tune with the changing realities of organizational environment, renewal effort needs to be taken up at regular intervals. Renewal can be more than one type as discussed below:

Step 1: Renewal on Evaluation

Evaluation exercise yields two kinds of results: (i) results of a particular level of leadership development programme (operational, middle or strategic) and (ii) results at satisfaction, competence and business level. Based on these results, unified concerns for improvement must be drawn. These concerns may warrant changes which may range from large scale to very minor in nature. For example, evaluation results may throw light on the inadequacy of leadership development objectives, which requires structural change in the leadership development strategy. It can point out excessive emphasis on a specific leadership attribute that has no great benefit either to organization or to the individual or group of employees. Renewal process must be used to perform as rejuvenator and reinforcer of leadership development programme.

Step 2: Systemic Renewal

The second type of renewal is more of a systemic review of leadership development programme on its implementation for a considerable duration, may be for a decade or so. This is meant essentially to take care of environmental changes. In other words, the entire strategy of leadership development must be renewed since leadership development objectives as articulated and action plans as executed might have cost the contextual and strategic backdrop. This facilitates to inject new life and energy into the programme. The basic principle of renewal is to treat leadership development programme as a dynamic process that requires continuous appraisals and modifications.

INTERVENTION 2: LEADERS LEAD INSTITUTIONALIZATION OF PERFORMANCE MANAGEMENT

Leadership is primarily responsible for institutionalizing performance management in an organization. In a tautological sense, leadership anchors the design and execution of performance management strategies such as reward, measurement, career, culture, competence and team-based performance management strategies. These strategies and their interventions and drivers are presented in detail in relevant chapters. This second intervention of leadership-based performance management strategy focuses on how leaders lead the said strategies by deploying a range of drivers with the principal aim of optimizing performance. These are discussed here:

DRIVER 1: COMMUNICATING

The foremost important driver is that leader must communicate clearly and specifically the expectations and targets. Effective leadership institutionalizes performance work culture through communicating with people and providing them robust understanding of vision, mission, objectives, values and ideas. People surge up with great performances on the inspiration and communication of leadership. In order to reach people and involve them mentally, leaders use a range of communication skills that include written, oral, visual and behaviour. They use every opportunity amply to share with people and impress upon them the structure and spirit of performance management strategies, interventions and drivers.

FIGURE 8.3 Drivers of the intervention capitalizing on leadership strategy in institutionalization of performance management.

DRIVER 2: GENERATING COMMITMENT TO PERFORMANCE MANAGEMENT

Leadership institutionalizes performance management system through generating commitment of employees to the structure and intent of performance management. This, is done through demonstration of performance management results to the individual and collective employees and to organization. Leaders leverage development orientation of performance management strategies, interventions and drivers to enhance commitment of employees. Bringing oneness among employees, and enabling them to see common interests by managing their expectations are some of the techniques leaders prefer in building employee commitment.

DRIVER 3: EMPOWERING

Leadership uses the method of interpretation rather than method of control in institutionalizing performance management. Employees are trusted, belief in their abilities is illustrated and their confidence and commitment to perform exemplarily are duly recognized. Leaders only provide examples and broad directions and interpretations wherever required in leading people through high performance work practices. Employees are made masters of their own journey and invited to write their scripts.

DRIVER 4: CULTIVATING INDIVIDUAL AND COLLECTIVE TALENTS

Though leadership ensures the development of individual and collective talents through execution of competency-based performance management strategy with military precision, it assumes greater responsibility in this area of performance management. The crux of institutionalizing performance management lies in talent management of people.

A leader performs a variety of roles in this context: a coach, mentor, teacher, counsellor, technical specialist, consultant and a role model. He/she puts developing talent high on the agenda and this forms their routine work schedule. Briefly stating, leaders institutionalize performance management by devoting themselves for development of employees' talent on continuous basis. They look at both individual level and group/trade level development needs and address them suitably by instilling learning culture. Leaders facilitate individual employee to gain a sense of identity and groups to derive a purposeful and highly functional direction.

DRIVER 5: INSTITUTIONALIZING THROUGH NETWORKING

A leader performs roles of a partner, consultant, resource person, liaison person, guide and a friend of organization to institutionalize performance management. A leader stands as moderator and articulator of employees and organizational interests. The chief objective of network role is to attain semblance among all stakeholders of an organization as far as design and execution of performance management strategies, interventions and drivers are concerned. This balance would be achieved through exchange of dialogues and keeping control over internal and external pressures.

DRIVER 6: SETTING SELF AS EXAMPLE

Leading performance management as example rather than as exception is the key to successful institutionalization of performance management. It has often been the experience with many systems in organizations, particularly at the stage of implementation that leaders seek exceptions to self in terms of applicability of system to them. Ineffective leaders view that their positional privilege must provide them few concessions and still others see exceptions as testimony to the validity of their leadership. This is in complete contrast to the spirit of performance management. Leaders leading by setting themselves as an example is the essence of performance-oriented leadership. Leadership in the context of performance management believes in deeds rather than words in institutionalization of strategies, interventions and drivers. People follow what leader does and not what they advise. For example, position of leadership is also subject to measurements, evaluations, assessments and renewals. Leaders must participate in this process like any other participant in the organization. Leadership is seen as a role with broader responsibility and concerns instead of traditional understanding of a role with positional power and arbitrary authority.

DRIVER 7: TAKING COMPLETE AND PERSONAL RESPONSIBILITY

Performance driven leadership takes a complete and personal responsibility in institutionalizing performance management. Unstinted responsibility reflects in its active role in design and execution of performance management strategies, interventions and drivers. Leadership owns up failures in the same stance that of success. In reality, matured leadership declares its responsibility for failures, shares success and credits team for breakthrough achievements. This attribute alone enables leadership to steer performance management practice as managing owner and whom people can look up to in realizing their potential into scintillating performance.

DRIVER 8: CREATING BENCHMARKS

Role of leadership in the context of performance management institutionalization is setting/coordinating creation of benchmarks in various spheres of organizational activities. Leadership inspires people to constantly look for finding new ways to improve current performance levels. This involves leadership possessing robust understanding of systems, practices and processes of all functional areas in the organization and casting performance management practice as a catalyst in creating new standards in such functional areas. Leadership channelizes performance management strategies to evolve benchmarks in functional areas like operations, commercial, marketing, quality management. This process is a double-edged sword since it enables redefining standards of functional performance on one side, and institutionalization of performance management on the other side.

DRIVER 9: MAKING TOUGH DECISIONS

Leadership of performance focus is not liberal but fair and firm are the trademarks. Leaders indulge in tough decision making to institutionalize performance management. This attitude and capability for sustaining pressures and strain of taking tough decisions strengthen the effort in creating performance excellence. Leaders follow typically two approaches: they develop right standards of performance and also evolve rigorous parameters to measure attainment of such targets. Secondly, they constantly take action in order to improve performance as most of the aspects/functions in organizations generally would not improve in the first or second attempt. Tough decisions may temporarily attract criticism, resistance and tend to be perceived as negative. However, in medium and long terms, decisions are appreciated since they are highly positive and deliver great performance results to organizations and their employees.

DRIVER 10: INSTILLING PERFORMANCE MANAGEMENT BY IMPROVING ORGANIZATIONAL CAPABILITY

Performance minded leadership endeavours to institutionalize performance management through improving organizational capabilities. Leaders of this class give equal emphasis to the past, present and future of the organization and people instead of being driven by any single period/phase. Performance management and organizational capabilities are managed as dependent on each other. Improved organizational capability smoothens institutionalization of performance management, since it can endure sharp and tough measures and also augment performance efforts with allocation of resources. Likewise, performance management strategies, interventions and drivers ultimately result in enhancing organizational capabilities. Leaders always look for improving organizational capabilities since it is the best visible form of institutionalizing performance management.

SUMMARY

Leadership is not only a factor, but also the objective of performance management. This is the prime argument of this chapter. It is a factor because leaders perform a critical role in conceptualization, development, execution, evaluation and revitalization of performance management, which is called institutionalization of performance management in this book. It is the objective since a systematic performance management strategy is expected to contribute for building pools of leadership talent at every level in the organization.

Leadership theories such as four systems theory of management leadership, managerial grid, cognitive leadership, situational leadership, charismatic leadership, path-goal leadership, transformational leadership, and nurturant task leadership theory offer great lessons for building leadership-based performance management strategy. Lessons for building performance centric leadership include:

(i) Focus on results with people orientation
(ii) Consistent personality with flexible orientation
(iii) Multifaceted orientation
(iv) Aptitude with attitude

(v) Charisma
(vi) Situational sensitiveness
(vii) Managing expectations of people
(viii) Organizational leadership synchrony
(ix) Master in mechanics of organizational business
(x) Defining leader-follower roles.

These theories also present various forms, styles, range, orientations, skills, competencies and attributes of leadership. Leaders drive revolution of performance management through the process of:

(i) Setting direction
(ii) Defining performance management strategies, interventions and drivers
(iii) Mobilizing resources
(iv) Positioning leadership as key factor
(v) Leading change
(vi) Motivating people
(vii) Delivering results.

Strategy of leadership-based performance management comprises two interventions and 20 drivers. First intervention is *nurturing performance-oriented leadership*. This intervention is initiated with the help of 10 drivers such as:

(i) Objectives formulation
(ii) Leadership competency dictionary
(iii) Measuring current level of leadership
(iv) Assessing the need for leadership development
(v) Developing tailor-made leadership development programme
(vi) Selection of leadership development participants
(vii) Choosing leadership development methodology
(viii) Executing leadership development programme
(ix) Evaluating leadership development programme
(x) Renewing leadership development programme.

Second intervention is called as leaders lead institutionalization of performance management. A set of 10 drivers catapults this intervention into reality. These are:

(i) Communicating
(ii) Generating commitment
(iii) Empowering
(iv) Cultivating individual and collective talents
(v) Networking
(vi) Setting self as an example
(vii) Taking complete and personal responsibility
(viii) Creating benchmarks
(ix) Making tough decisions
(x) Improving organizational capability

The chapter also throws light on what is leadership and what it is not in the context of performance management. Popular misconceptions about leadership practices are also illustrated to clarify the strategy and structure of leadership-based performance management.

KEY WORDS

Following are the key words discussed in this chapter.

- Performance stimulated leadership
- Managerial grid
- Situational leadership
- Transactional leadership
- Charismatic leadership
- Strategic leadership
- Somatic markers
- Leadership competencies
- Nurturing performance centred leadership
- Measuring leadership effectiveness
- Leadership development agreement

- Four systems of management leadership
- Cognitive leadership
- Path-Goal leadership
- Transformational leadership
- Nurturant task leadership
- Skilled incompetence
- Leadership attributes
- Leadership index/dictionary
- Leaders institutionalizing performance management
- Leadership development workbook
- Renewal of leadership

DISCUSSION QUESTIONS

1. What is leadership-based performance management? Discuss significance of leadership in performance management.

2. Briefly present the theoretical aspects of leadership and their lessons for building performance stimulated leadership.

3. Effectiveness of leadership is contingent upon compatibility between leadership style and the situation. Analyze this statement with the support of related theories and examples.

4. How important is followers' quality in leadership effectiveness? Discuss with examples.

5. Discuss different types of leadership and their suitability to present day organizations.

6. Compare and contrast charismatic leadership with transformational leadership.

7. What are the various approaches of leadership?

8. What is the structure and content of leadership-based performance management strategy? Write a summary illustrating essential features.

9. What are the attributes and competencies of leadership?

10. How can a leadership nurturing intervention be developed? What are the important steps that should be followed in developing a leadership development programme?

11. How does leadership lead institutionalization of performance management strategies, interventions and drivers?

CASE STUDIES

1. Steve Hotels Ltd. is a five star hotel located in a metropolitan city in India. This hotel has grown from an obscure lodging place to a reputed five star deluxe hotel with an annual turnover of Rs. 1000 million. The hotel could reach to this stage due to the vision, hard work and competent leadership of the promoter, namely Umesh Oberoi. He is the coordinator of different departments and takes all small and big decisions related to functioning of the hotel. However, the hotel growth is stagnated during last three financial years and in fact, it had shown a negative trend in the last financial year. This year hotel occupancy rate is expected to be 30 per cent lower than the hotel's average occupancy during the last 15 years.

   Oberoi noticed that reasons for declining sales is mainly indecisiveness of people in all departments such as foods and beverages, banquet management, services like housekeeping, marketing, relationship with corporate clients and under realization of credit bills. This has happened since employees at all levels look forward to Oberoi for decisions. In his absence, employees leave issues/problems unattended as they see their role is only to follow instructions of promoter of the hotel instead of keeping customers satisfied. Oberoi is growing old and his availability in future to manage the hotel affairs will be limited to a day or two in a week. He realized that people need to be trained and empowered to take decisions and there must be multiple leaders to manage the ever-growing complexities in hotel management.

   Now, discuss the following issues based on the above case:
   (i) How Oberoi's leadership style that helped to turn a small lodging place into a five star deluxe hotel is becoming a stumbling block in further growth of the hotel?
   (ii) How a leadership development programme can help to remove indecisiveness among employees?
   (iii) Nurturing leadership can be a potential solution to overcome problems that the hotel is facing, especially in view of falling health of the promoter and his restricted availability for decision-making. Discuss how developing leadership is relevant here. If relevant, how should a leadership development programme be made in the context of present case?

2. Silicon Solutions Inc. is a software company that has clients spread across globe. Currently about 3000 people are employed in the organization. Broadly, they work in three departments. These are (i) software development and implementation department, (ii) business development department and (iii) service departments like finance, human resource, administrative and company affairs. Human resource department with the help of a multinational consultant put in place a corporate strategy aligned performance management system. Though performance management policy framework

is sound, pragmatic and well-crafted, the organization is stranded with implementation problems mainly in anchoring and institutionalizing the system. Human resource department alone was made responsible for execution of the new performance management and this has been found to be responsible for slow and ineffective implementation. Line managers like software developers, business development managers, finance executives weren't actively involved in the implementation. Top management became sensitive to this lapse and decided to involve all managers to institutionalize performance management system. All managers are made primarily responsible for pushing the new system. However, managers are not quite clear how to go about it in institutionalizing the performance management system.

You have been invited to guide managers in regard to the behaviour and tactics and drivers that they must follow to fulfil their responsibility of performance management institutionalization successfully. Discuss how and what drivers you will suggest them in this regard. Illustrate how the intervention of leaders leading institutionalization of performance management and its ten drivers can enable managers in this context.

3. Gram Bijlee Vikas is a non-government organization committed to facilitate electrifying all villages in selected districts of Chattisgarh. In the first phase, seven districts of Chattisgarh were identified for this purpose. About 700 people are expected to work in these districts. These employees are classified into three groups: village level implementers, mandal level coordinators and district level managers. The organization proposed to build leadership for successful implementation of the task in these districts.

Discuss what level of leadership development is required in employees? Why and how?

SUGGESTED READING

Argyris, Chris (1987). "A leadership dilemma: skilled incompetence." *Business & Economic Review,* **1**, pp. 4–11.

Bass, Bernard (1990). "From transactional to transformational leadership: learning to share the vision." *Organizational Dynamics*, Winter, pp. 19–31.

Blake, Robert and Jane Mouton (1964). *The Managerial Grid.* Houston: Gulf Publishing.

Evans, Martin G. (1970). "The effect of supervisory behaviour on the path-goal relationship." *Organizational Behavior and Human Performance*, May, pp. 277–298.

Farkas, Charles De, Phillipe Backer and Allen Sheppard (1995). *Maximum Leadership.* London: Orion Books.

Fielder, Fred (1971). *A Theory of Leadership Effectiveness.* New York: McGraw-Hill.

Goleman, Daniel (1998). *Working with Emotional Intelligence.* New York: Bantom Books.

Hersey, Paul and Kenneth H. Blanchard (1982). *Management of Organizational Behavior.* Englewood Cliffs, NJ: Prentice-Hall Inc.

House, Robert, J. (1971). "A path-goal theory of leader effectiveness." *Administrative Science Quarterly*, September, pp. 321–338.

House, Robert, J. (1978). "A 1976 theory of charismatic leadership." In J. Hunt and Larson (Eds.), *Leadership: The Cutting Edge*, pp. 189–207.

Likert, Rensis (1967). *The Human Organization*. New York: McGraw-Hill.

Sinha, Jai B.P. (1979). "The nurturant task leader." *ASCI Journal of Management*, **8**(2), pp. 109–119

Vicere, Albert A. and Robert M. Fulmer (1996). *Leadership by Design*. Massachusetts: Harvard Business School.

AUTHOR INDEX

SUBJECT INDEX